The Arthurian Handbook
SECOND EDITION

Norris J. Lacy and Geoffrey Ashe
with Debra N. Mancoff

Garland Publishing, Inc.
New York & London
1997

Library of Congress Cataloging-in-Publication Data

Lacy, Norris J.
    The Arthurian handbook. — 2nd ed. / Norris J. Lacy and Geoffrey
Ashe, with Debra N. Mancoff.
        p.   cm.— (Garland reference library of the humanities ; v. 1920)
    Includes bibliographical references and index.
    ISBN 0-8153-2082-5 (alk. paper). – ISBN 0-8153-2081-7 (pbk. :
alk. paper)
        1. Arthurian romances—History and criticism.   2. Knights and knight-
hood in literature.   3. Arthurian romances—Illustrations.   4. Kings and
rulers in literature.   5. Knights and knighthood in art.   6. Kings and rulers
in art.   7. Arts.   I. Ashe, Geoffrey.   II. Mancoff, Debra N., 1950– .
III. Title.   IV. Series: Garland reference library of the humanities ; vol.
1920.
PN685.L3   1997
809'093351—DC21   97-17495
                                                              CIP

Cover illustration: Edward Burne-Jones, Tapestry: *Verdure with Deer and Shields.*
By permission of Birmingham Museums and Art Gallery

Cover and book design by Karin Badger

Printed on acid-free, 250-year-life paper
Manufactured in the United States of America

The Arthurian Handbook

SECOND EDITION

Garland Reference Library of the Humanities
Volume 1920

Arthurian Britain

TABLE OF CONTENTS

iLLUSTRATIONS

PREFACE TO THE SECOND EDITION

This is the second edition of *The Arthurian Handbook*, a critical survey of the Arthurian legend in all periods and languages. Like the first edition, it deals extensively with the complex question of Arthurian origins and with the early development of the legend. Later chapters study Arthurian literature (from Geoffrey of Monmouth to the present) and the expression of Arthurian themes in the other arts: manuscript and book illustration, painting, sculpture, tapestry, opera, film, and other media.

In the main, the organization of this edition is similar to that of the 1988 original, but there are a number of additions and changes. The most evident is the layout of the volume, which often provides boxes and sidebars to offer additional information on authors and themes. The new edition is also more extensively illustrated than was the earlier one. Textually, the most significant change is in Chapter IV, on Arthurian themes in the nonliterary arts. Debra Mancoff, who served as a consultant for the original volume, has now reworked much of that chapter, specifically the sections that deal with the visual arts, both medieval and modern. The remainder of that chapter (music and film) is the work of its original author, Norris J. Lacy.

In other chapters, revisions range from stylistic adjustments to substantial rewriting. In the chapter dealing with modern literature, there has been revision of the poetry section, and in that chapter and the following (on the arts), the material has been brought up to date by the discussion of novels, stories, films, and other creations that have appeared during the years since *The Arthurian Handbook* was first published.

From language to language, and often within a single language, Arthurian names can take many forms. In speaking of the character in general, we have used the form that is most familiar in English (or one of those forms, since there are sometimes two customary forms, as in Iseut/Isolde or Modred/Mordred). In reference to particular texts, we use the form preferred by their authors.

As in the original edition, each chapter is followed by brief bibliographical notes organized by subject. These references are identified only by author's last name and, in some cases, by indications of chapter or page number; they are, however, keyed to the bibliographies at the end of the volume, where full information is given.

In updating the volume, we have exercised the same degree of selectivity as in the original (see Preface to the First Edition). We have made no effort to discuss or even to mention a great many of the recent contributions to the elaboration of Arthurian themes. A single statistic will dramatize the futility of trying to do so: in the period 1990–95, and in English alone, well over eighty Arthurian novels and even more short stories were published, and the flood shows no signs of abating. Rather than clutter these pages with unending lists of names and titles, we have chosen to discuss, as we did in the original, a few of the items that possess unusual artistic merit or illustrate trends in Arthurian literature, art, music, and film. (Readers in search of more nearly complete coverage are referred to the updated paperback edition of *The New Arthurian Encyclopedia* [Garland, 1996].)

In addition to renewing our acknowledgments to the persons named in 1988, we wish to thank reviewers, students, and friends who offered comments on and evaluations of the first edition. Our thanks go also to Kevin J. Harty for information concerning films and for providing some of the stills reproduced here, to Phillip Boardman for information about modern literature and about music, and to Edwin V. Lacy, Jr., who provided assistance with the genealogical charts.

N.J.L., G.A., D.N.M.

PREFACE TO THE FIRST EDITION

This book is a critical survey of the Arthurian legend. It deals with all periods, from the fifth and sixth centuries through the Middle Ages and to the present, examining Arthurian origins, the development of the legend in chronicles and other sources, the interpretation of Arthurian themes in literature, and their treatment in the other arts.

We have tried to write for a broad audience, including students and the general reader who may be fascinated by King Arthur and eager to have more information about him. We hope, however, that the book will also be of interest to scholars. The breadth and brevity of our presentation will of course limit scholars' interest in regard to their own specialization, but we anticipate that they will find useful information about areas and aspects of Arthuriana with which they do not deal directly.

Readers often ask two questions about Arthur. The first almost invariably concerns Arthur's historicity: "Who was he?" or "Did he exist?" If it is an inquiry about the existence of the legendary king, with his Camelot and Round Table, the question is easily answered: no such king lived. The monarch of literary invention, however, may have had a real original, and his existence and identity are considerably more complex matters. Their investigation, involving both historical facts and informed conjecture, constitutes our first chapter, on Arthurian origins.

The second question is in its way no less difficult. Those who read a certain version of the Arthurian legend will frequently ask: "Is this really the way the story goes?" This question does not necessarily imply a belief in the historicity of the events and characters in question, but it at least assumes that there is a standard or "orthodox" form of the legend. Of course, for English-speaking audiences Malory's work and retellings of it virtually constitute such a standard version, but other texts, before and after his, offer variants that sometimes differ strikingly from the story he tells.

Depending on the text at hand, Merlin may, for example, be imprisoned by Nimue, or he may voluntarily retire from the world; Mordred may be Arthur's nephew or his illegitimate son; Arthur may have no children, or only Mordred, or also a legitimate son, or also a daughter; Guinevere's lover is usually Lancelot but occasionally Bedivere instead. This fluidity, characteristic of both medieval and modern treatments of the legend, accounts for much of its vitality and richness, but it also makes it difficult if not impossible to define "authentic" and "inauthentic" elements of that legend. Chapters II and III present a great many of the literary versions of the story, from the very earliest to the present; our discussions often point out influences and borrowings but just as often emphasize an author's departures from traditional accounts. Chapter IV surveys interpretations of Arthurian themes in arts other than literature: in tapestry and stained glass, in sculpture, in painting and book illustration, in music, in film and television, and in the decorative arts.

Although we have treated a variety of periods and subjects, we do not purport to offer here an exhaustive history of Arthurianism. Not only would the scope of the legend make that virtually impossible, but the attempt to do so would yield little more than an inventory of titles and authors, many of them holding no interest for anyone but a specialist in that field. We have attempted, rather, to convey a sense of the development of the legend without encumbering the reader with endless details. We thus provide the necessary information about history, archaeology, literature, and art, and we pause in the process to discuss in more detail the most important Arthurian moments, monuments, and authors. We hope thus to have offered a useful critical survey of the long process that transformed the Arthurian legend from the reference to a *dux bellorum* into the fully elaborated history, society, and ideology familiar to countless devotees of Arthur.

A few more notes and caveats are in order. First, the selectivity mentioned here is applied with particular rigor to the chapter treating modern literature. That is a decision made out of necessity: the absolute flood of twentieth-century Arthurian works, especially in English, requires us to omit a great many titles; our choices are arbitrary to an extent, but we have attempted to include the best and the best-known works, as well as certain others that make some interesting or significant contribution to Arthuriana. Admittedly, though, by no means everything deserving of mention has found its way into these pages; conversely, a few items that scarcely merit discussion have been included to make or illustrate a point.

Our understanding of what is Arthurian has intentionally been very broad. Some works follow such "Arthurian" characters as Gawain and hardly mention Arthur himself. Others, such as Gottfried von Strassburg's *Tristan*, are not literally Arthurian at all, and in fact the Tristan legend itself involves the graft of an independent body of narrative material onto the Arthurian legend. Such grafts and the opposite phenomenon, in which a motif like the wasteland can be split off and exploited for its allusive or mythic value in a non-Arthurian text, are fundamental characteristics of Arthuriana through the centuries. For our purposes, we thus consider such works fully as "Arthurian" as the most traditional retelling of the whole story of King Arthur.

Finally, the dividing line between early and modern literature, between Chapter II and Chapter III, is not clear and absolute. The reason is that the sixteenth century gave us a great many texts that adapt or translate earlier material (and therefore belong to Chapter II), while others may break with medieval conceptions and methods and set a new direction. Thus, a literary work from the sixteenth century may be discussed in either chapter, depending on the character of the text in question.

The principal authorship of portions of the *Handbook* is as follows: Geoffrey Ashe for Chapter I and the Glossary of authors, characters, terms, and places; Norris J. Lacy for Chapters II, III, IV (see Preface to the Second Edition), and V. Each chapter is followed by brief notes that offer the principal sources for the major subjects presented in the chapter. These references, identified by author's last name and in some cases indications of chapter or page number, are keyed to the appropriate bibliography at the end of the volume, where full information is given.

In recognizing the assistance and advice of others, we inevitably omit many who have made a significant contribution by discussing with us Arthurian matters in general or this book in particular, or by bringing an idea or a title to our attention. To all those, we acknowledge our debt and apologize for our silence. There are, however, several persons whose substantial contributions cannot go unacknowledged: Raymond H. Thompson, for his advice concerning the difficult area of modern fiction in English and his kind permission for us to rely strongly on his book *The Return from Avalon* and his contributions to *The New Arthurian Encyclopedia*; Ulrich Müller, for providing invaluable information about Arthur in modern drama, musicals, and fiction; Debra N. Mancoff and Ernst Dick, for reading portions of the manuscript and offering useful critiques; and J. Theodore Johnson, for information concerning modern French material. We are grateful for their assistance but wish to emphasize that the responsibility for the choice and treatment of material in the book is ours. We also express our gratitude to the General Research Fund of the University of Kansas, for grants that facilitated Norris Lacy's contributions to this volume. Finally, it is with pleasure that we acknowledge the encouragement and assistance of our editor, Gary Kuris of Garland Publishing.

N.J.L., G.A.

CHRONOLOGY

Tbe eARLY peRIOD

This chronology (pp. xviii–xxv) lists most important Arthurian events, authors, and works of art. The dates given after authors' names refer either to all their Arthurian works (in which case a range of dates is listed) or to a single

		Literature	
History, Chronicle, Archaeology	Art	Celtic	French
3rd– 9th c.	Britain separated from Empire (410)			
	Vortigern (r. 425–50)			
	Arthur (r. 455–75, according to Geoffrey)			
	Ambrosius Aurelianus (r. ca. 460)			
	"King of Britons" crosses into Gaul (468)			
	Seige of Mt. Badon (between 500 and 518)			
	Gildas (540)			
	Gododdin (ca. 600) (may be earliest mention of Arthur by name)			
	Nennius (9th c.)			
11th c.			*Mabinogi* (1050)	
			Culhwch (11th c.)	
12th c.		Perror Relief (1st Arthurian sculpture, 1100)		

important composition. In either case, given the impossiblity of dating many medieval texts with precision, the dates here are approximate and are provided simply to give a general idea of comparative chronology.

Dutch, German, Scandinavian	Hispanic, Italian	Latin	English

		Literature	
History, Chronicle, Archaeology	Art	Celtic	French
12th c. cont.	William of Malmesbury (1125)			
	Henry of Hunting-don (ca. 1129)			
		Modena Archivolt (1st half 12th century)		
	Geoffrey of Mon-mouth (ca. 1136) (1st mention of Merlin by that name)			
				Wace (1155; 1st mention of Round Table
		Otranto Mosaic (1165)		Chrétien (1160–80) (1st mention of Grail, Bleeding Lance, Camelot, Lancelot)
				Marie de France (1170)
				Thomas (1175)
	Layamon (1190)			
	Discovery of Arthur's Grave (Glastonbury, 1190 or 1191)			Béroul (1191)
	Giraldus Cambrensis (1193)			
13th c.			Three Welsh Romances (13th century)	Robert de Boron (1200) (1st men-tion of Sword in Stone, in *Merlin*)
				Perlesvaus (1200)

Dutch, German, Scandinavian	Hispanic, Italian	Latin	English
Eilhart von Oberge (1180)			
		Andreas Capellanus (1185)	
Gunnlaugr Leifsson (1200)		*De Ortu Waluuanii* (1200)	
Wolfram von Eschenbach (1210)		*Historia Meriodoci* (13th c.)	

| | | Literature | |
History, Chronicle, Archaeology	Art	Celtic	French
13th c. cont'd			Vulgate (1215–35) (1st mention of Galahad by name)
	1st illuminated Arthurian MSS (1220s)		
			Prose *Tristan* (1250)
	Chertsey Abbey Tiles (1270)		
14th c.	Winchester Round Table (1st half 14th century)		
	Wienhausen Embroideries (1310–40)		J. de Longuyon (1st list of Nine Worthies, 1310)
			Perceforest (1330)
	Cloisters Tapestry (1385)		*Meliador* (1380)
15th c.	Runkelstein murals (1400)		
	Pisanello (1395–1455)		
	Louvre tray (early 15th century)		
	La Manta murals (1420)		

Dutch, German, Scandinavian	Hispanic, Italian	Latin	English
Gottfried von Strassburg (1210)			
Wirnt von Grafenberg (1215)			
Hákon IV (r. 1217–63)	*Jaufré* (1220)		
Heinrich von dem Türlin (1225)			
Wigamur (1250)			
Maerlant (1261)			
Albrecht von Scharfenberg (1270)			
Penninc (1280)	*Tristano Riccardiano* (1280)		
Herr Ivan Lejonriddaren (1303)	*Zifar* (1300)		*Sir Tristrem* (1300)
	Vives (1313)		
	Amadís (orig. version, 1340)	*Arthur and Gorlagon* (1320)	
	Tavola Ritonda (1340)		
	Pucci (1380)		Alliterative and Stanzaic *Mortes* (late 14th c.)
Saga of Tristram ok Isodd (1400)	*El Cuento de Tristán de Leonís* (1400)		*Sir Gawain and the Green Knight* (1400)

		Literature	
History, Chronicle, Archaeology	Art	Celtic	French
15th c. cont.	Sorg's *Tristan* (1st printed Arthurian book illustrated with woodcuts, 1420)		
	Wynkyn de Worde, 1st illustrated Malory (1498)		
16th c. Polydore Vergil (1512–13)			P. Sala (1525)
Leland identifies Cadbury Castle as Camelot (1542)	Burghley Nef (1527–28)		
17th c.			

Dutch, German, Scandinavian	Hispanic, Italian	Latin	English
			Lovelich (1450)
Ulrich Fuetrer (1467)			Malory (1470)
	Boiardo (1490)		
	Montalvo (1508)		
	Ariosto (1516)		
Hans Sachs (1543–53)			
			T. Hughes (1588)
			Spenser (1590, 1596)
	Cervantes (1605)		

THE MODERN PERIOD

The chronology for the modern period (ca. 1600 to the present, pp. xxvi–xxxv) omits dates, which can easily be found in the body of the appropriate chapter. Instead we group works by centuries (for the seventeenth and

	History and Archaeology	The Arts
1600–1699		
		Purcell/Dryden, *King Arthur*
1700–1799		
		Mortimer, *Discovery of Prince Arthur's Tomb*
1800–1849		
		Dyce, Queen's Robing Room (1848–68)
		Founding of P.R.B.
1850–1859		Rossetti's 1st Arthurian painting *(King Arthur's Tomb)*
		Oxford Union Murals
		Moxon Tennyson
1860–1869		
		Dunlop Windows
		Wagner, *Tristan und Isolde*

eighteenth centuries), then by the first half of the nineteenth; thereafter we proceed by decades. The chronology lists a good many, but by no means all, of the works discussed in this book. Particularly for the second half of the twentieth century we have in many cases limited ourselves to a single title per author.

Literature		
English, American	French	German
Jonson, *The Speeches at Prince Henry's Barriers*		
Drayton, *Poly-Olbion*		
Blackmore, *Prince Arthur, King Arthur*		
Fielding, *Tom Thumb*		
R. Hole, *Arthur*		
Frere, *The Monks and the Giants*		Wieland, *Merlins weissagende Stimme*
Peacock, *The Misfortunes of Elphin*		Immermann, *Merlin*
Tennyson, *Idylls* (1834–85)		
Morris, *The Defence of Guenevere*		
	Quinet, *Merlin L'Enchanteur*	

	History and Archaeology	The Arts
1870–1879		Cameron, photographs (1st publ.)
		Woolner, sculptures
		Burne-Jones, *The Beguiling of Merlin*
1880–1889		Burne-Jones, *Arthur in Avalon* (1881–98)
		Wagner, *Parisfal*
		Goldmark, *Merlin*
1890–1899		Founding of Kelmscott Press
		Beardsley's illustrations for Dent *Morte D'Arthur*
		Abbey, Boston Public Library murals (1890–1901)
		Waterhouse, *Lady of Shalott*
		Chausson, *Le Roi Arthus*
1900–1909		Pyle, illustrations
1910–1919		Boughton's choral works (1911–45)

Literature		
English, American	French	German

English, American	French	German
Lanier, *A Boy's King Arthur*		
Swinburne, *Tristam of Lyonesse*		
Twain, *A Connecticut Yankee*	Founding of *La Revue Wagnerienne*	
Hovey, *Launcelot and Guenevere*		
Comyns Carr, *King Arthur*		
		Vollmöller, *Parcival*
	Bédier, *Tristan et Iseut*	
	Apollinaire, *L'Enchanteur pourrissant*	Mann, *Tristan*
Rhys, *Lays of the Round Table*	Claudel, *Partage de midi*	
Housman, *Sir Aglovale*		Stucken, Grail Cycle (1902–24)
		Ludwig, *Tristan und Isolde*
		Kralik, *Der heilige Gral*

	History and Archaeology	The Arts
1910–1919 cont.		Brickdale, illustrations
		Crane, illustrations
1920–1929		
		Connick, Princeton University Chapel windows
		Bédier/Artus, *Tristan et Iseut*
1930–1939	Radford's Excavations at Tintagel	
1940–1949		Cocteau, *L'Éternel retour* *A Connecticut Yankee* (film)

| Literature | | |
English, American	French	German

Rackham, *Romance of King Arthur*

    Boulenger, *Les Romans de la Table Ronde*

Robinson, *Merlin*

Cabell, *Jurgen*

        Hauptmann, *Merlins Geburt* (1917–44)

Robinson, *Lancelot*

Eliot, *The Waste Land*

Machen, *The Secret Glory*

Hardy, *The Queen of Cromwell*

    Guénon, *Le Roi du monde*

Erskine, *Galahad*

Robinson, *Tristram*

Masefield, *Midsummer Night*

Powys, *A Glastonbury Romance*

Jones, *In Parenthesis*

    Cocteau, *Les Chevaliers de la Table Ronde*

Williams, *Taliessin Through Logres*

White, *The Sword in the Stone*

    Gracq, *Au Château d'Argol*

Joyce, *Finnegans Wake*

Deeping, *The Man Who Went Back*

	History and Archaeology	The Arts
1940–1949 cont.	International Arthurian Society founded	
1950–1959		
1960–1969		Lerner and Loewe, *Camelot*
	Excavations at South Cadbury (Alcock, 1966–70)	Disney, *The Sword in the Stone*
		Camelot (film)
1970–1979		
		Monty Python and the Holy Grail
		Wakeman, *The Myths and Legends of King Arthur*
		Bresson, *Lancelot du Lac*
		Rohmer, *Perceval le Gallois*

Literature		
English, American	French	German
Williams, *Region of the Summer Stars*		
Lewis, *That Hideous Strength*		
	Gracq, *Le Roi Pêcheur*	
Jones, *The Anathemata*	Vian, *Le Chevalier de neige*	
Malamud, *The Natural*		
	Pinget, *Graal Flibuste*	
White, *The Once and Future King*	Benoit, *Montsalvat*	
Steinbeck, *The Acts of King Arthur* (publ. 1976)		
Cooper, *Dark Is Rising* (1965–77)		
Deal, *The Grail*		
Sutcliff, *Sword at Sunset*		
Stewart, *The Crystal Cave*	Briant, *Le Testament de Merlin*	
Norton, *Merlin's Mirror*		
Laubenthal, *Excalibur*		
Canning, *Crimson Chalice*		
Monaco, *Parsival*		de Bruyn, *Tristan und Isolde*
Berger, *Arthur Rex*		Harder, *Parzival*
Percy, *Lancelot*		
Hunter, *Perceval and the Presence of God*		Werkhaus Moosach, *Der Fall Partzifall*
Vansittart, *Lancelot*	Roubaud/Delay, *Graal-Théâtre* (1977–)	

	History and Archaeology	The Arts
1980–1989		Romero, *Knightriders*
		Boorman, *Excalibur*
		Syberberg, *Parsifal*
1990–		Gilliam, *The Fisher King*

| Literature | | |
English, American	French	German
Bradshaw, *Hawk of May* Godwin, *Firelord* Newman, Guinevere trilogy (1981–85)		Dorst, *Merlin oder das wüste Land* Harder, *Recht mitten durch*
Cherryh, *Port Eternity* Bradley, *The Mists of Avalon* Chant, *The High Kings* Stewart, *The Wicked Day* Lodge, *Small World* Powell, *The Fisher King* Yolen, *Merlin's Booke* Davies, *Lyre of Orpheus* Woolley, trilogy (1987–91)	Roubaud, *Le Roi Arthur* Le Dantec, *Graal-Romance* Weingarten, *Le Roman de la Table Ronde* Barjavel, *L'Enchanteur*	
Barthelme, *The King* Byatt, *Possession* Murdoch, *The Green Knight* Griffiths, *Lay of Sir Tristam* Updike, *Brazil*	Rio, *Merlin*	Muschg, *Der rote Ritter*

GENEALOGY

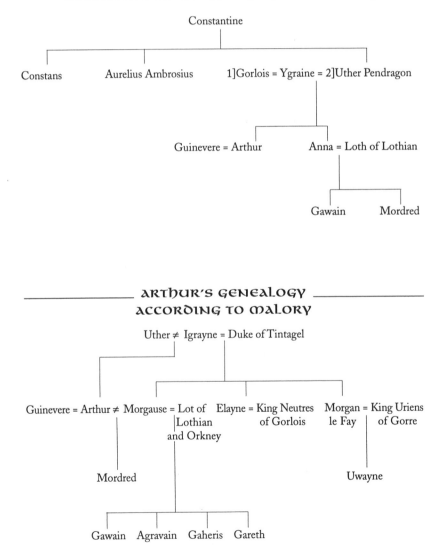

ARTHUR'S GENEALOGY ACCORDING TO GEOFFREY OF MONMOUTH

Constantine

Constans Aurelius Ambrosius 1]Gorlois = Ygraine = 2]Uther Pendragon

Guinevere = Arthur Anna = Loth of Lothian

Gawain Mordred

ARTHUR'S GENEALOGY ACCORDING TO MALORY

Uther ≠ Igrayne = Duke of Tintagel

Guinevere = Arthur ≠ Morgause = Lot of Elayne = King Neutres Morgan = King Uriens
Lothian of Gorlois le Fay of Gorre
and Orkney

Mordred

Uwayne

Gawain Agravain Gaheris Gareth

ARTHUR'S GENEALOGY
ACCORDING TO THE FRENCH VULGATE MERLIN

```
         Constant                    Duke Hoel

      ┌──────────┬──────────────────────┐
  Pendragon                             │
Seneschal's daughter ≠ Leodagan = ?    2]Uther = Ygraine = 1]Duke of Tintagel
      ┌──────────┬──────────┐               ┌──────────┐
 False Guinevere    3]Guinevere = Arthur ≠ 1]Morgause = Lot  Morgan* = King Neutres
                         2]Lisanor ≠
                                                              Galescalain
                    Loholt      Mordred
                                         ┌──────┬──────────┬──────────┐
                                      Gawain  Agravain  Guerrehet  Gaheriet
```

*Elsewhere in the text, the wife of Neutres is identified as Ygraine's daughter Blasine, rather than as Morgan. Still elsewhere, Blasine is Ygraine's half-sister.

GALAHAD'S ANCESTRY
ACCORDING TO THE FRENCH VULGATE*

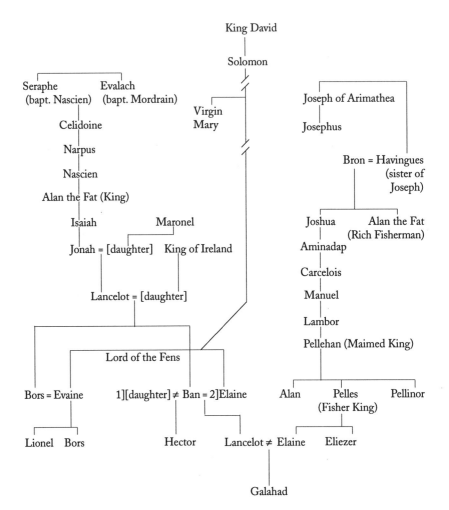

*From romance to romance, or even within a single one, genealogical details are sometimes confusing or contradictory. Joseph of Arimathea and Josephus appear to head the line of Fisher Kings, although the information about their line is sketchy, as are details concerning Lancelot's descent, through his mother, from David and Solomon. Galahad's mother is traditionally called Elaine but is often unnamed; sometimes Pelles and the Fisher King are distinct and Elaine is the daughter of the former and the niece of the latter.

PARZIVAL'S ANCESTRY
ACCORDING TO WOLFRAM VON ESCHENBACH

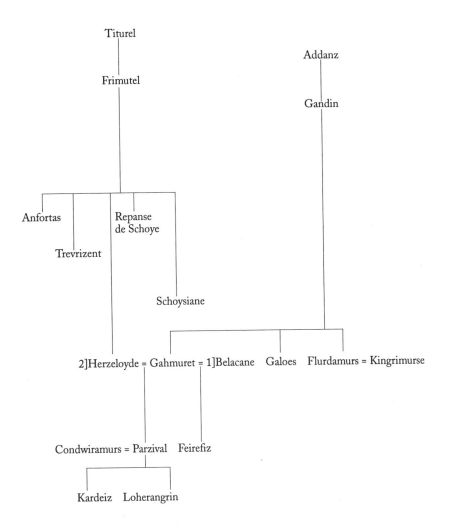

ḄERALÒRY

Heraldry, the use of a coat of arms to identify a knight and a family, developed in the twelfth century, that is, well after the "Arthurian period." It quickly became so firmly engrained in medieval consciousness that, by the time many of the Arthurian romances were composed, it was simply taken for granted that any great knight must be associated with a crest. As a result, coats of arms were created for King Arthur and for many of his knights.

Arthur's full coat of arms usually included thirteen crowns, two greyhounds, and the motto "Pendragon," all of it surmounted by a dragon. However, as in the Cloisters Tapestry and other visual representations, his device was often simplified to three crowns arranged on a shield or banner.

Heraldic tradition often varied with time and geography, and the description of a knight's arms might differ radically from text to text. The most obvious example may be Gawain, who, in the continental tradition, most often had a shield bearing an eagle (sometimes double-headed); in the Middle English *Sir Gawain and the Green Knight*, his shield carried the image of a pentangle, an "endless knot" with multiple symbolic meanings, such as the perfection of his five senses, his five virtues, and the five wounds of Christ.

a. Coat of arms of King Arthur, full arms, late version, French style.

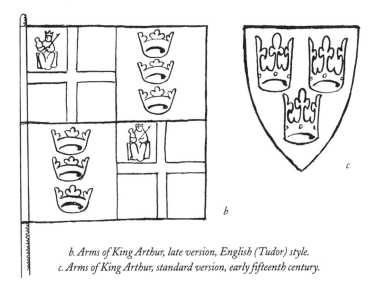

b. Arms of King Arthur, late version, English (Tudor) style.
c. Arms of King Arthur, standard version, early fifteenth century.

Heraldic drawings by Helmut Nickel; reproduced by permission of Helmut Nickel.

*d. Arms of Gawain, earlier version. e. Arms of Gawain, later version.
f. Gawain's shield (the pentangle).*

*g. One version of Sir Kay's arms. h. Arms of Sagramours le Desrée.
i. Arms of Yvain.*

*j. Arms of Lancelot du Lac. k. Arms of Tristram of Lyonesse.
l. Arms of Mordred, later version.*

Heraldic drawings by Helmut Nickel; reproduced by permission of Helmut Nickel.

The Arthurian Handbook

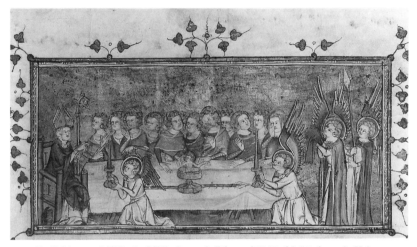

Grail Liturgy. MS Paris, Bibliothèque de l'Arsenal 5218, fol. 88, from the Vulgate
Quest for the Holy Grail. In the presence of Galahad and of the Holy Grail,
Josephus, the first Christian bishop, descends from heaven, carried by angels.
As he begins to celebrate Mass, a child descends from above and enters the mass wafer.
Then a figure of the bleeding, crucified Christ emerges from the Grail,
gives communion to Galahad and his companions, and explains that the Grail
is the dish from which the Savior ate the lamb with his disciples at Easter.

chapter 1

Origins

King Arthur is the central figure of one of the most famous cycles of legend. His name evokes a whole cluster of characters and themes. First is the King himself, magnificent monarch of a glorious realm. Beside him is Guinevere, his fair and high-spirited queen. Close by is Merlin, the enchanter who contrives his birth, guides him from the beginning, and sets him firmly on his throne. We may think, too, of Excalibur, his wonderful sword. Of Camelot, his royal city. Of the Knights of the Round Table, vowed to uphold the noblest ideals. Of Lancelot, the most splendid among them, torn by his love for the Queen. Also of another love affair, the doomed passion of Tristan and Iseut (Isolde). The story of the Grail Quest and the saintly Galahad enshrines a spiritual mystery. At the close is the treason of Mordred, followed by the tragedy of Arthur's downfall and his passing away to Avalon. Yet even that is not quite the end, because of the prophecy of his return, "King that was, King that shall be."

The Arthurian legend is multifaceted, a literature in itself, built up by romancers and poets during the Middle Ages in Europe. But it did not expire afterward. Many authors have handled it since, developing its themes or, conversely, turning it into a fairy tale for children. Several modern writers have satirized it, or given it new meanings, or tried to reconstitute a reality underlying it. Such questings are all valid, each in its way, and they have enlarged and enriched the legend. The essential creation, however, is medieval, and King Arthur's Britain is an idealized medieval kingdom, a sort of chivalric Utopia.

The legend reflects features of medieval storytelling in its more sophisticated forms. To begin with, it is collective, the work of many authors elaborating a shared body of material. King Arthur himself is unusual among legendary heroes in having a biography produced by a single writer, Geoffrey of Monmouth, who published his highly imaginative account in 1136 or a year or two later. But other writers added characters and themes to the structure in all the main languages of Europe. Some of the most important of them were French, such as Chrétien de Troyes. Some were German, such as Wolfram von Eschenbach. Some were English, although the greatest and best known of these, Sir Thomas Malory, came late on the scene, in the fifteenth century, remolding and improving stories already told and inter-weaving them in a unity not attained before.

Medieval storytellers seldom strove to be original. Originality was not favored as highly as it came to be in later times. Medieval minds valued authority and tradition; medieval authors often claimed to be drawing on previous authors, adapting or translating, even when they were not. Story-tellers tended to work with recognized bodies of material. And the Arthurian legend in its great medieval development was one such body, the main con-stituent of one of three principal "matters," referred to as the Matter of Brit-ain. Alongside it were the Matter of France and the Matter of Rome. The Matter of France meant chiefly a cycle of heroic tales concerning the em-peror Charlemagne, his mighty companion Roland, and the peers of France, round about the year 800. The Matter of Rome meant classical antiquity and could be stretched to cover the Trojan War and Alexander the Great.

Before King Arthur was widely publicized, the Matter of France had produced a major epic, the *Song of Roland*. But during the twelfth century, the Matter of Britain, dominated by Arthur, surpassed it in popularity. The tales of Charlemagne and his peers were martial and masculine, and a soci-ety advancing in culture wanted something with a wider variety. It wanted glamour, love, courtliness, magic. It wanted themes of more interest to women. Political forces were active, too. The French kings, who claimed to be Charlemagne's heirs, enjoyed the prestige and august ancestry that the Mat-ter of France conferred on them. The Anglo-Norman kings, lately enthroned in England, welcomed the cycle of Arthur as a retort. It gave their island realm a similar glory, and their dynasty a similar dignity, supposedly inher-ited from another majestic ruler.

If we ask the obvious question "Did King Arthur exist?," it is clear that the Matter of Britain is more mysterious than the other two Matters. With Charlemagne, or a classical hero like Alexander, the question can be given a straight answer: "Yes." The hero existed and can easily be discerned behind all fantasies about him. Historical records, older than the fantasies, are sufficient to prove it. With King Arthur, the case is otherwise. "Yes" and "No" are both misleading. "Yes" is misleading because, with Arthur, the emphasis is different. All the imaginative focus is on the legend. That is what Arthur's name evokes, and to say "Yes, King Arthur existed" implies that the monarch of romance was real, with all the panoply of his court. In that literal sense, he was not. But here we confront a second feature of medieval storytelling, at least the more literary kind, which precludes an unvarnished "No" as well and makes it hard to decide what the answer ought to be.

Romancers not only cared little for originality, they cared little for authenticity. The Matter of Britain shows their attitude in an extreme form. Historical novelists today, telling stories based on the characters and events of a past age, normally try to get it right. They find out how people dressed, what they ate, what sort of houses they lived in, what work they did, what topics they discussed. Medieval romancers did not. They updated. They considered their patrons and readers—mostly of the nobility, or at any rate upper-class—and told stories that those patrons and readers could understand, stories about things belonging to their world, however anachronistic the result. They wrote of chivalry and heraldry, of love affairs following prescribed patterns, of knights wearing showy armor and fighting in tournaments, of witches and magicians such as their audiences believed in. A few facts of history could not be changed (for instance, that people who lived before Christ were not Christians), but generally speaking, whatever the real or supposed historical setting, a story would emerge in the garb, so to speak, of the author's own time.

So while King Arthur in his familiar guise is plainly fictitious, that alone does not disprove his historicity. The figure of Arthur may be the result of updating and medievalizing a tradition that was truly ancient, and have originated in a real person. To say "No, he didn't exist" is a snap dismissal that the facts do not warrant, suggesting that the Arthurian legend is a baseless medieval fiction. The issues are more complicated. Perhaps the updating, the medievalizing, may seem to make it impossible to break through to an underlying reality. Yet the reality may be there all the same.

Medieval storytellers believed that it was. An authentic Arthur had existed indeed, a long time before. Most of them probably did not care much. Their main interest was in weaving fictions about his reign, fictions that, although anachronistic, grew into a literature with a validity of its own. But they did accept, if in a vague way, that the reign was there to be fictionalized. They and their audiences viewed Arthur's kingdom rather as people now regard the Wild West. We know, if in our own vague way, that for a few decades the West was wild, that there were cowboys, sheriffs, gunfights, and so forth, that such persons as Billy the Kid and Calamity Jane existed. Yet for the ordinary reader or viewer of westerns, history does not matter much.

Novelists like Owen Wister and Zane Grey, followed by Hollywood and the makers of television programs, transformed the West into a recognized realm of the imagination, the scene of adventures of certain kinds, with many fictitious inhabitants and a few real ones more or less fictionalized. On the one hand, this realm of the imagination is what most people know. On the other, it is understood that there is something behind it all, even if comparatively few are interested. This is roughly how it was, in the Middle Ages, with Arthur's Britain. Like the Wild West, it was a realm of the imagination, but its creators would have denied that they were simply inventing out of nothing.

A glance back at a remoter past is enough to sustain their claim in some degree. There is no doubt that their stories were based, at however many removes, on something real. The fruitful question to ask is not "Did King Arthur exist?" but "What facts is the legend rooted in, how did it originate?" Inquiry on that line may suggest, in the end, that Arthur was a real individual . . . or it may not.

We may begin by identifying the period when medieval authors conceived him to have flourished. While they offer few dates that even pretend to be exact, his reign lies within a limited span. Geoffrey of Monmouth, whose account purports to be historical, gives clues that would put a large part of it between, roughly, A.D. 455 and 475. Incompatibly, he also gives the year 542 for Arthur's departure, although that may be simply an error, as it is certainly an error when another author, paraphrasing Geoffrey in French, turns it into 642. Elsewhere, the Quest of the Holy Grail is stated to have begun in the 480s, and Arthur's name is linked with a real battle fought about 500. However inconsistent these dates may be, they place the reign somewhere between, say, 450 and 550, in a most obscure period. The scarcity of records, due to wars and plagues and other troubles, is one reason for the Arthurian legend's flowering. There were so few facts to contradict it.

Britain, which had been part of the Roman Empire, broke away for practical purposes somewhere about 410, and its inhabitants, the Britons, passed almost beyond the ken of the Empire's historians. During the ensuing decades, a different people began encroaching on them. The new claimants to British territory were Angles, Saxons, and Jutes, closely akin and often called collectively Saxons, who came from across the North Sea. Some had probably been in the island for years, but now they arrived in much larger numbers, multiplied, and expanded their settlements. They were eventually to create the country called England, "Angleland," and become the English, but their early progress was gradual. The Arthurian timespan puts the King in a phase when the Britons still held most of the land, and he is depicted, plausibly to at least this extent, as a king over them. He is also associated with Brittany across the Channel, which began to be colonized at this time by Britons—whence its name.

Who were these Britons, reputedly Arthur's subjects, neither Roman nor English? They were one of several peoples of Celtic stock like the Irish. Established in the island during the last centuries B.C., they succumbed to Roman conquest and received the stamp of Roman civilization. Left to their own devices after 410, they slowly broke up politically and lost ground to the Saxon settlers. But the Welsh, Cornish, and Bretons are descendants of these Britons who have kept an identity and have languages derived from the Britons' Celtic tongue, which survives also in many place-names in England, where the Britons, though overwhelmed and dominated, were not wiped out.

From the Arthurian point of view, the question is what happened in that transition period where the King is said to belong and whether he can be detected in it with any confidence. Certain beliefs about it were fundamental to the legend in its formative days. Post-Roman Britain was said to have fallen into the power of a disastrous ruler called Vortigern. The first Saxons arrived because he was harassed by enemies from the north and invited Saxons to settle in Britain as auxiliary troops. Their leader was Hengist. When more and more of the savage heathens poured in without permission, Vortigern lost control and fell under the domination of Hengist, whose hordes ravaged the country. Finally, the Britons recovered, thanks to new leaders, and Arthur was the greatest leader of all. He routed the Saxons and subdued them. His reign was founded on victory over these and other enemies and the restoration of peace. While he lived, the Britons were in the ascendant, and the Saxons were confined to a limited area and were not dangerous. It was only after his passing that the pendulum began to swing back. When they advanced again, the advance was permanent, because there was now no Arthur to stop them.

These beliefs can be shown to have some basis. Whatever the truth about King Arthur himself, the legend is rooted where medieval authors supposed it was, in Britain's post-Roman history. Let us go over that history more carefully. It is vague and ill-documented. The little that can be said depends on a hazardous reconstruction from a medley of sources. Nevertheless, the blank is not total.

Roman Britain, Britannia, corresponded approximately to modern England and Wales, plus a semicontrolled portion of Scotland. Beyond were the unconquered and turbulent Picts. Britannia's end came in confusion. It is often said that the central government gave up trying to hold this outpost and withdrew the legions. Actually, the change was more complex, a sort of unplanned declaration of independence in two stages. Almost cut off from Rome by a Teutonic invasion of Gaul (now France), the army in Britain set up an emperor of its own, a soldier named Constantine. He had a son, Constans, who left a monastery to join him. In 407, they took most of the troops to the Continent, hoping to master the anarchy and reach an agreement with Honorius, the much-reduced emperor in Italy. Four years later, they were both dead. The Britons, represented by city councils and regional governing bodies, had already broken with them and begun taking defensive measures against barbarians assailing Britain itself, chiefly the Picts, and Saxons from across the North Sea, who were raiding but not yet settling in considerable numbers.

After these events, Britain was still theoretically part of the Empire, but in practice Honorius had let it go, and the fiction was gradually abandoned. At least one British plea for imperial aid was unsuccessful. The administrative system went on functioning for a while, and there was a slow growth of regional governments under officials and commanders whose descendants were to become minor kings. A fragile unity persisted for fifty or sixty years. As with the Celts of Ireland, Britain's regional rulers apparently acknowledged a "high king" above them, at least in name. This is where the man known traditionally as Vortigern comes in. There is little doubt that he existed, since he is mentioned by Anglo-Saxon writers who were certainly not influenced by British legends. "Vortigern" is a Celtic title or designation, meaning simply the "over-chief" or "over-king." There is little doubt, either, that he did play a part in establishing the Saxons in Britain, although archaeology shows that their advent was piecemeal and widespread and that the story of Vortigern's deal with Hengist is a simplified and dramatized version. They had been known for a long time as marauding pirates, and some of their early settlement may have been mere squatting. However, Vortigern's alleged treaty, giving Saxons an authorized foothold as auxiliary troops, is consistent with Late Roman procedures. He, and perhaps other Britons, evidently employed them as *foederati*, barbarians allotted land and maintenance in return for behaving themselves, keeping order, and repelling other barbarians.

Further immigration, probably without leave, increased the Saxons' numbers. In the 440s, they were dominating parts of the country, such as Kent and East Anglia, and spreading through Lincolnshire and southwest from the Wash. Their inflated demands for supplies could not be met, and they mutinied. Toward the middle of the fifth century, Britain was drifting into a time of trouble, with Saxon bands raiding at will, and Picts, no longer opposed, acting in concert with them. Many of the Roman towns became derelict as their inhabitants scattered into the countryside for safety and subsistence. The movement of Britons across the Channel to the land known as Armorica, the movement that turned most of it into Brittany, began at this time as a flight of refugees, although it presently became more considered and less panic-stricken.

By 460 or thereabout, the Saxons were at last tired of raiding or discouraged by British resistance to it. They withdrew to their settlements in the eastern part of the island. Vortigern was dead, and the Britons were finding new leaders, seemingly from that part of the population that kept a tincture of Roman civilization and sentiment. A regional ruler called Ambrosius Aurelianus—a Roman name, eloquent of his parents' sympathies—organized a counterattack against the Saxon enclaves.

Meanwhile, it appears, another high king (at least in his own estimation) had claimed the succession to Vortigern. He is the only Briton of his time, apart from an ecclesiastic or two, who figures in continental records. The reason lies in a continental involvement. During the 460s, the Roman Empire was crumbling throughout the west. Various nations had seized large portions of Gaul. Among these, the Franks and Burgundians were still fairly docile. But there were Saxons in the Loire Valley as well as Britain, and Euric, the king of the Visigoths, held much of Spain and was menacing Gaul from the south. Leo I, who reigned in the eastern part of the Empire, appointed a western colleague named Anthemius, who tried to retrieve the situation. Anthemius may have been told of a pro-Roman trend among the Britons. At any rate, he negotiated a British alliance. In 468, the "King of the Britons" crossed to Gaul with twelve thousand ship-borne troops.

So at least early records indicate. The most recent historians to discuss this affair call it puzzling, and in some ways it is, but parts at least of the puzzle can be eliminated. Confusion has been caused by a doubt as to where the King of the Britons came from. Some have tried to reduce him to a "Breton," a chief of emigrants in Brittany. There is, however, no evidence for anything like enough Britons having emigrated, so far, to field a large army. Present opinion inclines toward the plain sense of what is said, that he started from some power base in Britain.

The objection has been an assumption that if he did come directly over, he must have been a mere chieftain leading a wandering warband, and it is hard to see how or why a warband numbering thousands could have simply wandered across the Channel. True, but in fact there is no great problem. The early testimony to his being invited into Gaul by the western emperor, bringing his force by sea (as "Bretons" would not have done), and being officially received as an ally is quite plain. After arrival, he may have recruited among his "Breton" countrymen and even treated them as still his subjects, but there can be no serious doubt as to his starting point in the island. As for his being a mere chieftain at the head of a mob, the answer lies in a fact only lately realized, the significance of the way continental writers refer to him.

They call him not only the "King of the Britons" but Riothamus. This latinizes a British form *Rigotamos*, which would have meant "supreme king" or "supremely royal," and is most probably a title or assumed style asserting a high-kingship just as "Vortigern" does, though perhaps a less effective one. (It does become a name later, as, likewise, "Vortigern" does, but with reference to other persons.) Ambrosius Aurelianus may have been a general in this king's service, whose action to contain the Saxons had been successful enough to justify taking troops overseas. Certainly, that move suggests that the home front was thought secure and that the king, with temporarily widening horizons, did plan his expedition in consultation with Rome.

He pushed up the Loire into central Gaul. Treachery, however, was working against him. Arvandus, Gaul's imperial prefect or governor, tried to make a deal with the Visigoths by which they would crush the British army and divide up Gaul with the Burgundians. His scheming was detected, but the Visigoths acted on his proposal and defeated the King of the Britons near Chateauroux. No imperial force had arrived to aid him. About 470, he made his way with a remnant of his army into the nearby territory of the Burgundians, who had held aloof from the plotting and were still friendly. No more is heard of him, and this was doubtless the end of even vestigial claims to a British high-kingship.

One sideshow was the overthrow of the Saxons in the Loire Valley. Britons may have taken part in a decisive battle near Angers. Deprived of further Gallic prospects, Saxons began to enter Britain at new points along the south coast. In other parts of the island, their fellow Saxons were consolidating, seemingly without conflict with the local inhabitants. Small Saxon kingdoms were taking shape, and the Britons, no longer united, were forming small kingdoms of their own. But Ambrosius's counterattack, and the fresh coastal incursions, led to a fluctuating warfare that smoldered on for years till a British victory brought a lull and stability in most areas. Meanwhile, clerics from Wales were beginning to migrate to Brittany, where they helped to organize the slowly growing communities of Britons, preparing the ground for a larger emigration that followed.

Obscure as all this is, one conclusion emerges. The unique Arthurian legend is grounded on a unique train of events. During the fifth century, barbarians of many kinds were overrunning the Empire in the west. Besides the Saxons, there were Vandals, Alans, Suevi, Goths, Franks, Burgundians, Huns. Some were repulsed, some were brought temporarily under control, some were victorious and carved out domains for themselves. Generally speaking, however, the peoples of the imperial provinces remained passive. The Britons alone achieved self-rule—whether deliberately or because it was thrust on them—before the barbarians moved in. The Britons alone fought back when they did. The Britons alone recovered, for an appreciable time, through their own efforts. Twice at least, they more or less mastered the situation. Such feats are not accomplished without leadership, and it is unlikely that Ambrosius alone accounts for everything. The presentation of Arthur as a leader of independent Britons, in the right period, overcoming the right enemies, attests a knowledge of this unparalleled British rally.

Still, the time gap is wide. Six centuries elapsed, so far as we can tell, before the knowledge generated a full and coherent story of his reign. How was it transmitted? And if we study the process of transmission, does it give us any glimpses of a real Arthur, or does he look like an afterthought, a creature of the imagination inserted in a phase of British success as a symbolic hero and then credited with impossible glories?

GILDAS

Although much has been lost, we can catch sight of knowledge being handed down, together with fantasy and fable, in the Latin writings of a few clerics. Gildas, a sixth-century monk from the north, produced a book entitled *De Excidio Britanniae*, "Concerning the Ruin of Britain." By his country's "ruin," Gildas means the Saxon invasion, regarded as a divine judgment for the Britons' sins and shortcomings. Regrettably, he is not a historian, and most of his book is a diatribe against persons living in his own time (before 550; it is hard to be more precise), including five regional kings. But he prefaces this tract with a retrospect of events in Britain since the Roman conquest. He treats his countrymen as a poor lot, and the Romans, imperceptively, as alien overlords who came and went. Nevertheless, he shows the lingering of a Roman inheritance not only in his style but in references to Britons as "citizens" and to Latin as "our language"—that is, our official and written language, the British being spoken only. He also takes it for granted that his readers are nominally Christians, which they were, as heirs of the Roman Empire's conversion.

Gildas's retrospective prelude is rhetorical, short on facts, and sometimes wrong. When he reaches the post-Roman period, he is annoyingly reluctant to name names, and it is doubtful whether he knows much that lies beyond living memory. However, he speaks of post-Roman Britain as having a governing council headed by a *superbus tyrannus*. The word *tyrannus* implies a doubtfully legitimate authority rather than oppression. Gildas's phrase means in effect "preeminent ruler" and alludes to the high-kingship. In the passage where the *superbus tyrannus* is mentioned, Gildas says it was he, with his councillors, who invited the Saxons in. This is the oldest written version of the Vortigern story, which we can see developing more or less in conformity with the likely facts.

Gildas goes on to tell of the arrival of more Saxons, their exorbitant demands for supplies, and their revolt, spreading fire and devastation right across to the western sea. It is all very lurid but probably closer to truth than falsehood. He is dramatizing scattered raiding, spread over a longish period, as a single universal catastrophe. This is a first step in the creation of the context of Arthur as a national savior, a rescuer from dissolution.

He goes on to note the migration to Brittany, the Saxons' eventual withdrawal, Ambrosius Aurelianus's counteraction, and the to-and-fro warfare culminating in a victory that brought partial peace. He calls it the "siege of Mount Badon" and makes a cryptic statement about its date that is usually taken to mean that it happened in the year of his own birth and that he is writing in the forty-fourth year after it. While his words have been read in other senses, no credible reading can shift the battle enormously far from the year 500. Gildas is speaking of an event within living memory, and his testimony to Badon is important. It is also acceptable as explaining a fact revealed by archaeology: that while the Saxons continued to multiply and consolidate, their actual advance halted in most areas for several decades. Besides its real historical value, the reference to Badon is another step toward the conception of an Arthurian salvation.

Gildas gives no hint as to where Mount Badon was. By inference, it was in southern England, because there were not enough Saxons anywhere else for a victory over them to have had significant results. Hills close to the Roman city of Bath have been favored, and so has the ancient hill-fort of

Badbury Rings in Dorset. Possibly the best candidate is another hill-fort, Liddington Castle near Swindon, which has a village of Badbury at its foot and overlooks important roads. Another of Gildas's omissions is more frustrating. His narrative outlines a series of events into which Arthur could fit and comes in fact to be portrayed as fitting. It shows a pattern becoming established in British minds, the destined matrix of the Arthurian legend. But it says nothing of Arthur.

That silence is all too depressingly in keeping with its general character. The unnamed king who is probably Vortigern, and Ambrosius Aurelianus, are the only specific Britons whom Gildas mentions between the breach with Rome and his own time. He is preaching, not writing history for its own sake, and he singles out individuals only when they are relevant to the sermon. He mentions the king as the fool who brought the Saxon scourge on his people. He mentions Ambrosius—as a commander only, no royal rank is implied—mainly to remind Britons that their forebears found leadership that gave them a second chance, and yet the degenerate princes of the present have thrown it away.

The protracted warfare and the triumph at Badon make it fairly clear, without going outside Gildas's text, that he is recalling a period when there were other leaders besides Ambrosius. Furthermore, Ambrosius's own nonroyalty implies the existence of kings. Gildas's Arthurian silence is exactly that: a silence. Perhaps Arthur was not one of the leaders and indeed did not exist. Perhaps Gildas regarded him as irrelevant to the sermon, or as, for some reason, "bad" and undeserving of credit. Or perhaps Arthur was already beyond living memory and Gildas knew nothing of him. Gildas omits obviously important people who were, such as the pretender Constantine and Riothamus. There are too many unknowns to allow a conclusion.

BEÒE, NENNIUS, ANNALES CAMBRIAE

In 731, the Anglo-Saxon scholar Bede wrote a history including a brief treatment of the same period. As far as the Britons are concerned, Bede sheds no further light, or hardly any, because he takes nearly everything from Gildas and has no independent account to offer. One of his few contributions is unhappy, a date for the Saxons' advent that is too late and that misled historians until recently. But he refers to the king who invited them as, explicitly, Vortigern, and he adds one important detail doubtless drawn from the traditions of his own people, their alliance with the Picts in the fifth-century onslaught. Other traditions from the same source have gone into the *Anglo-Saxon Chronicle*, which is considerably later than Bede. It, too, names Vortigern and gives uncertain particulars about the early settlements and the fighting with Britons. It names one or two British leaders whom the Saxons defeated, but none who defeated the Saxons. Ambrosius therefore does not appear in it. Nor does Arthur, who would have been remembered, if at all, as having done likewise.

In this case, his absence is not due to his never having been mentioned anywhere, because, by the time the *Chronicle* was compiled, he had. A little after the year 800, at the monastery of Bangor in North Wales, a book had been put together called the *Historia Brittonum*, "History of the Britons." Some copies have a preface in which a Welshman called Nennius claims responsibility for it. Hence, the book is often referred to by his name. It is written in a Latin much poorer than Gildas's, although some medieval authors absurdly supposed it to be his. Nennius says that he has "made one heap of all he has found" amassing old manuscripts and collecting oral traditions. Whether or not the preface is authentic, and Nennius actually is the compiler, that is the impression the *Historia* gives. It is encouraging to this extent, that Nennius does seem to be passing on genuinely older materials and not inventing.

We find here the account of fifth-century Britain carried far beyond Gildas. It is still crude and disjointed, but the enduring outline has been sketched. Vortigern is said to have been king during a vague forty-year period after the end of Roman Britain, and he has become more clearly the villain, solely to blame for opening the door to the Saxons. Hengist, we are told, landed at the head of a party of exiles, and Vortigern settled them in Kent and employed them as soldiers, not foreseeing the expansion and catastrophe that would follow. Some notes at the end of the main text give a few dates, the years being defined in Roman style by the names of the consuls. Vortigern is said to have risen to power in 425, and the first authorized Saxon settlers are assigned to 428. These dates may not be far wrong. But many incidents are fabulous-looking indeed, such as Vortigern's infatuation for Hengist's daughter and a treacherous massacre of British nobles at a peace conference. Another character briefly takes the stage, Vortigern's eldest son, Vortimer, who leads an army against the Saxons but dies.

Ambrosius reappears, very oddly. Vortigern is said to have been afraid of him. The reason lies in a fairy-tale episode. Vortigern tries to build himself a stronghold among the mountains of Snowdonia in northwest Wales. The walls keep crumbling. Magicians tell him that he must find a boy without a father, kill him, and sprinkle his blood on the foundations. A boy is found whose mother claims to have had intercourse with no man. Brought to the site, he gives a display of paranormal powers, revealing that the walls have been subsiding because of a hidden pool with two fighting serpents in it, one red, one white, symbolizing the Britons and Saxons. This teenaged prodigy turns out to be the young Ambrosius, referred to by his Latin name and also by the Welsh style "Emrys gwledig." The word *gwledig* originally meant a regional ruler, and Nennius says that Vortigern, shaken, made Ambrosius overlord of western Britain (more plausible hints elsewhere suggest that his area of authority was in the south). Strangely, Nennius does not speak of him later as a military leader at all but only, in a passing phrase, as prominent among the kings of the British nation, at some unspecified date. Arthur enters the scene by name shortly afterward, in a single chapter.

> In that time, the Saxons strengthened in multitude and grew in Britain. . . . Then Arthur fought against them in those days with the kings of the Britons, but he himself was leader of battles. The first battle was at the mouth of the river that is called Glein. The second and third and fourth and fifth upon another river that is called Dubglas and is in the district Linnuis. The sixth battle upon the river that is called Bassas. The seventh battle was in the Caledonian Wood, that is, Cat Coit Celidon. The eighth battle was in Fort Guinnion, in which Arthur carried the image of St. Mary, ever virgin, on his shoulders and the pagans were turned to flight that day and a great slaughter was upon them through the virtue of Our Lord Jesus Christ and through the virtue of St. Mary the Virgin, his mother. The ninth battle was waged in the City of the Legion. The tenth battle he waged on the shore of the river that is called Tribruit. The eleventh battle took place on the mountain that is called Agned. The twelfth battle was on Mount Badon, in which nine hundred and sixty men fell in one day from one charge by Arthur, and no one overthrew them except himself alone. And in all the battles he stood forth as victor.

The passage is thought to be based on a lost Welsh poem in Arthur's praise. In other words, a hero carried forward from a panegyric of unknown date has been slotted into the disaster-and-rescue pattern. If he actually lived then, the poem could not have been composed in his lifetime, because the Welsh language itself had not evolved out of the British. Arthur's status is unclear. He is the war leader—*dux bellorum* in the Latin—among the regional rulers, but as what? A high king or simply a commander-in-chief?

"Arthur at the Siege of Gaunes." French MS 1, fol. 244v. Reproduced by courtesy of the Director and University Librarian, the John Rylands University Library of Manchester.

The introductory "In that time" is unhelpful. Nennius mentions the death of Hengist, but in a parenthetical remark that is no use for dating. "That time" seems to be in the middle or later fifth century, because the Badon victory, somewhere about 500, comes at the end. No more can be said on the point with any confidence.

Several of the place-names have vanished from the map. Others can be identified fairly credibly, and they do bear some relation to the apparent fifth-century facts. Probably the River Glein is the Glen in southern Lincolnshire, and the "district" or "region" Linnuis is Lindsey, the central and northern portion of the same county. Archaeology shows early settlement by the Angles in these parts, so the area would have been logical for a campaign against them. The Caledonian Wood, or forest of Celidon, was in southern Scotland, and the City of the Legion, in this context, is almost certainly Chester. These latter sites, the ones where the location is most nearly sure, would both point to the anarchic period of the Saxon revolt, around the middle of the fifth century. Celidon is so far north that it implies Arthur was fighting Pictish allies of the main enemy, and while Bede speaks of such an alliance in the revolt, none is mentioned in the decades ensuing.

Chester is so far west that it implies Arthur was opposing a Saxon raid right across the country, and while Gildas speaks of such raids in the revolt, none is mentioned later.

Nennius's far-flung geography shows Arthur being pictured as a national rather than a local leader. That is not impossible, especially if he flourished when the Roman roads were still in good repair. Possibility, however, is not certainty, and the unknown poet whom Nennius seems to follow may have credited him with victories that, even on the assumption of his existence, were not his. Badon is the crux. This is the decisive success that Gildas had attested, without naming the leader who won it. By Nennius's time, it has become a battle of Arthur's, his crowning triumph. But the Arthur who triumphs is incredible, slaying nine hundred and sixty men single-handed. He is already a figure of legend. There is a consequent doubt as to how far his connection with Badon, or indeed the battle list as a whole, can be accepted as any sort of history; and the doubt is reinforced by the suspiciously long stretch of time that the battles seem to cover.

Further questions are raised by an appendix attached to the *Historia Brittonum*. This may be later than the rest, but not much. It is a list of "Marvels of Britain," that is, strange phenomena. Two of them concern Arthur.

One is a heap of stones in Buelt in south-central Wales, where the name Builth Wells survives today. On top of it is a stone marked with a dog's paw print. The dog is said to have been Cabal, the hound of "Arthur the soldier" or "warrior," and to have set his foot on it during a boar hunt described in a collection of Welsh tales called the *Mabinogion*. Arthur piled up the heap of stones with the marked one on top, and that stone cannot be removed, because, after a day and a night, it always reappears on the heap. The other marvel is in the old district of Ercing, which covered much of what is now Herefordshire. It is a tomb near a spring, the source of the River Gamber. The man in the tomb is Amr, a son of Arthur, and Arthur himself slew him there and buried him. No light is shed on this otherwise unknown tragedy. The tomb is marvelous because, every time you measure it, it is a different length—anything from six feet to fifteen—and, the writer assures us, "I have tried it myself."

In ninth-century Wales, then, Arthur is a famous figure and associated with battles that at least fit into the historical picture, but also with superhuman feats and bizarre local lore. The next century yields another Latin document, a chronicle known as the *Annales Cambriae*, or Annals of Wales, which is copied after the *Historia Brittonum* in the most favored

manuscripts. Basically, this is a table of five hundred thirty-three years starting with a Year 1 best taken as 447. Against some of the years, events have
been written in, posted from older chronicles. Several of the entries near the
beginning have been taken from an Irish source. At Year 72 (that is, 518 or
thereabout) we have the first British one:

> The battle of Badon, in which Arthur carried the cross of Our Lord Jesus
> Christ for three days and three nights on his shoulders, and the Britons were
> victors.

And at Year 93 (539 or thereabout):

> The strife of Camlann, in which Arthur and Medraut fell. And there was
> plague in Britain and in Ireland.

The Badon item, again, has a legendary look, though it can be rationalized. "Shoulders" may be a mistranslation of a Welsh word for "shield," as
perhaps also in Nennius's sentence about the eighth battle. The cross could
be an emblem, or one of the many pieces of the True Cross reputedly found
in Jerusalem. Yet the three days and nights remain peculiar. The other entry
is the first known allusion to a disaster that looms large in Welsh tradition.
Medraut is the man who becomes Arthur's enemy and destroyer in later
literature, his treacherous nephew, Modred or Mordred. However, it is not
stated here that he was a relative or a traitor or even that they fought on
opposite sides. The difficulties over dating recur. The year 518 seems incompatible with Gildas, who wrote when the battle was within living memory,
and an Arthur still an active warrior in 539 cannot be reconciled with an
Arthur made out to have been a war leader far back in the fifth century,
perhaps as early as the Saxon revolt.

"Camlann" is derived from a British word *Camboglanna*, "crooked
bank" (of a river), or less probably *Cambolanda*, "crooked enclosure." There
was a fort called Camboglanna on the Roman wall across northern Britain.
It may have been the one now called Birdoswald above the suitably crooked
River Irthing. Yet Arthur's fatal battle is never located in the north. The
"Modred" form of his enemy's name is Cornish, early references to their
quarrel place it in Cornwall, and rivers called "Camel" and "Cam" are found
in the southwest. To add to the doubts, Merioneth in Wales has a small
valley called "Camlan" and a river of the same name. The many allusions to
this battle suggest strongly that it happened, but it cannot be pinned down,

with or without a real Arthur in it. Since everybody else mentioned in the *Annales Cambriae* seems to have been real, the mention of Arthur and Medraut suggests that they were, too. But an allusion under Year 57 (ca. 504) to a bishop dying at the age of three hundred fifty also suggests that the particulars in the early entries are not unassailable.

SAINTS' LIVES

Wales's last Latin contribution, before the grand medieval flowering, is a group of "lives" of saints that introduce Arthur. The church in Wales had no canonization procedure, and the title of "saint" was bestowed freely, especially on founders of religious communities. Traditions of such a founder would be handed down in the community, and eventually a Life might be committed to writing. Most of these productions have little genuine biography in them. As a rule, it is swamped by legends, miracles, and would-be edification. One recurrent feature is a type of incident in which the saint achieves ascendancy over a powerful layman, who has been causing trouble and is duly put in the wrong and humbled. Arthur is cast in that role several times.

The Lives in which he figures were written at the monastery of Llancarfan in Glamorgan, during the eleventh and early twelfth centuries. That of Llancarfan's own founder, St. Cadoc, brings him in twice. We are told that when Cadoc's mother-to-be, Gwladys, a princess of Brecknock, was eloping with the man she intended to marry and her father was pursuing the couple, they came to a hilltop and found Arthur playing dice with his warriors Cai and Bedwyr—who, like Medraut, reappear in medieval romance, as Kay and Bedivere. Arthur looked upon Gwladys lustfully, but his companions urged that they should aid people in trouble, and when her father caught up, Arthur told him she was outside his jurisdiction and free. She married her lover and Cadoc was their firstborn. Many years later, when Cadoc was abbot of Llancarfan, he gave sanctuary for seven years to a man who had killed three of Arthur's soldiers. Arthur at last discovered where he was and, accompanied by an armed force, parleyed with Cadoc across the River Usk. He claimed that the abbot had no right to grant sanctuary for such a long time. The dispute was submitted to arbitrators, who awarded Arthur a hundred cows as compensation. He demanded that they should all be red in front and white behind. Cadoc miraculously provided such a herd, and Arthur's men drove them across a ford in the river, but the cows changed into bundles of fern. Abashed at this further miracle, Arthur conceded Cadoc's right to grant long-term sanctuary.

The Life of St. Padarn, whose monastery was near Aberystwyth, has a short and surprising episode in which the saint is harassed by "a certain tyrant named Arthur, from foreign parts," who covets a fine tunic belonging to Padarn and tries to carry it off. Padarn says, "Let the earth swallow him up," and it does. Arthur is engulfed to the chin and has to beg the saint's forgiveness before he can extricate himself. The Life of St. Carannog tells how the saint had a floating altar that drifted down the Bristol Channel to the coast of Somerset opposite Wales, where Arthur reigned as co-prince with Cato or Cadwy, another person who reappears in romance, as Cador. Presently, Carannog arrived himself. His altar was nowhere to be seen. Arthur was trying to catch a giant serpent that was devastating the neighborhood. He promised to reveal where the altar was if Carannog would subdue the serpent. The saint summoned the monster and banished it, whereupon Arthur confessed to having taken the altar himself and attempted to use it as a table. Resenting the sacrilege, it had thrown off everything he put on it. He gave it back and donated a plot of land to the saint. Outside Wales, a Breton Life of St. Efflam has an incident rather like this. About 1130, a monk of Llancarfan named Caradoc wrote a Life of Gildas, who counted as a saint in the Welsh church. It relates how Gildas's brother Hueil troubled the north with freebooting and piratical deeds. Arthur captured him and put him to death. Gildas was grief-stricken and furious. Arthur finally acknowledged that he had gone too far, and they were reconciled. Later, when Gildas was at the monastery of Glastonbury in Somerset, the local king Melwas carried off Arthur's wife and kept her in a stronghold near the monastery. Her husband came to recover her with troops from Devon and Cornwall, but the marshy country round about made the place difficult of access. Gildas and the abbot prevented him from attacking and negotiated a peace that restored the lady painlessly.

The last of these stories is significant as showing themes of the medieval legend evolving. It is the first assertion of a linkage of Arthur with Glastonbury, later to be claimed as his place of burial and involved in the saga of the Holy Grail. It is also the first version of a persistent motif, the abduction of Guinevere. Generally, however, the interest of these monastic fables is peripheral. Since they cast Arthur in a stock role, to show the saint's superiority in virtue or spiritual power, they are not plausible history even if the marvels are discounted.

Yet a few implications are worth noting. First, they emphasize a fact already evident, that the Welsh stretched out Arthur's career impossibly far. Carannog points to the fifth century, and so does a passage in another Life, that of St. Illtud, which mentions the saint visiting Arthur's court. But Cadoc can hardly have been abbot of Llancarfan much before the middle part of the sixth. His alleged clash with Arthur suggests that the Camlann entry in the *Annales*, making Arthur an active warrior in 539, may be only one instance of a wider process of prolongation. Second, a view of Arthur that allows him to be made a foil for the saints is at odds with the *Historia Brittonum*, where he carries a holy image into battle and conquers by celestial aid. Likewise, the *Annales*. Welsh clerical tradition about him was clearly not unanimous. Finally, the hagiographers disagree as to his status. He is a military chief, or a local ruler, or an upstart tyrant, or, in the Lives of Cadoc and Gildas, king of Britain—although even in the last two he is far from having absolute or unchallenged power. While all this could be mere incoherence and inconsistency, it could also correspond to a real career dimly recalled at different stages and an Arthur of no very exalted origins who fought his way upward to a high but uncertain authority. That was the story of quite a number of emperors, and it would have been possible in the Britain of the fifth century, although the climax, the high-kingship as we might say, would be an anachronism in the sixth. A phrase in one text of the *Historia Brittonum* prefaces the reference to Arthur as warleader by saying that there were "many more noble than he." It may not be wholly negligible.

BARDS AND GODS

To sum up, Wales supplies Latin materials showing that ideas about post-Roman Britain were handed down in the monastic writing rooms. Some of them have a sort of basic rightness, but they are fanciful and confused, with no clear sequence or succession. The allusions to Arthur are entangled with legend and not fully compatible. They are also scarce. But this last objection cannot be invoked to dismiss him, because, when we turn to the vernacular, it becomes plain that far more was said about him in other quarters. Around the few Latin texts is the penumbra of a popular saga. Arthur made an impression that gathered strength, and long before the twelfth century, he loomed larger as a hero of Celtic imagination than as a character in the histories, or pseudo-histories, of the monks.

We are catching glimpses here of what was, in effect, a proto-Arthurian literature, and it raises the issue of early Welsh literature in general. Much of it had an ancestry in the Celts' druidic past. Essentially, the druids were shamans or medicine men, but in their heyday they were far more, an elaborately trained priesthood, counselors to rulers, custodians of poetry and mythology. Women as well as men could join the order, though their concern perhaps was more with the magical side. The druids' doctrines on immortality interested philosophers in the classical world, but their darker practices, such as human sacrifice, and their enmity to Rome brought their suppression wherever Rome could accomplish it. In Celtic Gaul, the order was virtually broken. In Britain, however, it is said to have had its principal colleges, and the druidic heritage did not altogether expire among the Britons and their descendants.

Welsh bards kept some of it alive and created new poetry in their language as it emerged out of British. Gildas mentions bards singing the praises of a king in North Wales (he complains, characteristically, of their "mouths stuffed with lies and liable to bedew bystanders with their foaming phlegm"). The first major group was in the Cumbrian kingdom of Rheged in the north, where Taliesin and Aneirin flourished toward the end of the sixth century. Both left poetry that has survived, in verse forms already well developed and meant to be sung, a fact implying musical composition. Bards like these were honored figures attached to royal courts, and, supposedly, gifted with inspiration denied to most mortals. Storytellers of a more ordinary stamp took up their themes and spun popular tales about heroes of ancient myth and later legend. These spread widely along what was still a Celtic fringe outside the power of the Anglo-Saxons. The people of British stock in Wales and the north were called Cymry, meaning "fellow countrymen." The Cornish did not count as Cymry but shared many traditions and had others of their own, as did the Bretons, descendants of the emigrants who had turned that part of Gaul into the Lesser Britain, or Brittany.

As Christianity took a firmer hold, it squeezed out belief in the gods and goddesses of the druidic era. But Celtic Christians viewed the old divinities and their myths with a tolerance and even attachment that few of their co-religionists shared. Throughout most of the Roman Empire, the church had suffered a series of persecutions at the hands of pagan authorities abetted by the priests of the pagan cults. They detested the old religious order as evil and its deities as malign spirits deceiving the human race. But in Britain the persecutions had been half-hearted and brief, and they never affected Ireland at all. Although Irish druids opposed the mission of St. Patrick, and clerics in both islands (including Patrick himself, who was British) inveighed against false gods, there was no general sense of a black-and-white conflict. A great deal of pagan mythology survived in storytelling, and sometimes gods and goddesses reemerged disguised as kings, queens, enchanters. Brennus and Belinus, Nodons, and Matrona and her son Maponus became Bran and Beli and Nudd and Modron and Mabon, with new myths and attributes. Some of the places of holiness and power preserved their spell or transmuted it. The otherworld of Celtic myth, Annwfn as the Welsh called it, continued to flourish as (to use science-fiction language) a parallel universe, with known points of access, such as Lundy Island. So while some of the Welsh literature that has come scantily down to us is straightforward panegyric or elegy, much of it is wild, fantastic, and bewildering, and also, at least for latter-day readers, obscure.

The few authentic poems of Taliesin are in the straightforward class, more or less. They extol a northern king, Urien, and his son Owain, who temporarily checked the encroaching Angles. Aneirin composed, under the title *Gododdin*, a series of laments for a company of British nobles who assembled in the little kingdom of Manau Guotodin, around Edinburgh, and rode south to Catraeth—probably Catterick in Yorkshire—where they fell bravely in battle against the same enemy. The date of this campaign is about 600, and the *Gododdin* poems, or those that are genuinely Aneirin's, belong to that time. One stanza mentions a warrior named Gwawrddur as having "glutted the ravens" (that is, killed adversaries) "though he was not Arthur." The apparent sense is that he was a great fighter even though not equal to the greatest of all. Arthur is clearly proverbial for prowess in war. While this interesting stanza may be an addition by a later poet, there is no cogent reason for thinking so. Whoever is responsible, he says no more on this point and does not imply that Arthur was one of the northerners himself, or contemporary with them.

Another poem, dating in its present form from the tenth century but probably a rehandling of an older original, celebrates a king called Geraint and his valor in a battle at Llongborth. His domain was in the south and southwest, comprising the kingdom of Dumnonia or Dyfneint. "Devon" is derived from this name. Its royal house had several Geraints, and the poem betrays a confusion among them, but the Geraint in question is likely to belong to the late fifth century. "Llongborth" means "warship port" (Gildas speaks of the "long ships" of the Saxons), and the best candidate for the battle site is Portchester on the Hampshire coast, where the *Anglo-Saxon Chronicle* notes a contested landing in 501. The date is very doubtful, but the Saxons did occupy Portchester's Roman fort, and the action may have been the one that involved Geraint. The poet speaks in the character of an eye-witness, and in one stanza he turns aside to salute another leader.

> In Llongborth, I saw Arthur's
> Brave men who cut with steel,
> The emperor, ruler in toil of battle.
> That is all. He returns to Geraint and stays with him.

These lines are unlikely to have been put in after Arthur became a preeminent literary hero. An interpolator would have said more. All we get is the bare reference to his men—to a force fighting under his name along-side Geraint—and the word "emperor," in Welsh *ameraudur*, derived from the Latin *imperator*. It may mean "commander-in-chief," but it was some-times employed in Ireland to mean a high king. Whatever his status, Arthur is pictured here much as in the *Historia Brittonum*. He is a war leader, and a band of troops associated with him is acting in concert with a regional ruler, one of the "kings of the Britons."

As already remarked, the battle list in the *Historia* itself is thought to be based on a lost poem praising Arthur at length. Bards praised other he-roes in similar style, sometimes while they lived, sometimes afterward, even long afterward. Nennius (or whoever latinized the poem) believed it to be factual, and some of these panegyrics, such as Taliesin's, undoubtedly are. Yet, while most of the Latin version is fairly sober, it will be recalled that the last sentence, about Badon, shows fantasy creeping in. Indeed, that frequently happens. Taliesin may also have remained fairly sober, but that is far from true of poems that came to be ascribed to him, and he himself is given a strange legendary career including a magical birth. As for Arthur, apart from stray allusions underlining his general and growing fame, the rest of the Welsh matter invests him with a fairy-tale quality that severs historical links almost entirely.

In one poem, he arrives at the Gateway of a fortress and is challenged by the gatekeeper, Glewlwyd Mighty-Grasp, who demands that he name all his companions. At this point, Arthur is evidently at the head of a force but not a supreme ruler, since he has no authority over the gatekeeper. His prin-cipal follower is Cai, as in the Cadoc legend, and he names nine others. One is Bedwyr, again as in the Cadoc legend, and Arthur refers to Bedwyr's war-like feats "on the shores of Tryvrwyd." This is the unknown river called Tribuit in the battle list, but while the poem gives the list this scrap of support, it furnishes no clue to the river's whereabouts. Another follower is described as "Uthr Pendragon's man," Uther Pendragon being Arthur's father in medieval narrative, although there is no hint of it here. Arthur reverts to Cai and praises him in detail for his superhuman capacity as a drinker and for his prowess in slaying monsters and witches. The most fearful of the monsters is Palug's Cat, which lived in the island of Anglesey and ate one hundred and eighty warriors.

Among the poems ascribed to Taliesin is *The Spoils of Annwfn*—actually composed in the tenth century. Pre-Christian in its imagery, it gives an obscure account of a raid on the otherworld or underworld made by Arthur in quest of a magic cauldron. He sails with his companions in his ship Pridwen through a region of waterways and islands and uncanny strongholds. Three shiploads of warriors undertake the voyage; only seven men return. Their perilous pursuit of a wonder-working vessel foreshadows the Grail Quest and may have gone into the making of that complex theme. The most interesting line mentions the cauldron's custodians: "By the breath of nine damsels it is gently warmed." This, too, looks like an advance hint at the Grail, which is carried by maidens, and there may be a specific link with actual Celtic sisterhoods. A Roman geographer of the first century A.D., Pomponius Mela, tells of nine priestesses living on an island off Brittany, who cured the sick and had magical powers.

The Stanzas of the Graves, a poem listing the burials of famous men, observes casually that Arthur's grave is a mystery. Although this could be a plain statement of fact if the site was forgotten, it looks like an early phase in the growth of the folk belief that Arthur had no grave because he never died.

FRAGMENTS OF A SAGA

As for Welsh storytelling apart from poetry, it drew on a rich body of legend and folklore, but most of the early tales are lost. The *Mabinogion* assembles a few survivors. Besides these, we possess a kind of index tantalizingly suggesting how much has vanished. It takes the form of a series of "triads," recorded in several versions, of varying content and authenticity. A triad in this sense was a device to aid memory. Storytellers grouped characters and plot summaries in threes, under a heading covering all three, such as "Three Generous Men" or "Three Futile Battles." In this way, a storyteller could mentally organize his repertoire. Having told the tale of the first generous man, futile battle, or whatever, he could go on to the second as an encore, and the third after that.

Some of these miniature lists are late and influenced by medieval literature, but some are early enough to be eloquent. Arthur occurs in a good number of them, and, more than once, unexpectedly. It goes without saying that he is a renowned warrior, but he is also one of the Three Frivolous Bards, a label explained in another context by an account of his making up a verse that offended Cai. He is guilty of one of the "Three Wicked Uncoverings," or "Unfortunate Disclosures." This was the exhumation of the head of the prehistoric king Bran, buried on Tower Hill in London as a protection against foreign evils. Arthur dug it up, saying Britain should not rely on such talismans but on the military effort under his leadership. The result was that, after his passing, the Saxons conquered.

A triad headed "Three Unrestrained Ravagings" gives the alleged reason for Arthur's quarrel with Medraut, leading up to the fatal battle of Camlann. Medraut raided Arthur's hall in Cornwall, where his followers "consumed everything" and he struck Arthur's wife, Gwenhwyfar. Arthur retaliated by raiding Medraut's hall. This episode sounds like a feud of equals. Although the triad amplifies the Camlann entry in the *Annales*, it remains clear that the notion of Mordred as a treacherous and rebellious subordinate is a non-Welsh theme grafted on from outside. Camlann is mentioned in other triads, but they ignore the victory of Badon. Arthur's role as a Saxon crusher seems not to have counted for much in the evolution of his saga, however crucial it was in giving the initial impulse. Notable, too, is the fact that although the Welsh claim Arthur as theirs, they never locate his home in Wales. He lives at Kelliwic in Cornwall, perhaps the hill-fort Castle Killibury, and is also found once or twice in Somerset.

Gwenhwyfar, or Guinevere, is not restricted to her part in her husband's quarrels. She appears in her own right in several triads, including an extremely curious one, the "Three Great Queens of Arthur's Court," which asserts that all three were named Gwenhwyfar. The background may be a fragment of myth no longer understood about the Great Goddess of Celtic antiquity manifesting herself in three forms.

Arthur's frequency of appearance in the triads is a sign of his popularity as a hero. So is the fact that he and persons in his circle are added to several of the triads as a fourth. The triad of the "Three Famous Prisoners," having noted who they were, goes on to say that there was another prisoner more famous than those three, namely Arthur, and to list his imprisonments—perhaps in the course of early guerrilla adventures, who knows? Guinevere is unkindly added to the triad of the "Three Faithless Wives" as a fourth more faithless than the three, because she deceived a better man.

The triads mention other characters of romantic fame, notably the members of the tragic love triangle, King Mark, his wife, Iseut, and her lover, Tristan. They are called March, Essyllt, and Drystan. The chief triad concerning them summarizes a tale in which Tristan guarded Mark's pigs while the swineherd took a message to Iseut for him, and Arthur attempted a raid but failed to capture a single pig. The impression is oddly primitive, though pigs were more dignified animals in Celtic society than they have become since.

One early Welsh tale of Arthur is preserved complete in the *Mabinogion*. Its title is *Culhwch and Olwen*. A barbaric, colorful, sometimes comic production, this tale dates in its present form from the eleventh century or a trifle before. It shows that by then Arthur had become a figure of towering stature, and many other characters had been annexed to his saga, some historical, some taken from ancestral myth, some wildly anachronistic, and some incredible, such as three kings of France. There are few hints of a real context and no indications of the Roman Empire, despite references to widespread travel and even to Arthur conquering Greece.

Culhwch (pronounced Kil-hooch, with the *ch* as in the Scottish "loch") is a young nobleman under a spell, doomed never to marry unless he weds Olwen, the daughter of Ysbaddaden, the Chief Giant. He foresees difficulties and rides off to seek the help of Arthur, who is his cousin. The gatekeeper of the court is Glewlwyd Mighty-Grasp, the same who obstructs Arthur in the poem. Arthur has apparently taken Glewlwyd into his own service, but the gatekeeper is just as obstructive as of old when it comes to admitting Culhwch. The suitor has to argue and threaten his way in.

Culhwch hails Arthur as "sovereign prince of this Island," but again there is ambiguity about his status. One reason why Culhwch's prospects are uncertain is that Arthur has no authority over the giant. Ysbaddaden in fact claims some sort of authority over Arthur, although the point is never developed. The story lists the members of Arthur's court, giving anecdotal details, often of a fabulous kind, about them. Cai and Bedwyr, the future Sir Kay and Sir Bedivere, head the list. Gildas is present with his brothers, and so is the incompatibly late Taliesin, together with northern heroes of his time. Guinevere is "the first lady of this Island." Another lady is the mythical Creiddylad, daughter of Lludd, from a cloudy antiquity. Totally fantastic characters include Sgilti, who can run along the treetops, and Sugyn, who can drink up the sea till three hundred ships lie stranded.

Arthur pledges his help to Culhwch. Olwen, it transpires, is willing to marry him, but her father, the Chief Giant, objects strongly. He, too, is under a spell, doomed to die when his daughter weds, and several suitors have disappeared already. In keeping with fairy-tale logic, he cannot veto the match, but he makes absurd conditions meant to avert it. To prepare bread for the wedding feast, Culhwch must clear away a wood, plow, sow, and reap, all in one day. To boil the meat, he must fetch a special cauldron from Ireland. To hold the milk, he must get some magic bottles in which no liquid turns sour. He must overcome witches and monsters, and to trim the giant's hair, he must take a comb and scissors from between the ears of Twrch Trwyth, a king changed into a giant wild boar for his sins.

Arthur and his men fulfil the conditions by various amazing feats. The climax of the tale is the hunting of Twrch Trwyth. This is the same hunt mentioned in the "marvels" attached to the *Historia Brittonum*, during which the dog Cabal put his foot on the stone. After a long chase, fatal to several hunters, the comb and scissors are wrested from the boar. Culhwch claims his bride, both the spells run out, and an enemy cuts Ysbaddaden's head off.

Culhwch and Olwen is told with enormous gusto and many allusions to other tales now lost, allusions that mesh to some extent with the triads. Arthur's Cornish home Kelliwic is mentioned. So, in anticipation, is the battle of Camlann, but not Badon. As in the triads, Arthur's warfare against the Saxons is no more than an implication. While his power and freedom of action presuppose their containment, nothing shows how this was achieved.

The Welsh saga attests his fame among the Britons' descendants before the medieval reshaping that created the legend in its familiar form. Another sign of that fame is the proliferation of folklore. Up and down Britain, from the Isles of Scilly far into Scotland, there are at least one hundred and sixty places with Arthurian lore attached to them. This imposition of Arthur on the landscape had begun by the ninth century, when the two "marvels" were recorded in Buelt and Ercing. In 1113, when some French priests were traveling through Devon and Cornwall, according to Hermann of Tournai, people told them they were in Arthurian territory and pointed out Arthur's Chair and Arthur's Oven, probably rock formations or prehistoric stone huts. In modern times, four hills have been noted called Arthur's Seat, six stones called Arthur's Stone, eleven others called Arthur's Quoit. There are reputed battlefields and earthwork Round Tables. There are (unfortunately) five bodies of water into which the King's sword was thrown away.

While some of this folklore is due to medieval or modern fancy, it is grounded in the early saga rather than the later romance. The Arthur of local legend is seldom found in well-known cities or historical settings, and where anything specific is said about him, he is sometimes not so much a medieval monarch as a sort of titan, a *Culhwch and Olwen* character, sitting on hills and hurling rocks for miles. Moreover, few of his folklore locations are in the more English parts of England. The lore has seldom struck root there, despite his literary renown. It spreads along the Celtic fringe where the saga took shape, in areas that kept a Celtic identity longest and in some cases keep it still.

One persistent folklore theme, which makes its mark on the Arthurian map, is the belief in the King's survival and promised return. *The Stanzas of the Graves*, with its cryptic statement that Arthur's grave is a mystery, is echoed by the Anglo-Norman historian William of Malmesbury, who observes in 1125 that "Arthur's tomb is nowhere beheld, so that ancient songs fable he is still to come." William does not commit himself as to how ancient the songs were, but the belief was current before 1125. It takes several forms, the best known being two: that Arthur is living in the enchanted island of Avalon, the "place of apples," or that he is asleep in a cave, often accompanied by his knights or his treasure. Both versions were probably derived from a Celtic myth recorded by Plutarch in the first century A.D.,

ARTHUR'S SURVIVAL AND RETURN

Traditions vary widely in their treatment of the question of Arthur's survival and return. The possibility of such a return was reflected in the works of authors as early as William of Malmesbury (1125) and Wace (1155), and such a belief must have been a feature of popular lore even earlier. Wace wrote that, "if the chronicle does not lie, Arthur was mortally wounded in his body. He had himself carried to Avalon to heal his wounds. He is still there, and the Britons are still awaiting him." Most medieval chroniclers rejected the belief, but their very rejection gave evidence of its hold on the popular imagination.

Only a few medieval texts (the short English romance *Arthur*, the *Alliterative Morte Darthur*, and Malory) use the formula *Rex quondam rexque futurus* popularized by T.H. White's version: *The Once and Future King*. Caxton's Malory expresses reservations about the possibility, noting that "men say that he shall come again" but adding that "I will not say it shall be so."

Wherever the possibility of a return is held open, it is said that Arthur, grievously wounded, is taken away to a place called Avalon, to have his wounds healed. Avalon has most often been identified with Glastonbury.

about a banished god lying asleep in a cave in a far-off western isle, with attendant deities around him. As with some other mythic motifs, this one came to be applied to a human hero, dividing in the process.

Arthur's immortality seems to have started as a Breton belief and spread to Cornwall and Wales. The Bretons stressed the island conception, whether or not they used the name Avalon, and Avalon became Arthur's retreat in literature, but popular lore in Britain preferred the cave legend. Collection and collation of all the instances known to folklorists show that Arthur, or his knights, or both, are asleep in at least fifteen places. These include the Somerset hill-fort Cadbury Castle and sites across Wales, through the north of England, and near Melrose in Scotland. Two real caves bear his name, in the Forest of Dean and on Anglesey, but the usual story is that the cave is a magical one that can be found and entered only under peculiar conditions, perhaps through the agency of a wizard, and often with unhappy results for the person who enters.

The earliest documentation for an undying Arthur is a narrative written by Hermann of Tournai about the English journey, already mentioned, of a party of French priests in 1113. They were raising funds to rebuild a church, and they brought holy relics with them, to encourage the sick to come forward in search of healing and make donations. In Bodmin, Cornwall's chief town, a man with a withered arm approached the relics. For some reason, King Arthur was mentioned, and the man declared that he was still living. The Frenchmen, who knew of the same notion in Brittany, were amused, but bystanders supported the claim and a fight broke out. A curious point here is that, although the Cornish belief was so strong, Cornwall has no cave legend. An island in the Scillies called Great Arthur may hint at its Avalonian rival. However, the favored idea in Cornwall is that Arthur turned into a bird, probably a raven.

Whatever its origin in this case, the cave legend became a medieval folklore motif in other countries, with other characters. Arthur himself was said to be in Mount Etna, and a number of national heroes were also asserted to be asleep in a cave. One of the most famous was originally the German emperor Frederick II, although he later became Frederick I, Barbarossa. Such tales, at least in Europe, may have been inspired by the literary renown of Arthur himself. A byproduct of Arthur's immortality is his participation in the Wild Hunt. He and other legendary and mythical figures were said to emerge from whatever retreat they occupied and to career through the clouds summoning the spirits of the dead to join them. In Wales, the leading huntsman was Gwyn ap Nudd, son of the British god

Nodons. Mentioned in *Culhwch and Olwen*, he is the lord of Annwfn and has a hidden palace inside Glastonbury Tor, the hill above the town.

NO SMOKE WITHOUT FIRE?

So we come round again to fundamental issues. We have defined the historical situation in which the Arthurian legend is remotely rooted. We have seen traditions about it being handed down, clumsily, fancifully, but with a tenuous hold on the facts. And we have seen Arthur embedded in those traditions and growing to impressive proportions, before the medieval legend even began. But does all this saga and poetry and quasi-history give any plain clues as to when and how he came in, and whether he was a real person?

The "no smoke without fire" argument is valid up to a point. This is a major phenomenon, and somehow it had a beginning. "Fire" of some kind there was. However, that alone does not mean that the first impulse came from the career of an individual. It might have come from a poet's imagination. Modern examples show the uncertainty of inferences about characters who have passed into folklore. In America, tall tales are told of Davy Crockett and Paul Bunyan. Davy Crockett existed, Paul Bunyan did not. The most salutary example of all is Sherlock Holmes, another character in modern folklore, not superhuman but the hero of a saga comprising dozens of stories and films, so vivid that people discuss his exploits as if they actually happened and even pretend to reconstruct his biography, debating when he was born and what university he went to. Yet, in this case, we know exactly how the saga began, and we know that Holmes is fictitious.

One clue does tell us roughly when Arthur's story was launched: his name. "Arthur" is a Welsh form of the Roman name Artorius. A man called Artorius, whether real or invented, cannot be dated much later than the post-Roman period when Britons were still being called by Roman names ("Ambrosius," for instance). Moreover, with this particular name, something exceptional happened. When the custom in general had almost died out, "Arthur" made a comeback. In the later part of the sixth century, a number of Arthurs are on record in Wales and the north. They presumably were named after an earlier Arthur who by then had become a hero of widespread reputation.

Arthur's origin, then, does lie more or less in the time of the Britons' temporary recovery. He is not a character picked up or invented long afterward and imposed on the period retroactively. Whoever or whatever he was, he began his career in it and was celebrated fairly soon after it. His henchman Cai confirms the point. "Cai" is probably another Roman name, Caius.

Thus far, the question of his reality remains open. Oddly, a fact that tells in favor of reality is one that looks utterly fanciful, the cave legend. However mythic its inspiration, it has an aspect that was pointed out by the folklorist Jennifer Westwood. Arthur is not the only sleeper in a cave. The same is told of other national heroes, the emperor Frederick being the most eminent. And it appears that in every other case, at least in Europe, the sleeper is historical. One or two may be open to doubt, but the motif never attaches itself to definitely fictitious or fairy-tale characters. By analogy, Arthur, too, is real or at any rate has always been regarded as real. To claim otherwise is to claim a glaring exception for which there is no evidence.

The Historical Quest

Considerations like these take us a little way, but not far. Attempts have been made to prune away all the legendary accretions and reach a firmly attested "historical Arthur." Some scholars have stressed the phrase *dux bellorum*, "war leader," in the *Historia Brittonum* and envisaged a commander-in-chief rather than a king, the leader of a personal corps sustaining British resistance in different areas. R.G. Collingwood suggested that the imperial military office of *Comes Britanniarum*, Count of the Britains, continued or was revived after the end of Roman authority, and Arthur in that capacity led a force of imperial-type cavalry, to which the pedestrian Saxons had no answer. The most durable part of Collingwood's theory has proved to be the cavalry notion. In the absence of stirrups, which did not reach western Europe till later, mounted warriors could not have had the impact that medieval knights were to have, but they would have enjoyed an advantage through mobility, surprise, and moral effect. This is a conjecture that many still find attractive, but no more than that. There is no hard evidence for it.

Kenneth Jackson, while rejecting the main Collingwood thesis, speculated about the war-leader idea and identified some of the battle sites. He showed that these were far-flung and that Arthur was represented as active throughout the former Roman Britain, a belief that could suggest that the anti-Saxon effort was led for a time by someone called Artorius who made a strong impression, a "commander of genius" probably based in the southwest, within striking distance of the major Saxon settlements. The archaeologist Leslie Alcock argued much along Jackson's line, relying on the *Historia Brittonum* and the *Annales Cambriae*, especially the latter. He judged that the British high-kingship went on after Vortigern and suggested that Ambrosius and Arthur were generals in the service of a high king or kings. John Morris, in *The Age of Arthur*, enlarged this military Arthur into a kind of emperor. Another school of thought, one of its most distinguished members being Rachel Bromwich, found it easier to interpret Arthur as a northern leader and not originally so important. The main argument was that the earliest relevant matter deals chiefly with northern events and characters. On this showing, much of the Arthur saga began in the north and was relocated.

The search for Arthur by such methods came to an inconclusive halt in 1977, when David Dumville published a trenchant attack on all the Welsh matter as historical evidence. Despite some objections, his critique was effective, and attention was also drawn to other difficulties. It has to be confessed, for instance, that the attempt to cut out legend and isolate plain historical statements can never convince. No Welsh reference to Arthur can be proved close enough in time to be trustworthy. Nor is there any document, even among the earliest, that can be accepted with any confidence as free from legend. The cutting-out leaves no plain statements at all. Nennius's battle list reads fairly plainly up to a point, and then the assertion that Arthur slew nine hundred and sixty men single-handed at Badon calls its whole testimony in question. In the *Annales*, the Badon entry is likewise suspect. The Camlann entry looks better and has even been claimed as the single irreducible datum. But it cannot be proved earlier than the tenth century, and in any case to explain the Arthurian phenomenon from this one item is no explanation. It puts Arthur so late that virtually everything else must be rejected. It implies that the entire legend arose from a petty chief, one among dozens, with no record of victory or anti-Saxon campaigning, fatally squabbling with another petty chief in deep obscurity. This is merely replacing one mystery with another. There is no intelligible way in which an Arthur confined to the Camlann entry could have been the starting point of the saga, could have blotted out the fame of the leaders who did win victories.

The doubt over the testimony does not mean that the battles are fictitious or that the linkage of a real Arthur with them has to be spurious. It does mean that in themselves they lead to no safe conclusion about him. The *Annales* entries throw a further problem into relief, the way his career is spread over an impossible stretch of time. His two roughly locatable battles, Celidon and Chester, make sense only in the context of the Saxon revolt, with its Pictish alliance and its cross-country raiding. In other words, they put his leadership in the 450s or '60s. But his presence at Badon would make him still lead forty or fifty years later, and his presence at Camlann, if the *Annales* are trusted, would make him active as a centenarian. The Life of St. Cadoc stretches him further yet.

It may well be that a real Arthur flourished somewhere in the long time range, and everything discrepant is later fantasy weaving or the result of stories becoming attached to him that were first told of others. But where to put him in the time range? What is needed is a chronological fix: a statement clearly synchronizing him with known history outside Britain. That is what the Welsh material never supplies. It never says that he campaigned when such-and-such a person was emperor or died when such-and-such a person was pope. It leaves him hanging or drifting, in a temporal void.

Its inadequacy is proved in the end by the dissensions of scholars who have tried to use it. Some have made out Arthur to be a national leader; others see him as a local one inflated by legend. Some have put him in the north, on largely literary grounds; others have put him in the southwest, partly because it is only there that even legend gives him a birthplace or a headquarters or a grave and partly because it is only there that archaeology offers any support for tradition. There have been disagreements over his date and over his connection with Badon, supposedly his supreme triumph, yet never credited to him by Gildas or by the early Welsh poems and stories.

His elusiveness has inspired theories claiming to account for the facts without any real person. Since a few of the British gods were semihumanized as heroes of legend, it has been argued that Arthur was such a god, and that even if a man of that name existed he is irrelevant, since the Arthurian stories are adapted from myths of the divine being. There is, however, no trace in Britain of a god called "Artorius" or anything else that could have evolved into "Arthur," and the known gods who did become legendary characters were never given a detailed career in a serious historical setting. A notion that Arthur was the god of a patriotic pagan revival in the fifth or sixth century, having been unknown in the pagan past, is refuted by the silence of Gildas, who denounces the officially Christian Britons for every sin under the sun except apostasy and would have denounced revived paganism if there had been any.

In practice, the "god" interpretations of Arthur have contradicted each other even more flagrantly than the human variety. A kindred attempt to make out that "Arthur" really means "bear," and that he is a bear-hero of a type found in other mythology, has proved a blind alley. Comparison shows that he is simply not a bear-hero. He certainly undergoes what might be called mythification, and some of his companions certainly are survivors from the old pantheon. But no one who has tried to get rid of him as a human being has given a convincing account of the data without him. Most impartial followers of the debate over the Welsh matter have been inclined to accept that a real person is lurking in it somewhere. They have found it somewhat easier, on balance, to believe that he existed than that he did not.

A WAY OUT?

That conclusion is a lame one. Its lameness, however, could be a result of question begging. It has too often been assumed that if Arthur existed, his activities, and any historical tradition of them, were confined to Britain. It would follow that there can be nothing of historical interest outside the island, meaning, in practice, outside the orbit of the Welsh. Yet the best early narrative of fifth-century Britain is not in a Welsh work but in a Breton one, and it touches on Arthur.

This is the *Legend of St. Goeznovius.* "Goeznovius" latinizes the name Goueznou, in Welsh Gwyddno. The saint in question was one of the many clerics who went over to Brittany. He has no Arthurian relevance himself, but the author of his *Legend* starts with a preface giving the background to the saints' migration, the word "saint" being used, as in Wales, in a broad and general way. He states his name as William and the date of composition as 1019. His work was long dismissed as Arthurian evidence, on the ground that the date was spurious and it was merely copied from the later and greater book of Geoffrey of Monmouth. Léon Fleuriot, however, has upheld William's date, and even if his arguments are mistaken, *Goeznovius* cannot be explained as a copying from Geoffrey and implies another source; William indeed mentions it and calls it the *Ystoria Britanica*. Obviously, a text like this cannot be used as direct evidence for events half a millennium earlier. But its quality favors a respectful attitude toward whatever tradition may underlie it and a readiness to ask in what direction this points.

In William's words:

The usurping king Vortigern, to buttress the defense of the kingdom of Great Britain that he unrighteously held, summoned warlike men from the land of Saxony and made them his allies in the kingdom. Since they were pagans and of devilish character, lusting by their nature to shed human blood, they drew many evils upon the Britons.

Presently, their pride was checked for a while through the great Arthur, King of the Britons. They were largely cleared from the island and reduced to subjection. But when this same Arthur, after many victories that he won gloriously in Britain and Gaul, was summoned at last from human activity, the way was open for the Saxons to go again into the island, and there was great oppression of the Britons, destruction of churches, and persecution of saints. This persecution went on through the times of many kings, Saxons and Britons, striving back and forth....

In those days, many holy men gave themselves up to martyrdom; others, in conformity to the Gospel, left the greater Britain that is now the Saxon's homeland and sailed across to the lesser Britain [i.e., Brittany].

Here at last is Arthur in a straightforward narrative, with some rhetoric but nothing palpably legendary. Moreover, it is far better history than anything else. Apart from Arthur himself, all the main features of the story are correct, so far as present knowledge goes. Vortigern invites the Saxons in as auxiliaries. They revolt and cause trouble. Finally, they retire, or are driven, into a confined area. After a shift in fortune, Saxons begin entering Britain at new points. There is now no longer a single British king, and the country is broken up into small kingdoms, British and Saxon, engaging in a to-and-fro warfare. The saints emigrate to Brittany. All these things apparently happened, more or less, and in that order.

Since William seems to be drawing on sound information, what about his witness to Arthur? He puts him in as the King of the Britons before the breakup, Vortigern's successor. There is no hint of anyone else between. Thanks to Arthur, after the Saxons' mid-century revolt ("presently," *postmodum*, implies *soon* after), they desist from raiding and are contained. It is after his departure—made slightly cryptic, but not necessarily supernatural—that the new Saxon incursions begin. They fall into place as the landings along the south coast, which, according to the *Anglo-Saxon Chronicle*, started during the 470s. That is confirmed by the fluctuating warfare, spoken of by Gildas as going on from Ambrosius's counterattack till Badon, but not after. William therefore places Arthur just before these developments, in or around the 460s.

He takes him to Gaul, a new and non-Welsh factor, pointing to continental tradition that reached Brittany but not Wales. Alone, this is not factual documentation, but it leads directly to matter that is. In conjunction with the dating, it suggests who is meant by Arthur here. As we saw, a man described as the King of the Britons did campaign in Gaul during the late 460s. He is referred to as "Riothamus," probably an honorific or assumed royal style, and leaves open the question of personal name. His reality is proved by the survival of a letter to him from a Gallo-Roman author, Sidonius, and also by the outline of his campaign that emerges from other writings of Sidonius, from the Gothic historian Jordanes, and from the Frankish historian Gregory of Tours. Jordanes calls him the "King of the Britons" as *Goeznovius* calls Arthur, and his silent disappearance from history matches the *Goeznovius* phrase about his being "summoned from human activity."

It is plausible to suppose that William's Arthur is the same person. There may have been a belief that "Arthur," or to be precise Artorius, was his name. It may actually have been his name. Alternatively, it could have been given to him as a nickname or sobriquet, at the time or in retrospect. Two Roman emperors are best known by nicknames, Caligula and Caracalla. In this case, a definite source can be proposed. One earlier Artorius is on record in Britain, Lucius Artorius Castus, who held an army command. In A.D. 184 he took a force from Britain over to Armorica, the country that later became Brittany, to suppress a rising. This event could have been remembered (there is some slight evidence that it was), and a fifth-century Briton taking a force over to the same country or thereabout could have been nicknamed, or hailed in panegyrical verse, as a "second Artorius." An Arthurian link with this general has been suggested also by way of a kind of saga in Britain itself, taking shape, hypothetically, among descendants of auxiliary troops under his command. That would account at least for his name being known, and ready to hand for some poet extolling a later leader.

In any event, *Goeznovius* points to another way of viewing the origins. The king known as Riothamus did exist. The question is whether the Arthurian legend began with a tradition, correct or not, telling of this man—perhaps the last British high king, with an audacious career and a tragic and mysterious end—under the name Arthur. This would mean placing the original Arthur-figure near the beginning of the time range. To do so leads to manifest problems, but there is no way of placing him that does not.

We must pass on, however, to the medieval eruption, while not neglecting the chance that even the effusions of the twelfth century may shed more light on the possibility that *Goeznovius* raises.

GEOFFREY OF MONMOUTH

Concerning the creator of Arthur's "biography," the framework of medieval romance, little is known. Geoffrey was presumably born at Monmouth in southeast Wales. He was of Celtic stock, although not necessarily Welsh, since many Breton families returned to their ancestral island with the Norman Conquest, and Geoffrey certainly shows an interest in Brittany and Breton matters. A cleric, he was teaching at Oxford between 1129 and 1151 and was consecrated bishop of St. Asaph in Wales but probably never went there. He died in 1154 or 1155.

Writing in Latin, he first appeared before the public with a cryptic series of "Prophecies of Merlin" *(Prophetiae Merlini)*. Though most of these were inventions of his own, he ascribed them to an obscure wanderer mentioned in Welsh legend as an inspired madman. Merlin's literary role as a mighty sage and court magician was to come later, through his development by Geoffrey himself and the romancers. Toward 1138, Geoffrey incorporated the "Prophecies" in his major work, the *History of the Kings of Britain (Historia Regum Britanniae)*.

This is one of the most influential books of the Middle Ages, and there is nothing else quite like it. Geoffrey begins by expanding a Welsh legend found in Nennius, according to which the island of Britain, then called Albion, was colonized in the late twelfth century B.C. by a party of Trojans under the leadership of Brutus, great-grandson of Vergil's hero Aeneas. They exterminated the giants who were then the only inhabitants, and renamed the island "Britain" after their chief. Geoffrey traces the imagined British monarchy through a long series of kings, and a queen or two, till he comes to Julius Caesar and the Roman invasions. After this, he is somewhat constrained by facts, but he patriotically reduces the Roman sovereignty to a vague protectorate, with the line of British kings going on.

In the fifth century, with Britain's separation from Rome, he moves into shadowy territory. He introduces a king called Constantine, who restores order after barbarian incursions but is assassinated. The disastrous Vortigern makes his entrance. Geoffrey portrays him as an unscrupulous magnate bent on achieving supreme power. He persuades Constantine's eldest son, Constans, who is a monk, to leave his monastery and assume the crown. Constans, a puppet in Vortigern's hands, is soon murdered, after which Vortigern rules openly. Geoffrey more or less follows Nennius's account of the invitation to Hengist, the Saxon dominance over the king, the massacre of British nobles, the abortive counterattack by Vortigern's son Vortimer, and Vortigern's flight to Wales. He improves the tale of the collapsing fortress, enlarging the red and white serpents into dragons, and turning the prophetic youth into Merlin, who thus makes his debut in major literature. Merlin utters his prophecies, and the usurper is doomed. Constantine's two surviving sons restore the legitimate royal line. The elder, Aurelius Ambrosius, has a brief reign in which the main event is the transfer of Stonehenge, with Merlin's aid, from Ireland to Salisbury Plain, where it stands today. Uther, called the Pendragon, succeeds him. Both struggle against the Saxons in Britain with successful but indecisive results.

Geoffrey now comes to Arthur himself, whose reign is the climax of the *History*. King Uther, he says, was holding court in London when he conceived a violent passion for Ygerna, the wife of Gorlois, duke of Cornwall. Observing his advances, her husband took her away from the court without asking leave and immured her in his castle on the Tintagel headland in Cornwall. Uther treated the departure as an insult and led an army to Cornwall to ravage the ducal lands. While Gorlois was busy fighting, Uther sought the help of Merlin, who changed him into an exact replica of the duke. Disguised as the lord of Tintagel, Uther freely entered the castle and slept with Ygerna. Arthur was thus begotten. The real Gorlois had fallen in battle, so Uther could return to his true shape and marry the lady. (Geoffrey does not say that their son was born at Tintagel, but this has been the usual assumption.)

Arthur succeeded to the throne while in his teens. He launched a campaign against the Saxons and crushed them at Bath (Geoffrey's interpretation of Badon), wielding a sword called Caliburn that was forged in the enchanted island of Avalon. They were henceforth confined to a small area. He then subdued the Picts and Scots and conquered Ireland and Iceland. He also married Guinevere.

EXCALIBUR

Arthur's sword is called Caliburn by Geoffrey of Monmouth. The early French tradition made Excalibur the property of Gawain before it belonged to Arthur, but most later versions reserved it exclusively for Arthur. Originally, too, it was distinct from the Sword in the Stone and was a sword given to Arthur by a hand that emerges from a lake. However, some later accounts, especially in the modern period, identify Excalibur with the Sword in the Stone.

"Battle Scene." French MS 1, fol. 224v. Reproduced by courtesy of the Director and University Librarian, the John Rylands University Library of Manchester.

Twelve years of peace and prosperity ensued. Arthur formed an order of knighthood that became celebrated throughout the nations. He was popular with all classes at home, and Britain rose to a high level of civilization and prestige. Among his followers were Kay, Bedivere, and Gawain. At length, he took to warfare again, conquering Norway and Denmark and wresting much of Gaul from the Roman Empire, which still held that country, though feebly. After several years of campaigning and consolidation, he held court with great magnificence at the former Roman town of Caerleon-upon-Usk in Wales. Geoffrey's long and splendid description foreshadows the Camelot of romance. A Roman demand for tribute and the return of his conquests, addressed to him by the western Roman ruler Lucius, provoked a fresh war. Leaving his nephew Mordred in charge at home, jointly with Guinevere, he shipped an army to Gaul. After a diversion caused by a fight with a giant living on Mont-Saint-Michel, he pressed forward and defeated the Romans. The decisive battle took place in the neighborhood of Burgundy, and he pushed on into that region with a view to conquering more of the Empire. However, he was recalled by news that Mordred had proclaimed himself king, induced the Queen to live in adultery with him, and made a deal with the Saxons. Arthur returned and routed the traitor by the River Camel in Cornwall but was grievously wounded himself and carried away to the Isle of Avalon for his wounds to be healed.

There is no commitment as to the King's eventual fate. Geoffrey leaves the door open for the folk belief in his immortality without actually affirming it. The *History* goes on afterward, closing with the triumph of the Saxons in the seventh century. Several parts of it were to supply themes for later authors—it is the source of the story of King Lear, for instance—but the Arthurian portion, comprising about one-quarter of the whole, was by far the most influential. Once this glorious episode was established, much matter from Wales, Cornwall, and Brittany was attached to it.

Geoffrey's motives in his flight of imagination are none too clear. He may have taken a hint from William of Malmesbury, who had recently written of the reputed discovery of the tomb of Gawain and had urged the need for a reliable account of Arthur. Geoffrey doubtless wanted to glorify the ancestors of the Welsh, Cornish, and Bretons and to insinuate, through the prophecies put in Merlin's mouth, that they still had a future. Perhaps he also wanted to flatter the Norman conquerors by giving their island realm a splendid pedigree and making out that their territories in France had been under the same crown before. Whatever precisely he was doing, he did it with a verve and narrative skill that were rare in his time.

Where did he get it all? And does he shed any further light on Arthurian origins?

He is not a historian. Even apart from the normal anachronistic updating, he can be checked against known history, chiefly in the Roman period, and it refutes him utterly. His word can never be taken, unsupported, for any fact. Yet, except in parts of his pre-Roman story, he is not a pure fantasist either. The same checking process that destroys him as a historian also shows that he uses history, exaggerating, inflating, contorting, inverting, but seldom fabricating at any length out of nothing at all. He draws on

DEPARTURE FOR AVALON

Arthur, wounded, is taken onto a barge with many fair and noble ladies on it. His last words were spoken to Bedivere; they were, according to Malory, the following: ". . . for I will into the vale of Avalon to heal me of my grievous wound. And if thou hear nevermore of me, pray for my soul."

Roman authors before the fifth century and on Gildas and Bede after it. In the fifth century itself, besides his evident use of the *Historia Brittonum* and the *Annales Cambriae* or something similar, he has several characters based on persons who were real or reputedly so. King Constantine is suggested by the imperial pretender of that name, who was proclaimed in Britain in 407 and whose son Constans did leave a monastery. Vortigern and Vortimer are from Nennius. Aurelius Ambrosius is Ambrosius Aurelianus, lifted out of Gildas or Bede and transposed. Mordred (Geoffrey spells it "Modred") is the Medraut of the *Annales* and triads. Geoffrey mentions two Gallic bishops, Germanus and Lupus, who visited Britain in 429, and at least one emperor—possibly another, and a pope also, although less certainly because the names do not quite correspond.

Significant also is the overall character of his conception of Arthur. The King is far more than a mere expansion of the war leader of the Welsh. Despite all updating, he is a British version of a kind of messiah persistently imagined and hoped for in Late Roman antiquity, the *Restitutor Orbis*, or World-Restorer, who would end civil strife and usurpation, subdue the barbarians, defeat the Empire's enemies, and bring back peace and prosperity. Even when the end was in sight, three of the last ineffectual western emperors were hailed in succession as the destined savior. In Geoffrey's imagination, a lately Roman Britain actually finds its *Restitutor* in Arthur. His Arthur is closer to the ideals and aspirations of the fifth century than to those of the twelfth.

Geoffrey claims in a preface to have translated the entire *History* from a "very ancient book written in the British language" given him by Walter, archdeacon of Oxford. The "British language" could mean either Welsh or Breton, the latter being more likely in this context. While no such book has survived, and the claim is preposterous as it stands, there are grounds for suspecting a lost source in Geoffrey's account of Arthur. When he is dealing with Vortigern, the villain of the fifth century, he simply expands the Welsh matter as supplied by Nennius. When he is dealing with Arthur, the hero, he does something conspicuously different.

Only a fraction of the story, comprising Arthur's early campaign against the Saxons and the final denouement, is based on known Welsh matter. A far larger proportion—fully half, in fact—is taken up with the Gallic warfare, which Geoffrey clearly regards as important. Even in the denouement itself, while he uses the tradition of Medraut and Camlann, he transforms the situation by superimposing the non-Welsh motif of a traitorous deputy ruler conspiring with barbarians. The "Prophecies of Merlin" even suggest that he first conceived Arthur's demise quite differently, locating it in Gaul.

"Arthur Tarries at the Castle of Dover After Sending the Body of Gauvain to Camelot and Before Going to Fight Mordred." French MS 1, fol. 255v. Reproduced by courtesy of the Director and University Librarian, the John Rylands University Library of Manchester.

Arthur's final destination, in Welsh, is the isle of Avallach, and Geoffrey's "Avalon," *Insula Avallonis*, does not precisely latinize this but echoes "Avallon," the name of a real place in Burgundy, the region of Gaul where Arthur's continental career ends. It looks as if Geoffrey is combining the Welsh story with another that he had in mind previously.

To dismiss half of Arthur's reign as baseless and irresponsible fancy would be to assume that in this part of his work Geoffrey is doing something that he does not do anywhere else after the entry of Julius Caesar: inventing a long and important episode out of absolutely nothing. It is more likely that he did have a lost source for the Gallic business, a document that he may have exaggerated into his "ancient book," especially if it contained other matter as well.

If we admit this as a possibility, and look at the Gallic episode in that spirit, things begin to emerge. Notably, it supplies what the Welsh materials never do, a chronological fix. Three times, Geoffrey names the Roman emperor—not the person whom Arthur fights in Gaul, but the faraway eastern one—as Leo. This can only be Leo I, who reigned from 457 to 474. Other indications of time, such as the sequence of reigns and generations from

Constantine, cohere quite well, and the seemingly garbled names of a pope and another emperor, if they are what they appear to be, not only converge with the rest but narrow down the date of the main Gallic war with surprising exactitude, to the years 469-70.

Did Geoffrey use a lost document locating Arthur in Gaul during those years? We are clearly back with the possibility raised by *Goeznovius*, that Riothamus, who campaigned in Gaul precisely then, was believed to have been named Arthur. A survey of his career, to the slight extent that it is known, goes far to confirm Geoffrey's use of some record of it. Riothamus took a British army to Gaul at the right time. He advanced to the neighborhood of Burgundy. He was betrayed by a deputy ruler, the prefect Arvandus, who conspired with barbarians. He is last glimpsed fading out of view after a fatal battle, with no recorded death. His line of retreat not only takes him into Burgundian territory, where Arthur's Gallic career ends, but points him in the direction of the actual Avallon. Besides the names and dates, Geoffrey has all these themes, although in his characteristic way he takes them out of history and converts them into literature.

Two objections resolve themselves easily and, indeed, supportively. For Geoffrey, the Romans are Arthur's enemies; for Riothamus, they were allies, however untrustworthy and, in the end, absent. Geoffrey, however, has to make Arthur confront the world's greatest power and win, momentarily recreating the Empire around himself, and the change in the character of the war is like changes Geoffrey makes in the character of other wars. Furthermore, in the prelude to the second continental campaign, one of Arthur's subkings speaks of going overseas to fight Romans *and Germans*. Riothamus's real Germanic opponents are still vestigially in the text, though they are forgotten afterward. The other difficulty is that Geoffrey says Arthur passed away in 542. This is so wildly inconsistent with almost everything else that we might suspect what is common in medieval texts, the garbling of an exact numerical date, and it has in fact been shown that recognized processes of error, found in other texts, could have produced 542 when the correct year was 470, the very one in which Riothamus drops out of sight.

The gap of time is wide, yet the coincidences are too many to dismiss, and *Goeznovius*, pointing the same way but not merely saying the same things, suggests a common source far back—a bridge. As for Arthur-Riothamus himself, to coin a term, the evidence is contemporary or early. It may now appear that he is the starting point for at least a part of the Arthurian legend, the King's activity over the Channel in Gaul. In other words, he accounts for fully half of the official "biography" that Geoffrey created, a much larger part than the Welsh matter accounts for. Nor does the theme stop there. It remains a major constituent. Arthur holds court in Brittany, and extends his power beyond, in the work of several of the chief romancers: Chrétien de Troyes, Wolfram von Eschenbach, Malory.

The question arises whether we might go farther and see Riothamus as the starting point of the legend as a whole, the inspiration of the Welsh matter, too, Arthur complete. Several medieval chroniclers, by placing Arthur's reign in and around the 460s, hint at a tradition to that effect. One, who extends a chronicle by Sigebert of Gembloux, comes close to asserting the Arthur-Riothamus identity. Another calls Arthur's betrayer "Morvandus," showing that somewhere along the line the name of Riothamus's betrayer, Arvandus, may have been preserved. "Morvandus," Mordred-Arvandus, oddly echoes the fusion of themes which Geoffrey, on this showing, perpetrated.

The Welsh matter fails to prove any other "historical Arthur" to compete with Riothamus. He is the only documented person who does anything Arthurian. Nothing is at present known of him in Britain before he shipped his army to Gaul. But that action may be thought to imply a recruiting ground of his own in the Arthurian West Country. As nominal high king in succession to Vortigern, he might have played a part in the Saxons' containment and fought the more locatable of the twelve battles, Glein, Linnuis, Celidon, and Chester, which all fit better in the middle of the fifth century than the later part. On the other hand, a leader who vanishes in Gaul about 470 can hardly have commanded at Badon and Camlann. Arthur's association with those battles, and the Welsh tendency to pull him into the sixth century, might be dismissed as pure legend weaving. Still, there are other explanations.

One is that while Riothamus is the starting point, the King Arthur of legend is a composite combining his deeds with those of at least one other leader. This, as we shall see in a moment, is the solution of even graver time difficulties with Merlin. Another conjecture follows from the Welsh poem about the battle at Llongborth, which has "Arthur's men" fighting alongside Geraint. Some translators have rendered it "Arthur and his men," making him present in person. For various reasons, it seems that this reading is mistaken. No such presence is affirmed. The poet refers to a force fighting under Arthur's name in his absence, perhaps after his passing. But if modern scholars can disagree as to whether he is said to be there himself, and some decide wrongly, so might any Welsh bard or storyteller have done when transmitting an allusion to "Arthur's men." If it was believed that such a force could have survived him, and kept up its strength by recruiting new members, a similar poem could have spoken of "Arthur's men" at Badon, aiding some other leader as at Llongborth; and it could have been similarly misconstrued, planting the notion that "Arthur and his men" were at Badon when it was only the men. Likewise, a lament for Camlann, telling how "Medraut stirred up strife and Arthur's men perished" or words to that effect, could have become a lament for the perishing of "Arthur and his men." In that way, poetry could have given Arthur a phantom existence prolonged for many years.

Little more can be said. If the question "Did Arthur exist?" is pressed, it is defensible to reply: "The Arthur of Geoffrey and the romancers is a legend, but he has a real original, the British king who went to Gaul." That is as far, at present, as the probing of history will take us. Whether Arthur has other originals, how far he is a product of mythification, to what extent we should forget history altogether and consider him as a sort of golden-age symbol, are still more palpably matters of opinion.

Τηε "ηιςτορικαλ αρτηυρ"

There have been numerous attempts to identify either the historical Arthur or a figure who served as the model for the King of legend and literature. The former have been largely unpersuasive: evidence is simply lacking that there was ever a King Arthur. Prominent among the latter efforts—to identify one or more figures upon which the legend may be based—is Geoffrey Ashe's Riothamus theory, discussed in these pages. (See bibliography for this and other theories.)

Two other theories are Graham Phillips's and Martin Keatman's identification of Arthur as a leader of the Votadini, a Celtic people in the North, and specifically as Owain; and what is known the "Sarmatian Connection," developed and refined progressively by Helmut Nickel, Scott Littleton, Anne C. Thomas, and Linda Malcor. The Sarmatians were Iranian horse-nomads from the Caucasus. In A.D. 175, a number of them were hired as military auxiliaries by the Roman Empire and sent to Britain. The Sarmatian warriors, who were armored cavalry, had beliefs and practices reminiscent of the Arthurian legend; among them were a dragon battle ensign, veneration of a naked sword set in the ground or in a platform, and a sacred cauldron. Even today, there is a legend among the Ossetians of the Caucasus concerning a great hero (Batraz), whose marvelous sword is to be thrown into the sea before his death.

MERLIN

Geoffrey's other major creation was the archprophet and wonderworker of Britain. Here, likewise, he was not creating out of a void. In the first phase of his literary work, he knew dimly of a Cumbrian seer named Lailoken whom the Welsh called Myrddin. Lailoken, or Myrddin, was said to have incited an inter-British battle at Arfderydd (now Arthuret on the Scottish border) about the year 575. Demented by the carnage and his own guilt, he was afflicted, like similar figures in other folklore, with a gift of prophecy and wandered in the forest of Celidon making strange pronouncements. The Welsh claimed that he had consolingly foretold a Celtic resurgence.

Geoffrey latinized the name as "Merlin" (Merlinus), changing a consonant so as not to echo a French improper word, and concocted new prophecies that the seer was alleged to have uttered. It was in ignorance as to when Myrddin, or Merlin, lived, that he introduced him as the youth who prophesied before Vortigern in the 430s or thereabout, substituting him for Ambrosius in that role. Having done so, he ascribed mysterious arts to him as well, crediting him with the transplantation of Stonehenge and the contrivance of Arthur's birth.

After putting all this in the *History*, Geoffrey learned more about the original Myrddin, including the fact that he lived much later. He poured his new knowledge into a further work, a long Latin poem entitled *Vita Merlini*, the "Life of Merlin." One passage tells of Arthur's voyage to Avalon, describing it at some length as the "island of apples" (the usual, although not undisputed, etymology), ruled over by the enchantress Morgen at the head of a sisterhood of nine. As in the Welsh poem *The Spoils of Annwfn*, there are reminiscences of actual pre-Christian sisterhoods. Morgen is the lady who becomes Morgan le Fay in Arthurian romance. Geoffrey makes her a benign healer who takes charge of Arthur as a patient. The romancers' blackening of her character is still far off.

In this final work, Geoffrey tried to reconcile the Myrddin or Merlin of authentic legend with the role he had assigned to him in the *History*. It could not be done. To anybody knowing the background, Merlin was obviously living in two periods more than a century apart. Writers who followed Geoffrey, such as the learned Gerald of Wales (Giraldus Cambrensis), realized that his Merlin was a composite, as Arthur, too, may have been.

"Myrddin" is derived from *Moridunum*, the old name of Carmarthen in southwest Wales. In Welsh, Carmarthen is Caer-fyrddin, the Myrddin-town, the *m* changing to *f* in keeping with Welsh rules. Geoffrey, however, makes out that the town was the seer's birthplace and was renamed after him.

It is rather puzzling. On the face of it, Myrddin originated as a mythical figure ignorantly invented to explain the name of the town, but if so, why should the northern prophet Lailoken have been identified with him? There may have been some association of this part of Wales with prophetic powers, so that a prophet was a Myrddin-man. The Stonehenge connection has its interest here. It has often been claimed that the story of Merlin bringing it by sea from the west preserves a grain of factual tradition, since the bluestones (though not the greater sarsens) actually were brought by sea from the west, from a Welsh quarry in the Prescelly Mountains. What has not been noted so often is that if this is correct, the place of origin was not too far from Carmarthen. Some ancient sacredness of this part of Wales, involving both the seer and the monument, seems a possibility. There are geologists, however, who say that although the bluestones did come from the Prescelly Mountains, they have apparent points of origin that are scattered over a fair-sized area, not confined to an identifiable quarry, and could have been conveyed to Salisbury Plain by movements of ice in a remote past.

Once Merlin was launched, he proved too alluring for subsequent romancers to drop. Not at once, but as the Arthurian legend grew in scope, he became far more than Geoffrey had made him. By the middle of the thirteenth century, Merlin is a devil's son with powers foreign to normal humanity. He not only arranges Arthur's birth but sustains him in his rise to sovereignty, provides him with Excalibur, devises the Round Table, and prepares the way for the Quest of the Grail.

ARTHURIAN PLACES

Throughout the rest of the Middle Ages, Geoffrey's *History* was widely accepted as being, in substance, true. Chroniclers copied from it, and romancers, to the slight extent that they cared about historical fact, conceived their plots as fitting into its framework, especially into the spell of peace when Arthur formed his order of knighthood. Credulity was perhaps excused by Geoffrey's manifest erudition, when, in the absence of printed books, it was not always easy to detect his irresponsible use of it. His knowledge extended to the map. He located major events in cities that actually were important during the Roman era and doubtless for a while afterward, and in at least one case he either made an astonishingly good guess or was aware of a place's post-Roman importance when no serious historian was aware of it till the twentieth century.

That place was Tintagel, which he chose as the site of Gorlois's stronghold, where Arthur was begotten. Tintagel raises the whole issue of archaeology. Generally speaking, the archaeology of the period sheds no light on individuals, although it illuminates the process of Saxon settlement and the lifestyles of the Britons. It does, however, show that certain places where Arthurian stories were located did count for something at about the right time, so that a case exists for factual tradition rather than pure fancy.

At Tintagel itself, the headland on the north Cornish coast has ruins of a castle. When Geoffrey wrote his *History*, it had not yet been built, and the headland was presumably bare. But excavations by Ralegh Radford in the 1930s revealed traces of a much earlier occupation. Pottery imported from the eastern Mediterranean, used for luxury goods, such as wine, and datable to the late fifth century or the sixth, proved the presence of a fairly opulent household. Radford interpreted the settlement as a monastery, but rethinking in the light of later discoveries suggests that it was a princely stronghold and that Tintagel may have been

Tintagel Ruins. A British Tourist Authority photograph.

Glastonbury Abbey Ruins. A British Tourist Authority photograph.

the home of a fair-sized population. That implies nothing about Gorlois or Ygerna, but it does make it likely that Geoffrey knew in some way of Tintagel's importance and located Arthur's beginnings in a spot deemed worthy of him.

Geoffrey does not score so conspicuously anywhere else. However, similar work at the hill-fort Dinas Emrys in Snowdonia, the scene of Vortigern's ill-starred building project, has established a post-Roman presence. The same has been asserted of Castle Dore near Fowey in Cornwall, in an area where romancers set the Tristan-Iseut story and an inscribed stone commemorates a Briton whose name was a form of "Tristan." But this claim now appears doubtful.

The famous case of Glastonbury in Somerset is more complicated. Its monastery grew around a very old church. Before Geoffrey, William of Malmesbury wrote a history of the place and noted some extreme local claims about the church's antiquity, pushing back its building to the second century A.D. or even the first. Geoffrey himself does not mention Glastonbury, but after his time the church's builder was named as Joseph of Arimathea, the rich man who obtained the body of Christ and laid it in the tomb. Joseph also figured in romances about the Grail, and the Grail theme, Glastonbury, and stories of Arthur and his knights were intertwined. But Arthur had been linked with the place independently and before, first in Caradoc's tale of the abduction of Guinevere by Melwas, and then through a claim by the monks to have found his grave, in 1190 or early the following year. One

Marker of King Arthur's grave, Glastonbury Abbey. A British Tourist Authority photograph.

William Camden, drawing of the "leaden cross." From
William Camden, Brittania *(1607, 1610). Courtesy of*
Kenneth Spencer Research Library, University of Kansas.

result of their announcement was a belief that Glastonbury, as Arthur's last earthly destination, was the true Avalon.

Modern excavation in Glastonbury Abbey has confirmed that the monks dug where they said and found an early burial, though nothing shows whose it really was. There seem to have been Celtic monks on the abbey site substantially before the arrival of the Saxons, which occurred in the seventh century—that is, after their conversion, so that Christian continuity was unbroken. On the Tor, the oddly shaped hill above the town, it has been shown that a settlement existed in the sixth century and perhaps the fifth. This has been interpreted as a small fort—the citadel of Melwas?—or as another monastic site. As at Tintagel, the main point is that the Arthur connection, however fabulous the details, corresponds to a real and relevant antiquity.

Cadbury Castle, also in Somerset, is on a different footing. This Iron Age hill-fort does not figure in medieval Arthurian writings. In 1542, however, the traveler John Leland stated that it was Camelot, Arthur's principal home. A good deal of local folklore has been recorded since, including a version of the cave legend. Camelot, named as such from the late twelfth century onward, is a medieval fiction, but its peculiar character as a place personally Arthur's, rather than a national capital, would allow it a possible factual basis. The hill could have been the headquarters of a fifth-century king, the original Arthur, so far as such a person existed. The possibility was given more weight in the 1950s by finds of imported pottery, as at Tintagel. Excavations in 1966–70, directed by Leslie Alcock, disclosed that the hill had been inhabited up to the Roman conquest, then cleared of people by the conquerors, and then reoccupied. About the 460s or somewhat later, probably not much later than 500, it was refortified with a girdling stone wall sixteen feet thick and nearly a quarter of a mile long, in a framework of timber beams. Buildings included a gatehouse, and a timber hall on the summit plateau. Though many more hill-forts were excavated afterward, and post-Roman occupation was established in some of them, nothing like the stone-and-timber defensive system is known anywhere else in England or Wales during that period; a few instances in Scotland are much smaller and have no gatehouses. Cadbury is unique in size, sophistication, and implication as to the amount of labor involved.

Alcock's interpretation of the site was at first military but shifted in a political direction. Cadbury looks like the residence of a king with resources

South Cadbury. Photograph by Simon McBride. Published by permission of Simon McBride.

of manpower unparalleled in the Britain of his time. It continued in use for some decades, but not for very long. While it yields no names, it may have a tentative link with the Arthur-Riothamus hypothesis. If we look in history for someone who could have been its royal refortifier, the King of the Britons who went to Gaul is the only documented candidate. His army proves that he had large resources of manpower, and his cross-Channel contact suggests that his home ground was close to the southern sea routes.

Study of Arthurian lore along these lines leads to certain conclusions about the geography. While stories of Arthur are spread out over hundreds of miles, it was remarked long ago that he has only one birthplace, only one grave. For practical purposes, Tintagel and Glastonbury have no real competitors. Both are in the West Country. Archaeology, besides giving them a degree of substance, has added Cadbury, a third West Country site, as a credible home; and it offers no comparable home anywhere else. Whether or not anything historical follows, this part of Britain is where the legend's roots go down deepest.

NOTES

(References are to the appropriate section of the Bibliography.)
Post-Roman Britain
    Alcock (1), Chapters 1–5.
    Ashe (3), pp. 26–59.
    Campbell, Chapter 1.
    Morris, Chapters 3–7.
    Wood, pp. 251–62.
Riothamus (in History) and His Aftermath
    Alcock (1), pp. 112–13.
    Ashe (2), pp. 310–13 (details of primary sources here), (3), pp. 52–59; and
        art. "Riothamus" in Lacy et al.
    Campbell, p. 37.
    Fleuriot, pp. 168–69, 172–73.
    Jackson, p. 457.
    Morris, pp. 90–92.
    Wood, p. 261.
Gildas
    Ed. cit. Alcock (1), pp. 21–29.
    Lapidge and Dumville, passim.
    Loomis, pp. 2–3 (discussion by K.H. Jackson).

Historia Brittonum and Annales Cambriae
"Nennius."
Alcock (1), pp. 29–41.
Bromwich, Jarman, and Roberts, pp. 25–28, 88–93.
Thomas Charles-Edwards, "The Arthur of History," in Bromwich, Jarman, and Roberts, eds., pp. 15–32.
Arthur's Battles
Alcock (1), pp. 55–71, 80–88.
Ashe (3), p. 118.
Loomis, pp. 4–10 (discussion by K.H. Jackson).
Welsh Saints' Lives
Chambers, pp. 80–85, 243–48, 262–64.
Morris, pp. 120–22.
Tatlock (1).
Early Welsh Literature
Chambers, pp. 59–80.
Jarman and Hughes, Vol. 1, Chapters 1–3, and pp. 106–11.
Lacy et al., art. "Celtic Arthurian Literature" (by Patrick K. Ford).
Loomis, Chapters 1–2 (by K.H. Jackson).
Mabinogion
Morris, pp. 104–06.
The Welsh Triads
Bromwich, passim, also in Loomis, Chapter 5.
Arthurian Locations
Lacy et al., art. "Topography and Local Legends" (by Geoffrey Ashe).
Westwood, pp. 5–8, 18–21, 29, 292–93, 306–08, 313–15.
Arthur's Survival
Chambers, pp. 217–32.
Loomis, Chapter 7.
Arthur's Name
Loomis, pp. 2–4 (discussion by K.H. Jackson).
Historical Arthur, Theories and Criticisms
Alcock (1), pp. 80–88, 359–64; (2), 15–18.
Ashe (3), pp. 73–85, and art. "Arthur, Origins of Legend" in Lacy et al.
Bromwich, art. "Arthur" in notes on Triads.
Dumville.
Lacy et al., art. "Scholarship, Modern Arthurian," Section 4 (by Marylyn J. Parins).

Loomis, Chapter 1 (by K.H. Jackson).

Morris, pp. 103–41.

Goeznovius

Ashe (2), pp. 304–10, and art. "Goeznovius, Legend of St."
in Lacy et al.

Chambers, pp. 92–94, 241–43.

Fleuriot, p. 277.

Tatlock (1), pp. 361–65.

Lucius Artorius Castus

Fleuriot, pp. 47–48.

Loomis, p. 2 (discussion by K.H. Jackson).

Geoffrey of Monmouth's History

Ed. cit. and (2).

Ashe (3), pp. 3–26.

Loomis, Chapter 8 (by J.J. Parry and R.A. Caldwell).

Tatlock (2), passim.

Riothamus (in Possible Relation to Arthurian Legend)

Adams, pp. 157–64.

Ashe (2), pp. 313–23; (3), pp. 96–124; and art. "Arthur, Origins of Legend"
in Lacy et al.

Fletcher (1st edition), pp. 82–83, 172, 185.

Fleuriot, pp. 118, 176.

Chronicles

Ashe (3), pp. 106–11, and art. "Chronicles, Arthur in" in Lacy et al.

Fleuriot, pp. 118, 227.

Llongborth Poem

Ashe (3), pp. 121–23.

Loomis, p. 13 (discussion by K.H. Jackson).

Morris, pp. 104–06.

Merlin

Bromwich, art. "Myrddin" in notes on Triads. Geoffrey of Monmouth (3).

Jarman and Hughes, Vol. 1, pp. 102–06, 117–18.

Loomis, Chapter 3 (by A.O.H. Jarman) and pp. 75–79, 89–93 (discussion by
J.J. Parry and R.A. Caldwell).

Tolstoy, passim.

Tintagel

Ashe (4), Chapter 3 (by C.A. Ralegh Radford).

Padel.

Dinas Emrys
    Alcock (1), pp. 214–15.
    Ashe (4), Chapter 4 (by Leslie Alcock).
Castle Dore
    Alcock (1), p. 212.
    Ashe (4), Chapter 3 (by C.A. Ralegh Radford).
    O.J. Padel, "Some South-Western Sites with Arthurian Associations," in
        Bromwich, Jarman, and Roberts, eds., pp. 240–43.
Glastonbury
    Alcock (1), pp. 73–80.
    Ashe (1), passim, and art. "Glastonbury" in Lacy et al.
    Ashe (4), Chapters 5 (by C.A. Ralegh Radford) and 6 (by Philip Rahtz).
    Carley, pp. xlviii–lx.
    Rahtz, passim. (esp. chaps. 4–7).
    Scott, pp. 1–5, 23–26, 29, 34–35.
    Westwood, pp. 18–21.
Cadbury
    Alcock (1), pp. 219–27; (2) and (3), passim.
    Lacy et al., art. "Cadbury-Camelot" (by Geoffrey Ashe in consultation with
        Leslie Alcock).
    Westwood, pp. 5–8.

"Fire Consumes an Occupant of the Perilous Seat": The Perilous Seat is reserved for the chosen
Grail knight; only Galahad can occupy it, and anyone else who tries immediately loses his life.
French MS 1, fol. 109v. Reproduced by courtesy of the Director and
University Librarian, the John Rylands University Library of Manchester.

chapter ii

Early Arthurian Literature

By the time the first Arthurian romances were composed, in the second half of the twelfth century, the conception of King Arthur and his court was firmly established, having been set by Arthurian chronicles and probably by oral tradition, as described in Chapter I. Curiously, however, from the very beginning the Arthur of romance differs significantly from the warrior-monarch presented by chroniclers. Perhaps Arthur has become the victim of his own military and political successes, as recounted in chronicle material; he has already conquered his foreign enemies (except for Rome). In the romances, the court is often a static political entity, with Arthur as a passive figure at its head. In the first Arthurian romances, the works of the French poet Chrétien de Troyes, the King has few if any enemies, and even later, when writers concentrate on his downfall, his only enemies are within: Mordred, for example, and especially Lancelot and Guinevere—those who were closest to him but whose illicit love eventually leads to the ruin of the Arthurian realm.

Thus, in the romance tradition, especially on the Continent, Arthur has generally given up the warrior's role. He occasionally participates in hunts, and often in feasts and other social events, but his function is largely to provide others with both the opportunity and the impetus for quests, journeys, battles, and other adventures. He is a patriarch, or at least a benevolent middle-aged monarch, and although he frequently presides over the court or the Round Table, we may just as often find him inactive: distracted, dejected, or simply asleep.

Nonetheless, the Round Table continues to inspire knights, and the greatest ambition of many is to become a part of Arthur's court. The romancers may seem to be presenting chivalry as the noblest state to which a man might aspire. A good many of the romances to come will, however, give us reason to question that inference, or to reject it outright.

Arthurian romance may be seen as a literary investigation of chivalry and love: of their separate value, their relationship to each other, and the relationship of Arthurian chivalry to morality and, eventually, to spirituality. A good number of romances will demonstrate that chivalry is capable either of serving society or of disrupting it. Similarly, courtly love (a combination, usually adulterous, of passion and adoration, requiring the man to give unstinting service and devotion to the woman) may ennoble, but it can also jeopardize a friendship, a marriage, or the Round Table society.

All this leaves King Arthur in an ambiguous position. He is a great and renowned king, to be revered and served—but he is also the head of an order that will prove to be a dead end. Having reached chivalric perfection, his order must either decay from within or be supplanted by a higher form

Historiated O: arrival at court. Large initials within which a scene is painted were seen in many Arthurian illustrated manuscripts. MS 805, fol. 35v. The Pierpont Morgan Library, New York.

*"Lady Arming a Knight." MS fr. 2186, fol. 8v. Paris,
Bibliothèque Nationale.*

of chivalry and a higher conception of morality. The following pages will survey the development of Arthurian romance and will trace, briefly, the dual process of perfection and degeneration.

FROM CHRONICLE TO ROMANCE

Although Arthurian romance—the fictional treatment of Arthur and his knights, the Round Table and Grail, and courtly love and chivalry—was born in the second half of the twelfth century, it had its roots in earlier chronicles and legends. Some of the early texts dealing with "Arthur," such as Gildas's *De Excidio Britanniae*, the *Annales Cambriae*, and "Nennius's" *Historia*

Brittonum, either develop the background against which the Arthurian legend will evolve or devote short passages (such as Nennius's list of Arthur's twelve battles) to the monarch.

That the legend of Arthur had been growing steadily is indicated clearly by William of Malmesbury, who in his *Gesta Regum Anglorum* (1125) laments the fact that so many fictional details had been added to the reality of Arthur's existence. Around 1129, Henry of Huntingdon composed his *Historia Anglorum*, in which, following Nennius's list of battles, he offers a brief account of Arthur between the events of 527 and those of 530. About the same time, the *Chronicon Montis Sancti Michaelis in Periculo Maris* ("Chronicle of Saint Michael's Mount") notes that Arthur was king of Britain in 421.

It was Geoffrey of Monmouth who, in his *Historia Regum Britanniae* (ca. 1136), developed in considerable and authoritative detail the career of Arthur (including Merlin, Guinevere, and the establishment of a chivalric order—though not of a Round Table) and thus largely determined the direction that the chronicle tradition would take thereafter. The majority of chroniclers, such as Pierre de Langtoft, Robert Mannyng of Brunne, and John Hardyng, accepted Geoffrey's account of Arthur as substantially correct and reliable and followed it closely; however, a few—Ranulph Higden, Giraldus Cambrensis, and William of Newburgh—subjected his version to skeptical scrutiny and sometimes concluded, as William did in his *Historia Rerum Anglicarum* (1196-98), that Arthur was a fictional creation. Some works, such as Giraldus's *De Instructione Principum* (1190s) and John Capgrave's *Abbreuiation of Cronicles* (1462-63), updated the Arthurian story to recount the late twelfth-century discovery of the King's grave at Glastonbury.

Since Arthur, in Geoffrey's *Historia*, had been an enemy of the Scots, Scottish chroniclers faced a dilemma. Their resentment aroused by Arthur's war against the Scots was exacerbated by the fact that the Plantagenets had in effect claimed Arthur as an English king. Thus, the Scottish view of him was, not surprisingly, mixed. Although most Scottish chroniclers accepted Geoffrey in the main, they scrutinized his work closely and tended in many cases to transform its spirit or the character of Arthur. A model for both favorable and unfavorable presentations of Arthur was provided by John of Fordun's influential *Chronica Gentis Scotorum* (1385), in which Scottish history is both presented fully and glorified. John expresses strong admiration for Arthur himself but argues that, owing to the circumstances of Arthur's conception, Scots (Gawain and Mordred) should have occupied the British throne.

Certain Scottish chronicles, such as John Barbour's *Bruce* (late fourteenth century) and Blind Harry's *Wallace* (ca. 1478), express almost unreserved admiration for Arthur; others, especially toward the end of the Middle Ages and beyond, were far less sympathetic. The *Chronicle of Scotland in a Part* (ca. 1460) is harshly critical of Arthur, and Hector Boece, in *Scotorum Historiae* (1527), presented him as a corrupt and licentious leader; George Buchanan's late *Scoticarum Historia* (1582) goes even farther than Boece in condemning Arthur.

The chronicles, even when presented as fact or as speculation on fact, regularly included the kind of imaginative elements decried by William of Malmesbury, and those composed on the Continent often presented Arthur less as a historical ruler than as a hero of romance. It was Geoffrey of Monmouth who invented certain of those imaginative details and expanded on many others; to a considerable extent, Geoffrey was writing fiction in the guise of history. His chronicle was translated into numerous languages, the most influential version being the work of a Norman writer named Wace, who in 1155 composed the *Roman de Brut* ("Romance of Brutus," the title identifying the first in the line of kings whose history the work traces). Wace's translation was itself adapted into Middle English by Layamon.

———————— DISCOVERY OF ARTHUR'S GRAVE ————————

Giraldus Cambrensis (or Gerald of Wales), in *De Principis Instructione* (1193), tells of the 1190–1191 discovery of Arthur's grave at Glastonbury. Henry II, having been told the location of that grave, informed the abbot, who ordered an excavation in Glastonbury Abbey's cemetery. The excavation unearthed a lead cross with the inscription "Hic iacet sepultus inclitus Rex Arturius in Insula Avalonia": "Here lies buried the renowned King Arthur in the Isle of Avalon." Farther down was discovered a coffin containing the bones of a large man and perhaps those of a woman. It was assumed that the bones were those of Arthur and Guinevere. Giraldus describes the man's size: "You should know that Arthur's bones were huge. . . . His shinbone, when placed on the ground by a monk next to that of the tallest man there, reached three fingers beyond that man's knee."

In 1278, the remains were placed in a tomb before the high altar in the main abbey church. They disappeared after the monasteries were dissolved in the sixteenth century.

_____ Tḅe ꞄouNꝺ Table _____

Arthur fashioned the Round Table
Of which many tales are told.
There sit his knights,
Each one equal to the next:
They sit equally at the Table
And are equally served.
None of them can boast
That he sits ahead of the next.
None has a favored position,
And none is excluded.

(Wace, *Brut*, lines 9751–60)

"Translator" is not an entirely accurate term for Wace. Although his verse chronicle did indeed purport to be a translation of Geoffrey's work, in fact it very nearly completed the transition from chronicle to romance. Wace related not only many episodes from Arthur's life but also conversations, anecdotes, reactions, feelings. He may, however, be most notable for a single striking innovation: he was the first to write about the Round Table, a symbol of chivalric equality that quickly became a larger symbol—of chivalric distinction, devotion, and accomplishment.

Although Wace, like other chroniclers, arranged his material chronologically to construct a biography of Arthur and to situate Arthur in the line of British kings, much of the content and the method of the Brut thus belongs unmistakably to the world of fiction rather than history. Little distance, in time or technique, separates Wace from the writers of romance, and within a decade or two will appear some of the masterpieces of Arthurian fiction.

celtic liteꞄatuꞄe

The customary assumption that Chrétien de Troyes composed the first Arthurian romance is accurate if we are thinking in terms of courtly or chivalric romance organized around the notion of Arthur as a feudal monarch. Yet Celtic tradition had developed a body of Arthurian material, especially in Welsh, well before the time of Chrétien. How long before is difficult to determine, since the problems of dating Celtic texts by linguistic or other means make chronology uncertain. Among the important manuscripts that preserve the Celtic Arthurian works, the Black Book of Carmarthen dates from around 1200; the White Book of Rhydderch, from the early fourteenth century; the Red Book of Hergest, from nearly a century later. Yet fragments of certain texts contained therein appear in earlier manuscripts, and some of them may have taken form during the tenth or eleventh century, or even before. Several of these works were discussed in Chapter I.

For example, although the earliest manuscript of the Welsh *Culhwch and Olwen* dates from the fourteenth century, the work itself is obviously much older than that, and the story may have existed in much the same form during the eleventh century or before, making it perhaps the earliest fully developed Arthurian story in Welsh. It may also be the most important. The tale recounts the prodigious tasks accomplished by Culhwch, with the assistance of Arthur and his men, in order to win and wed Olwen. Unlike the King presented by Chrétien, the Arthur of this text takes an active role in battles, hunts, and rescues, and the work makes prominent use of magic, the supernatural, and Celtic mythological elements.

Earlier still, Celtic texts give evidence of an established Arthurian legend, although, again, the dates of most are uncertain. The *Gododdin*, generally ascribed to the late sixth century (although perhaps later), praises a certain warrior but comments that "he was no Arthur." A poem entitled *The Stanzas of the Graves* notes that the location of Arthur's grave is a mystery. The Welsh triads, which were groupings of three names (along with a characterization of those named) intended to record traditional lore, preserve references to Arthur, Guinevere, Tristan, Mordred, and others; Arthur's importance is indicated both by the frequency with which he appears in the early triads and also by the composition of later triads that clearly capitalize on the vogue of Arthurian subjects. The Book of Taliesin, a manuscript dating from about 1275 but preserving poems that are clearly far older than that includes a number of texts that mention or discuss Arthur. The best-known poem from this collection (named for a sixth-century poet who himself became a character in early Welsh poetry) is *The Spoils of Annwfn*, which describes an expedition undertaken by Arthur and his followers to a city, representing the Celtic otherworld, to obtain a magic cauldron.

A number of characters and events later integrated into the Arthurian matter were already, in Celtic lore and literature, the subjects of well-established independent legends. For example, long before he became Arthur's tutor and wizard, Merlin, or Myrddin, was known as a seer who issued political and other prophecies, and some sources identify him as Lailoken, a madman in the Caledonian Wood, living in fear and longing for earlier and happier days.

A Welsh poem entitled *Dialogue of Arthur and Gwenhwyfar* is actually a dialogue between Gwenhwyfar (Guinevere) and Melwas, and Cei (Kay) also appears in the poem. Melwas may be related to the Meleagant who abducts the Queen in Chrétien's *Lancelot*. The verse is obscure and might originally have been accompanied by linking or explanatory prose sections, now lost. The older of the two manuscripts that transmit the poem dates from the sixteenth century, but the work itself was doubtless composed much earlier.

Although Welsh Arthurian literature consists largely of indigenous compositions and certain works (e.g., *Branwen*, discussed below) whose relationship to continental romances is unclear, a few Arthurian texts were translated into Welsh during the fourteenth to sixteenth centuries. Only one is complete: *Y Seint Greal* (late fourteenth century) is a translation, in a single work, of the French *Queste del saint Graal* and *Perlesvaus*.

ϾꞀABINOGI

Amid the profusion of legends, poems, and prophecies, the Welsh title most familiar to readers will be the *Mabinogion*, a term used to designate eleven stories first made known in English through the 1837-49 translation by Lady Charlotte Guest. The title is a misnomer, although a thoroughly customary one. The term *mabinogi* (of uncertain meaning, although it may identify stories about the Celtic god Maponos) should properly be applied only to the first four stories in Lady Guest's translation: the Four Branches of the Mabinogi. Of those four, the second, entitled *Branwen*, is of most interest here: in this text we find the character Bendigeidfran (or Bran the Blessed), taken by some scholars as the prototype of the Fisher King, who in texts after Chrétien will be given the name Bron. Bran, like the Fisher King, had suffered a spear wound, as a result of which Britain had become a wasteland. Arthur himself does not appear in this story (or in the other three branches of the Mabinogi), but a number of the characters in them are associated with the King in Celtic tradition.

In addition to the Mabinogi proper, Lady Guest's text included four independent tales and the three Middle Welsh prose tales often identified simply as "the three Welsh romances." The former group includes, most notably, *Culhwch and Olwen* and *The Dream of Rhonabwy*. In the former story, Culhwch is required to accomplish a number of seemingly impossible feats before marrying Olwen, the daughter of a giant who imposes the completion of the tasks as a precondition of winning the bride. The feats are accomplished, and the giant is killed, with the help of Arthur's men. The story provides a long list of the members of Arthur's retinue, and many of them are names that are otherwise unknown (and that doubtless reflect traditional lore now lost); the court also includes some familiar names, such as Cei, Bedwyr, and Gwalchmai (Kay, Bedivere, and Gawain). In the second half of the work, Arthur himself takes the primary role, indulging in hunts, quests, and the making of war and peace.

The Dream of Rhonabwy is a satirical dream-vision that initially paints a picture of the Arthurian era as a heroic period and then deflates that myth. It includes fascinating and enigmatic episodes, such as a chess-game between Arthur and Owain and battles between ravens and Arthurian knights.

THE THREE WELSH ROMANCES

The three romances, *Geraint and Enid*, *Owain* or *The Lady of the Fountain*, and *Peredur*, probably date from the thirteenth century. They use both Celtic themes and traditional Welsh rhetorical methods, but readers conversant with French romances may find them more accessible than other Welsh texts, both because their spirit is closer to that of chivalric romance and, specifically, because they are essentially analogues of Chrétien de Troyes's *Erec et Enide*, *Yvain*, and *Perceval*. The Welsh and French romances tell the same basic story, although events may be added, reordered, or altered by one or the other; one of the most radical differences concerns an episode in *Peredur*—but entirely lacking in Chrétien's work—in which the hero spends fourteen years ruling with the empress of Constantinople. Another striking difference between *Peredur* and *Perceval* involves the Welsh counterpart of Chrétien's Grail: a platter bearing a human head. The relationship between the Welsh and French compositions has never been conclusively established. The possibility of a direct influence of the French on the Welsh, although it cannot be discounted entirely, is remote. Even if the Welsh authors derived their romances from those of Chrétien, they adapted very freely and transformed their tone and spirit. It appears far more likely that both the Welsh author(s) and Chrétien drew on a common body of narrative material.

IRISH ARTHURIAN TALES

Arthurian themes acquired only modest popularity in medieval Ireland. Irish tradition has transmitted to us only a single work that is a direct translation of a known Arthurian story; the *Lorgaireacht an tSoidhigh*

Naomhtha ("Quest of the Holy Grail") is a rendering of the French Vulgate *Queste*, or perhaps of a lost English translation. It includes some details that are not found in the extant French manuscripts and so may well reflect the original version of the *Queste*. The Irish text is preserved in three fragmentary manuscripts, which together represent about two-thirds of the *Queste*.

In addition to this translation, several Irish compositions from the fifteenth century on make prominent use of Arthurian motifs, characters, or settings. In the *Eachtra an Mhadra Mhaoil* ("Adventures of the Crop-Eared Dog"), the son of the King of India, having been transformed into a dog, regains his human form with the help of Sir Bhalbhuaidh (Gawain). A woman transformed into a deer provides the subject of *Céilidhe Iosgaide Léithe* ("Visit of the Gray-Hammed Lady"), which takes place at Arthur's court. Irish literature also preserves, in a poem in *Duanaire Finn*, a version of the chastity test involving a mantle. An obscure but fascinating Irish tale, postmedieval but of uncertain date, is *Eachtra an Amadain Mhoir* ("Adventures of the Great Fool"), which is distantly related to the story of Perceval and to *Sir Gawain and the Green Knight*.

A sixteenth-century Irish tale, *Eachtra Mhacaoimh an Iolair* ("Adventures of the Youth Carried Off by an Eagle"), contains an Arthurian section, and the seventeenth-century *Eachtra Mhelora agus Orlando* ("Adventures of Mhelora and Orlando,") is cast in an Arthurian framework and was likely inspired by Ariosto's *Orlando Furioso*.

Irish Arthurian texts are not numerous, but some scholars have emphasized the possible role of Irish lore in the formation of Arthurian legends. According to these theories, the traditional Fionn stories from Ireland may provide analogues (if not actual models) for the characters of Mark, Arthur, and Perceval, and the adventures of the young Fionn bear a narrative resemblance to events in the Middle English *Sir Perceval of Galles*. In addition, the Irish tales of Diarmaid and Grainne appear to be related to those of Tristan and Iseut.

BRETON

There may well have been at one time a significant body of Breton Arthurian material, but little remains. The most notable extant example is *An Dialog Etre Arzur Roe D'an Bretounet Ha Guynglaff* ("Dialogue Between Arthur and Guynglaff"), a Breton composition in which Guynglaff, a sort of "wildman of the woods" who is also a prophet and magician, is questioned by Arthur about the events that will precede the end of the world.

After answering those questions, Guynglaff predicts invasions, wars, and catastrophes that are to occur during the 1580s. As that date indicates, the extant version of the *Dialog* dates from the sixteenth century, but it may be derived from a traditional and considerably older work.

CONCLUSION

Celtic tradition is far more complex and rich than these remarks suggest. In addition to the texts mentioned above, the Celtic lands have preserved an important store of Arthurian folklore and legend. Traditionally, certain scholars have emphasized Celtic influences on continental versions of the Arthurian story, although the extent of those influences is a subject of strenuous controversy.

An example of that controversy involves one of the important theories concerning the origin and meaning of the Grail (and of related material, such as the Grail procession and the Fisher King). The most persistent proponent of Celtic theories, Roger Sherman Loomis, emphasized the relationship of Bran, his wound, and the wasting of his land, to the equivalent in French romance: the Fisher King, whose name the *Didot-Perceval* gives as Bron. Loomis argued that a drinking horn, or horn of plenty (*corn*), that belonged to Bran was mistranslated into French as "body" (that is, the Corpus Christi or sacramental wafer) through the confusion surrounding the nominative form *cors*, meaning both "horn" and "body." The Celtic theories, to which these brief comments cannot do justice, have provoked passionate debate; while acknowledging the intrinsic value and interest of Celtic legends and texts, many scholars now deemphasize the theories of Celtic origins, and some discount those theories entirely.

The Celtic Arthurian matter proves problematic for a variety of reasons. First of all, much of it exists in the form of highly enigmatic poems or in the tantalizingly brief references offered by the triads. Moreover, much of it is difficult to date with any assurance and in many cases its relationship to continental Arthuriana is uncertain. There have been scholars who ascribed to French romances, and to virtually every sequence and symbol within them, a Celtic source. Few would now go that far, and there have been a number of vehement attacks on Celtic theories. Yet, even if we cannot accept without reservation the notion of Celtic origins and transmission, it is reasonable to acknowledge that Celtic lore and, in particular, Welsh literature preserve an important store of Arthurian material and provide striking analogues to continental Grail themes and other motifs.

french literature

Despite the difficulty of dating Celtic Arthurian texts, it is clear that many of them predated the appearance of Arthur in French and other literatures. Yet Arthurian romance, in the form that much of western Europe would know it throughout the Middle Ages—an episodic narrative, involving the adventures, and usually the loves, of a hero of Arthur's court—first appeared and flourished in France. French writers combined traditional material and motifs with innovative themes and literary forms to forge what was known as the *matière de Bretagne* ("Matter of Britain"). And if France was the dominant force in the creation and development of Arthurian romance, the dominant figure in that development was Chrétien de Troyes.

chrétien de troyes

Chrétien wrote five Arthurian romances that set the shape and direction of Arthurian literature for some time to come. He also wrote two lyric poems on Arthurian subjects, and he may also have been the author of a non-Arthurian romance entitled *Guillaume d'Angleterre*. We know little of Chrétien himself. He either came from Troyes or spent some time there; he was associated in some way with the court of Marie de Champagne (to whom his *Lancelot* is dedicated), and later he claimed as patron Philippe de Flandre. He wrote his romances during the second half of the twelfth century, and although their exact dates are the subject of controversy, they must fall between the mid-1150s and Philippe's death in 1191.

The fact that Chrétien signed his works may indicate pride of authorship, and he explicitly confirmed that pride in a prologue to his first Arthurian romance, *Erec et Enide*, assuring his audience that a narrative garbled by other writers will be transformed, at his hand, into a *molt bele conjointure*, "a pleasing and effective composition." His story, he concludes, will be remembered as long as Christendom endures; that the line puns on his own name (Chrétien, *chrétienté*) does not diminish his evident confidence in his posterity.

His Arthurian romances are all in the standard French narrative form of the period: octosyllabic lines of rhymed verse. Those works, in addition to *Erec et Enide*, are *Cligés*; *Lancelot* or *Le Chevalier de la charrete* ("The Knight of the Cart"), which presents the love of Lancelot and Guinevere and which Chrétien left to Godefroy de Leigny to finish; *Yvain* or *Le Chevalier au lion* ("The Knight with the Lion"), the composition of which may have overlapped that of *Lancelot*; and the uncompleted *Perceval* or *Le Conte del Graal* ("The Story of the Grail"), in which Chrétien introduces the Grail into world literature. *Perceval* also follows Gauvain (Gawain) through extensive adventures, and some scholars have suggested, though unconvincingly, that Chrétien had intended for those adventures to become a separate romance.

In terms of their contribution to our knowledge of Arthur, the most striking fact about Chrétien's romances is that, unlike the chronicles, they present the King as a secondary character. The romances focus on other characters, who give their names to the works, and Arthur has acceded (or receded) to the position of patriarch. The King only rarely initiates action and even more rarely participates directly in it. Yet his court remains the ideological and geographical center of the characters' world. Erec journeys elsewhere to find a bride, but they then return to Arthur's court. Cligés is a Greek prince, but he cannot be happy until he is accepted at Arthur's court. Perceval lives a bucolic life in the woods until he learns of knights and the court, and he is then irresistibly drawn to Arthur, "the king who makes knights."

More important, the ideals and codes of conduct accepted and practiced by Arthurian knights inspire Chrétien's characters and give form to his stories. At the risk of oversimplifying, we may say that those knights are expected to serve God, King, justice and morality, their ladies, and the cause of all who are in need. They are expected to develop their military skills, perfect their moral state, and exhibit appropriate social behavior. Yet the drama of Chrétien's romances derives from a discrepancy between the theory and the practice of Arthurian chivalry. Perceval, for example, falls into error and sin because, in order to become a knight, he rejects his youthful simplicity and purity in favor of a code of behavior that he cannot understand.

Other characters may assume a discrepancy where none exists, between their public obligations as knights and their personal, private existence as husbands or lovers; that is the failing of both Erec and Yvain. Erec's love for Enide causes him to neglect his public, chivalric duties until he overhears her lamenting the situation. Yvain represents the other side of the coin: he leaves Laudine immediately after their wedding, to seek chivalric adventures with Gauvain, and he fails to return on the agreed date. The resulting crises experienced by both Erec and Yvain require a lengthy period of repair and expiation before they can work out a proper balance of love and chivalry. During that period, Yvain rescues a lion from a serpent, and the

_____ CHIVALRY _____

"Chivalry," a term originally related to a horseman or mounted soldier (Fr. *chevalerie* from *cheval*, "horse"), quickly came to have a far wider application. Quite early, it referred also to the moral and military code of the knight, whom medieval manuals of chivalry exhorted to love and serve God, king, and companions in arms; to pursue justice; to protect the poor and the weak; to flee from pride; to remain clean in flesh and pure in spirit. Some such manuals give more specific rules of chivalry, involving basic fair play; for example, a knight on horseback should never attack one who is on foot, and a combatant must accord rest or respite to any opponent who requests it. Indications are that practice often fell short of the theory.

In the twelfth century, courtly love was combined with chivalry to produce a social ideal of service to love and to the lady. During the following century, the French *Quest for the Holy Grail* contrasted the traditional notion of chivalry ("earthly chivalry") with what the author called "celestial chivalry." The latter, taking God as the sovereign to be served, promoted an ideal of moral and sexual purity so rigorous as to disqualify all knights except Galahad.

_____

grateful lion, a symbol of devotion and faithfulness, accompanies him through his remaining adventures.

At least, such a balance between chivalry and love is possible in those romances. In *Lancelot*, on the other hand, the public and private domains, the martial and sentimental, are *not* compatible, and Lancelot's problem is different from Erec's or Yvain's. Lancelot perceives the same conflict, but in this romance it is real: love must rule supreme.

The crisis occurs (in one of the most familiar episodes from Chrétien's romances) when, in search of the abducted Guinevere, Lancelot has the chance to find her sooner by riding in a cart usually reserved for criminals. Before stepping up into the cart, he hesitates for a mere instant—for "two steps"—only to learn later in the poem that an instant is too long. As Guinevere explains, "Were you not ashamed and fearful because of the cart? By delaying for two steps, you showed yourself unwilling to ride in it. That is why I did not want to see you or speak with you" (lines 4,484–89). That is, he has briefly placed his concern for his honor and reputation before blind obedience to the dictates of love, and he nearly loses Guinevere as a result. Instead of establishing an eventual balance between love and chivalric concerns (pride, honor, reputation), Lancelot must later show himself willing to

COURTLY LOVE

This term, coined during the nineteenth century, identifies an ideal and a code of love as it was extolled by lyric poets and explored by romance authors from the twelfth century onward. A complex phenomenon, courtly love includes the adoration of the lady, the desire to serve her devotedly, and the notion that such service ennobles the lover. It is often assumed that courtly love was necessarily adulterous, but some authors (e.g., Chrétien de Troyes in several of his romances, though not in his *Lancelot*) effected a synthesis of courtly and conjugal love.

The "theory" of courtly love is contained in *De amore* ("On Love"), by Andreas Capellanus, a twelfth-century contemporary of Chrétien who described "courts of love" that adjudicated questions of amorous duty and service. Andreas also included a long list of love's "rules," in which he affirmed that love and marriage are incompatible and described the actions and reactions appropriate to lovers. Though intended as an ironic treatise, Andreas's composition has often been taken at face value.

---

suffer public humiliation in order to prove that he unequivocally values love and the Queen over himself.

With the possible exception of Cligés (whose story both recalls the Tristan-Iseut-Mark triangle and shows the characters trying, unsuccessfully, to craft a workable alternative to it), Chrétien's heroes all experience a personal crisis, entailing loss and pain and requiring a difficult expiation. The characters' adventures eventually lead to the maturing of their understanding and to an enhancement of their moral and personal worth.

The unfinished *Perceval* provides the most complex expression of the paradigm established by Chrétien. The crisis occurs when Perceval observes

"Lancelot Riding in the Cart." MS 806, fol. 158. The Pierpont Morgan Library, New York.

the Grail procession: a youth enters a hall with a bleeding lance and is followed by youths carrying candelabra, then by a young woman bearing the Grail. The procession excites Perceval's curiosity, but having earlier been informed that a knight should not talk excessively, he refuses to ask about the Grail. He later learns that, had he inquired, his question would have cured the maimed Fisher King. Curiously, he also learns that his failure was due to an earlier sin, which he committed by leaving his mother and thereby causing her to die of grief. Whatever may be the precise connection between the two events (that is, how his leaving his mother could have caused his tragic silence in the Grail Castle), it is apparent that in this romance Chrétien goes well beyond creating a character whose understanding of chivalry is deficient.

Although Perceval is initially naive and unenlightened, it is precisely when he follows the rules of Arthurian chivalry that he falls into error and sin. The implication is inescapable: this romance constitutes an indictment of Arthurian chivalry, not only as it had come to be practiced at court but perhaps in its theoretical conception as well. Since Chrétien never completed the romance, we cannot know how the work would have ended, but the religious dimension that appears late in the hero's adventures points to a conclusion in which Perceval would doubtless have surpassed Chrétien's other characters. The remainder of the work would surely have led him to a spiritual perfection, rather than a social or chivalric one.

Chrétien set the course of Arthurian literature in the Middle Ages, and not only because he was the first to write Arthurian romances. He introduced the Grail into the Arthurian world, and he presented the love story of Lancelot and Guinevere. Yet he also exerted an important influence by his technique as well as by his themes. He is an engaging and skilled writer, adept in the establishment of character, in style and in the creation of striking images, and in the arrangement and unfolding of events. He can also be a fine writer of comedy, and moments of appealing humor lighten the serious treatment of chivalric themes and personal crises. That humor, evident in all his romances, becomes especially prominent in the last, where the early scenes show Perceval as a bumpkin, awed by the world around him; once he finds his way to court, his initial chivalric efforts result in a comedy of errors in which he succeeds in spite of himself, before Chrétien turns to the high seriousness of the Grail Castle and the religious fervor that will inspire the final (and uncompleted) Grail Quest.

THE GRAIL

The Grail is first mentioned by Chrétien de Troyes, in his final romance; for Chrétien, it is a "very holy thing," but it is not yet the Chalice of the Last Supper and the cup in which Christ's blood was collected at the Crucifixion; that identification would be made by Robert de Boron. Chrétien's Grail was a platter or vessel that held a single mass wafer.

Robert's transformation of the Grail into the Chalice is the innovation that has proved most productive; few are the medieval and modern Grail narratives that reject that identification. However, in Wolfram von Eschenbach (*Parzival*), the Grail is a precious or semi-precious stone, and in the Welsh *Peredur*, the object corresponding to Chrétien's Grail, though it does not carry that name, is a platter holding a human head.

1.   A maiden—
beautiful, noble, and well attired—
was carrying a grail.
When she entered the hall,
with the grail,
there was such a great light
that the candles lost their brightness,
just as the stars do
at the rise of sun or moon.
The grail was of fine gold,
and there were many precious stones
set in the grail;
they were the richest on earth,
and they undoubtedly surpassed
all other stones.

Chrétien de Troyes, Perceval (ca. 1190)

2.   "And what will be the fame
Of the Vessel that pleases you so?
Tell us, what is it called
When it is named by its proper name?"
Petrus answered, "I have no wish to conceal it:
He who wishes to name it
Properly will call it Grail."

Robert de Boron, Roman de l'estoire dou Graal (ca. 1190)

THE GRAIL, cont. on page 74

TҌE GRAIL, *cont. from p. 73*

3. Peredur sat beside his uncle, and they talked. He saw two young men enter the hall and go into another room; they carried an enormous spear with three streams of blood flowing from the point to the floor. . . . After a brief silence, two young women entered, carrying a large platter containing a man's head, covered in blood.

Peredur (early thirteenth century?)

4. [Parzival] asked the hermit to tell him about the Grail. . . . "Many brave knights dwell with the Grail at Munsalvaesche. When they ride out, as they often do, it is in order to seek adventure. These templars do this for their sins. A valiant host lives there, and I will tell you what sustains them: a stone of the purest kind. If you do not know it, I will name it for you here. It is called *lapsit exillis*. . . . The stone gives a man such power that his flesh and bone are immediately made young. The stone is also called the Grail."

Wolfram von Eschenbach, *Parzival* (ca. 1200)

5. Then Josephus appeared to begin the sacrament of the Mass. After a brief delay, he took from the vessel a host made in the form of bread. And when he raised it up, a figure in the form of a child descended from above; his red countenance seemed to burn like fire. As he entered the bread, those present saw clearly that the bread took on the form of human flesh. After he had held the host for a long time, Josephus returned it to the Holy Vessel. . . . Then he took the Holy Grail to Galahad, who knelt down and received his Savior with a joyous heart and with hands clasped.

Queste del saint Graal (ca. 1125)

6. And then it seemed [to Galahad and his companions] that there came an old man and four angels from heaven. He was clothed in the likeness of a bishop and had a cross in his hand. And the four angels bore him in a chair and set him down before the silver table upon which the Sangreal was. And it seemed that he had on his forehead letters that said, *You see here Joseph, the first bishop of Christendom, the same one our Lord succored in the city of Sarras in the spiritual palace.* Then the knights marvelled, for that bishop had died more than three hundred years before. . . . Then they looked and saw a man come out of the holy vessel who had all the signs of the Passion of Jesus Christ, bleeding all openly. . . . "This is," said He, "the holy dish

wherein I ate the lamb at the last supper, and now you have seen what you most desired to see. But you have not seen it as openly as you will see it in the city of Sarras in the spiritual palace. Therefore, you must go there and take with you this holy vessel, for this night it will depart from the realm of Logres, and it will never be seen here again.

Sir Thomas Malory, "The Tale of the Sankgreal" (1470)

7.   The cup, the cup itself, from which our Lord
Drank at the last sad supper with his own.
This, from the blessed land of Aromat—
After the day of darkness, when the dead
When wandering o'er Moriah—the good saint,
Arimathæan Joseph, journeying brought
To Glastonbury, where the winter thorn
Blossoms at Christmas, mindful of our Lord.
And there awhile it bode; and if a man
Could touch or see it, he was heal'd at once,
By faith, of all his ills. But then the times
Grew to such evil that the holy cup
Was caught away to Heaven, and disappear'd.

Tennyson, "The Holy Grail" (1867)

8. Half the knights had been killed—the best half. What Arthur had feared from the start of the Grail quest had come to pass. If you achieve perfection, you die. There had been nothing left for Galahad to ask of God, except death.

T.H. White, *The Ill-Made Knight* (1940)

9. It was the type of bowl they call sometimes a cauldron, or a grail of the Greek fashion, wide and deep. It was of gold, and from the way he handled it, very heavy. There was chasing of some sort round the outside of the bowl, and on the foot. The two handles were shaped like birds' wings. On a band round it, out of the way of the drinker's lips, were emeralds, and sapphires.

Mary Stewart, *The Last Enchantment* (1979)

THE GRAIL, *cont. on p. 76*

ThE GRAIL, *cont. from p. 75*

10. King Arthur assembled his knights to urge them ever to continue their Quest for the Holy Grail, for down that path and down no other lay fame and glory.

Now know you that not one of those knights was certain in his heart exactly what a grail was, save that it was Holy and the object of Quests, but as no man durst confess his ignorance, each bethought himself the only one so stunted in knowledge.

Nicholas Seare, *Rude Tales and Glorious* (1983)

11.   ARTHUR: Please go and tell your master that we have been charged by God with a sacred quest; if he will give us food and shelter this night, he can join us in our quest for the Holy Grail.

FRENCH KNIGHT: Well, I'll ask him, but I don't think he'll be very keen. He's already got one, you see.

ARTHUR: What?

GALAHAD: He says they've already got one.

ARTHUR: Are you sure he's got one?

FRENCH KNIGHT: Oh yes. It's very nice.

(*Monty Python and the Holy Grail*,
dir. Terry Gilliam and Terry Jones (1975)

PERCEVAL CONTINUATIONS AND ThE GRAIL

Both because Chrétien's *Perceval* was unfinished and because of the appeal of the Grail Quest as a theme, the way was now clear for poets to compose sequels to his work in order to bring that quest to a conclusion. The quest is in theory infinitely expandable, and the authors of the so-called Continuations were nothing if not expansive. There were four Continuations, in verse, following alternately the story of Perceval and that of Gauvain, whose adventures had been juxtaposed to those of Perceval in Chrétien's romance. The First Continuation (ca. 1200), once attributed to "Wauchier de Denain," is a Gauvain-Continuation. The Second, signed by "Gauchier de Donaing" and also dating from about 1200, follows the further adventures of Perceval, who tries but fails to repair a broken sword, the flaw in which represents Perceval's own imperfection. The Third Continuation, from about 1230, is the work of Manessier; it continues Perceval's story, relating the successful mending of his sword and his becoming Grail

King. The Fourth Continuation (which in some manuscripts was inserted between the second and the third) was composed by Gerbert de Montreuil, who, writing at about the same time as Manessier, provided a transition by bringing Perceval back to the Grail Castle in preparation for the repairing of the sword. Taken together, the Continuations added nearly 60,000 lines to Grail literature.

ROBERT DE BORON

In Chrétien's work, the Grail had been a mysterious dish containing a single mass wafer capable of sustaining life—in this case, the life of the Fisher King's father. The Fisher King himself had suffered a wound in the thigh or genitals, and his kingdom had at the same time been transformed into a wasteland. Perceval's failure to inquire about a procession that included the Grail and a bleeding lance prevented the cure of the Fisher King and the restoration of his land. Chrétien's Grail was a mysterious object and an enticing symbol, but it was not the Holy Grail as we would soon come to know it; in fact, when Chrétien first mentions it, it is a common noun—*a grail*—and only later does he describe it as a holy object.

Around the end of the twelfth century or during the first years of the thirteenth (that is, soon after the composition of *Perceval*), the poet Robert de Boron wrote *Le Roman du Graal*, known also as the *Joseph d'Arimathie*, in which he transformed the Grail into a sacred relic whose meaning is clear: it is the vessel used by Christ at the Last Supper and the one in which Joseph of Arimathea collected Christ's blood after the Crucifixion. The bleeding lance, moreover, became the spear with which Christ's side was pierced. Robert thus linked the Arthurian story to that of Christ, and the Round Table became the third of a series that included also the table of the Last Supper and a table set up by Joseph (at the direction of the Holy Spirit) to celebrate the service of the Grail.

Robert possessed far less talent than vision: his verse is flat and monotonous, and the literary value of his work is negligible. Nonetheless, he made a brilliant and inspirational addition to Arthurian literature, by integrating the Grail into a sort of universal history leading from the Crucifixion (and even from the Fall of Man, treated in the prologue) to a future when the Grail would be delivered to its intended guardian in the Vales of Avalon.

Robert also composed a verse *Merlin* romance and probably a *Perceval* as well. Only a fragment of the former survives, and none of the *Perceval*. Yet all three of Robert's works were recast in prose by an unknown adapter

"*Christ Gives Book to Author,*" *from* L'Estoire del saint Graal.
Rennes MS 255, fol. 1. Bibliothèque Municipale, Rennes.

soon after they were written. The prose versions, known as the Prose *Joseph*, the Prose *Merlin*, and the *Didot-Perceval*, were influential in the later composition of the Vulgate (or Lancelot-Grail) Cycle of French romances.

In addition to this prosification of Robert's *Merlin*, we also have a prose continuation known as *Le Livre d'Artus* ("The Book of Arthur"), which coincides in the beginning with the Merlin portion of the Vulgate but soon launches into a long series of adventures involving Gauvain. Another continuation of the *Merlin* is the thirteenth-century *Suite du Merlin* ("Merlin Continuation"); this work, which recounts such events as Arthur's acquisition of Excalibur, Mordred's birth, and the enchantment of Merlin by Niniane, provided the basis for Malory's "Tale of King Arthur." Another French Merlin text, *Les*

Group of six images from L'Estoire del saint Graal: *"Our Lord breathes breath into a hermit; An animal leads a hermit to a kneeling holy man; Joseph asks Pilate for Our Lord's body; Our Lord gives a book to a hermit; A hermit writes in a book; Joseph puts Our Lord into the sepulcher and collects the blood from his wounds in a vessel."*
Bonn MS 526, fol. 1r. Universitäts- und Landesbibliothek Bonn.

Prophecies de Merlin ("Merlin's Prophecies," ca. 1270), is unrelated either to Geoffrey of Monmouth's text of the same title or to the work of Robert.

THE DIDOT-PERCEVAL AND PERLESVAUS

The *Didot-Perceval* (so-called for the nineteenth-century owner of one of the manuscripts) is an early example of French prose, dating from around 1200 or soon after. It offers a compressed version of Perceval's early adventures and then follows his exploits as he undertakes, with eventual success, the Grail Quest. The romance borrows heavily both from Chrétien's text and from the Second Continuation; following the conclusion of the Grail Quest, it turns abruptly to an account, similar to that given by Wace, of Arthur's conquests, his betrayal by Mordred, and his being taken away to Avalon.

Chrétien's work inspired not only the Continuations but also such works as the independent (i.e., noncyclic) prose romance entitled *Perlesvaus*, or *Li Hauz Livres du Graal* ("The High History of the Grail"), dating, as does the *Didot-Perceval*, from the first decade of the thirteenth century. This long work establishes itself as a sequel to *Perceval* (although not a direct continuation of Chrétien's romance) by noting that Britain and Arthur himself have suffered because Perceval failed to ask the Grail question. Perlesvaus is an extension of Perceval and yet, as the name indicates, somehow different: he is a character who obeys a moral imperative, not a chivalric one.

In this romance, Gauvain and Lancelot fail Grail quests (the latter because of his affair with Guinevere), and Perlesvaus eventually frees the Grail Castle from its enemies. The romance also offers a full-length account of Loholt (Arthur's and Guinevere's legitimate son), of his death, and of the Queen's consequent death from grief. Finally, we learn that Arthur goes to Avalon to grieve at the tomb of Guinevere, and Lancelot as well resolves to find Avalon (traditionally associated with Glastonbury). The work has a militantly religious flavor, and its emphasis on the supernatural is combined with an insistent depiction of bloody warfare; yet, despite the bloodshed and grief, the development of the *Perlesvaus* (unlike that of the Vulgate Cycle soon to follow) anticipates an eventual triumph and a restoration of peace and the land's fertility.

Perlesvaus, despite its comparatively early date, is one of the masterpieces of medieval prose, and although it was soon overshadowed by the Vulgate Cycle, it would twice be printed during the sixteenth century (in 1516 and 1523), where it stood, as a component in a three-part cycle, between the *Estoire del saint Graal* ("Story of the Holy Grail") and the *Queste del saint Graal* ("Quest for the Holy Grail"). In addition, the Anglo-Norman romance *Fouke Fitz Warin* (ca. 1256) includes the story of Arthur's squire, Cahus, in a sequence the author apparently took from *Perlesvaus*.

THE VULGATE CYCLE AND POST-VULGATE

Alongside such romances as *Perlesvaus*, the thirteenth century produced great Arthurian cycles, characterized by imposing length and increasing complexity (e.g., multiple quests and interlaced adventures). The cycle

"Souls Delivered from Hell," from Vulgate Merlin. This scene, the Harrowing of Hell, is not depicted in the Merlin but is the provocation for the council where devils plan the birth of Merlin. Rennes MS 255, fol. 101. Bibliothèque Municipale, Rennes.

SWORÖ IN TÞE STONE

One of the most famous motifs in Arthurian legend is that of the Sword in the Stone (or anvil), and the most famous version is Malory's. At Christmastime, there appeared in the churchyard a great stone, on which was a steel anvil a foot high. In the anvil was imbedded a naked sword, and there were gold letters around the sword: "Whoso pulleth oute this swerd of this stone and anvyld is rightwys kinge borne of all Englond." All the men try and fail to draw the sword. Arthur, only a boy and squire to Kay, is sent to fetch the latter's sword; when he finds the door locked, he takes instead the sword from the anvil. Despite his feat, and three later repetitions of it, the barons of the land are reluctant to be ruled by a mere boy, particularly one thought not to be noble. Eventually, however, he is accepted and begins his reign.

---

known as the Vulgate Cycle, the Lancelot-Grail, the Prose *Lancelot*, or the Pseudo-Map Cycle (because of its false attribution, in the text itself, to Walter Map, who actually died before the works were composed), dates from around 1215–35. The cycle consists of five distinct but interrelated works. The *Estoire del saint Graal* and *Merlin* were undoubtedly written after the other three but stand before them in the chronological sequence established within the cycle. The body of the cycle includes the *Lancelot* Proper, *La Queste del saint Graal*, and *La Mort Artu* ("The Death of Arthur").

The question of authorship of the Vulgate has long concerned scholars. Some (e.g., Ferdinand Lot) have suggested that the cycle may have been the work of a single author, who composed it over a relatively brief time. The proponents of that theory cite as evidence the precise chronology at work throughout the romances and the narrative unity achieved by the technique known as *entrelacement* ("interlace"). This term designates a method of composing, used in rudimentary form by Chrétien and more systematically by the *Perlesvaus* author, by which a number of themes and sequences may be advanced simultaneously: uncompleted narrative threads may disappear for long periods and then reappear one or many times, often recalled by an event or even an image or word. As a result, the work incorporates an elaborate web of connections, extending backward and forward and tying together numerous characters and stories so successfully that some scholars could not conceive of the cycle having been composed by more than a single author.

Jean Frappier proposed the theory of authorship now accepted, at least in its broad outlines, by most critics: that of a single "architect," who planned and outlined the last three romances and probably wrote much or all of the *Lancelot* Proper. The authors of the *Queste* and the *Mort Artu* followed the architect's plan; the *Estoire* and the *Merlin* were composed later

"First Kiss of Lancelot and Guinevere." MS 806, fol. 67.
The Pierpont Morgan Library, New York.

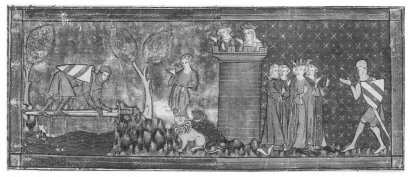

"Lancelot Crossing the Sword Bridge"; "Guinevere with King Baudemagus"; "Baudemagus
Meeting Lancelot." MS 806, fol. 166. The Pierpont Morgan Library, New York.

"Lancelot Rescues Guinevere." MS fr. 342, fol. 186. Paris, Bibliothèque Nationale.

"Arthur Convokes the Grail Questers." French MS 1, fol. 114v.
Reproduced by courtesy of the Director and University Librarian,
the John Rylands University Library of Manchester.

and added to the beginning of the cycle. The identities of the architect and the authors remain a matter of conjecture.

The *Estoire* develops the Joseph of Arimathea connection, by adding the story of his son Josephe (Josephus), who would become the first Christian bishop. At Joseph's death, the Grail is passed to his nephew Alain, who is the first Fisher King. The *Merlin*, situated second in the Vulgate's sequence, narrates the magician's role in arranging the events that lead to Arthur's conception, to his drawing the sword from the stone, and to his military victories. This work also presents the Round Table, providing it with religious associations by making it the replica of the table of the Last Supper. The *Merlin* is prolonged by a continuation (the *Suite-Vulgate*) recounting Arthur's marriage to Guinevere, the story of Merlin and Viviane, and the birth of Lancelot.

The *Lancelot* Proper, the large central core of the Vulgate, draws on

Chrétien's *Charrete* and other sources to depict the early training of Lancelot and his adventures in the love service of the Queen. According to this romance, Lancelot comes to Logres (England) as a young man to join the knights of the Round Table. He quickly distinguishes himself as the best among them, but he also falls hopelessly in love with the Queen and undertakes a lengthy series of adventures in an attempt to prove his worth and win her. (It is in this portion of the cycle that the use of *entrelacement* is most elaborate and effective.) Unfortunately, the same adventures that prove his worthiness as a knight also include some failures that arise from his sin with Guinevere and that will make it impossible for him to achieve the Grail.

The *Queste* recounts the choice and progress of Galahad (the son of Lancelot) as perfect Grail knight. As a descendant of both King David and of the Grail Kings, Galahad represents the fusion of Arthurian story with sacred history. The *Queste* narrates the adventures of various other questers (Perceval, Gauvain, Hector, Bors), but it is Galahad, soon known as "the best knight in the world," who successfully concludes the Grail Quest. The *Queste* is followed by the *Mort Artu*, the Arthurian apocalypse. Lancelot and Guinevere resume their adultery, and we are told that "now he loved her more than he ever had, and she loved him no less." Their sin eventually leads Arthur and Gauvain to begin a war against Lancelot, and the King is betrayed by his illegitimate son Mordred, who kills Arthur and is killed by him. The final

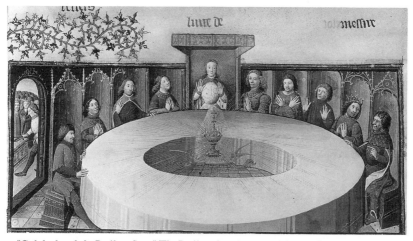

"Galahad and the Perilous Seat." The Perilous Seat is reserved for the chosen Grail knight; only Galahad can occupy it. MS fr. 120, fol. 524v. Paris, Bibliothèque Nationale.

pages narrate those deaths, as well as those of Yvain, Lionel, Gauvain, Guinevere, Lancelot, and others. Bors, one of the few surviving knights, retires to a hermitage. The Vulgate Cycle and the Arthurian world are at an end.

The Vulgate may have had as one of its guiding principles the literary investigation of the value and effects of courtly love, although the Grail Quest was an equally prominent focus. Courtly love can be an ennobling emotion, but the Vulgate demonstrates its destructive power as well. Ostensibly, it is Mordred's treason that precipitates the ruin of the Round Table, but that treason is simply the final, inevitable step in a long sequence of events set in motion by the love of Lancelot and Guinevere. While that love inspires great feats of prowess on Lancelot's part, it also jeopardizes the Grail Quest and eventually brings about a holocaust for which no remedy is possible.

The importance and influence of the Vulgate Cycle are incalculable. Not only is it intrinsically valuable for its vision, scope, and technique, but parts of it were translated or adapted into other languages, especially German (the *Prosa Lancelot*) and Dutch *(Lancelot-Compilatie)*. Hispanic translators used it to an extent, although they were more drawn to the Post-Vulgate (see below). Portions of it were translated into Welsh. Abridged versions of

"Combat between Lancelot and Gauvain."
MS fr. 120, fol. 590v. Paris, Bibliothèque Nationale.

*"After Entrusting Guinevere to Mordred, Arthur Assaults Lancelot." French MS 1,
fol. 240v. Reproduced by courtesy of the Director and University Librarian,
the John Rylands University Library of Manchester.*

the Vulgate were prepared in French during the fifteenth century *(Histoire du sainct Graal abregée)* and the sixteenth *(Histoire de Lancelot du Lac)*. The Italian *Chantari di Lancelotto* offers an account of the fall of Camelot that is ultimately related to the *Mort Artu*, while the Italian *Lancillotto del Lago* is a translation of a Vulgate *Lancelot* printed in Paris in 1533. But nowhere is the importance of the Vulgate so clearly established as in its role as the principal source of Malory's *Le Morte Darthur*, whose enormous influence on English and American Arthurian literature ensures its own immortality and, indirectly, that of its source.

The Vulgate was followed quickly by the Post-Vulgate, a cycle dating from 1230–40 and sometimes called the "Pseudo–Robert de Boron" cycle. The Post-Vulgate is not preserved intact, but it has been largely reconstructed, partially on the basis of extant translations in Spanish and Portuguese. The overall structure of the cycle resembles that of the Vulgate, with a major difference: there are an *Estoire*, a *Merlin*, a *Queste*, and a truncated *Mort Artu*—but there is no distinct *Lancelot* romance. Although portions of the romances follow the Vulgate closely (and, indeed, the same *Merlin* romance is part of both cycles), the author(s) of the Post-Vulgate substituted Arthur for Lancelot as the central character, the apparent intention being to deemphasize the story of Lancelot and Guinevere's adulterous love and to concentrate instead on the Grail.

In both narrative development and the motivation of events, the Post-Vulgate has a tighter structure than the Vulgate and thus avoids the duality of the earlier cycle, which had to trace the effects both of the adultery and of the various events that culminated in Mordred's treason. The Post-Vulgate author also presents an uncompromising moralistic rigor that interprets misfortunes and suffering as the result of divine punishment for sins, whether committed by design or inadvertently. Admirable in its singlemindedness, the Post-Vulgate lacks the interplay of sacred and profane themes, as well as the rich narrative texture, of the Vulgate.

TRISTAN AND ISEUT

While Arthur and the Grail Quest were being treated at length, another theme and set of characters were proving to have great popularity. The story of Tristan, Iseut, and Mark, originally part of a different tradition, was soon attached, however loosely, to the Arthurian legend. During the late twelfth century, both Béroul and Thomas d'Angleterre composed Tristan romances in French, although both poems survive only in substantial fragments. Critics traditionally assign these two works, and most Tristan romances in other languages, to one of two versions, known as the courtly (Thomas) and the primitive or common (Béroul). Many scholars assume the existence of an archetype, now lost, from which both versions derive. Such an archetype would have told of the love potion drunk by mistake by Tristan and Iseut, the wife-to-be of his uncle, King Mark, and would have traced the effects of this love, from their miserable exile to Tristan's marrying Iseut of the White Hands (simply because her name recalls that of his beloved) to the tragic death of the lovers.

We know nothing about Béroul except that he wrote a romance of Tristan and Iseut, of which we now possess a single long fragment of some four thousand five hundred lines, preserved in a single manuscript. Although his work (along with the German romance of Eilhart von Oberge, discussed below) belongs to the so-called primitive version, it could well postdate Thomas's more courtly romance, and it might even date from the last decade of the century. The remaining fragment of Béroul's text opens with the famous tryst of the lovers under a tree in which Mark is hiding to spy on them; Iseut's alert cleverness saves the two and eventually leads the king to apologize for ever suspecting them. Following this adventure, the work offers a number of episodes in which the lovers' enemies, including a dwarf, spy on them and betray them to Mark, whereupon they use their ingenuity or Mark's gullibility to exculpate themselves. Nonetheless, to be together

"Tristan and Isolde Beneath the Tree," appliqué; German, fourteenth century.
Courtesy of Victoria and Albert Museum, London.

they eventually have to lead the lives of fugitives in the forest, moving every day and living on whatever they can find or catch. The waning of the love potion makes them wish to rectify at least the material effects of their exile. To reconcile herself with Mark, Iseut deceitfully, but effectively, swears an ambiguous oath before God in order to convince others of her innocence. The romance contains episodes of brutal realism, such as Iseut's being given to a colony of lepers for their pleasure, but such realism is balanced by fre-

quent humor and levity and, despite textual problems and internal contradictions, by a vigorous and appealing narrative method.

Thomas's work, dating perhaps from around 1175, is also preserved
in fragmentary form, but in nine distinct fragments, rather than the single
long one that offers Béroul's text. Thomas's romance is thoroughly and seriously courtly in nature; it indulges frequently in a refined analysis of emotions, particularly the love and anguish of the protagonists. Thomas tends to
eschew indelicate or shocking episodes (such as the leper-colony scene that
Béroul appears to relish); he adds scenes intended to emphasize the raptur-
ous nature of Tristan's love; and he largely transforms the love potion into a
symbolic representation of the birth of love. Thomas's text served as a source
for Gottfried von Strassburg's *Tristan*; other compositions that draw on the
same tradition include the Italian *La Tavola Ritonda* ("The Round Table")
and the English *Sir Tristrem*.

Episodes of particular note in Thomas's romance include Tristan's
unconsummated marriage to Iseut of the White Hands (to whom he was
attracted because of her name, but whom he married in a futile attempt to
forget his mistress). The text also preserves the famous death scene: Tristan,
lying near death, sends for Iseut, who can heal him; he asks that the ship
have a white sail if she is aboard, a black one if she is not. As the ship
is approaching shore, Tristan's wife lies to him, telling him the sail is
black. He dies of sorrow and despair, and Iseut, finding him dead upon
her arrival, embraces him and, "body to body, mouth to mouth," dies
of grief.

Since the Tristan story was by nature episodic (involving brief encounters, separations, reconciliations, and further separations), a number of
writers offer us the account of a single episode or a restricted sequence of
events. Various texts have Tristan returning to court in disguise to see Iseut
(in two short poems entitled *La Folie Tristan*, "Tristan's Madness," preserved
in manuscripts in Bern and in Oxford); assuming the role of a minstrel
(Tristan Menestrel, inserted into the Fourth Continuation of *Perceval); or
imitating birdcalls to offer her a pretext for joining him outside *(Tristan
Rossignol*, "Tristan the Nightingale"). However, the best known of such narratives, *Chevrefueil* ("Honeysuckle"), relates a secret and passionate rendez-
vous of the lovers in a forest. This brief (118-line) and lyrical evocation of
desperate love, symbolized by the intertwining of the honeysuckle and the
hazel ("So is it with us, my love: you cannot live without me, nor I without
you"), is the work of France's first woman of letters, Marie de France, who
wrote during the second half of the twelfth century.

THE PROSE TRISTAN

The lengthy Prose *Tristan,* dating from the mid-thirteenth century, exists in two versions (attributed, probably falsely, to Luces de Gat and Helie de Borron), and its preservation in numerous manuscripts and printed editions attests to its enormous popularity. The romance develops the lovers' story in great detail, beginning with the story of Tristan's ancestors and including numerous adventures taken, sometimes with little change, from the Vulgate romances and other texts. In this work, Mark becomes a villain (who, according to some versions, kills Tristan), whereas Tristan is a member of the Round Table, a friend of Lancelot, and an active participant in the Grail Quest. Thus, while Béroul's and Thomas's poems were only marginally Arthurian, the Prose *Tristan* completes the fusion of the Tristan story with those of Arthur, his knights, and the Grail. The work makes frequent but inconsistent use of the kind of structural interlace exploited to such advantage in the Vulgate, and its structure is comparatively loose and episodic. It recounts numerous adventures, jousts, and battles, but it rarely offers introspective examinations of love or deals with such questions as the nature and moral implications of chivalry; significantly, though, one character, Dinadan, does express frequent doubts about the value of jousting and even of love. The popularity of the Prose *Tristan* led to its adaptation or translation into a number of other languages and to its extensive use (notably by Malory) in English.

BRETON LAIS

Alongside the lengthy episodic romances of the period stand a number of brief works generally known as Breton lais. These are short narratives that in some cases may have been based on earlier lyrics; certain of them have been lost, with only their titles (e.g., *Merlin le sauvage,* "Merlin the Wildman") known to us. In addition to *Chevrefueil,* Marie de France wrote one other Arthurian lai, *Lanval.* In this poem, Lanval is loved by a fairy maiden who requires that their love be secret. Guinevere makes advances to him, and in repelling them he reveals his love; the Queen then publicly accuses him of making similar advances to *her* and, when she refused them, of having insulted her by saying he loved someone far better and nobler than she. Lanval is to be punished unless he can prove his claim, and at the last minute his lady arrives to save him. A related Breton lai, *Graelent,* is a setting of the same theme as that of *Lanval* but is not explicitly Arthurian.

Other Arthurian lais include settings of the Arthurian chastity test, a theme that would become very popular in subsequent years and in various literatures. Robert Biket's *Lai du cor* ("Lai of the Horn"), dating perhaps from the third quarter of the twelfth century, is an irreverent and humorous anecdote involving a drinking horn that, because it is made to spill its contents on all cuckolds, soaks Arthur. A related tale, involving a cloak that stretches or shrinks in order to fit ladies guilty of infidelity, provides the subject matter of *Le Mantel mautaillié* ("The Ill-Fitting Mantle," also known as the *Lai du cort mantel*, "Lai of the Short Mantle").

Tyolet, written toward the end of the twelfth century, is a bipartite lai; the second half may have been the original work, to which the author fitted an "Arthurian" preface. That preface is a reflection of the early history of Perceval, as the hero is brought up in the forest by his mother, only to discover the attractions of knighthood and find his way to Arthur's court. The second half recounts a quest for a stag with a white foot, and although Tyolet is not known in other Arthurian texts, he is established in this lai as a knight at Arthur's court and is surrounded by Gauvain, Keu, Ewain (Yvain), and other familiar figures.

GAUVAIN ROMANCES

Although the best-known romances from the late twelfth and thirteenth centuries deal with the Grail Quest and focus on Perceval, Lancelot, and Galahad, a number of writers chose instead to follow other paths, and one of the popular subjects was Gauvain. Throughout Chrétien's work, he had played a significant role (as a consummate knight but usually as a foil for the hero), and in *Perceval* he clearly has obvious defects, notably pride, impetuousness, and frivolity. Later poets seized on his flaws and composed a number of "non-Grail" verse romances, most of them relatively short, in which, without being an object of derision, Gauvain becomes either a somewhat comical figure or a means of charting the progressive decline of chivalry.

Gliglois (first half of the thirteenth century) has Gauvain lose the lady he loves to a squire who serves her more humbly and devotedly. Paien de Maisières, in *La Mule sans frein* ("The Mule Without a Bridle," late twelfth century), comically transforms him into an uncharacteristically devoted knight but has him unstintingly pursue a largely pointless quest. In *Le Chevalier à l'épée* ("The Knight with the Sword"), the author, who may also be Paien de Maisières, plays on the traditional view of Gauvain by surrounding him with people more faithless than he.

Gauvain's character is further explored (either comically or by ironic insistence on his virtue and constancy) in several thirteenth-century romances,

"*A Knight Who Wishes to Kill Gauvain Gives Poisoned Fruit to Guinevere, but She Offers It to Another Knight.*" *The episode illustrated here is from the* Mort Artu; *the knight (Avarlan) hates Gauvain for unexplained reasons. French MS 1, fol. 223r. Reproduced by courtesy of the Director and University Librarian, the John Rylands University Library of Manchester.*

including *La Vengeance Raguidel* ("The Vengance of Raguidel"), perhaps by Raoul de Houdenc, and *Hunbaut*, one of the few romances to depict a Gauvain who evolves, perhaps ironically, from his traditional frivolity to uncompromising virtue and fidelity. On the other hand, the author of *Yder* offers a striking departure from tradition in presenting him throughout as unreservedly worthy of praise (only the author of the *Perlesvaus* had offered a similar view). Although Gauvain, in most of these romances, is a secondary character whose function is to emphasize the qualities of another knight, *Meriadeuc* (or *Le Chevalier aux deux épées*, "The Knight with Two Swords") and *L'Atre périlleux* ("The Perilous Cemetery") make him the central hero of the stories.

In addition to Gauvain himself, his son became the subject of romances. In the best of these works, Renaut de Bâgé's *Le Bel Inconnu* ("The Fair Unknown," written ca. 1185–90), the son is named Guinglain; he is a young but gifted knight who succeeds in liberating a lady who has been transformed into a serpent. (A romance entitled *Fergus*, composed by Guillaume le Clerc during the first third of the thirteenth century, appears to be in part an imitation of *Le Bel Inconnu* but does not deal with Gauvain's son.) Less successful than Renaut's romance, Robert de Blois's *Beaudous* (written during the second half of the thirteenth century) follows the out-lines of the earlier work but introduces some new features, such as the mar-riage of Gauvain. In addition to Guinglain and Beaudous, Gauvain's son sometimes bears other names: "Lionel" in the First Continuation of Chrétien's *Perceval*, "Giglan" and "Gyglain" in a sixteenth-century French work by Claude Platin and in the *Roman de Laurin*, "Gyngalyn" in the English *Libeaus Desconus*, and "Wigalois" in a German romance of that title (for the English and German, see below).

SEVEN SAGES OF ROME

The work known as *Les Sept Sages de Rome* ("The Seven Sages of Rome") is a series of Old French prose romances, existing in various and complicated versions and combinations, dating from the thirteenth and four-teenth centuries and derived from a text composed during the twelfth cen-tury or before. The cycle consists of serial narratives in the tradition of Scheherazade; that is, an empress tries to seduce the young prince and is sentenced to death; to prevent the sentence from being carried out, she tells a series of stories and is answered by tales told by the prince's tutors, the Seven Sages. The structure and premise of the *Sept Sages* have nothing to do with Arthurian literature, but several texts belonging to the Seven Sages tradition are infused with an Arthurian spirit or, in some cases, are cast in a specifically Arthurian mold. Foremost among them is one of the continua-tions of the cycle, the *Roman de Laurin*, which concerns the emperor of Constantinople (Laurin), who travels to Arthur's court and there under-takes adventures involving knights of the Round Table: Arthur, Mordred, Gauvain, Gyglain (Gauvain's son), and others.

Other works in the cycle, without being cast in an Arthurian con-text, are obviously influenced by Arthurian themes or motifs. The *Roman de Cassidorus*, which follows the *Laurin* in the cycle, includes a sequence that clearly recalls the Knight with the Lion theme from *Yvain*. Similar "knight with the lion" sequences occur in the *Roman de Pelyarmenus* and the *Roman de Helcanus*, while the concluding romance of the cy-cle, the *Roman de Kanor*, uses a setting of the cart motif from Chrétien's *Lancelot*.

Redactions or translations of the Seven Sages cycle are known in Latin and in numerous vernaculars: English, Dutch, Icelandic, Swedish, Welsh, Spanish, German, Russian, and Polish. The Italian version, the *Sette savi di Roma*, is discussed below.

LATE-MEDIEVAL ROMANCES

By the end of the thirteenth century, French romance authors were no longer writing in verse. The single exception is the fourteenth-century *Meliador*, by Jehan Froissart (best known as a love poet and a chronicler). Froissart composed an early version of *Meliador* between 1365 and 1369; most of that version is lost, but a revision, done between 1383 and 1388, has left us over thirty thousand lines of octosyllabic verse. The romance presents a series of tourneys arranged to enable knights to win the hand of Hermondine of Scotland; the victor is Meliador. The work is set in the period preceding the stories of the most familiar heroes of Arthurian romance—Lancelot, Perceval, and the others—although we meet certain Arthurian characters, and one tourney takes place at Camelot.

In many ways, it is unfair to lump together the Arthurian romances of two centuries and call them "late-medieval romances," as though they were all alike. Yet while they have distinct identities and offer different emphases, they also present certain common characteristics that we would be unlikely to find regularly in romances of a much earlier period. Like *Meliador*, many romances of the late Middle Ages were increasingly lengthy and complex works that often extend the boundaries, temporal as well as geographical, of the Arthurian romance. *Perceforest*, a romance of staggering proportions, relates that Alexander the Great establishes the work's hero as the new British king and that the civilization founded by Perceforest is eventually destroyed by Caesar. *Ysaïe le Triste* moves forward rather than backward: in this romance, Tristan's son inhabits a post-Arthurian world where the King's chivalric system represents a decided anachronism.

Alongside those compositions, the late Middle Ages have left us also vast compendiums of Arthurian material, such as the "Compilations" of Jean Vaillant, Michel Gonnot, and Rusticiano da Pisa, works that combine numerous Arthurian sequences drawn for the most part from earlier prose texts. The romance *Palamedes* consisted of two large divisions, devoted to Tristan's father (Meliadus) and to Guiron le Courtois, respectively. The two parts were sometimes separated and, during the sixteenth century, were published as distinct romances, each half titled after its primary character. During this time, a number of earlier romances were reworked or expanded, some new romances were written about earlier heroes (Erec and Yvain, for example), and Chrétien's *Cligés* and *Erec et Enide* were adapted into prose, with a number of changes designed to make the works conform to contemporary tastes.

The popularity of Arthurian themes during the later Middle Ages led to the frequent insertion of such themes (or Arthurian motifs or characters) into basically non-Arthurian works. *Le Roman de Silence,* by Heldris de Cornuälle, is the story of a young woman raised as a man; the romance is Arthurian only because the final scene features Merlin. *Ly Myreur des histors* ("The Mirror of Histories," ca. 1375) is a universal history that includes an account of Arthur's life and death (and a number of strange episodes, such as Guinevere's death at Lancelot's hands, after which Mordred eats her body in an attempt to forestall starvation). Finally, *Le Chevalier errant* ("The Wandering Knight," ca. 1400), by Tommaso III, Marquis of Saluzzo, is a long, often rambling romance in which Arthurian stories are told and Arthurian characters, such as Tristan, Lancelot, and Morgan, appear.

In general, French Arthurian literature at the end of the Middle Ages was characterized by expansion, in both length and scope. Authors or compilers tended to multiply quests and adventures, sometimes linking them only loosely to the structure of the work; they expanded the Arthurian world to present the predecessors and successors of traditional characters (although we should remember that it was Robert de Boron, far earlier, who led the way by connecting the Grail with biblical history and with the future). Scholars have often criticized the French Arthurian romances of the later Middle Ages for formlessness and their authors for prolixity. It is certain that most of these compositions lack the subtlety and structural clarity of Chrétien's works and the chronological and thematic intricacy of the Vulgate. However, considering that serious study of late French romance is a recent development, we may simply be unaware or unappreciative of the principles and methods that produce such works. In any event, the great popularity they achieved suggests that they were ideally suited to the tastes of the time, and once printing permitted the easy dissemination of literary works, Arthurian romances were among the texts most frequently published.

ROUNÒ TABLES

Beginning in the thirteenth century, nobles often organized festive events involving dancing and jousting in imitation of King Arthur and his knights. In many cases, the participants took the names and coats of arms of Arthurian knights, and in the fifteenth century René d'Anjou built a complete "Arthurian" castle for the Round Table he hosted.

GERⱮAN LITERATURE

Far more than in France (or in the Celtic world), the writers of medieval German romance have left us their names. We do know Chrétien de Troyes's name, of course, and those of Robert de Boron, Béroul, and Thomas, and certain others. Beyond those, however, we have mostly anonymous works, both cycles (the Vulgate, Post-Vulgate, and Prose *Tristan)* and numerous individual romances, from the *Perlesvaus* to *Perceforest* and including the majority of Gauvain romances. When we turn to German literature, we find not only that the three greatest Arthurian authors are named— Hartmann von Aue, Wolfram von Eschenbach, Gottfried von Strassburg— but that most others are as well. It is true that we know comparatively little about some of these authors, but the frequency with which they identify themselves makes the occasional anonymous romance (e.g., *Wigamur)* conspicuous.

That the German poets offer us their names is more than a trivial detail, for along with names we have, to a greater or lesser extent, personalities. Not only do certain authors tell us something about themselves (e.g., Wolfram's claim to be illiterate), but some of them mention one another; Gottfried discusses Hartmann, Wolfram, and others, and he and Wolfram conducted a literary feud of sorts. German courtly epic or *Artusepik* ("Arthurian epic") continues the process begun by the French, investigating the value of the Arthurian world and the efficacy of chivalry. More than in the French tradition, however, we have a strong sense of a continuing debate among the German authors, as they compose works that often seem designed to answer or refute previous ones, both German and French. The romances of Hartmann and Wolfram reacted to, rather than continued, Chrétien's. Some of the poets, like Wolfram, reject the Gallic implications of chivalric decay, while others go farther than the French toward a rejection, implicit or sometimes explicit, of the Arthurian world.

ⱵARTⱮANN VON AUE

Hartmann von Aue may have been the first author of German Arthurian romance. He was a learned court poet who has left us two Arthurian compositions, *Erec* and *Iwein*, the first dating perhaps from about 1180, the second from around 1200. These texts offer the narratives found in Chrétien's works, but they are not simply translations. *Erec*, for example, expands or alters episodes from Chrétien's *Erec et Enide* and occasionally modifies the sequence of events. In certain instances, where Hartmann departs from Chrétien's text, he follows the Welsh *Geraint*, a fact that suggests not necessarily that he knew the Welsh (which is unlikely) but that he drew on sources other than Chrétien and that one of those sources may have influenced the author of *Geraint* as well. *Iwein*, on the other hand, follows Chrétien's narrative closely. The changes that do occur are in many instances clarifications or explanations of events.

In both romances, Hartmann shows himself to be concerned with moral issues: he criticizes Enite as well as Erec, and in the second romance he indicates that Iwein's irresponsible behavior is condemned not only by his wife (through a messenger), but by Arthur himself. Throughout the romances, Hartmann praises the virtues of honor, propriety, and proper chivalric comportment; and he traces the progress of his heroes toward the full acquisition of those virtues and of the maturity that will let them assume their responsibilities and discharge them properly.

WOLFRAM VON ESCHENBACH AND HIS SUCCESSORS

Shortly after 1200, Wolfram von Eschenbach composed one of the greatest monuments of medieval literature: *Parzival*. He adapted Chrétien's *Perceval* story, completing it and also prefacing it by two books that relate the story of Parzival's parents, Gahmuret and Herzeloyde. The work is long—some twenty-five thousand lines—and complex, and it is written in a style that is elliptical, densely detailed, and sometimes obscure, generally lacking in the "crystalline" clarity so valued by Gottfried (see below), who praised that quality in Hartmann. Wolfram criticizes Chrétien de Troyes for what he considered an inadequate treatment of the narrative, and he claimed as his more reliable source one "Kyot, the Provençal," whose identity is unknown and whose very existence is doubted by many scholars. In addition to *Parzival*, Wolfram has left us two fragments known as *Titurel*, dealing with Schionatulander and Sigune, two of the characters from *Parzival*; he also wrote a non-Arthurian romance entitled *Willehalm* and a number of lyric poems.

We know little of Wolfram beyond what we can deduce from his work. He was a Bavarian and apparently a soldier or knight, although not a wealthy one, rather a "professional writer" dependent on the patronage of nobles. He spent some time at the court of Hermann of Thuringia, among others, and he may have traveled a good deal. His writings reveal extensive and detailed knowledge of a variety of subjects (e.g., precious stones) that he could most likely have derived only from written sources. Thus, although oral composition, by dictation, is by no means unheard of in the Middle

Ages, we should probably give no credence to his claim to be illiterate, a claim he may have made to distinguish himself from those (Gottfried or Hartmann?) who rely too heavily on their literary sources or who boast of their learning. Moreover, Wolfram's poem has an intricately balanced, mathematically precise structure, which offers an additional argument against his claim of illiteracy.

The most significant difference between *Parzival* and Chrétien's *Perceval*, beyond the simple fact that *Parzival* is complete, resides in the relationship of the Arthurian world to the Grail society. In Chrétien's poem, they appear to be mutually exclusive: Perceval has to distinguish himself from other knights and reject the Arthurian code in order to pursue the Grail. The two realms constantly overlap, however, in *Parzival*. For example, the guardians of the Grail, known as "templars," are knights who may leave to assume vacant thrones throughout the world and may return later; although they may not marry, the Grail King himself is allowed to do so. Wolfram conceives of the Grail realm as superior to that of worldly chivalry, but they are not separate and mutually exclusive realms.

Whereas the Welsh *Peredur* had presented us a tray containing a human head (although without calling it a Grail), and Chrétien had made the Grail into a tray containing a mass wafer, Wolfram's Grail is a stone. He calls it a *lapsit exillis* (an enigmatic term that evokes "stone," "fall," and "exile") and relates it to sacred history: it was to this object that angels were banned if they remained neutral in the struggle between God and Lucifer. Now the Grail is in a castle, Munsalvaesche, that no one can find by force of will or effort. The Grail sustains the lives of those who guard it, but the current Grail King, Anfortas, suffers from a painful wound that cannot be cured until a stranger arrives and asks the Grail question. The stranger is Parzival, but his deficient moral development during his first visit prevents him from asking the question and necessitates a long process of purification and maturation on his part. Parzival, we are told, is "a brave man slowly wise."

Wolfram commands admiration primarily by his vision and the scope of his work. He has transformed an uncompleted romance into an enormous epic of human and divine achievement. He has answered the questions left by Chrétien de Troyes, and although some readers may regret that the enigmatic quality of Chrétien's romance has evaporated in its transformation into German, Wolfram has clearly created one of the masterpieces of medieval literature, one that some consider second only to Dante's *Divine Comedy*.

More than a century after Wolfram, Philipp Colin and Claus Wisse adapted into German two of the French continuations of Chrétien de Troyes's

Perceval. The result, known as *Der nüwe Parzefal* ("The New Parzefal"), was inserted into Wolfram's *Parzival* between Books XIV and XV. It more than doubled the length of the work, adding over thirty-six thousand lines; it also concentrated heavily on Gawan and emphasized the value of adventure and traditional chivalric endeavor over the moral purification that Wolfram's poem had required of the Grail hero.

During the fifteenth century, the story of Parzival, taken from Wolfram, also inspired Ulrich Fuetrer (see below), who incorporated it into *Das Buch der Abenteuer* ("The Book of Adventures," 1473–78). And Wolfram's influence would not end with Ulrich, for literary adaptations and modernizations of his romance continued to appear throughout the nineteenth and twentieth centuries. The most influential of those works is surely Wagner's musical drama *Parsifal*, which has introduced Wolfram's story to a century of opera lovers.

GERMAN TRISTAN ROMANCES

The Tristan material also attracted the attention of German poets, who produced romances of exceptional quality. German texts never effected the full fusion of the Arthurian and Tristan legends, as French tradition had done, and many scholars do not in fact count them as Arthurian works. They are included here not only because they drew on French Tristan models or on the same sources as the French but also because, as early as Hartmann's *Erec*, Tristan regularly appeared as a member of Arthur's court in a good many other German romances.

Germany can claim the distinction of preserving the oldest completed Tristan romance. Some time between 1170 and 1190, Eilhart von Oberge composed *Tristrant*. His work belongs to the same tradition, the primitive or common version of the legend, as does Béroul's. The two use the same general plot, and it is likely that they have a common source, although it is also possible that Eilhart made a free adaptation of the French text. Eilhart's poem is *completed*—but not necessarily *complete* if measured against Béroul's romance, from which it omits or reduces some scenes, such as the equivocal oath or the death of the dwarf at Mark's hand. The episodes preserved in both romances show some striking differences of detail, and Eilhart's romance, bringing the story to a conclusion, also preserves such episodes as that of the second Isolde, not included in the French fragment.

Despite the weakness of the characters' psychological motivation, Eilhart's poem is worthy of admiration. It is nonetheless overshadowed by the *Tristan* of Gottfried von Strassburg, composed at the beginning of the thirteenth century. The greater popularity of Gottfried's poem is due largely to his superior talent but may also be related to the fact that he continues the courtly version of the story, as related by Thomas d'Angleterre. Unfortunately, Gottfried's *Tristan* breaks off (after nineteen thousand five hundred lines) before the hero's marriage to the second Isolde.

Although little is known about Gottfried's life, we learn a good deal about his ideas and tastes from the work itself, especially his literary opinions and stylistic views. In a section of *Tristan* traditionally called "the literary excursus," he discusses a number of poets and expresses his clear preference for Hartmann von Aue over a certain poet—doubtless Wolfram von Eschenbach—who confuses obscurity with profundity, who has to "include commentaries along with his stories."

Gottfried was a learned and cultured poet and an admirable stylist. It was perhaps natural for him to be attracted to the courtly version of the Tristan legend, rather than to the version followed by Béroul and Eilhart. The psychological analysis, the introspective monologues, and the more cultivated climate of the courtly tradition drew him to Thomas's romance. His text offers about five-sixths of the entire story, and by a happy accident the portion missing from his work is the very material of Thomas's *Tristan*. Thus, the two poems together provide a complete recounting of the courtly form of the legend.

The Tristan of Gottfried's work is less interested in traditional chivalric pursuits like battles or adventures than in courtly pleasures. From his childhood, he was gifted at chess, music, hunting lore, and languages; Gottfried seems to have thought of him more as poet than as knight. The love potion plays a role in the romance, but that role is not the same as in the "primitive" version; here, while it may indeed have caused Tristan and Isolde to fall in love, it has primarily a symbolic rather than a biological function. Symbolism and allegory are prominent throughout the text, and nowhere more strikingly than in Gottfried's elaborate explanation of the architecture of the lovers' temple, whose components represent such virtues as constancy and purity.

The lovers in Gottfried's work suffer, as had those in Béroul's romance, but in different ways. Béroul's lovers had suffered physically from their privations, and their love bound them together without bringing them peace and happiness. In Gottfried, although the lovers pine for each other, their anguish is ameliorated by their love, which sustains them throughout their ordeal; while in the "lovers' cave," they do not even require food, for the beloved's gaze provides sufficient nourishment: "they cared for no food except that from which the heart took desire, the eyes delight, and the body pleasure."

Curiously, the German romance offers some episodes that we might have expected the refined poet to omit. Corresponding to an equivocal oath sworn by Iseut to establish her innocence in the primitive version is a trial by ordeal in which she has to carry hot irons in order to exculpate herself. When she is unharmed, Gottfried draws a conclusion about the pliancy of Christ, who adapts himself to the circumstances at hand, in this case showing Isolde innocent of the adultery she had committed. Even more striking may be the attempt by Isolde to murder her faithful servant Brangane, who had sacrificed her virginity to save her lady's reputation and perhaps her life. Such scenes give evidence of Gottfried's willingness to follow his story where the psychological imperatives of his characters lead him: subtlety, delicacy, and symbolism may dominate, but Gottfried fully understands that the story also involves sin, guilt, and treachery.

"Tristan." MS fr. 99, fol. 56r. Paris, Bibliothèque Nationale.

Gottfried's *Tristan* is usually taken to be the "classic" version of the legend. In conception, in characterization, and in style it is the product of a brilliant poet whose accomplishment has been an inspiration to many. The Tristan story in general, and Gottfried's romance in particular, proved to be enormously popular, and other writers, such as Ulrich von Türheim and Heinrich von Freiberg, ca. 1235 and 1285, respectively, drew on Eilhart's poem in order to provide conclusions to Gottfried's *Tristan*. In later centuries, still others would adapt or update Gottfried's work or use it as inspiration for related works, and indeed, as Wagner's opera *Tristan und Isolde* proves, that inspiration was not limited to literature.

DERIVATIVES OF ThE FRENCh VULGATE

Around 1250, an anonymous translator (or perhaps more than one) prepared the *Prosa-Lancelot*. Derived from the Vulgate *Lancelot*, this prose work deals with events from Lancelot's life and death and narrates the Grail Quest and the death of Arthur. Galahad, Lancelot's son, is the knight who replaces Perceval as the destined hero of the Quest, and the author suggests that the Arthurian system must give way to a higher conception of chivalry and thus to a superior order of knights.

Ulrich Fuetrer composed an abridgment of the Prosa-*Lancelot*, the *Prosaroman von Lanzelot* (ca. 1467), which included a Grail story and the death of Arthur. During the 1480s, he revised the work under the title of *Der strophische Lanzelot*. His *Buch der Abenteuer* (1473–78) was adapted from Albrecht von Scharfenberg's *Der jüngere Titurel* (see below); it included not only the story of Parzival but also those of Lohengrin, Merlin, and others, as well as narrative material drawn from Heinrich von dem Türlin's *Crône* (see below). A second *Buch der Abenteuer*, which offers an expansion of his *Lanzelot* and the addition of miscellaneous stories, followed within the next decade.

ROMANCES OF ENTERTAINMENT

As early as 1200, German writers composed a series of Arthurian works that, although they pale beside the accomplishments of Hartmann, Wolfram, and Gottfried, achieved considerable popularity during the Middle Ages. First, there are works known as "Romances of Entertainment" *(Unterhaltungsromane)*. The *Lanzelet* (ca. 1200), by the Swiss author Ulrich von Zatzikhoven, is chronologically the second German Arthurian romance, preceded only by Hartmann's *Erec*. Unlike Chrétien's Lancelot romance, *Lanzelet* offers a full biography of the hero, beginning with his abduction, when less than two years old, by a water fay and his rearing by a group of women. Although his numerous adventures include his championing Ginover (Guinevere), there is no suggestion of an adulterous love between her and Lanzelet.

Wirnt von Grafenberg's *Wigalois* (ca. 1210–15), which has as its hero Gawein's son Wigalois, bears a strong resemblance to *Le Bel Inconnu*. Although the work is a romance of adventures, relating enchantments and other marvelous occurrences, Wirnt's emphasis is on moral and didactic concerns; his intent is Christian rather than Arthurian, and Wigalois undertakes adventures to serve God rather than to win glory at Arthur's court. Wirnt insists that the greatest knights are those who have God on their side, and the hero's successes are often due to God's direct intervention.

MISCELLANEOUS THIRTEENTH-CENTURY ROMANCES

Following Ulrich and Wirnt, German authors of the thirteenth century produced a series of Arthurian or pseudo-Arthurian descendants of earlier and greater works. Many of these not only recast and multiply traditional Arthurian themes but also combine them with classical or other motifs. About 1230, Heinrich von dem Türlin wrote *Diu Crône* ("The Crown"), and he may also be the author of *Der Mantel* ("The Mantle"), an adaptation of *Le Mantel mautaillié*. *Diu Crône* is a lengthy compilation—thirty thousand lines—of material drawn from various sources. Ostensibly, it is a biographical romance, and the author announces his intention to tell the story of Arthur. However, after recounting Arthur's birth and childhood, and certain other adventures, Heinrich turns to Gawein, who is the epitome of chivalric polish and success. Gawein, whose accomplishments are prodigious, is presented in fact as the model to be emulated, while Arthur appears to fade by comparison. The romance evinces decidedly uncourtly tendencies, the most striking example of which is doubtless the rape of Ginover by Gasozein.

At about the same time, ca. 1220–30, Der Stricker composed *Daniel von dem blühenden Tal* ("Daniel of the Flowering Valley"). Daniel is attracted to Arthur's court, and in Arthur's service he sets out to combat evil. His universe is the precourtly world of magic. Daniel is direct and sometimes ruthless, and Arthur takes a direct hand in the action of the work. Sometime after the middle of the century, Der Pleier responded to Der Stricker in *Garel von dem blühenden Tal*. This work and Der Pleier's other Arthurian romances, *Meleranz* and *Tandareis und Flordibel*, promote courtly ideals and present Arthur and his court, as well as the romances' protagonists, as models for chivalric and social comportment.

The anonymous *Wigamur*, perhaps written about 1250, is replete with extraordinary events and characters, including a sea-monster who takes Wigamur away to an underwater kingdom. The work also includes a battle between a vulture and an eagle; after Wigamur intervenes to rescue the eagle, the grateful animal (like Iwein's lion) follows him faithfully, causing him to be known as the Knight with the Eagle. This romance is notable in that it does not appear to have a chivalric "thesis"; the Arthurian court often appears to be concerned with little more than feasts and tourneys. The impression, however, is not that the author is attempting to show the vanity of courtliness but that he is simply entertaining his audience with the engaging and comical account of his hero's adventures.

Most authors of German romances had debated, at least implicitly, the value of Arthurian chivalry and courtly ethics. Some had endorsed them almost without question; some, like Wolfram, had shown how the Arthurian ethic might be fused with a mystical and religious ideal; still others had seen courtliness as a simple code of manners and social behavior (and had thereby devalued it). Yet few writers had expressly undercut the Arthurian court. One who did was Albrecht von Scharfenberg, in *Der jüngere Titurel* ("The Younger Titurel," ca. 1270). Albrecht develops the characters found in Wolfram's *Titurel*; he also exploits many of the situations and motifs of *Parzival* and even identifies himself a number of times as "Wolfram," and only once as "Albreht." As a result, the romance, which achieved great popularity, was long attributed to Wolfram von Eschenbach, even though the character and intent of *Der jüngere Titurel* are completely unlike Wolfram's.

A didactic spirit pervades this work, and it is didacticism aimed against Arthur. Chivalric efforts may succeed, but successes are hollow and without value: Arthurian knights, and Arthur himself, win battles and wars, but the Round Table society disintegrates nonetheless. Glory on the battlefield and splendor in society are of no value. Albrecht contrasts the Arthurian world with the Grail kingdom and condemns the former as spiritually inferior, a secular kingdom that, however glorious it may be, offers only a pale reflection of the kingdom of eternal life. But when setting about to discard Arthur and his court, *Der jüngere Titurel* does not even permit them to perish, as in other accounts, through war, treason, or the tragic effects of a sinful love. Rather, the King suffers a greater indignity: he is simply forgotten, and he and the court disappear at the end of the work. Apparently, they are now irrelevant relics of a past age; at the very least, they are ineffectual inhabitants of the world created by Albrecht.

CĐASTITY TESTS

In addition to *Der Mantel*, mentioned above, German literature preserves several other settings of Arthurian chastity tests. Several date from the fifteenth century. The anonymous play *Der Luneten Mantel* ("Lunet's Mantle"), concerning a cloak that reveals infidelity, may be derived from *Der Mantel*. A drinking horn betrays unfaithful wives in *Dis ist Frauw Tristerat Horn von Saphoien* ("This is Frau Tristerat of Savoy's Horn"), as it had in Robert Biket's *Lai du cor*.

While most such chastity tests, in various literatures, concern either the drinking horn or the ill-fitting mantle, the German *Das Vasnachtspil mit der kron* ("The Shrovetide Play with the Crown") involves a crown that causes unfaithful husbands to grow horns.

CONCLUSION

German Arthurian literature, like the French (and perhaps even more), has suffered from the fact that its greatest masterpieces are among the earliest Arthurian texts. Few French writers could compete successfully with Chrétien de Troyes, but the Germans who wrote after the very early years of the thirteenth century had to contend with the greatness not of one remarkable writer but of three. As a result, these three inspired a great many texts that could not equal them. Yet, even though the German Middle Ages never again produced the equal of Hartmann, Wolfram, or Gottfried, they nonetheless gave us a number of romances that contributed to the continuing debate on the efficacy of chivalry and to the progressive elaboration of the Arthurian legend.

SCANÒINAVIAN LITERATURE

Compared with French or German medieval literature, Arthurian literature in the North consists of a limited body of work, including both narratives and ballads. Among those texts are some important translations and adaptations, particularly of romances and lais imported from France. In dealing with Scandinavian literature about Arthur or his knights, we are concerned principally with Norwegian and Icelandic texts, and with Icelandic copies or adaptations of Norwegian works.

The oldest example of Scandinavian Arthuriana may be the *Merlínusspá* ("Prophecy of Merlin," ca. 1200), by the Icelandic monk Gunnlaugr Leifsson: this work is an Old Norse verse translation of Geoffrey of Monmouth's

Prophetiae Merlini, with some added material and some condensations and modifications, mostly minor except for a significantly shortened ending. A free translation of Geoffrey's *Historia Regum Britanniae* was provided by the *Breta Sǫgur* ("Sagas of the Britons," early thirteenth century), written in either Iceland or Norway; one of the two extant manuscripts of this work, a compilation known as the *Hauksbók*, includes the *Merlínusspá*.

THE CONTRIBUTION OF HÁKON

We owe a good number of the extant Scandinavian Arthurian texts to the efforts of Hákon Hákonarson (Hákon IV, king of Norway 1217–63), who commissioned the translation of several French Arthurian poems. The earliest of these works, known as *riddarasögur*, or "chivalric stories," is *Tristrams saga ok Ísöndar* ("Saga of Tristran and Isöndar"), translated by one "Brother Robert" in 1226; not only is this the first work commissioned by Hákon, but it is also the only complete version of the "courtly" branch of the Tristan story (represented in France by Thomas d'Angleterre). Hákon also commissioned *Ívens saga* (a prose rendering of Chrétien's *Yvain*), *Strengleikar* ("Stringed Instruments"), and *Möttuls saga* (from *Le Mantel mautaillié*). *Möttuls saga* and a metrical version of it known as the *Skikkju rímur* ("Mantle Verses," fourteenth century) offer an account of the magic mantle that reveals the infidelity of wives. The *Strengleikar* collection offers twenty-one lais, eleven of them attributed to Marie de France; those eleven include *Geitarlauf (Chevrefueil)* and *Januals ljóð (Lanval)*, both of which present abridgments or alterations of their French source.

We also have, from the same period, translations of Chrétien's *Erec et Enide (Erex saga)* and *Perceval* (translated in two parts, entitled *Parcevals saga* and *Valvens þáttr*, respectively), and while it is not certain that these were commissioned by Hákon, that possibility cannot be excluded, as cannot the possibility that they were the work of the same Brother Robert who prepared the *Tristrams saga*.

All of these Norwegian translations, with the exception of *Geiterlauf* and *Januals ljóð*, are now known only in Icelandic manuscripts. We thus owe a great debt to Icelandic scribes for the simple preservation and transmission of the *riddarasögur*. At the same time, the loss of the Norwegian manuscripts complicates the process of evaluating the original translations. A comparison of the Icelandic and French works reveals that alterations, abridgments, and interpolations have been made, but it is likely that many of those changes took place not in their translation into Norwegian but in the subsequent transmission into Icelandic.

The Second Generation

Although many Scandinavian Arthurian texts are translations or adaptations from the French, those translations themselves stimulated and influenced significant literary activity. Many of the motifs from the first generation of works found their way into other texts. The Tristan translation and others exerted an influence of their own. In Iceland, the *Tristrams saga* inspired the *Saga af Tristram ok Ísodd* (ca. 1400), a work that also incorporates motifs drawn from the Scandinavian versions of Chrétien's romances. The Icelandic saga transforms its sources in such a way as to develop a variety of exaggerations, humorous details, and ironic reversals (including a comparatively happy ending), leading recent critics to consider it a parody of the Norwegian text and of romance conventions in general. An early fifteenth-century ballad, *Tristrams Kvæði* ("Poem of Tristan"), concentrates on the concluding episodes of the lovers' story, beginning with Tristan's injury and ending with the trees that grow from the two graves and intertwine their branches. Finally, toward the end of the Middle Ages, and well beyond, the Tristan material was incorporated into a number of Danish, Icelandic, and Faroese ballads. One of them, the Danish *Tistram og Jomfru Isolt*, exists in several versions, one of which presents Tristan and Iseut as brother and sister.

With a single exception, all the Scandinavian Arthurian narrative texts of the Middle Ages are associated with Iceland or Norway. That exception is the 1303 *Herr Ivan Lejonriddaren*, a Swedish translation of Chrétien de Troyes's *Yvain* into rhymed couplets. The translator, who may also have used the Norwegian *Ívens saga*, condenses the story but remains relatively faithful to his source.

Despite the limited number of Scandinavian Arthurian works that are extant, Arthurian literature obviously attained considerable popularity in the North. That popularity is attested both by the large number of manuscripts that preserve them and by the frequency with which Arthurian names and themes were recast in other texts that are not themselves Arthurian. The *Tristrams saga* in particular provided motifs (such as the Hall of Statues episode) that were later integrated into indigenous romances. Themes developed in Chrétien de Troyes's romances also proved popular, although it is uncertain whether they were taken directly from Chrétien, from his Norse translators, or from folklore. Two icelandic sagas incorporate analogues to the Joy of the Court episode in *Erec et Enide*, while the Grateful Lion theme from *Yvain* or *Ívens saga* found its way, in one form or another, into fully half a dozen Icelandic works. Other texts offer possible, but less than certain, reflections of the magic fountain *(Yvain)* and the rustic youth *(Perceval)*. The Icelandic *Samsons saga fagra* ("Saga of Samson the Fair"), a fourteenth-century work often considered to be Arthurian, includes a setting of the chastity test involving a mantle; it also presents its hero as the son of King Arthur of England—but it is a different King Arthur.

Scandinavian texts provide important evidence of the esteem in which French Arthurian literature was held during the Middle Ages, and they are also extremely instructive for anyone interested in the adaptation of texts to different tastes and cultures. It would, however, be unjust to consider Scandinavian Arthurian works nothing more than "evidence" about another literature; they are also valuable literary creations in their own right, and, as noted, they often inspired other works that would remain a prominent part of both the literary and the popular culture for centuries.

ÐUTCh LITERATURE

Like Scandinavian, Middle Dutch literature preserves translations and adaptations of French Arthurian works. In one case, that of the *Perchevael*, a thirteenth-century rendering of Chrétien's *Perceval*, the translation, although not preserved in its entirety, is quite close; others are adaptations rather than direct translations. The fragmentary *Wrake van Ragisel* ("Avenging of Ragisel," first half of the thirteenth century) is adapted from the French *Vengeance Raguidel*; only nine hundred lines of the adaptation remain, although an abridged version was included in the *Lancelot-Compilatie* (discussed below). *Ferguut* (verse, mid-thirteenth century) closely follows its source, the French *Fergus*, through some two thousand lines, after which it progressively diverges. Thomas's *Tristan* was also known through a Middle Dutch version, of which there now remains only a 158-line fragment.

Two translations and an adaptation were made of portions of the Old French Vulgate Cycle; one of these, a faithful verse rendering of the Vulgate *Lancelot–Queste–Mort Artu*, is preserved in an important manuscript known as the *Lancelot-Compilatie*, which contains ten Arthurian texts. The other translation is a literal prose version. The adaptation of the Vulgate is a free rendering in verse, entitled *Lantsloot vander Haghedochte* ("Lancelot of the Cave"); only about six thousand lines are extant out of the many thousands that the full text must have comprised.

MAERLANT AND VAN VELThEM

The most important name in Middle Dutch Arthurian literature is Jacob van Maerlant (ca. 1230–90). The first of his Arthurian works was probably *Torec*, a romance contained in the *Lancelot-Compilatie* and perhaps adapted or translated from a French romance that has not survived. Maerlant also composed the *Historie van den Grale* and the *Boec van Merline*, adaptations (ca. 1261) of Robert de Boron's *Joseph* and *Merlin*.

Near the end of his life, Maerlant began an adaptation of Vincent of Beauvais's *Speculum Historiale*, which includes the life of Arthur. In his adaptation, entitled *Spiegel Historiael* ("Mirror of History"), he added material drawn from Geoffrey of Monmouth's *Historia Regum Britanniae*. The work was apparently interrupted by Maerlant's death, but it was continued by Lodewijk van Velthem, who also composed a sequel to Maerlant's adaptations of Robert de Boron. That sequel, entitled *Merlijn-Continuatie*, was adapted from the French *Suite du Merlin*.

The INDEPENDENT ROMANCES

Five Middle Dutch romances are known that are not apparently descended from French originals. The most important of these is the *Roman van Walewein* ("Romance of Walewein" [= Gawain]), begun by Penninc and completed by Pieter Vostaert, both of them writing during the second half of the thirteenth century. The romance concerns Gawain's quest to recover a floating chessboard, a quest that is repeatedly interrupted by adventures and challenges before the hero accomplishes his goal. The other "independent" Middle Dutch texts, from the second half of the thirteenth century, include *Lanceloet en het Hert met de Witte Voet* ("Lancelot and the Deer with the White Foot"), a brief work that shares with the French *Tyolet* the motif of a quest for a deer's white foot; *Moriaen*, recounting dual quests (as the hero, a Moorish knight, seeks his father while Walewein and Lanceloet look for Perchevael); *Die Riddere Metter Mouwen* ("The Knight with the Sleeve"), which recounts Miraudijs's bride winning and the successful search for his father; and *Walewein ende Keye* (included in the *Lancelot-Compilatie*), in which Gawain performs numerous exploits to prove, contrary to Kay's contention, that the boasts he makes at court are not idle. His proof leads to Kay's exclusion from court.

Arthurian literature was obviously popular in the Netherlands during the 1200s; that century saw translations, adaptations, and the composition of new romances. For reasons that are not clear, that popularity waned strikingly during and after the fourteenth century, and with a few exceptions (such as a sixteenth-century *Merlijn* that is different from that of Maerlant) Arthur is largely absent from Dutch literature for several centuries thereafter.

SPANISH, PORTUGUESE, AND PROVENÇAL LITERATURE

TRANSLATIONS AND ADAPTATIONS

French sources exercised the strongest influence on Hispanic Arthurian literature. Many of the surviving Spanish and Portuguese texts are translations or adaptations of French Arthurian works, but unlike Scandinavian or Dutch translators the Hispanic ones appear not to have been drawn to the first generation of Arthurian romancers, such as Chrétien, Thomas, and Béroul. It was instead the large prose works and cycles of the thirteenth century—the Prose *Tristan*, the Vulgate, and the Post-Vulgate—that found Spanish or Portuguese translators. Some of the later French romances, such as *Palamedes*, were also known on the Iberian peninsula, and *Perceforest* was translated into Spanish, as *Historia del noble rey Persefores*, by Fernando de Mena in the sixteenth century.

The French Post-Vulgate was translated by Brother Juan Vives (or João Bivas) around 1313. His translation is now known through Portuguese and Spanish redactions and fragments, which have been used in part to reconstruct the Post-Vulgate itself, and portions of all three branches of the cycle are contained also in Lope García de Salazar's *Libro de las bienandanzas e fortunas* ("Book of Prosperity and Fortune"). The extant texts include a sixteenth-century Joseph of Arimathea romance (the Portuguese *Livro de Josep Abaramatia*), fourteenth-century fragments of *Merlin*, and a fifteenth-century Portuguese *Demanda do santo Graal*, along with a less faithful Spanish *Demanda del sancto Grial*. The *Estoria de Merlín* is a fragmentary fourteenth-century text that relates Merlin's birth and the early part of his life. An important Merlin text deriving from the Post-Vulgate, *El baladro del sabio Merlín* ("The Shriek of Merlin the Sage"), came to be considered the first part of the *Demanda*; extant in volumes published in 1498 and 1535, the work includes chivalric adventures and series of prophecies, some of them the traditional ones taken from Geoffrey of Monmouth, others concerning aspects of Spanish history.

The Tristan story also proved popular in Spain and Portugal. The French Prose *Tristan* and some of the Tristan material from the Post-Vulgate were translated or adapted several times, although most of the Hispanic texts may be derived from the French by way of intermediaries (Italian, Provençal, or other French texts). The earliest of such translations, from the fourteenth century, now exist only in fragmentary form. From the end of that century or the beginning of the fifteenth we have a fuller Tristan text, the Aragonese *El cuento de Tristán de Leonís,* and in the sixteenth-century *Don Tristán de Leonís y su hijo* ("Sir Tristan de Leonis and His Son"), the story of Tristan and Iseut's children is added to their own. The Hispanic Tristan texts generally emphasize the chivalric aspects of their material over the love theme, but an exception to this tendency is the *Carta enviada por Hiseo la Brunda a Tristán; Respuesta de Tristán* ("Iseut's Letter to Tristan; Tristan's Reply"). In this work, from the end of the Middle Ages, Iseut writes to Tristan to lament his marriage to Iseut of the White Hands; in return, Tristan writes to explain and defend his actions.

PROVENÇAL

In addition to the translation and adaptation of French material, Spain and Portugal also produced a significant body of indigenous Arthurian literature. First, there are two important Provençal verse texts, both of them of apparent Catalan authorship. *Jaufré,* a romance of about eleven thousand lines, was composed before 1225 by an anonymous author notable for his irony and humor. Its hero is probably the same character as Girflet in Chrétien de Troyes, and other names, themes, and motifs that occur both in *Jaufré* and in Chrétien suggest a strong influence of the latter on the Catalan writer. The Provençal romance, in which Jaufré undertakes a series of adventures in order to avenge affronts to King Arthur by Taulat, was apparently translated into French in the late Middle Ages, and that translation, now lost, probably served as the model for a Spanish prose romance printed during the sixteenth century and popular thereafter (see below). The other text in question is *Blandín de Cornualla,* from the late thirteenth century or the beginning of the fourteenth. This work, which recounts the adventures of two friends, Blandín and Guiot Ardit de Miramar, is not specifically Arthurian, but it reflects and perhaps parodies Arthurian themes and motifs.

Provençal plays another role in the growth of the Arthurian legend. The popularity of the legend in the south of France is indicated by the numerous references, in troubadour lyrics, to Arthurian themes and characters (especially Arthur, Tristan, Iseut, and Gawain). Certain of the poems contain references that are otherwise unknown to us and that may therefore derive from romances or legends now lost. Arthurian allusions are significantly more numerous in the Provençal troubadours than in the work of northern French lyric poets.

Other troubadour lyrics (although in this case Galician-Portuguese rather than Provençal) include the five anonymous *Lais de Bretanha,* which may date from the very late thirteenth century. These poems develop traditional lyric themes but also contain explicit links to the French Vulgate and Prose *Tristan* material.

INDIGENOUS WORKS

Indigenous Arthurian or pseudo-Arthurian works produced on the Iberian peninsula include, in addition to the romances discussed below, three narrative ballads (called *romances*) concerning specific knights. *Tres hijuelos había el rey* ("The King Had Three Dear Sons") and *Nunca fuera caballero* ("No Knight Was So Well Served") deal with Lancelot, while "Herido está don Tristán" ("Sir Tristan Lies Wounded") concerns Tristan and Iseut.

The earliest surviving chivalric romance from Spain, *Libro del Caballero Zifar* (or *Cifar*) ("The Book of the Knight Zifar"), written about 1300, perhaps by Ferrán Martínez, is not specifically Arthurian, but it includes some obviously Arthurian motifs and names, such as Yván, and episodes that parallel those of certain Arthurian texts.

During the fourteenth century, Guillem de Torroella wrote *La faula* ("The Tale"), a short verse text in Catalan, to recount the narrator's imaginary journey on a whale's back to an enchanted island where he finds a palace painted with Arthurian scenes and meets Arthur and Morgan le Fay. This work, which draws from the French Vulgate *Mort Artu* and other romances, shows Arthur being sustained by the Grail as he waits to return in the hour of Britain's need.

From the fourteenth century on, Arthurian allusions, names, and motifs find their way regularly into a number of texts, thereby blurring (even more than in some other literatures) the distinctions among strictly Arthurian works, chivalric romances clearly influenced by the Arthurian vogue, and non-Arthurian texts.

One of the best-known Spanish romances (indeed, one of the few likely to be known to nonspecialists) is *Amadís de Gaula*. The original version of the romance, composed around 1340, is anonymous. Drawing on material from the Post-Vulgate and the Prose *Tristan*, it begins prior to the reign of Arthur, includes a number of Arthurian motifs, and offers obvious parallels to the stories of Lancelot and Tristan. Garci Rodríguez de Montalvo, in a version of the *Amadís* published in 1508, condensed some of the material from the original text, changed the ending, and added an additional book in which he emphasized his views on amorous and moral values.

Tirant lo Blanc ("Tirant the Fair"), by Joanot Martorell and Martí Joan de Galba, is a Catalan romance (ca. 1460) about a descendant of Uther Pendragon who encounters multiple adventures in the course of freeing

Constantinople. Guinevere, Iseut, Morgan, and other characters appear in certain episodes, and the romance offers numerous allusions to such Arthurian themes as the Grail Quest. The work was translated into Castilian prose, in the early sixteenth century, as *Tirante el Blanco* and into Italian as *Tirante il Bianco* (first half of the sixteenth century).

No discussion of medieval Hispanic Arthurian literature should end without a mention of one of the world's great literary monuments, Cervantes's *Don Quixote* (1605, 1615). This work marks the conclusion of romances of chivalry. Cervantes, whose text provides reflections of Arthurian themes and characters, brilliantly parodies the conventions of romance by creating a "hero" who fancies himself a knight-errant and who finds himself blinded to reality by his chivalric fantasies—to emulate and surpass "the Round Table, the Twelve Peers of France, and the Nine Worthies." Quixote's problem is precisely that he reads too much and that he reads the wrong kind of books: romances, beginning with *Amadís*. Cervantes tells us that Quixote "so plunged himself into his reading that he spent entire nights and days at it; thus, through little sleep and much reading, he dried up his brain and completely lost his judgment." The "enchantments, quarrels, battles, challenges, wounds, amorous entreaties, loves, and other impossibilities" that filled his fantasies provide ample material for Cervantes's genius, producing a comic masterpiece that reduces the excesses of chivalric adventure to absurdity. Arthur survived Cervantes, but two centuries would pass before he was restored to his former glory.

ITALIAN LITERATURE

In addition to specifically Arthurian texts, either indigenous creations or translations, Italian literature includes an unusually large number of other works in which allusions to the Matter of Britain abound. The recurrence of Arthurian names and references in lyric and other texts shows that the legend of Arthur and his knights achieved great popularity in Italy, and that popularity is confirmed by Arthurian subjects that appear in nonliterary art, such as the Modena archivolt (see pp. 205–6). The most famous Arthurian reference in Italian literature is a passage in Dante's *Inferno*, Canto 5, where reading the story of Lancelot and Guinevere's kiss inspired the passion of Paolo and Francesca. The passage, presumably drawn from the Vulgate *Lancelot*, concludes with a reference to the character who brought Lancelot and Guinevere together: "the book and its author were a Galehaut."

"*First Kiss of Lancelot and Guinevere.*" MS fr. 118, fol. 291v. Paris, Bibliothèque Nationale.

TRISTAN AND ISEUT

The most popular Arthurian figures in Italy seem to have been not Lancelot and Guinevere but Tristan and Iseut, who were taken as symbols of fated, passionate, and undying love. Passing references to the lovers were frequent between the late twelfth and early fourteenth centuries, and Italian authors produced a number of narrative texts concerning Tristan. Most of these were drawn largely from French prose works, such as the Prose *Tristan* and material contained in the Compilation of Rusticiano da Pisa, but the Italian texts often used multiple sources, adapted with considerable originality.

Galehaut tapestry, northern French or Flemish, fifteenth century.
Courtesy of the Saint Louis Art Museum.

The earliest Italian Tristan romance is *Tristano Riccardiano* (late thirteenth century), drawn principally from the French Prose *Tristan*. After
speaking of Tristan's father, Meliadaus, and of Meliadaus's brother, Marco
(Mark), the *Tristano Riccardiano* then recounts Tristan's birth and early life,
concentrating on his chivalric adventures and on his marriage. During the
following century, the *Tristano Panciaticchiano* drew in part from the same
source used for the *Tristano Riccardiano*, recounting much of the same material but concentrating on the deaths of Tristan and Iseut and the sumptuous
tombs prepared for them by Mark. Other Tristan texts include the fourteenth-century *Tristano Veneto*, a relatively faithful translation of the French
Prose *Tristan*, with some additional material from Rusticiano da Pisa's Compilation.

In *La Tavola Ritonda* ("The Round Table," second quarter of the fourteenth century), the stories of Arthur's court and of Tristan are thoroughly
fused, with Tristan the central figure. This work, notable for being the only
complete Arthurian cycle in Italian and perhaps the most original Italian
presentation of the Tristan material, is an exemplar of the "courtly" version
of the Tristan legend as represented in France by Thomas. Its sources are
multiple, however: it is essentially a highly original reworking of the French
Prose *Tristan*, combining Arthurian sequences from that work with stories
from the *Palamedes*, the Vulgate *Queste*, and other sources to constitute an
embryonic Arthurian cycle.

The anonymous author of *La Tavola Ritonda* contrasts the reigns of
Uther and Arthur, emphasizing the Old and New Tables presided over by
the two kings, respectively. The principal focus remains on Arthur's rule and
the exploits of Tristan and Lancelot, and the work regularly emphasizes
chivalry and physical actions over courtly love. Tristan is indisputably the
hero of the romance, and he and Mark are enemies. The work adds an original sequence recounting Mark's murder of his nephew and the vengeance
taken by Arthur.

MISCELLANEOUS ARTHURIAN WORKS

Other specifically Arthurian texts, although not literary masterpieces,
give additional evidence of the vogue of Arthur in Italy. Merlin attracted the
attention of several writers. The *Sette savi di Roma*, the Italian version of the
Seven Sages cycle, existed in nine redactions; each of them included the
story entitled *Sapientes*, which emphasizes the role and character of Merlin.
That narrative was then used by Paolino Pieri, at the beginning of the thirteenth century, in his *La storia di Merlino*, a prose work that recounted Merlin's

youth and prophecies. The late-medieval *Vita di Merlino con le sue profetie* ("Life of Merlin, with His Prophecies"), although based on the prosification of Robert de Boron's *Merlin*, adds some prophecies that apparently refer to events of recent or contemporary Italian history. Even earlier, Rusticiano da Pisa had written a large Compilation, which stands as the first Arthurian romance written by an Italian; however, he wrote the work in French, and it is discussed above, with other French texts of the period. Other Arthurian works of note are the anonymous *Il novellino* (a collection of tales from about 1300 that includes stories about Lancelot, Merlin, and Tristan and Iseut) and the fourteenth-century encyclopedic poem entitled *Il dittamondo*, in which Fazio degli Uberti discusses Tintagel, London, and other sites in terms of their purely Arthurian associations.

CANTARI

Although the indisputably Arthurian works retain our primary interest, the most impressive fact about Italian Arthurian literature is, once again, the extent to which references to Arthur and his knights pervade other texts, to the point that it is not always possible to conclude that a certain work is really Arthurian. The most striking examples are the *cantari*, narrative poems sung or performed in public from the thirteenth century through the fifteenth. Most of the *cantari* were constructed on traditional themes, adapted to the needs of the moment or the audience. That is, they might relate stories that belonged to a non-Arthurian tradition, but Arthurian characters could easily be introduced, often in the form of passing references that indicate, more than anything else, the popularity in Italy of Arthur, Merlin, Lancelot, Tristan, and others. While some of these works are clearly Arthurian in subject and substance, others may be, more properly, considered pseudo- or neo-Arthurian texts.

One of the few authors of *cantari* whose name we know is Antonio Pucci (ca. 1310–88). His *Gismirante* recounts the bride winning by a knight of Arthur's court, who in the process also saves Arthur's court from starvation. His *Brito di Brettagna*, which derives from Andreas Capellanus's Arthurian tale (see p. 120), depicts the hero's efforts to earn his lady's love by bringing from Arthur's court a sparrowhawk, hunting dogs, and a list of the rules of love. Pucci is also occasionally (and unconvincingly) thought to be the author of the *Cantari di Carduino*, which may be the masterpiece of the genre. The work, in two parts, tells first a story strongly reminiscent of the first part of Chrétien's *Perceval*: a youth raised in the forest encounters knights by accident and leaves his mother to journey to Arthur's court to serve the

King. The second *cantare* has Carduino release an enchanted city from its spell and, by a kiss, change a serpent into a beautiful lady.

Other *cantari* that treat Arthurian themes include *I Cantari di Tristano* (six episodes from Tristan's life); *Li Chantari di Lancelotto* (also called *La struzione della Tavola Ritonda*, "The Destruction of the Round Table"), consisting of seven narratives that roughly parallel the French *Mort Artu* account of the ruin of Arthur's realm; *Quando Tristano e Lancielotto combattettero al petrone di Merlino* ("When Tristan and Lancelot Fought at Merlin's Tomb"); *La vendetta che fe messer Lanzelloto de la morte di miser Tristano* ("The Vengeance Taken by Sir Lancelot for the Death of Sir Tristan"); and the *Cantare dei Cantari* (ca. 1380), which preserves stories dealing with both Roland and Arthur.

CAROLINGIAN EPIC AND ARTHUR

In addition to the *Cantare dei Cantari*, Italian literature preserves texts that represent a fusion of Carolingian epic, involving Charlemagne and Roland, and Arthurian material. The Franco-Italian *Entrée d'Espagne* (first half of the fourteenth century) provides a prelude to the French *Song of Roland* but departs from epic methods in a long section that shows Roland as a knight-errant and that contains frequent references to Galahad, Meliadus, and other Arthurian characters. Arthurian motifs provide much of the material for *Li fatti di Spagna*, a fourteenth-century work that constitutes, in part, a recasting of and sequel to the *Entrée d'Espagne*.

Matteo Maria Boiardo (1441–94) composed one of the outstanding representatives of the Italian chivalric romance form in Italy, the *Orlando Innamorato* (Orlando being the Italian form of Roland, the nephew of Charlemagne). This work, which continues the *cantare* tradition, offers the narrative of Charlemagne's struggle with the pagans, but Boiardo sets it in a framework borrowed from Arthurian romance, complete with Arthurian characters and themes, involving chivalric adventures, magic, and mystery.

Boiardo's poem, although running to sixty-nine cantos, is incomplete, and in 1516 Ludovico Ariosto published a continuation of it entitled *Orlando Furioso*. Ariosto kept the fascinating tonality achieved in his predecessor's work by the combination of the Carolingian epic tradition and the Arthurian inspiration and themes. Borrowing from the *Tavola Ritonda*, the *Vita di Merlino*, various *cantari*, and other Arthurian works, and using methods of interlace developed by Arthurian authors, as in the French Vulgate, Ariosto follows his hero through a series of quests that bring him to greater maturity and responsibility. The *Orlando Furioso* is generally recognized as the greatest masterpiece of Italian chivalric romance.

During the late Middle Ages and the sixteenth century, a number of Italian works appeared that had sources or counterparts in other languages. One of them, the *Sette savi di Roma*, was mentioned above. *I due Tristani* ("The Two Tristans," published in 1555) is translated or closely adapted from the Spanish *Don Tristán de Leonís*, but it also includes a long interpolation in which Tristan and Iseut have two children, who bear the same names as their parents. The French *Perceforest* was translated into Italian as *Parsaforesto* and printed in 1556–58, and *Lancillotto del Lago* (1558-59) was the Italian translation of a French *Lancelot du Lac* printed in 1533.

LATIN LITERATURE

Although a number of Arthurian chronicles and saints' lives mentioning Arthur were composed in Latin, most romances and lais were written in the vernacular languages. There are, however, a few exceptions. The earliest (ca. 1185) is a prose text included in the *De Amore*, Andreas Capellanus's famous treatise on courtly love. Roger Sherman Loomis, in *Arthurian Literature in the Middle Ages*, refers to Andreas's narrative as an Arthurian romance, although its brevity and its inclusion in a larger work hardly justify that designation. Romance or not, it is Arthurian: the sequence tells of a contest at Arthur's court in which a young knight wins a hawk for his lady and then finds tied to the hawk a document listing the rules of love.

The most important Latin Arthurian romance is *De Ortu Waluuanii Nepotis Arturi* ("On the Rise of Gawain, Arthur's Nephew"), a prose text dating from the last quarter of the twelfth century or, conceivably, from the early thirteenth. John Bale attributed this work, probably incorrectly, to Robert of Torigni, abbot of Mont-Saint-Michel 1154–86. While many chroniclers include fictional elements that blur the line between history and romance, the author of *De Ortu Waluuanii* moves in the opposite direction, integrating Gawain's adventures into actual fifth-century events, such as the sack of Rome, and thus giving the appearance of history to the already legendary story of Gawain.

The illegitimate son of King Arthur's sister, Gawain is known only as the Knight of the Surcoat. The work first recounts his early training and adventures as a Roman cavalry officer. He wins fame through his successful defense of Jerusalem; then, seeking other challenges, he travels to Britain in order to serve Arthur and be accepted as one of his knights. Initially rebuffed by Arthur, the brash young knight defeats an enemy king in order to recover the Castle of the Maidens. Gawain's success leads Arthur to reveal the young man's name and lineage and to accept him into the royal family and court.

Bale also attributed the prose *Historia Meriadoci* to Robert of Torigni (and in fact it probably was by the same—unknown—author as *De Ortu Waluuanii*). Meriadoc, whose father was murdered, is raised by Kay and later, with Arthur's aid, avenges the murder. Among the episodes that follow is an adventure in which Meriadoc rescues a princess and wins her as his bride.

The third Latin Arthurian romance (or the fourth, if we include the text from Andreas's *De Amore*) is *Arthur and Gorlagon*, a prose text from the early fourteenth century, in which Arthur undertakes a quest to disprove Guinevere's contention that he does not understand women.

To this short list of works may be added several texts classifiable as either chronicle or romance. For example, Etienne de Rouen's *Draco Normannicus* ("The Norman Dragon," dating from ca. 1169) is a rhymed chronicle that includes letters between King Arthur and Henry II. The letters concern a dispute about authority over Brittany and reveal the immortality granted to Arthur by his sister Morgan. The prose *Vera Historia de Morte Arthuri* ("True History of Arthur's Death"), which exists in a fourteenth-century manuscript, recounts the wounding and death of Arthur and the miraculous disappearance of his body.

The contribution of Latin to Arthurian literature was significant but not extensive. However, Latin was, as noted above, the preferred language for many Arthurian chronicles, including the most influential of all: Geoffrey of Monmouth's *Historia Regum Britanniae*.

ENGLISh LITERATURE

Middle English literature is a fitting conclusion to this chapter, not only because it includes two of the greatest monuments of Arthurian literature, *Sir Gawain and the Green Knight* and Sir Thomas Malory's *Le Morte Darthur*, but also because Malory, marking the culmination of medieval Arthuriana, also exerted an immeasurable influence on the Arthurian tradition, especially English and American, of the modern world.

CHRONICLES

Inspired in particular by Geoffrey of Monmouth or in some cases by Wace, authors writing in English created a strong chronicle tradition. Most of them dealt seriously with the question of Arthur's historicity, and with a few exceptions they accepted his historical existence and presented him as a heroic figure. A good many important chronicles, such as the works of Thomas Bek of Castelford, Robert Mannyng of Brunne, John Capgrave, and John Hardyng, were written from the thirteenth century on. The earliest appearance of Arthur in English occurs, however, in Layamon's *Brut*, which dates from shortly after 1189. This long alliterative work, which also uses some rhyme and assonance, is by far the best and most important English Arthurian chronicle. Based on several sources, but principally on Wace, it is a vivid adaptation that nevertheless retreats from Wace's romance flavor. Layamon deletes many details related to love and courtliness to concentrate on the martial and often brutal aspects of Arthurian society.

A good many works stand somewhere between chronicle and romance, notable examples being the *Short Metrical Chronicle* and *Arthur*. Some manuscripts of the former (anonymous, ca. 1307) incorporate material devoted to Lancelot and Yvain, as well as to Arthur himself. *Arthur*, a brief and anonymous fifteenth-century verse chronicle, was apparently based on Wace, but it includes such additional material as Arthur's burial at Glastonbury. It is one of the medieval texts (along with Malory, the Alliterative *Morte Arthure*, and the chronicle *Scotichronicon* by John of Fordun as continued by Walter Bowers) that identify Arthur as "once and future king": *rex quondam rexque futurus*.

FORM

The customary division of romance (French and most others) into verse and prose will not suffice for Middle English compositions, where the usual division is into prose, alliterative, and rhymed romances, with the last group including tail-rhyme, ballad, and couplet varieties. Of the rhymed forms, only tail-rhyme requires comment here. A "tail" is a shorter line concluding a stanza; it thus provides a conclusion and a sort of rhythmic punctuation. It may rhyme with a line in the stanza, with the tail of another stanza, or with nothing. The long alliterative line, used in *Sir Gawain and the Green Knight*, the Alliterative *Morte Arthure*, and other works, is capable of considerable variation, but it consists basically of unrhymed lines divided into two halves by a pause. It will normally contain four stressed syllables (and any number of unstressed ones), and one or both of the stressed syllables in the first half-line will alliterate with the first one in the second half-line. The "classic" alliterative line may thereby be represented by the formula *a a / a x* (with *a* representing stressed syllables that alliterate with others), but a number of permutations (e.g., *a a / a a* or *x a / a x*) may occur. In the following discussion, the form of the work is noted in passing, but romances are grouped into general categories based on subject matter rather than form.

ROMANCES ABOUT ARTHUR AND OTHER KNIGHTS

A number of Middle English romances deal with Arthur's own life and adventures. One of the earliest, *Arthour and Merlin* (verse, mid-thirteenth century), recounts the birth of Merlin and his role in the accomplishments of Uther and of the young Arthur. The alliterative *Parlement of the Thre Ages* (second half of the fourteenth century) presents a dream involving a debate among three men (representing youth, middle age, and old age) in which the oldest one offers a summary of Arthur's life and death.

The Alliterative *Morte Arthure* is a late fourteenth-century composition that many scholars consider closer to epic than to romance. It is notable for the detailed realism, bordering on bloodthirstiness, with which the anonymous author depicts battles, wounds, and deaths. It is also unusual in establishing Arthur clearly and firmly as the central character, rather than as the peripheral figure he is in most romances. The poem narrates the consequences of demands made on Arthur by the emperor Lucius. Refusing to pay homage to Rome, Arthur enters into a war from which he emerges victorious, only to find himself betrayed by Mordrede. The poem includes, as a pivotal scene, a traditional treatment of the Wheel of Fortune motif: a dream in which Arthur sees the other eight of the Nine Worthies rise and fall on the wheel, foreshadowing both his own future glory and his downfall at Fortune's hands. Yet despite the crucial role of Fortune, the text also suggests that Arthur is in part undone by his increasing pride and ambition, and the anonymous author manages to create a strong sense of the tragedy of the King's fall. The poet appears to have drawn from Wace in particular, but Layamon, Geoffrey of Monmouth, and other chroniclers may have served as additional sources. Although the surviving text is corrupt, the work is an adept and forceful composition that many critics consider to be, at the very least, a minor masterpiece of narrative art and of the alliterative form.

The Stanzaic *Le Morte Arthur*, a fourteenth-century poem in eight-line rhymed stanzas, is artistically a more modest accomplishment than the

Alliterative *Morte*. It draws heavily on the French *Mort Artu*, although it either derives from a variant version of the French text or perhaps condenses it and adapts it rather freely. Like its source, however, the work attributes Arthur's death and the dissolution of the Arthurian world not only to Mordred's treason but also to the destructive force of the love of Lancelot and Gaynor (Guinevere).

Other works treating Arthur as the central figure include, at the end of the Middle Ages, the greatest of English romances, Malory's *Le Morte Darthur*, discussed below, and, during the sixteenth century, several ballads of only passing interest: "King Arthur and King Cornwall," "The Legend of King Arthur," and "King Arthur's Death."

Curiously, various knights who inspired a number of works in other languages each became the subject of a single English romance (not counting Malory); most of them are adaptations or translations of French material. For example, *Sir Tristrem*, a stanzaic poem from about 1300, is the only English text devoted fully to Tristan and Iseut. It is a much-condensed (and sometimes inept) version of Thomas's *Tristan*. The text identifies its author as "Tomas," but whether that is a reference to the author of its source or to the English adapter is uncertain.

Yvain and Gawain (fourteenth century) adapts Chrétien de Troyes's *Yvain*; and Chrétien's *Conte del Graal* may have provided the inspiration for *Sir Perceval of Galles*, a tail-rhyme romance from the early fourteenth century, although the result in English is a relatively crude composition that holds little interest. Similarly, only a single work, aside from the late ballad "Sir Lancelot du Lake," is devoted principally to Lancelot: the Middle Scots *Lancelot of the Laik* (late fifteenth century). Lancelot also provides the subject of portions of the Stanzaic *Morte Arthure* and, of course, of Malory's work.

GAWAIN ROMANCES

Far more popular than any of these characters was Gawain, the hero of a dozen romances composed during the late fourteenth century or thereafter. In the Stanzaic *Morte Arthure*, Malory's *Le Morte Darthur*, and parts of *The Jeaste of Sir Gawain*, Gawain resembles the Gauvain of many French romances: proud, frivolous, and less than heroic. In the other English works, he is a prominent and genuine hero, and even in the exceptional texts he generally remains valiant and courageous.

Several of these works deal with the making and keeping of vows concerning such matters as prowess, vigilance, or marriage. Among the romances that provide tests of Gawain's resolve and physical skills are *The*

Awntyrs off Arthure at the Terne Wathelyn (late fourteenth century); *The Avowing of King Arthur, Sir Gawain, Sir Kay, and Baldwin of Britain*, a tail-rhyme romance composed around 1425; and *Golagros and Gawane*, a stanzaic Scottish work (late fifteenth century) based on incidents from the First Continuation of Chrétien's *Perceval*. The Loathly Lady theme, involving Gawain's willingness to marry a hideous woman (who afterward becomes beautiful), is the subject of *The Wedding of Sir Gawain and Dame Ragnell*, a tail-rhyme romance from around 1450, and of the ballad "The Marriage of Gawain." In the *Wedding*, and also in Chaucer's *The Wife of Bath's Tale* from *The Canterbury Tales*, where the Arthurian hero of this tale is unnamed, the theme of the Loathly Lady is combined with a riddle motif, in which the protagonist must marry her in order to learn, in the Wife of Bath's words, "what thyng is it that wommen moost desiren."

Several Gawain romances deal with tests or beheading contests. The best known and best by far is *Sir Gawain and the Green Knight* (last quarter of the fourteenth century), which is discussed in detail below. *The Grene Knight* (ca. 1500) offers a condensed recasting of the story from *Sir Gawain and the Green Knight*. The beheading theme is found also in *The Carle off Carlile* (ca. 1500) and *The Turke and Gowin* (ca. 1500). *Syre Gawene and the Carle of Carlyle* (ca. 1400) is related to *The Carle off Carlile* but lacks the beheading scene; it presents instead a test of Gawain's valor and courage.

A final Gawain romance, the brief fifteenth-century *Jeaste of Syr Gawayne* adapts events from the French First Continuation of *Perceval* and emphasizes the hero's seduction of a maiden and his generosity and mercy to her family.

MISCELLANEOUS ROMANCES

The Grail theme attracted relatively little interest in England prior to Malory. The early history of the Grail, though not the later quests, is the subject of the semialliterative *Joseph of Arimathie* (ca. 1375) and of Herry Lovelich's *History of the Holy Grail* (ca. 1450, in couplets), both adapted from the French *Estoire*. Lovelich also prepared *Merlin*, a verse translation (ca. 1450) of the Vulgate *Merlin*, and much of the same material is included in another, anonymous, *Merlin* text from the same period.

Along with Lovelich and Malory, one of the few Middle English romancers whose name we know is Thomas Chestre, the author of two Arthurian works from the late fourteenth century. His stanzaic *Libeaus Desconus*, drawn from Renaut de Bâgé's *Le Bel Inconnu* and other sources, treats the theme of the Fair Unknown (Gawain's son Gyngalyn). Chestre also wrote the lay of *Sir Launfal*, telling essentially the same story as Marie de France's *Lanval*; Chestre's principal source, however, was an anonymous work entitled *Sir Landeval* (first half of the fourteenth century). *Sir Landeval* and two sixteenth-century lays, *Sir Lambewell* and *Sir Lamwell*, may have been drawn from a common source, a Middle English rendering, now lost, of Marie's *Lanval* or from a source used by Marie as well.

The Arthurian chastity test appears in *The Romance of Sir Corneus* (ca. 1450) and in a ballad entitled "The Boy and the Mantle." Both involve objects, a drinking horn or mantle, that have the power to reveal infidelities.

SIR GAWAIN AND THE GREEN KNIGHT

Most of these Middle English texts are reasonably interesting, and a number of them are the work of talented and skilled authors. It has, however, been their inevitable misfortune to be measured against standards and expectations formed by the two great English Arthurian masterpieces of the later Middle Ages: *Sir Gawain and the Green Knight* and the works of Malory.

A single manuscript preserves the *Sir Gawain and the Green Knight*; the same manuscript contains three other poems, *Patience*, *Purity*, and *Pearl*, that may be by the same author. Scholars have formulated various hypotheses concerning that author, but his identity has yet to be established. The work is composed in alliterative stanzas, each of which is concluded by a "bob-and-wheel"; the "bob" is a single line containing a single stress, while the "wheel" consists of four three-stress lines. The five lines of the bob-and-wheel rhyme *ababa*, making the romance an intricate combination of rhymed verse and unrhymed alliterative lines.

Divided into four sections, or "fitts," the romance is the story of Gawain's encounter with the Green Knight, a stranger who arrives at Camelot to propose a beheading contest: an opponent may strike his neck with an ax, but if he survives he will return the blow in a year. Gawain accepts the challenge and beheads the giant, who picks up his head and leaves. The following year, Gawain, on his way to the Green Chapel, where the beheading game is to conclude, is received by a generous host, named, as we later learn, Bercilak. For three consecutive days, the host goes out to hunt, leaving his wife to do some hunting of her own, with Gawain as the target of her blandishments. Unsuccessful in her erotic pursuits, she at least persuades him to accept a green sash or girdle that will protect him from harm. When Gawain arrives at the chapel and submits to his fate, the giant takes three swings of the ax, leaving him untouched twice and wounding him slightly the third time. The wound, he then learns, is retribution for his having secretly kept the sash. The Green Knight is Bercilak himself, and he reveals that he had arranged for his wife to tempt Gawain and that the events of the whole year were planned by Morgan le Fay.

Although the action of the work is relatively simple and straightforward, the events are skillfully arranged and linked. Mysteries abound, concerning, for example, the identity and role of an old woman Gawain meets at Bercilak's castle, the identity of the Green Knight himself, and the purpose of the contest. Such questions accumulate and effectively create suspense, but they are eventually answered: the old woman is Morgan le Fay; the Green Knight and Bercilak are one and the same; and Morgan's purpose in arranging the entire adventure was to test the Round Table and frighten Guinevere.

The poem makes use of three traditional motifs: the Beheading Contest, the Temptation, and the Exchange of Winnings (whereby Bercilak gives the game he killed to Gawain, who in return gives him the kisses he received from Bercilak's wife, but deceitfully withholds the girdle). These motifs initially appear to be unrelated to one another, and in fact the reader may for a time take the events at Bercilak's castle as a secondary plot without connection to the principal one. At the end, however, it becomes clear that the plot and structure of the work are entirely unified, and there are no loose ends or subsidiary plots. Even within individual episodes, the poem is well balanced and pleasingly constructed. The poet emphasizes symmetrical arrangements of events, such as the three hunts and the three temptations, but also the three ax-strokes (as well as three kisses on the third day, Gawain's crossing himself three times, reference to three hounds, etc.). Moreover, the hunts— for a deer, a boar, and a fox—provide an unmistakable and humorous parallel to the hunt taking place in the bedchamber, with Gawain as the prey (and a "foxy" one at that, for concealing the gift of the green girdle). The poet also makes effective use of symbols, such as the girdle or, especially, the pentangle (five-pointed star) on Gawain's shield, representing courage, virtue, and courtesy. In this case, symmetry emphasizes contrast: as the pentangle symbolizes Gawain's perfection, the sash represents his flaw—his *lack* of perfection. It has been noted too (by Howard) that the structure of sections II and III parallels that of section IV: the arming of the knight (with descriptions of the shield and girdle), a journey (to the castle, to the chapel), the description of each place, three temptations and three strokes, and a concluding confession in both sequences.

What is less clear is the symbolic association that should be attached to the Green Knight or, more precisely, to his greenness (and to that of the chapel and sash). Some scholars have related the character and the color to an *eniautos daimon* (a year or anniversary "demon") or to the survival of a vegetation myth, an interpretation that accords with the emphasis on seasons and on the death and immediate rebirth experienced by the giant. Such speculations may elucidate sources, but they tell us little about the poem itself, in which the relationship of the knight's greenness to that of the sash and chapel provides a theme and tonality more important than the origin of the color.

The romance is characterized by a mature and often brilliant art. The poet excels in the creation of character, in the development of suspense, and in the ability to narrate an engrossing adventure story that is also, tantalizingly, much more than simply an adventure story. *Sir Gawain and the Green Knight* is a compact, well-constructed work that stands as the best of the Middle English romances. Even Malory, while easily surpassing the *Gawain* poet in the scope and sweep of his work, does not eclipse him in quality.

SIR THOMAS MALORY

There were several Thomas Malorys known to have been alive when *Le Morte Darthur* was completed in 1469 or 1470. After much discussion in past years, it is now generally, though not unanimously, agreed that the work's author must have been Sir Thomas Malory of Newbold Revel (ca. 1416–71). We know little about his literary career but a great deal about his criminal activities, or at least the accusations concerning such activities. He was a knight who was imprisoned repeatedly (accused of theft, extortion, rape, and other crimes). It was not unusual at the time for such charges to be trumped up for political reasons, although there is no proof that they were not justified—or, for that matter, that they were—in Malory's case.

Le Morte Darthur was printed by William Caxton in 1485, "after a copye unto me delyverd, whyche copye Syr Thomas Malorye dyd take oute of certeyn bookes of Frensshe and reduced it into Englysshe." Caxton's version was the only one known until the 1934 discovery, at Winchester, of a manuscript that Eugene Vinaver subsequently edited and published in 1947. The title that has long been in general use, *Le Morte Darthur*, was Caxton's; the manuscript version indicates that only the final section should bear that title and that the entire work is *The Hoole Book of Kyng Arthur and of His Noble Knyghtes of the Rounde Table*.

There are significant differences between the two versions. Some episodes, such as the Roman war, are presented in far less detail by Caxton (or else are expanded in the manuscript), and in various scenes, his additions offer useful clarifications of events. His style, on the other hand, is often less vigorous than that of the manuscript and his vocabulary more refined and less direct (as witness, for example, Caxton's writing "buttocks" when the manuscript reading is simply "arse"). The very structure of the work is different in the two forms: Caxton's version consisted of twenty-one books and five hundred seven chapters, while the manuscript divides the work into eight books or tales, most of which are to a good extent self-contained though loosely attached to other books by continuing characters and themes.

The differences between the two versions have most often been taken to indicate that Caxton introduced changes into the work and that the manuscript more nearly represents Malory's actual composition. The opposing view has also had its partisans, however, and it is possible either that it is the Winchester manuscript that incorporates revisions or that there was good authority for any changes made by Caxton.

The most important conclusion to be drawn from a study of the Winchester manuscript in fact concerns Malory's very conception of his work. Before Vinaver edited and studied the manuscript, even the most passionate admirers of Malory faced a serious difficulty in trying to defend the unity of his *Morte Darthur*: there are internal contradictions that cannot easily be explained away. For example, Tristram's birth and youth are related in a tale that *follows* the account of his adult adventures. Elsewhere, a character may die only to reappear later.

Vinaver's study of the Winchester manuscript enabled him not to reconcile these contradictions but to conclude that, as elements of discrete tales, they simply do not present a problem. There is not, he concluded, any strong evidence that Malory conceived of his compositions as part of a single, unified long work. There is indeed some evidence to the contrary, particularly in the existence of colophons closing each book; Caxton suppressed all these colophons except the last. It may well be that when he completed his first book *(The Tale of King Arthur and the Emperor Lucius)*, Malory either had no intention of writing others or, if he did, he at least did not plan for them to constitute a direct continuation of the first. While the last two books may have been composed as a unified pair, the others must be seen as separate romances. It would therefore be more accurate and appropriate to speak not of Malory's work, but rather of his *works*.

Although remarkably influential, Vinaver's views did not put an end to discussion. Some scholars, without rejecting his conclusions out of hand, have qualified them by suggesting that certain loose connections do link the tales together and that at least a general structure exists for the set as a whole. They point to a general chronological continuity from tale to tale and to references that extend backward and forward in the works, providing predictions, not always accurate, of future events and recollections of past episodes. The web of connections is nothing like the elaborate structure of the French Vulgate Cycle, but it is prominent enough that we cannot easily think of the tales as being entirely unrelated to one another. The relationships among Malory's tales may be roughly the same as that of Chrétien de Troyes's *Lancelot* to his *Yvain*: although entirely discrete romances, they do present continuing themes and characters and even provide references in one to an event that occurred in the other.

In addition to the controversy surrounding the unity of *Le Morte Darthur*, there has also been considerable disagreement concerning Malory's use and transformation of his sources. Those sources are multiple: they include principally the French Vulgate and Prose *Tristan* (the "certeyn bookes of Frensshe" mentioned by Caxton) and the Alliterative and Stanzaic *Mortes*. Working from his French sources, Malory extracted from the interlaced stories a single, or occasionally a double, narrative thread and recounted it apart from others. The results are uneven—least successful in the Tristan segments, most in the final two books.

Even within individual books, he reordered much of the material from his sources and eliminated episodes and emphases. The result is a series of extended narrative sequences, sometimes overlapping, but less often interlaced than linked together end to end; within the series, it is possible to see a general arrangement of subject matter, an arrangement that supports the views of those who question the separateness of the books. To oversimplify greatly, we can discern in *Le Morte Darthur* three large movements, depict-

---

THE SWORD RETURNED TO THE LAKE

King Arthur, mortally wounded in the battle with Mordred, asks Sir Bedivere to throw Excalibur into the water. Twice, Bedivere, thinking it a shame to throw away such a fine sword, hides it and tells Arthur that he has done as commanded. Twice, Arthur rebukes him and again asks him to do his king's bidding.

Sir Thomas Malory says that, the third time, Bedivere "threw the sword as far into the water as he might; and there came an arm and a hand above the water and met it, and caught it, and so shook it thrice and brandished, and then vanished away the hand with the sword in the water. So Sir Bedivere came again to the king, and told him what he saw."

---

ing 1) The Rise of Arthur: his birth and early career, the role of Merlin in those events, Arthur's marriage to Guinevere, and the introduction of Lancelot; 2) The Glory of Arthur and the Round Table: the adventures of knights of the Round Table (Lancelot, Gareth, Tristram) and the Grail quests (Perceval, Bors, Lancelot, and especially Galahad); 3) The Fall of Fortune's Wheel: the ruin, precipitated by Mordred and by the love of Lancelot and Guinevere, of the Arthurian realm and ideal.

By many estimates, Malory's works form the pinnacle of Arthurian literature, the masterly culmination of the medieval legend and the greatest single source of inspiration for future writers who would be drawn to King Arthur. Malory tells his story directly and often powerfully, in a vigorous and appealing style and with a strong sense of dramatic cause and effect. He is frequently praised for having brought clarity and coherence to a diffuse mass of material borrowed from the French.

For all that, however, he is not without his critics. Some have criticized him for accentuating knighthood and military action while deemphasizing or misunderstanding courtly love or the courtly refinement of the authors he drew from. Others, far from praising his treatment of his sources, contend instead that he has mishandled much of the material, such as the Tristan story, provided by those sources, that he has added irrelevant details, and that he has disrupted the intricately interlaced structure of the French. A few have condemned him soundly: John Speirs, in *The Age of Chaucer* (Penguin, 1954), argues that Malory consistently misses the significance of his material, that his style is lifeless, and that he reduces rich and appealing stories to a "succession of sensations and thrills."

Instead of either praising Malory for imposing order on the supposed disorder of his sources or criticizing him for having impoverished a rich body of narrative literature, it may be more to the point to admit that neither narrative techniques nor literary tastes in fifteenth-century England were what they had been in thirteenth-century France. There is no reason why they should be the same and therefore no reason for Malory to content himself with reducing "certeyn bookes of Frensshe . . . into Englysshe." All the discussion of the relationship of his works to their sources, while useful and necessary, often has the effect of preventing an assessment of those works on their own terms. *Le Morte Darthur* is a most remarkable, if uneven, achievement. Both its intrinsic literary quality and the influence it has exerted on the imagination of writers and readers since its time establish it as one of the half-dozen most important Arthurian creations in any language.

CONCLUSION

In his preface to Malory's work, Caxton points out that Arthur "is more spoken of beyond the see, moo bookes made of his noble actes, than there be in Englond; as wel in Duche, Ytalyen, Spaynyshe, and Grekysshe, as in Frensshe." He might have added German, the Scandinavian tongues, and others, for few literatures, in the medieval world or the modern, have been untouched by the Arthurian legend.

The most substantial medieval Arthurian literature was French, and the influence of French texts on others also makes them central to the medieval development of the legend. German and English were not far behind (and the latter will be the primary influence on future Arthurian works). The importance of the Celtic material, in terms of sources, analogues, and influences, goes well beyond the number of extant texts. Scandinavian, Hispanic, and Italian were also prominent, and Dutch only slightly less so. The production of Latin literary texts about Arthur was slim but significant.

But the list is not exhausted. Greek (mentioned by Caxton) has given us *Ho Presbys Hippotes* ("The Old Knight," verse, ca. 1300), about an old man who defeats Gawain, Lancelot, Tristan, and Palamedes. *Melech Artus* ("King Arthur," prose, 1279) is a Hebrew text, extant in fragmentary form, based ultimately on the Vulgate *Merlin* and *Mort Artu* (although perhaps more directly on a French or Italian intermediary). A fourteenth-century Yiddish verse composition, *Ritter Widuwilt*, preserves the story of Wigalois; this work exists also in three seventeenth- and eighteenth-century redactions. We have a late thirteenth-century *Tristant* fragment in Low Frankish and a Middle Frankish translation, *Perchevael*, of the Dutch work of the same title. Two fourteenth-century Czech Arthurian compositions are extant, both of them in verse: *Tandariáš a Floribella* retells the *Tandereis* of Der Pleier, and *Tristram a Izalda* borrows from Eilhart von Oberge, Gottfried von Strassburg, and Heinrich von Freiberg. Finally, we have an anonymous sixteenth-century Slavic prose composition, *Povest' o Tryshchane*, also known as the Byelorussian *Tristan*, drawn most immediately from the Italian *Tristano Veneto*, but influenced also by the *Tavola Ritonda* and other Tristan sources.

If we add to this list translations, fragmentary texts, and the preservation of Arthurian stories in oral tradition, it is apparent that, although Arthurian legends were concentrated in western Europe, there were few places and languages untouched by them. The spread of those legends would continue in modern literature (most prominently in English and American texts). But even if Arthur's popularity had ended with the Middle Ages, the result would still have been one of the largest bodies of vernacular literature ever devoted to a single subject. Moreover, the medieval corpus includes an astonishing number of texts that demonstrate significant literary merit— and more than a few enduring masterpieces of world literature.

NOTES

(References are to the appropriate section of the Bibliography.)
The Character of Arthur
>   Morris, passim.

Chronicles
>   Fletcher, passim.
>   Lacy et al., art. "Chronicles, Arthur in" (by Geoffrey Ashe), "Chronicles in English" and "Scottish Arthurian Chronicles" (by Edward D. Kennedy).
>   Loomis, ed. Chapters 8–10 (by John Jay Parry and Robert A. Caldwell; Charles Foulon; Roger Sherman Loomis).

Celtic Literature
>   Lacy et al., art. "Celtic Arthurian Literature" (by Patrick K. Ford).
>   Loomis, ed., Chapters 2–5, 16 (by K.H. Jackson; A.O.H. Jarman; Idris Llewelyn ed., Foster; Rachel Bromwich; Foster).
>   Loomis (2), passim.
>   Murphy, pp. 37–39.
>   Piriou, pp. 473–99.

French Literature
>   Frappier and Grimm, passim.
>   Lacy et al., art. "French Arthurian Literature (Medieval)" (by Norris J. Lacy).
>   Loomis, ed., Chapters 27, 28 (by Cedric E. Pickford; Alexandre Micha).
>   Schmolke-Hasselmann, passim.

Chrétien De Troyes
>   Frappier (2), passim.
>   Lacy, esp. pp. 1-33.
>   Loomis, Chapter 15 (by Jean Frappier).

Continuations of Chrétien's Perceval
>   Loomis, ed., Chapter 17 (by Albert Wilder Thompson).

Gauvain Romances
>   Busby, passim.

Marie de France
>   Mickel, pp. 55–59, 81–84, 93–95, 126–28, 130–33.

Perlesvaus
> Loomis, ed., Chapter 20 (by William Albert Nitze).

Post-Vulgate
> Lacy et al., art. "Post-Vulgate Cycle" (by Fanni Bogdanow).

Prose Tristan
> Loomis, ed., Chapter 26 (by Eugene Vinaver).

Vulgate Cycle
> Burns, passim.
> Lacy et al., art. "Vulgate Cycle" (by E. Jane Burns).
> Loomis, ed., Chapters 22, 23 (by Jean Frappier; Alexandre Micha).

German Literature
> Gürttler, passim.
> Lacy et al., art. "German Arthurian Literature (Medieval)" (by Karin R.
> Gürttler).
> Schultz, passim. (Appendix offers useful summaries of less familiar German
> Arthurian romances, pp. 185–207.)

Eilhart von Oberge
> Lacy et al., art. "Eilhart von Oberge" (by Marianne E. Kalinke).

Gottfried von Strassburg
> Jackson, passim.
> Lacy et al., art. "Gottfried von Strassburg" (by C. Stephen Jaeger).
> Loomis, ed., Chapter 14 (by W.T.H. Jackson).

Hartmann von Aue
> Loomis, ed., Chapter 33 (by Hendricus Sparnaay).
> Wapnewski, passim.

Wolfram von Eschenbach
> Lacy et al., art. "Wolfram von Eschenbach" (by Sidney M. Johnson).
> Loomis, ed., Chapter 18 (by Otto Springer).
> Poag, passim.

Scandinavian Literature
> Kalinke, passim.
> Lacy et al., art. "Scandinavian Arthurian Literature" (by Marianne E.
> Kalinke).
> Loomis, ed., Chapter 35 (by Phillip M. Mitchell).

Middle Dutch Literature
> Besamusca, passim.
> Lacy et al., art. "Middle Dutch Arthurian Literature" (by Bart Besamusca).
> Loomis, ed., Chapter 34 (by Hendricus Sparnaay).

Hispanic Literature

    Entwistle, passim.

    Lacy et al., art. "Spanish and Portuguese Arthurian Literature" (by Harvey
       L. Sharrer); "Tristan in Spain and Portugal" (by Dayle Seidenspinner-
       Nuñez).

    Loomis, ed., Chapter 31 (by Maria Rosa Lida de Malkiel).

    Jaufré

    Loomis, ed., Chapter 30 (by Paul Rémy).

Italian Literature

    Gardner, passim.

    Kleinhenz, pp. 145–58.

    Lacy et al., art. "Italian Arthurian Literature" (by Christopher Kleinhenz).

    Loomis, ed., Chapter 32 (by Antonio Viscardi).

Latin Literature

    Loomis, ed., Chapter 36 (by Roger Sherman Loomis).

English Literature

    Hibbard, passim.

    Lacy et al., art. "English Arthurian Literature (Medieval)" (by Sandra Ness
       Ihle).

    Loomis, ed., Chapters 37–38 (by Robert W. Ackerman; J.L.N. O'Loughlin).

    Mehl, passim.

    Sir Gawain and the Green Knight

    Benson (1), passim.

    Burrow, passim.

    Howard, pp. 425–33.

    Lacy et al., art. "Sir Gawain and the Green Knight" (by Vincent J.
       Scattergood).

    Loomis, ed., Chapter 39 (by Laura Hibbard Loomis).

    Sir Thomas Malory

    Lacy et al., art. "Malory, Sir Thomas" (by Peter J.C. Field).

    Loomis, ed., Chapter 40 (by Eugene Vinaver).

    Lumiansky, passim.

    McCarthy, passim.

    Takamiya and Brewer, passim.

chapter III

Modern Arthurian Literature

Arthurian literature did not stop with Malory and resume with Tennyson. It is true that the popularity of Arthurian themes declined sharply after the close of the Middle Ages. Yet interest in Arthur never ceased entirely, and in fact the sixteenth century in particular saw a continuation of earlier interest, indicated by the popularity of ballads and the frequent republication and recasting of medieval romances. Moreover, a good number of original Arthurian works were composed from the sixteenth century through the eighteenth, and if that period is often considered a kind of "Dark Ages" of Arthuriana, such a reputation is due not to a simple lack of interest in the King but rather to the fact that, for whatever reason, the authors most drawn to the subject do not generally include the greatest poets, dramatists, and novelists. The period produced competent and interesting Arthurian works but none comparable to those of Chrétien, Wolfram, or Malory of an earlier age, or to those of Tennyson to follow.

England fared better than most countries: Dryden and Spenser composed Arthurian works of some significance. Yet Arthurian material in Shakespeare, for example, is limited to occasional references to Merlin and perhaps to his conception of a fairy realm, while both Jonson and Milton planned and then abandoned Arthurian projects. In Germany, only the name of Hans Sachs stands out clearly. In France, most writers from the late Renaissance through a good part of the eighteenth century rejected everything "medieval," including the Arthurian legend, which France itself had originally done so much to develop. Arthur failed to interest such writers as Ronsard, Molière, or Voltaire. Rabelais shows the influence of Arthurian texts, but only in frequent references to Arthurian names drawn in part from burlesque Gargantuan fantasies of the time.

Even though few of the greatest authors of the sixteenth, seventeenth, and eighteenth centuries are represented, the number of Arthurian texts during the period gives evidence that the subject matter continued to exert an almost uninterrupted influence. To a good extent, the sixteenth century, especially in France but in other countries as well, is characterized by the frequent expansion, revision, or modernization of earlier works, as well as translation and adaptation; we have already mentioned translations into Welsh, Italian, Russian, and other languages.

The sixteenth century left us many new Arthurian works, some of them important. Among the prominent writers were Edmund Spenser *(The Faerie Queene)*, Ariosto *(Orlando Furioso)*, and Hans Sachs (see p. 147). If to those we add a good many other significant poets, chroniclers, and romance writers, and a host of minor ones as well, it is clear that Arthur's popularity continued. Yet the legend was losing its earlier vitality, and the century to follow would find the King's fortunes in eclipse. In most countries, there are few extended periods in which we cannot find popular ballads, texts that we can characterize as Arthurian or at least pseudo-Arthurian, and a historical or antiquarian interest in the King or in Merlin and others.

Only the nineteenth and twentieth centuries would restore Arthur's earlier status and initiate a remarkable flowering of literature and art. Modern Arthurian literature in France and Germany is varied and rich, though not voluminous, while the same period has seen an explosion of English-language novels, plays, and poems about Arthur. The proliferation of Arthurian titles, especially in England and the United States, makes it impossible within the confines of a single chapter to offer a full treatment or even to mention most authors and works. Thus, whereas the most significant works will be discussed or noted in the pages to follow, we can mention many titles, especially from English and American literature, only in passing or not at all. Fuller information concerning postmedieval Arthuriana in English is offered in important books by Merriman, Starr, Taylor and Brewer, and Thompson, to which readers are referred (see Bibliography).

fRENCb LITERATURE

The French sixteenth century continued both the interest in Arthurian literature and the tendency toward compilations, translations, adaptations and modernizations, prosifications, and expansions of those stories. Examples include *Le Chevalier doré* (a condensation of *Perceforest*), the French prose *Amadis de Gaule* (translation by Nicholas de Herberay), a *Lancelot du Lac* printed in 1533, *Le Noble Chevalier Gauvain* (1540), *Perceval le Gallois* (1530), and versions of the *Perlesvaus* printed (as part of a Grail trilogy, along with the *Estoire del saint Graal* and the *Queste*) in 1516 and 1523. Some of these books went through as many as seven or eight editions and reprintings.

A few sixteenth-century writers composed original works. Pierre Sala (to whom we owe a new redaction of Chrétien's *Yvain*) was the author of a prose *Tristan*, dating from the 1520s, that combines original material with themes drawn from the French Prose *Tristan*, the *Queste*, the *Tavola Ritonda*, and other works. Jean Maugin composed a *Nouveau Tristan* ("New Tristan"), updated for "modern" tastes and published in 1554.

Besides providing material for the reading public, Arthurian texts influenced and fascinated certain Renaissance writers, among them François Rabelais (1494–1553). Even though Rabelais did not write an Arthurian romance, that influence is apparent in certain of his techniques and also in his references to the Grail and to such characters as Gauvain, Galehaut, Lancelot, Merlin, and Perceforest. Other writers from the Renaissance, while not composing Arthurian works, give us an indication of the esteem in which Arthuriana was held. Joachim Du Bellay praised "ces beaux vieulx romans" ("those beautiful old romances"), and Pierre de Ronsard, in the preface to his *Franciade*, suggested that Lancelot, Tristan, Gauvain, and Artus should serve as themes for France's national epics. As these examples suggest, Arthurian texts were considered to be important more as national history or linguistic material than as literary creations. Without disappearing entirely, interest in Arthur diminished significantly toward the end of the sixteenth century, and Montaigne condemned Arthurian romances as being fit only for the amusement of children.

During the following century, the importance and interest of Arthurian works were championed by Jehan Chapelain in his *La Lecture des vieux romans* ("The Reading of Old Romances") and by Marc Vulson, Sieur de la Colombière, in *Le Vray Théâtre d'honneur et de chevalerie, ou le miroir héroïque de la noblesse* ("The True Theater of Honor and Chivalry, or the Heroic Mirror of Nobility," 1648). Vulson's work, intended as a book of instruction for the young Louis XIV, draws lessons of nobility and chivalric procedure from events of the Arthurian story.

The authors of original Arthurian works of the seventeenth century showed a particular fondness for Merlin. The magician figured in a number of plays and ballets, few of them memorable. The influence of Cervantes is apparent in most of these creations, some of which adopt or adapt his title. Typical of these is *Don Quichot de la Manche*, a 1640 play (with ballet) by Guérin de Bouscal; like most of the Merlin pieces, this one contributed significantly to the decline of the sorcerer's reputation. Similar plays of the period include Mlle Béjart's *Don Quichot ou les enchantements de Merlin* ("Don Quixote or the Enchantments of Merlin," a 1660 reworking of Bouscal's piece), Rosidor's 1671 *Les Amours de Merlin* ("Merlin's Loves"), a 1687 *Merlin peintre* ("Merlin the Painter," probably by Thuellerie), Dancourt's 1690 *Merlin déserteur* ("Merlin the Deserter"), and others. Such creations kept Arthurian names alive but otherwise did little to glorify or perpetuate the Arthurian legend.

The following century saw reworkings and popularizations of Arthurian legend, often in summary form and generally of unremarkable quality, but important nonetheless. At the same time, some serious scholars were beginning to discuss the value of legend. One of the most notable advocates and disseminators of Arthurian material was La Curne de Sainte Palaye, who insisted that it was a valuable source of historical information. Yet, instead of seeking historical accuracy, authors who prepared adaptations or original compositions generally altered the tone and themes of their predecessors to make them correspond to contemporary tastes. Le Comte de la Vergue de Tressan, in *Extraits de romans de chevalerie* ("Excerpts of Chivalric Romances"), transformed the story of Tristan and Iseut from a tale of passion and tragedy into simple pastoral. The series entitled *Bibliothèque universelle des romans* (1775–89), in which Tressan's work appeared, published versions of numerous medieval works, including Arthurian and other romances.

THE NINETEENTH CENTURY

Modernizations of Arthurian works continued to appear during the nineteenth century, and these influential contributions to the knowledge of the Arthurian legend were complemented, especially during the latter part of the century, by important scholarly works. Although its popular success was modest, one of the most significant of such modernizations was *Les Romans de la Table Ronde*, an imposing five-volume work prepared between 1868 and 1877 by Paulin Paris, one of the great medievalists of his day.

Not surprisingly, a number of French writers used the Arthurian legend for personal or political purposes. In 1860, Edgar Quinet (1803–75) published *Merlin l'Enchanteur* ("Merlin the Magician"), which exploited Arthuriana to provide a vehicle for attacks on Louis-Napoléon. For this enormous epic (in twenty-four books and nearly nine hundred pages), Quinet chose Merlin as a symbol of the French nation, which after attaining a position of glory and preeminence had fallen into a dispirited and shameful disarray, from which the sorcerer rescued it. Merlin also represents Quinet himself, the victim of a lengthy exile from France during the period he saw as its decadence, while the infidel Hengist apparently represents Louis-Napoléon. During a long exile, Merlin traveled throughout the world, performing various exploits (such as establishing peace between France and Germany) and meeting numerous persons of note, including Robespierre, Mirabeau, Robin Hood, Archbishop Turpin (a historical figure who was also a character in the *Song of Roland*), Faust, Don Juan, and Hamlet's father. He caused a *bastille* to be built in Paris and announced that it would be inhabited by the newborn Messiah, named *Liberté*.

Victor de Laprade (1812–83) also wrote an Arthurian work as an expression of opposition to the Empire. *La Tour d'ivoire* ("The Ivory Tower," 1865) is an allegorized Grail Quest, in verse, with the quester's adventures providing allusions to the immorality of the regime in power.

THE INFLUENCE OF WAGNER

The last fifteen years of the nineteenth century and the early years of the twentieth saw a small explosion of works treating Arthurian themes or motifs. The dual influences of Wagner and Joseph Bédier account for much of this activity. A great many poems inspired by Wagner's operas appeared in the journals *La Revue Wagnerienne* (founded in 1885) and, to a lesser extent, *Le Saint-Graal* (1892). Among the works that offered "homage to Wagner" and that dealt with Wagner's Arthurian characters were poems by Edouard Dujardin (1861–1949), Stuart Merrill (1863–1915), Gabriel Mourey (1865–1943), and Paul Verlaine (1844–96). Some, like Merrill's "A l'Instant auroral" ("At Daybreak"), simply mention the characters in passing. Others were devoted to a depiction of specific persons or events. Mourey's sentimentalized *Tristan et Isolde* evoked the lovers "far from men, far from tomorrows, far from maybes"; Jean Ajalbert (1863–1947) in "Lohengrin" presents the Swan Knight's departure from Elsa; and a "Parsifal" sonnet by Verlaine (who, in *Sagesse*, had also written of his own imprisonment in terms of Arthurian themes and landscapes) emphasizes Parsifal's efforts to resist temptations and remain pure in order to succeed in the Grail Quest. A line from this poem—"Et O ces voix d'enfants, chantant dans la coupole!" ("And oh, those children's voices, singing in the dome!")—has become famous, not so much for Verlaine's poem itself but because T.S. Eliot later incorporated it into *The Waste Land*.

In *La Queste du Graal* (1892), Joséphin Péladan (1859–1918) collected "lyrical prose" excerpts from his novels and dedicated the resulting volume to Wagner. Péladan also wrote *Le Secret des troubadours* (1906, containing a section devoted to Parsifal) and a play entitled *Le Mystère du Graal*. Edouard Schuré (1841–1929) composed a drama entitled *Merlin l'Enchanteur*, while the Count Villiers de l'Isle-Adam (1838–89) included characters from *Parsifal* and a transposition of the *Liebestod* from *Tristan und Isolde* in his romanticized poetic drama *Axel*. In *Lohengrin, fils de Parsifal* (1886), Jules Laforgue (1860–87) translated Wagnerian material into a satirical prose work dealing with modern love and marriage.

ᴛꞪᴇ ᴛᴡᴇɴᴛɪᴇᴛꞪ ᴄᴇɴᴛᴜʀʏ

At the turn of the century, Joseph Bédier (1864–1938) published a reconstruction of the Tristan story that has established itself as the standard version of the legend. *Le Roman de Tristan et Iseut*, which has gone through hundreds of editions and has been translated into numerous languages, has proved to be one of the most important sources of inspiration for authors of Arthurian works. The popularity of Bédier's reconstruction, added to that of Wagner's *Tristan und Isolde*, stimulated additional interest in the Tristan legend and led in particular to several dramatic works that explored it.

Prior to the publication of Bédier's version of *Tristan et Iseut*, Armand Silvestre (1838–1901) presented a *Tristan de Léonis*, which met with only limited success. A more promising project was announced by Gabriel Mourey (whose poem on Tristan and Iseut is mentioned above), but it was never completed. Mourey had long been fascinated by the Tristan legend, and after the publication of Bédier's work he made detailed plans with Claude Debussy (discussed in Chapter IV, p. 251) for a Tristan opera. Only the outline and a few measures of the music were composed. In 1929, a *Tristan et Iseut*, credited to Bédier himself and to Louis Artus, with music by Paul Ladmirault, played to lavish praise from critics. Another Tristan play, *La Tragédie de Tristan et Iseult*, by Stéphane-Georges de Bouhélier-Lepelletier (better known as Saint-Georges de Bouhélier, 1876–1947), had a brief run at the Théâtre de l'Odéon in Paris in 1923; it is of interest more as testimony to the popularity of the Tristan legend than for its intrinsic value.

While the appeal of Arthur for the twentieth century has been weaker in France than in England or the United States, the legend has continued to attract a good deal of attention. In addition to modernizations and retellings, such as Jacques Boulenger's four-volume *Les Romans de la Table Ronde* ("The Romances of the Round Table") in 1922, the century has seen Arthurian works by major authors, including Guillaume Apollinaire (1880–1918), Jean Cocteau (1889–1963), and Paul Claudel (1868–1955).

Dante Gabriel Rossetti, Sir Tristram and La Belle Yseult Drinking the Love Potion
(1867). The Cecil Higgins Art Gallery, Bedford.

Apollinaire's first important prose work was *L'Enchanteur pourrissant*
("The Putrescent Magician," 1904). Drawn to the demonic aspects of Merlin, Apollinaire presents the enchanter as an antichrist. In a sense, the work,
which parodies scripture (including Christ's words), is an "antigospel" that
some critics have seen both as a violent attack on Christianity and as an
effort on the poet's part to exorcise the remnants of his own former faith.
The text presents the declaimed sentiments of various characters gathered
around the tomb holding the decaying body of Merlin. To this work is appended *Onirocritique* ("The Interpretation of Dreams"), which contains additional Arthurian allusions.

Cocteau used Arthurian material successfully in drama and film. His play *Les Chevaliers de la Table Ronde* ("The Knights of the Round Table," 1937; the initial title was "Blancharmure," "White-armor," a name for Galahad) contrasts the intoxicating effect of Merlin's spells with the liberating effect of Galahad; the play apparently uses the Arthurian legend as a metaphor for Cocteau's own opium addiction, with Merlin reflecting his "intoxication," and Galahad, his detoxification.

Twentieth-century French writers (and filmmakers) have shown considerable interest in the Tristan and Iseut legend. Cocteau's 1943 screenplay *L'Eternel Retour* transposed the Tristan and Iseut legend into a modern setting, where the events of the drama reflect and sometimes duplicate those of the traditional legend; the film was directed by Jean Delannoy and featured music by Georges Auric; it starred Jean Marais.

Partage de midi ("Division of Noon," 1905, definitive version 1948–49) is Paul Claudel's contribution to the Tristan legend and reflects in particular the influence of Wagner's *Tristan und Isolde*. It is the story of a tragic love that begins with a shipboard romance and ends in death for the lovers. An updating of the myth, it develops themes and structures clearly drawn from Wagner.

Another major author, Boris Vian (1920–59), composed an Arthurian drama entitled *Le Chevalier de Neige* ("The Snow Knight," 1953). Vian concentrates on Lancelot (the knight with the white, or "snow," armor) and Guenièvre and excludes such themes as the Grail Quest. The four-hour drama includes music composed by Georges Delerue, who, with Vian, turned the drama into an opera that was presented in 1957.

The Grail story has occupied the attention of a number of French writers. In *Le Roi du monde* ("The King of the World," 1925), René Guénon (1886–1951) proposed to examine the whole history of the Grail, from its origins in the emerald that fell from Lucifer's forehead through the Arthurian period to an anticipated future. Julien Gracq treated the Parsifal legend twice, first in *Au Château d'Argol* ("The Castle of Argol," 1939) and later in his 1945 play *Le Roi Pêcheur* ("The Fisher King"). Both of these show the influence of Wagner, while the second uses Wolfram as well; both place greater emphasis on Amfortas, the Grail King, than on Parsifal. One of the most striking examples of the transposition of an Arthurian theme into a modern context is the 1957 *Montsalvat* of Pierre Benoit (1886–1962), which depicts a Grail Quest occurring in occupied France.

Robert Pinget's novel *Graal Flibuste* (1955; definitive edition, 1966) is a curious piece of Arthuriana, if it is Arthurian at all. It offers only a vague and inverted reflection of Grail themes. The narrator makes a voyage, or undertakes a quest, to a strange wasteland, a land of "desolation and stench," in the middle of which is the castle inhabited by its monarch, Graal Flibuste (an untranslatable name that juxtaposes the Grail with the word for "piracy" or "buccaneering"). The novel is a parody of travel narrative, and the quest it depicts, if there is indeed a quest, is an odd, even absurd one: it is not clear why the narrator has come there or what, if anything, he is seeking; the journey seems to have no specific beginning or end; it does not seem to progress, and the character does not see, much less achieve, a Grail.

During the 1970s and 80s, attention shifted to Merlin, the subject of novels by Théophile Briant, Romain Weingarten, René Barjavel, and Michel Rio. Briant's *Le Testament de Merlin* (1975) appears at times to be more concerned with philosophy and poetry than with the Arthurian legend *per se*. Merlin, whom he situates at the historical and spiritual confluence of druidism and Christianity, is at the center of the novel and the Arthurian universe. It is he who had founded chivalry; it is he also, and not the King, who killed Mordred on Salisbury Plain and who returned Arthur's sword to the lake. His power prevented Arthur's death and allowed for the King's departure for Avalon; thereafter, he retired to Brocéliande to remain with Viviane and to offer revelations of esoteric truths to his young friend Adragante.

Romain Weingarten tells the Arthurian story from the point of view of Blaise (once Merlin's master and traditionally the scribe to whom Merlin dictated his prophecies). Weingarten's *Le Roman de la Table Ronde, ou le livre de Blaise* ("The Romance of the Round Table, or the Book of Blaise," 1983) presents most of the Arthurian story (except for Tristan and Iseut): the birth of Merlin and Arthur, the sword in the anvil, the establishment of the Round Table, the Grail Quest, and the death of Arthur. Using a method of interlace reminiscent of medieval texts, Weingarten narrates the adventures of Perceval (including his naive introduction to knighthood), Lancelot, Galahad, and Gawain. He does not take full advantage of the dramatic possibilities of the Lancelot-Guinevere-Arthur triangle, and the brief and factual account of Arthur's death is anticlimactic.

Among the best of the modern French adaptations of Arthurian legend is Barjavel's *L'Enchanteur* (1984). Merlin's life and his relationship to Viviane (including the sexual frustration that results from his need to concentrate his energies elsewhere) form one of the unifying threads of the novel, but its central focus is Grail history. According to *L'Enchanteur*, the Grail was originally a cup made by Eve to receive the blood flowing from

Adam's side; after the Fall an angel broke the Grail, which was later repaired and became the cup of the Last Supper and the vessel used by Joseph of Arimathea. Barjavel traces the efforts of Arthur's knights (Gawain, Lancelot, Perceval, and finally Galahad) to find the Grail and heal the wounded king.

These two emphases (Merlin and the Grail) are joined in a number of ways, including Barjavel's suggestion that prior to Arthur's reign the magician himself had sent knights on the Grail Quest and that he, not Arthur, had established the Round Table. Moreover, we are told that he served as Perceval's mentor, providing the naive youth with training in combat, courtliness, service, and religion. Much of the Arthurian material in the novel conforms to tradition and demonstrates a thorough knowledge of precedent texts; yet, as the substitution of Merlin for Gornemant (Perceval's usual tutor) suggests, Barjavel has provided a good many innovations. Among them are the information about Grail origins, details concerning Camelot (a city built in concentric circles around the castle) and Avalon (an island in a river beneath Stonehenge), Perceval's early knowledge that the Rich Fisher is his uncle, and the form of the Grail question: what is in it?

The interest of Barjavel's work derives to a good extent from this interplay between tradition and novelty and from the contrast between the high-mindedness of the Grail Quest and Barjavel's frequent recourse to linguistic playfulness and humor. Merlin himself is a more intriguing and complex character than in many works; although he directs the Grail Quest, he can also be amused and excited by his initial discovery of a nubile Viviane sleeping nude in the grass. One of the appeals of the novel is the simple fact that it reinterprets an impressive amount of Arthurian material, remaining faithful to the spirit of early accounts without retelling them slavishly.

In 1989, Michel Rio published *Merlin*, a short novel in which the magician, at age one hundred, offers a reflective and often lyrical account of Arthurian events (including Arthur's birth in A.D. 460) and of his own active but ultimately sad life.

While a number of writers were concentrating on Merlin, Jacques Roubaud returned Arthur himself to the center of attention in *Le Roi Arthur au temps des chevaliers et des enchanteurs* ("King Arthur in the Time of Knights and Enchanters," 1983), retelling first the story of Arthur's forebears and then the early stages of the King's own career. His novel is an amusing if slight account of the stories, told with simplicity, humor, and a certain charm. It affords some narrative interest because of the author's practice of allowing his narrator the kind of lapses, uncertainties, and commentaries on his sources that we might expect from a medieval storyteller. With Florence Delay,

Roubaud is the author of a drama sequence entitled *Graal Théâtre* (1977–), a project planned for ten volumes.

In 1985, Jean-Pierre Le Dantec published *Graal-Romance*, a novel that depicts efforts by a cleric to write the history of Arthur's reign ten years after the King's death. His problem is that those who talk of those days have differing recollections, and it is no longer possible to separate fiction from fact. Le Dantec's theme, the inevitable conflation of truth, legend, and perhaps self-deception, represents an implicit acknowledgment not only of the vagaries of memory but also of the complexity of the Arthurian story.

Virtually all the modern French Arthurian compositions—those discussed here and others as well—present considerable interest, but the diversity of subject and approach makes it difficult to characterize them (and especially those that have appeared since mid-century), beyond noting a particular interest in Merlin and a tendency to use the Arthurian legend as underlying structure for personal and sometimes idiosyncratic visions. Many of them are highly original, and certain of them (Barjavel's, for example) are accomplished and effective works of fiction that will surely stand the test of time; they indisputably constitute an enduring contribution to the Arthurian corpus.

GERCDAN LITERATURE

Interest in Arthurian literature in Germany waned after the Middle Ages (despite the legend's dissemination in chapbooks and a few isolated texts) until the mid-eighteenth century. The one great name during the intervening period is that of Hans Sachs (1494–1576). Sachs, a prolific composer of *Meisterlieder* (well over four thousand of them) and dramas, also served as the thoroughly fictionalized hero of Wagner's *Die Meistersinger von Nürnberg*.

Between 1545 and 1553, Sachs wrote a drama and seven *Meisterlieder* on Arthurian subjects. All of them concern the Tristan story except "Die Ehbrecherbruck" ("The Adulterers' Bridge"), a recasting of the traditional chastity test in which, instead of a cloak, crown, or drinking horn, it is a bridge that reveals the infidelity of others; in this instance, however, it confirms the Queen's faithfulness. Sachs's drama *Tragedia von der strengen Lieb, Herr Tristrant mit der schönen Königen Isalden* ("Tragedy of the Strong Love of Sir Tristrant and the Beautiful Queen Iseut"), composed in 1553, consists of seven acts, each of them presenting one major scene, from Tristan's defeat of the Morolt to the death of the lovers. The songs similarly present individual scenes, such as the tryst under the tree.

Modern German Arthurian literature flourished with particular vitality and intensity during three distinct periods and had three specific subjects. The periods are, roughly speaking, the first half of the nineteenth century, the years from 1870 to about 1920, and the 1970s to the present. The subjects are three characters: Merlin, Tristan, and Parzival. Treatments of Arthur himself and the entire Arthurian story are comparatively rare, and authors who deal with the Grail most often exploit its value as metaphor or allusion rather than as the occasion to recast the traditional story.

Arthurian poetry developed in Germany before drama and fiction. Beginning in the 1750s, writers like Johann Jacob Bodmer (1698–1783), Christoph Martin Wieland (1733–1813), and August Wilhelm Schlegel (1767–1845) undertook ambitious poetic projects on Arthurian subjects. Schlegel's contributions included an uncompleted verse translation, in ninety-one stanzas, of Gottfried's *Tristan*, and other writers also translated medieval German texts; many of the other works of the period, however, were translations or adaptations of material from Ariosto or of medieval French texts (sometimes taken from modern French summaries rather than the original). In some cases, Arthurian figures are reduced to minor characters, as they had been in France and England during the seventeenth and eighteenth centuries. Such is the case with *Leben und Thaten des kleinen Thomas, genannt Däumchen* ("Life and Deeds of Little Tom Thumb," 1811), by Ludwig Tieck (1773–1853); in this work, Merlin, from his grave, predicts the birth of Thomas, who will prove to be a valuable ally for Arthur.

A number of poets from the early nineteenth century chose Merlin as their subject. Most were drawn to the theme of his entombment rather than his general role in the Arthurian story. Wieland's 1810 *Merlins weissagende Stimme aus seiner Gruft* ("Merlin's Prophetic Voice from His Grave") has the magician lament the disappearance of the Arthurian world. Karl Immermann (1796–1840), from whom we also have a posthumously published *Tristan und Isolde* poem, uses Merlin as a symbolic figure in two poems in praise of nature, "Merlins Grab" ("Merlin's Grave") in 1818 and "Merlin im tiefen Grabe" ("Merlin in the Deep Grave") in 1833. Heinrich Heine (1797–1856), in an 1835 poem, uses Merlin as an image of the lover who is symbolically imprisoned by the lady. The association of Merlin with nature continues in a section of the 1843 *Waldlieder* ("Forest Songs"), by Nikolaus Lenau (1802–50), and in the "Merlin der Wilde" ("Merlin the Wildman," 1829) of Ludwig

Uhland (1787–1862), the latter of which depicts the forest as the principal source of Merlin's strength.

One of the few important dramatic settings of Arthurian material during the first half of the nineteenth century was Immermann's drama *Merlin, eine Mythe* ("Merlin, a Myth," 1832), which presents the efforts of the magician, despite his satanic origins, to save the world by installing Arthur as the Grail King.

At the end of the nineteenth century and the beginning of the twentieth, a number of poets wrote ambitious poems or poem cycles, in which the expression of ideas was sometimes a greater concern than the accuracy of the historical legend or the coherence of the characters. Examples include Karl Vollmöller's *Parcival* cycle (1897–1900) and Albrecht Schaeffer's verse novel *Parzival* (1922). *Die Gralsage* ("The Legend of the Grail," 1907), by Richard von Kralik (1852–1934), manages to create a certain epic sense but is weakened by overambition, as the poet treats the entire complex of Arthurian and Grail material. Kralik also composed a musical drama, *Der heilige Gral* ("The Holy Grail," 1912, inspired by Wagner's *Parsifal*), and a *Merlin* drama in 1913.

The beginning of the century also saw such plays as the 1900 *König Arthur*, by Friedrich Lienhard (1865–1929), and especially the Grail cycle of Eduard Stucken (1865–1936). This cycle, more impressive for its ambition than for the intrinsic quality of the writing, consists of eight dramas emphasizing the centrality of the Grail Quest: *Gawan* (1902), *Lanval* (1903), *Lanzelot* (1909), *Merlins Geburt* ("The Birth of Merlin," 1912), *Tristram und Ysolt* (1916), *Das verlorene Ich* ("The Lost Self," 1922, later retitled *Uter Pendragon*), *Vortigern* (1924), and *Der Zauberer Merlin* ("Merlin the Magician," 1924).

As some of the preceding titles suggest, the traditional popularity of Merlin in German Arthurian literature continued during this period. One of the most important literary figures of the period, Gerhart Hauptmann (1862–1946), wrote of Merlin in *Merlins Geburt* ("The Birth of Merlin"), the first chapter of his *Der neue Christophorus* ("The New Saint Christopher," but originally titled *Merlin*), which occupied him from 1917 to 1944. Like many of the German Merlin compositions (as well as those concerning Parzival, the Grail, and other Arthurian themes), Hauptmann's work cultivates the mythic aspects of its subject, coloring it with a significant degree of mysticism and nationalism. Hauptmann also wrote an unfinished drama on *Galahad* (1908–14) and versions of the *Lohengrin* and *Parsival* stories (1913, 1914).

In addition to the works of Vollmöller, Schaeffer, and Hauptmann, we have a good number of adaptations of the Parzival story, including those by Will Vesper (1882–1962) and Hans von Wolzogen (1855–1934). Most of these texts are inspired by Wolfram or adapted directly from his work, and most of them are undistinguished. The most successful may be the 1898 *Die Sage von Parzival und dem Gral* ("The Legend of Parzival and the Grail"), by Wilhelm Hertz (1835–1902).

Reasons for the particular attraction of German writers to Merlin are not clear, although they certainly involve the combined appeal of myth, mysticism, and mystery. On the other hand, most German authors of Arthurian works looked to their national past for inspiration, and the popularity of Parzival and Tristan can be traced directly to the influence of Wolfram and Gottfried and to the later but no less pervasive influence of Wagner. In terms of their influence, the position of these three in German Arthurian literature is analogous to that of Malory and Tennyson in English. (Curiously, the works of Chrétien de Troyes and the Vulgate Cycle have not generally provided modern French authors with the kind of authoritative versions of Arthurian legend available either to the Germans or the English. The major "Arthurian" influence on French authors of the late nineteenth century was Wagner.)

Many German writers, almost all of them working in drama, have been inspired to recast the Tristan material adapted from Gottfried. Among the few reworkings in prose are texts by Emil Lucka (1909) and Will Vesper (1911); dramatic versions include those by Immermann (published posthumously in 1841), Josef Weilen (1860), Ludwig Schneegans (1865), Albert Geiger (1906), Ernst Hardt (1907), Emil Ludwig (1909), Eduard Stucken (1916), and Maja Loehr (1919).

Most of these newer versions of the Tristan story concentrate on one or more of the high dramatic moments of the legend: the love potion, Isolde's ordeal, and the lovers' death. In most cases, the potion is not literally the cause of their love, which they have already experienced, and in some instances (e.g., Stucken) they drink the potion by error, thinking it to be poison. The death scene is handled with equal originality and with mixed results. Weilen has Tristan kill himself, while Isolde dies of grief. Stucken has Tristan kill her. In Loehr's drama, he stabs himself, while she takes poison; in Geiger's version, Tristan dies of a wound and Isolde's death is the result of the plague. These innovations have not improved on the early story of the black and white sails, but they dramatize the efforts of authors to renew the legend rather than resort to slavish retellings.

Two Tristan works are not retellings at all, at least not in the traditional sense. *Tristan*, a 1903 novella by Thomas Mann (1875–1955), takes place in a sanatorium and traces the effect of Wagner's music by presenting a woman who is caught up in a passionate love from which only death can release her. *Tristans Ehe* ("Tristan's Marriage," 1916), a curious work by Karl Albrecht Bernouilli, presents Marke as an American millionaire and traces Isolde's psychological problems after Tristan's disappearance.

Following a decline of interest in Arthur that began during the 1930s and continued into the 1960s, Germany saw a new surge of works exploiting Arthurian themes. This recent period of Arthurian activity includes a good number of additional reworkings of medieval material, by such authors as Ruth Schirmer (*Tristan*, 1969) and Günter de Bruyn (*Tristan und Isolde*, 1975).

At the same time, the translation of English and American Arthurian works, including those of T.H. White, Mary Stewart, and Marion Zimmer Bradley, and the openness of German authors to these and other sources, such as Malory, have stimulated them to treat subjects other than the Tristan, Parzival, and Merlin material. Maria Christiane Benning's *Merlin der Zauberer und König Artus* ("Merlin the Magician and King Arthur," 1980) goes beyond the usual treatments of Merlin to pursue broader aspects of the Arthurian legend. The poetry of Hans Carl Artmann, during the 1970s, has drawn on English and American sources and promises to continue the revitalization of German Arthurian literature.

In drama, one of the most important and impressive projects of the modern period is Tankred Dorst's enormous *Merlin oder das Wüste Land* ("Merlin or the Wasteland," 1981, written in collaboration with Ursula Ehler). This work offers the complete story of Arthur and the Grail, drawing on a wide variety of sources, from Malory to Immermann to Eliot. Dorst's pessimistic vision of Merlin's failure is unrelieved by hope for a future redemption.

Even writers who recast the traditional subjects now tend to choose new forms and forums. *Flechtungen: Der Fall Partzifall* ("Weavings: The Partzifall Case," 1978), by the experimental theater Werkhaus Moosach, juxtaposes the social or psychiatric situation of Partzifall with that of a modern schizophrenic; Nathalie Harder has adapted Wolfram's *Parzival* (1976–79) for puppet theater.

Among modern retellings of Wolfram's *Parzival*, one of the most remarkable is the three-volume *Der rote Ritter* ("The Red Knight," 1991) by Adolf Muschg, an important Swiss-German writer. In this ponderous but fascinating novel, Parzival is burdened by sin and is thus unqualified for membership in Arthur's court until he is redeemed by the Grail Quest and eventually chosen Grail King.

Germanic interest in Arthur remains strong. The later twentieth century has seen a broadening of the base of acceptable Arthurian subjects. For traditional and nationalistic reasons, Tristan and Parzival continue to command attention, but new sources of inspiration, especially Anglo-American innovations and reinterpretations of traditional material, have prepared the way for German authors to treat a broader range of Arthurian subjects and to take a revitalized King Arthur in promising new directions.

ENGLISH AND AMERICAN LITERATURE

In England, from the end of the Middle Ages on, Arthurian tales were regularly condemned as a waste of time and as a corrupting influence on those who read them. Yet many readers chose not to heed such condemnations and continued to turn to Arthurian tales for pleasure. The establishment of Round Tables (tournaments loosely modeled after those described in Arthurian romance) and of various societies that borrowed Arthurian names or themes confirms the King's lasting appeal. The chroniclers continued to debate the truthfulness of Geoffrey of Monmouth's presentation of Arthur. The extremes of the debate are represented by Polydore Vergil, who in his 1534 *Anglicae Historiae* treated Geoffrey's account with disdain, and by John Leland, whose *Assertio Inclytissimi Arturii Regis Britanniae* ("A Worthy Assertion of Arthur King of Britain," 1544) offered a spirited defense of the twelfth-century chronicler.

The sixteenth century also preserved the memory of Arthur in many ballads and adaptations of Arthurian themes, but new literary efforts were rare until the Arthurian revival near the end of the century. A number of plays, mostly minor, were written at that time; Thomas Hughes's *The Misfortunes of Arthur* (1588) is more notable than most.

Hughes's work, including dumb shows and choruses, draws primarily on Geoffrey of Monmouth's history in order to give a documentary or chronicle effect, but the author borrows motifs and details from other sources. The most prominent of such borrowings is the theme of Arthur's incest with his sister Anne (the result of which is, of course, Mordred); this theme is probably taken from Malory, but with changes that transform its import. *The Misfortunes of Arthur* still holds a modicum of interest for readers, but it pales beside Edmund Spenser's epic *The Faerie Queene*, the most ambitious and important Arthurian project of the century.

EDMUND SPENSER

Spenser (1552–99) has been both praised as the greatest nondramatic author of the English Renaissance and criticized as the author of an "unreadable" allegorical epic. Although he composed other poems, *The Faerie Queene* is his best-known work, and it was the central project for much of his artistic life. It was begun at least by 1580, but of the twelve planned books only six were completed at Spenser's death; the first three were published in 1590, three more in 1596. An additional fragment, known as the Mutabilitie cantos, was published in 1609.

The Faerie Queene in both form and character is a combination of medieval allegory with Italian epic, as practiced, for example, by Ariosto. Arthur is not king, but Prince Arthur, and the poem recounts his quest for Gloriana, the Faerie Queene whom he saw in a dream vision and who, in Spenser's system of references to contemporary persons and institutions, represents Queen Elizabeth. Each book of the epic was designed to illustrate a particular virtue: holiness, temperance, chastity, friendship, justice, and courtesy.

Further, the central character of each book acquires and exhibits the virtue in question, and Spenser himself supplied the proper associations in a 1589 letter to Sir Walter Raleigh: Book One centers on the Red Cross Knight, who represents Holiness and who is also St. George. Other characters exemplify different virtues (e.g., Britomart is Chastity, Artegall is Justice, Guyon is Temperance) or institutions (Duessa, for instance, being Roman Catholicism, the target for much of Spenser's Protestant invective). Arthur himself, as Spenser notes, represents "magnificence in particular," for that virtue "is the perfection of all the rest, and conteineth in it them all."

The poem can be read as chivalric or romantic narrative, as spiritual allegory, or, particularly in Book 1, as a political and religious commentary on Elizabethan England. As a chivalric poem, it is loosely episodic, with characters joining one another against an enemy, being separated by evil forces, finally vanquishing their opponents; there are abductions, enchantments, battles. As a traditional allegory, the poem traces the Christian's struggle with evil and temptation and the efforts that, along with the gift of grace, bring about his eventual salvation.

Arthur's quest and the adventures he encounters provide a shape and a thematic unity to the narrative. He is its hero, and he is intended to exemplify the ideal nobleman. Yet, even though Arthur is present in every episode, he is a pale figure; his role is a thin unifying thread, and the focus of the poem, which we might expect to remain on Arthur himself, is dispersed over other characters and themes. Other than Arthur, Merlin is the only traditional Arthurian character to fill a significant role, with Tristram playing a small part in the action. Spenser surely knew Malory's work, but he made only occasional use of it; instead, he invented details of Arthur's youth, and he took his conception of Merlin from Ariosto.

Spenser's poetry is uneven. It is often flat and unappealing, but it can at other times be rich, full, and evocative. His invention of the form now known as the Spenserian stanza (nine lines: eight of five feet, one of six, rhyming *ababbcbcc*) is an important innovation. His vision, his technical achievement, and his often rich and flowing language justly merit for him a reputation as the finest narrative poet of his age. Although his contribution to Arthuriana is limited and idiosyncratic, his epic clearly merits our attention, and indeed by most estimates it was the last great Arthurian work in England until Tennyson.

Between Spenser and Tennyson, however, a good number of authors, including such important figures as Dryden and Fielding, were drawn to the legend of Arthur, giving us Arthurian texts that while hardly immortal offer more than passing interest. The first such work is perhaps Ben Jonson's masque *The Speeches at Prince Henry's Barriers* (1610), in which Merlin and Arthur offer praise of recent English monarchs. Also deserving of note is the *Poly-Olbion* of Michael Drayton (1563–1631). Drayton composed this 1612 poem to treat topographical features of England. Because many of these had legendary or literary associations with Arthurian themes, Drayton had occasion to pause frequently to recount stories related to Arthur, whose historicity he accepted without question.

During the seventeenth century, a number of works took Merlin as their subject, suggesting that, as in France at the time, the magician's popularity outstripped the King's. Indeed, Arthur was hardly taken seriously by now; ballads treated him as nothing more than material for children's stories and songs. Of particular note are ballads concerning Arthur's dwarf Tom Thumb and a prose *History of Tom Thumb, the Little* (1621). Among the works that accorded Arthur more dignity, Martin Parker's *The Most Famous History of That Most Renowned Christian Worthy Arthur King of the Britaines* (1660) achieved some success in its day, but now it is notable less for its literary value than for its documentary interest, including its listing of a hundred and fifty knights of the Round Table.

Three of the great writers of the seventeenth century, Ben Jonson, John Milton, and John Dryden, intended to write major Arthurian works. Milton abandoned his plan for an epic; Jonson completed only the minor

Arthurian work already noted *(The Speeches at Prince Henry's Barriers)*; Dryden (1631–1700) executed his plan, but the result is not among his greatest accomplishments. His 1691 dramatic opera *King Arthur: or, The British Worthy*, with music by Henry Purcell, is Arthurian in little more than name. Dryden, drawing from numerous sources, presents the struggle of Arthur and the Saxon Oswald for the possession of Great Britain and Emmeline, the blind daughter of the Duke of Cornwall.

At the end of the century, Richard Blackmore (1654–1729) published his epic *Prince Arthur: An Heroick Poem in Ten Books* (1695). Recounting Arthur's successful campaign to reclaim the crown after Uter's demise, the poem includes Lucifer's opposition to Arthur, Arthur's protection by angels, various dream-visions, and summaries of biblical and British history. *Prince Arthur* was followed two years later by Blackmore's second Arthurian epic, *King Arthur*, in which Arthur executes Clotar (who represents Louis XIV) and inaugurates a new era of peace.

THE EIGHTEENTH CENTURY

During the first half of the eighteenth century, little Arthurian literature appeared in England. Most of the texts that were published are notable, if at all, only for historical reasons: they provide evidence of the continuing decline of Arthur, who, as had often been the case during the preceding century, was often relegated to folktales and children's stories. In many instances, he was merely a foil for authors whose attentions were turned in other directions. The best example is the *Tom Thumb* of Henry Fielding (1707–54).

Fielding was interested less in the Arthur of Geoffrey of Monmouth than in the trivialized kind of folklore king who consorted with Tom Thumb. In 1730, he presented a two-act play, *Tom Thumb, A Tragedy*, redone the following year as *The Tragedy of Tragedies; or the Life and Death of Tom Thumb the Great*. Intended as an indictment of the excesses of contemporary drama and stagecraft, *Tom Thumb* offers a series of love triangles or, rather, chains: Arthur is in love with the Queen of the Giants, but both she and Arthur's queen love Tom Thumb, while Tom, who has defeated the giants in battle, is in love with Arthur's daughter Huncamunca. At the end, after numerous complications, various characters kill one another, Arthur commits suicide, and Tom Thumb is eaten by a cow. Fielding's drama, amusing in itself, is a far cry from Malory's account of the once and future king.

Aaron Hill's "pantomine opera" *Merlin in Love: or, Youth Against*

Magic has little to do with the traditional character of Merlin and, like Fielding's drama, virtually nothing to do with the traditional Arthurian legend in general. It does, however, have an undeniable if simple charm. The work, printed in 1760 but composed perhaps as early as 1740, was apparently never performed. It is the story, told to the accompaniment of songs and dances, of an elderly Merlin courting Columbine; in love with Harlequin, she repels Merlin's advances and uses his wand to transform him into an ass.

The middle of the century witnessed a flurry of new, pseudo-historical interest in the Middle Ages. However, that interest was generally colored by a disdain, inherited from Voltaire and others, for a Middle Ages thought to be a time of ignorance and barbarity; and it was initially expressed in reworkings of earlier though postmedieval material, especially of *The Faerie Queene*. Only in 1765, with Thomas Percy's *Reliques of Ancient English Poetry*, did earlier Arthurian literature begin to command serious attention. In this anthology, Percy published a number of Arthurian texts, including some that briefly present the events of Arthur's birth, military successes, and death. John Pinkerton, in his *Scotish Poems* (1792), republished sixteenth-century versions of *Gawan and Gologras* and *Sir Gawan and Sir Galaron of Galloway*.

Thomas Warton, who had a strong antiquarian interest in the Arthurian story, examined the legend in some detail in his *History of English Poetry* (1774–81). Warton also published poems inspired by the Winchester Round Table and by Arthurian associations with Stonehenge; his most important poem is "The Grave of King Arthur" (1777), which treats the King's burial in Avalon. William Hilton also indulged a serious interest in Arthur in the unperformed *Arthur: Monarch of the Britons, A Tragedy* (1759). This play, which makes an earnest effort to use medieval sources faithfully, deals with the war between Arthur and Mordred.

The thirty years that separate Hilton's work from *Arthur: or, The Northern Enchantment*, published in 1789 by Richard Hole, saw a definite and important change in the attitude toward Arthur. Hilton's pre-Romantic poem tells of Arthur's struggle to take power held by Hengist. It involves tests, enchantments, and the transformation of Hengist into the likeness of Arthur, whereupon he is killed by one of his own men. Hole's work, although minor, is important as an expression of a new approach to Arthur, who from that time on will be seen less as a distant king worthy of antiquarian curiosity than as a monarch capable of stirring the imagination and inspiring original poems and romances.

THE NINETEENTH CENTURY

Even though the production of Arthurian texts had never been entirely interrupted, the nineteenth century saw an extraordinary flowering of interest in Arthurian subjects. This resurgence, occurring both in literature and in the other arts, resulted from the coincidence of two trends: the publication of medieval texts and a number of historical treatises gave Arthur the intellectual respectability that permitted the rehabilitation of the legend, and pre-Romantic and Romantic interpretations of that legend gave it an essential vitality and appeal. The third essential ingredient was the activity of a great poet: Tennyson.

The Arthurian Revival owed a great deal to such men as Joseph Ritson and David Laing, who in the years following 1800 published editions or collections of medieval English texts and who in some cases provided solid and scrupulous examinations of the Arthurian legend. Another important name in the revival is George Ellis (1753–1815). Beginning in 1801, with publications like *Specimens of the Early English Poets* (2nd edition) and the 1805 *Specimens of Early English Metrical Romances*, Ellis gave a coherent summary of Arthurian legend, based on an examination of Geoffrey of Monmouth and others; he also printed detailed résumés of important Arthurian texts, from Chrétien de Troyes's *Lancelot* to the Stanzaic *Le Morte Arthur*, filling in gaps in the story by material borrowed from other sources. A similar process was followed a few years later by John Dunlop, in the *History of Fiction* (1814). Another essential step in the process was the availability of Malory's works, which, having been last printed in 1634, were issued in three different editions during 1816 and 1817; once Tennyson turned his full attention to Arthur, his work and Malory's would provide the dual sources of inspiration for virtually all the English-speaking writers and artists to come.

But prior to Tennyson's presentation of a heroic and tragic Arthur, the King was still to suffer a good deal at the hands of other writers. John Thelwall (1764–1834), in his 1801 romance *The Fairy of the Lake*, presents a muddled drama involving the abduction of Guenever by her father, Vortigern, who has incestuous designs on her, while Vortigern's wife, Rowenna, casts an enchantment on Arthur. The work portrays a weak Arthur, who must be rescued by the Lady of the Lake.

John Hookham Frere's burlesque epic *The Monks and the Giants* (1817–18), published under the pseudonym "William and Robert Whistlecraft," offers amusing portraits of Arthurian characters and themes and is important as well for having revived the *ottava rima* form in English. Its contribution to Arthurian literature is slight, however, since instead of developing Arthurian themes in any substantial way, it simply indulges in mild humor at their expense. Frere goes well beyond Thelwall's efforts, but we are still a long way from Tennyson.

The greatest poets of the time, including Byron, Shelley, and Keats, appear to have been indifferent to Arthurian legend. Tennyson is the obvious exception, of course, and Walter Scott to a lesser extent. Scott (1771–1832) should be especially mentioned for the role he played in the general popularization of medieval or medievalized themes; moreover, in addition to his 1804 publication of the medieval *Sir Tristrem*, with a new ending of his own invention, Scott ventured into Arthurian legend with his verse tale *The Bridal of Triermain*, which combines the story of Gyneth, Arthur's and Guendolen's daughter, with a Sleeping Beauty theme.

Others who made at least limited use of Arthurian themes were Blake and Wordsworth. William Blake (1757–1827) used Arthurian elements in his epic poem *Jerusalem, the Emanation of the Giant Albion*, but the character of the work is largely non-Arthurian. Wordsworth made nontraditional use of the legend in "The Egyptian Maid; or The Romance of the Water Lily" (1835), involving the actions of Merlin and the Lady of the Lake (here named Nina) and the marriage of Galahad and the Egyptian Maid.

Thomas Love Peacock (1785–1866) made a modest contribution to Arthurian literature in his poem "The Round Table; or, King Arthur's Feast" (1817), in which Merlin summons all future British rulers in an attempt to entertain Arthur, and a more substantial one in his 1829 romance *The Misfortunes of Elphin*. In the latter work, Peacock, using previously untranslated Welsh materials, made satirical statements about nineteenth-century British economy, the church, and industrialized society by contrasting them to the Wales of the sixth century. In certain ways, his method foreshadows that of Mark Twain (see below), although the latter is both less concerned with historical accuracy and more effective in the creation of humorous effect.

ALFRED, LORD TENNYSON   Tennyson (1809–92) immersed himself in the Arthurian legend, and his poetry was in large part responsible for the great flowering of Arthurian poetry and art during the Victorian period. Tennyson was drawn to the past in an attempt to illuminate and perhaps to repudiate the present; much of his poetry reacts against the prevailing mechanistic view of nature and the ugliness of an increasingly industrialized society. His concern was thus less with medieval ideals than with the Victorian moral condition, and the best mirror for that condition was King Arthur, known to the poet through Malory and other sources.

For much of his life, Tennyson was absorbed with two Arthurs. One was King Arthur; the other was Arthur Henry Hallam, the poet's closest friend, who died in 1833, at age twenty-two, and who was the subject of Tennyson's *In Memoriam*. The two Arthurs were never entirely separate in Tennyson's mind or in his poetry. His grief for his friend surely contributed to the intensity of his Arthurian vision, while King Arthur remained to an extent a metaphor that helped to immortalize Hallam.

Tennyson's Arthur is presented to us primarily through the *Idylls of the King*, a composite work built up gradually over the years. Prior to the *Idylls*, Tennyson wrote "Sir Launcelot and Queen Guinevere" (1830; only a fragment exists) and his first published Arthurian text, "The Lady of Shalott" (1832), both of which emphasize the power of awakening love. He also wrote two Arthurian poems in 1834: "Sir Galahad" deals with Galahad's chastity and his love of God, while "Morte d'Arthur" follows Malory closely in recounting the King's downfall.

With two new poems, "Vivien" and "Enid," Tennyson began what was to become the *Idylls*, although they were not all composed in the order in which they now stand. These two illustrate, respectively, the destructive and the ennobling aspects of love, the first leading to the ruin of Merlin, the second, taken from the Welsh story of Geraint, evoking the ideal order being created by Arthur but hinting already at its eventual failure; these poems, with Vivien renamed Nimue, were published together in 1857 as *Enid and Nimue: The True and the False*. The next poem, "Guinevere," presents the Queen as a complex individual torn between her ideals and duty on the one hand and her passion on the other. That was followed by "Elaine" (the Lady of Shalott story, taken this time from Malory), which illustrates the destructive effect Guinevere's adultery works on others.

"The Holy Grail" follows the adventures of six Grail questers but concentrates on Percivale, to depict his failure and to suggest, not that the quest has the power to ennoble and perfect, but that the absence of the Grail and thus the very necessity for a quest were related to the sin now gnawing at the heart of Arthur's realm. Tennyson introduced a new generation of knights in "Pelleas and Ettarre," after which he provided a beginning for his series ("The Coming of Arthur," recounting his birth) and an ending ("The Passing of Arthur," a slightly rewritten version of "Morte d'Arthur"). Later additions to the series were the melancholy "The Last Tournament" and the happier "Gareth and Lynette" (added to the *Idylls* in 1873), and "Balin and

Balan" (incorporated into the series in 1885). These poems, with "Enid" divided into two works, constitute the twelve books of Tennyson's epic. Late in his life, he composed his final Arthurian poem, entitled "Merlin and the Gleam"—not part of the *Idylls*—and he planned but never wrote a drama concerning Tristram.

Tennyson's is not a happy or optimistic epic. Melancholy and a sense of foreboding are only rarely relieved by a lighter tone, and even then, as when "Gareth and Lynette" depicts Camelot as Arthur would have had it, the reader has been so conditioned by the surrounding text that gaiety and idealism appear laced with irony and an expectation of failure.

Reality and truth are uncertain, and in any event reality pales beside legend and story, as witness the account of Arthur's birth. In straightforward, almost routine fashion, Tennyson tells us, altering the traditional account of Arthur's conception out of wedlock, that Uther, who loved Ygerne, killed her husband and wed her; immediately after his birth, the infant Arthur is delivered to Merlin and then to the elderly couple who will rear him. Yet Tennyson also tells us that there was a popular version of the story of Arthur's birth, and that version, as legend and poetry, was the more appealing: it was rumored that the baby appeared from the sea. The power of the waves increased,

> Till last, a ninth one, gathering half the deep
> And full of voices, slowly rose and plunged
> Roaring, and all the wave was in a flame:
> And down the wave and in the flame was borne
> A naked babe, and rode to Merlin's feet,
> Who stoopt and caught the babe, and cried,
> "The King! Here is an heir for Uther!"

It is Bedivere who affirms the former, less dramatic story, and casts doubt on the latter. Yet what matters is to recognize the web of legend and rumor that surrounded Arthur from the very beginning and that must put into question the legitimacy both of Arthur and of stories about him.

Hints of Camelot's fall begin to appear almost from the beginning. Such lines as "A doubtful throne is ice on summer seas" powerfully convey the transitoriness of royalty. The statement that "Arthur and his knighthood for a space / Were all one will" emphasizes both the common will established by Arthur's reign and the certainty (indicated by "for a space") that such a harmony cannot endure. In "Merlin and Vivien," the ageless embodiment of wisdom, the enchanter who taught and advised Arthur, is imprisoned by Vivien. The Grail Quest is undertaken recklessly by knights who do not possess Galahad's purity and devotion, and they are doomed to fail.

Throughout the *Idylls*, Tennyson condemns illicit love. Lancelot and Guinevere, despite efforts to reform, are destined to continue their adultery, and instead of elevating or ennobling them it brings about both their own ruin and, because Modred has exposed them, that of the Arthurian world. Arthur, who has tried to avoid facing the truth, must now condemn the Queen and undertake a war against Lancelot. The sinners suffer, but others must suffer with them. In "The Last Tournament," the Arthurian realm borders on anarchy, and Mark murders Tristan as the world crumbles around them all.

The land once again is barren and wintry. Arthur, in despair, lies close to death. In "The Passing of Arthur," the sad cycle is complete, and the world has reverted to its pre-Arthurian state. At the end, the King describes his passing in the same way he announced his accession: "The old order changeth, yielding place to new."

This somber and brooding vision of Camelot's ruin is depicted in some remarkably beautiful verse. Tennyson excels in creating poetic effect through the manipulation of sound combinations and rhythmic patterns; the following passage from "The Coming of Arthur" depicts a scene of violent and confused action and then resolves it, in the last three lines (and especially by the enjambment with "silenced"), into an evocation of tranquillity and peace:

> Then, before a voice
> As dreadful as the shout of one who sees
> To one who sins, and deems himself alone
> And all the world asleep, they swerved and brake
> Flying, and Arthur call'd to stay the brands
> That hack'd among the flyers, "Ho! they yield!"
> So like a painted battle the war stood
> Silenced, the living quiet as the dead,
> And in the heart of Arthur joy was lord.

That same idyll concludes with alliterations that effectively but deceptively suggest permanence and finality: Arthur, "in twelve great battles overcame / The heathen hordes, and made a realm and reign'd."

Although some critics have proclaimed the *Idylls* the greatest narrative poem since *Paradise Lost*, the poet has his detractors, including those who accuse him of infidelity to the fundamental spirit of the Arthurian legend. This charge of inauthenticity, almost of sacrilege, has been leveled especially at "The Last Tournament," in which Tennyson, according to some, has succeeded only in transforming the tragic love story of Tristan and Iseut into a sordid intrigue. It is true that the tone of Tennyson's idyll differs radically from that of the medieval legend, but it is also true that the design of his work requires just such a change, and the accusations of his critics are tantamount to a proscription against the use of his sources as inspiration dictates.

Other reservations are more defensible. If few poets could equal Tennyson in his creation of poetic effect, we may nonetheless be justified in wondering whether the haunting, often lovely verse that envelops the text in a misty glow is the most appropriate form for the depiction of an apocalypse, of a Camelot fated to fall. Tennyson's romanticizing and overuse of certain poetic devices are at times distracting. On the other hand, we could argue that the very beauty of the poetry powerfully and effectively underlines the bitterly ironic futility of Arthur's life.

If the *Idylls* have a serious flaw, it is for some readers Tennyson's failure to offer a positive alternative to the materialism he was rejecting. Although he looked to the past as remedy for present ills, the promise of Camelot proved to be an illusion or at best a brief respite from the darkness and savagery that preceded it and into which the world quickly sank again upon Arthur's passing. Tennyson does not replace that failed promise by another. Readers may in fact be distracted by his very attempt to use the past as little more than a mirror for the excesses and evils of his own day. Yet it is possible to read the poems simply as visions of a past and doomed glory, whether or not we wish to see them as a counterpoise to Tennyson's age or to our own, whether or not we take the poet's vision as a portent of calamity. Great poetry survives its context.

TENNYSON'S INFLUENCE   The influence of Tennyson's poetry was enormous. It served as the primary source of Arthurian inspiration for the early efforts of the Pre-Raphaelite painters (see Chapter IV, p. 221), and it was only with the Oxford Union project that the influence of Malory became dominant in their work. Yet Malory's works, though republished in 1816–17, could not have achieved their new vogue had not Tennyson popularized the Arthurian story. Modernizations of Malory's works appeared during the second half of the century, and that of James Knowles, published in 1862, was dedicated to Tennyson. Poetry written in imitation of Tennyson was plentiful but generally undistinguished; compositions like Edward Bulwer-Lytton's *King Arthur* (1848), George du Maurier's *A Legend of Camelot* (1866), Thomas Westwood's *The Quest of the Sancgreall* (1868), Ernest Rhys's "The Tale of Balin and Balan" (1897), and any number of others are persuasive proof of Tennyson's influence but otherwise are today little more than footnotes in literary history.

Arthurian poetry that developed independently of Tennyson, or even as a reaction against him, often proved more successful than imitations. A number of poets reacted against certain of his conceptions or methods, but even this negative influence confirms his importance. William Morris (1834–96), in *The Defence of Guenevere, and Other Poems* (1858), rejected Tennyson's concern for the poetic reflection of contemporary moral issues and developed a "purer" if artistically less successful Arthurianism. In "The Defence of Guenevere," the Queen offers her own defense against accusations made by Gauwaine. Her defense, however, is not a denial, or only partially so:

> this is true, the kiss
> Wherewith we kissed in meeting that spring day,
> I scarce dare talk of the remember'd bliss,
>
> When both our mouths went wandering in one way,
> And aching sorely, met among the leaves;
> Our hands being left behind strained far away.

No matter: as the poem ends, her rescuer arrives on a roan charger: "The knight who came was Launcelot at good need."

The same volume contains three other Arthurian poems. Morris's "King Arthur's Tomb," inspired in part by a watercolor done by Dante Gabriel Rossetti, is less known than "The Defence of Guenevere" but is at least its poetic equal. The others are "Sir Galahad, a Christmas Mystery" and "The Chapel in Lyoness." An additional poem by Morris, "A Good Knight in Prison," has Arthurian overtones, owing to the brief presence of Launcelot, but its subject is another knight, Sir Guy. (Morris's contribution to Arthurian visual arts is discussed on pp. 223 and 230.)

Other poets whose work asserts their independence from Tennyson, but not a lack of influence, include Matthew Arnold (1822–78) and Algernon Charles Swinburne (1837–1909). In his 1852 poem *Tristram and Iseult*, Arnold provided the first modernization of the Tristan story in English, and his handling of Arthurian legend represents a departure from early Tennysonian conceptions. His principal theme is the destructive nature of unbridled passion, which leads to instability, grief, and death. Yet he constructs his poem in such a way as to indicate, sometimes through explicit interpretation offered by his narrator, that legends from the past can be a mirror for the modern world. If that implies that such uncontrolled passion should be avoided, Arnold also suggests that the modern inability to experience passion at all, the inability to feel anything profoundly, is no less dangerous and tragic.

Although Swinburne wrote some early Arthurian poems and a late *The Tale of Balen* (1896), his Arthurian masterpiece was *Tristram of Lyonesse* (1882), in which his disdain for Tennyson's handling of the material led to a powerful and lyrically successful exploration of the lovers' passion. Swinburne emphasizes the innocence of the lovers until they "quaffed Death," drinking the potion because of simple thirst; that the potion is drunk by error does not prevent them from bearing a burden of guilt. Nor does it prevent their eventual condemnation, and if Tristram finally places himself in God's hands, this repentance or resignation provides more a sense of poetic closure than a relief from the tragic consequences of their love.

Numerous other poets of the nineteenth century were drawn to Arthurian themes, though few of their works carry the interest of those already discussed. Ralph Waldo Emerson (1803–82) devoted five engaging but slight poems to Merlin, whom he presented primarily as a poet, though one whose work produced practical results: "The rhyme of the poet / Modulates the king's affairs" (*Merlin II*, ll. 1–2). His and other Arthurian poems of the period are of value only as a witness to the extraordinary appeal of the legend once the modern world rediscovered King Arthur.

ᘉARK TWAIN Arthurian literature of the 1800s was dominated by poetry; until late in the century, we have only occasional plays, and novels are scarcer yet. Of the few notable novels, Peacock's has been mentioned, and during the last half of the century, only Mark Twain's 1889 *A Connecticut Yankee in King Arthur's Court* stands out.

Peacock, Tennyson, and others had composed Arthurian works that dramatized a distinction between the nineteenth century and an earlier age; Twain's novel represents the culmination of such an impulse. Twain (pseudonym of the American Samuel Clemens, 1835–1910) set his Arthurian story in A.D. 528, to which his main character, the nineteenth-century Yankee Hank Morgan, is transported as a result of an accident. With his superior knowledge and technology, Morgan easily puts Merlin's fraudulent magic to shame and then, by impressing the King and his people, establishes himself (under the name "the Boss") as a person of power and influence.

Finding the Arthurian period a time of brutality and ignorance, he sets about trying to civilize the barbarians, but eventually the joke turns on the modern world, as Boss's technological advances fail to mask the fact that we simply possess more efficient instruments of barbarity: along with schools and telephones, he introduces revolvers and Gatling guns. By the end of the novel, the Boss's work has been undone, Camelot lies in ruins, and Arthur is dead. Twain's novel teaches a cruel and pessimistic lesson, but the story itself is comedy as much as satire and social commentary. It is consistently amusing and sometimes hilarious, and its critique of the age of chivalry is relieved by a portrait of a good-hearted, if somewhat simple, King Arthur.

THE TWENTIETH CENTURY: DRAMA

Arthurian drama flourished during the last years of the nineteenth century and the early part of the twentieth. In 1895, J. Comyns Carr's *King Arthur*, with costumes by Edward Burne-Jones and music by Sir Arthur Sullivan, was an impressive success in London, though by no means a great play. In the same year, Henry Newbolt (1862–1938) wrote *Mordred: A Tragedy*, which was never performed. Across the Atlantic, Richard Hovey (1864–1900), in addition to using Arthurian themes in lyric poetry, was composing an ambitious cycle of Arthurian plays collectively entitled *Launcelot and Guenevere: A Poem in Dramas*. The cycle, intended to comprise nine plays in three groups of three, was not completed. The first group consists of the 1891 *The Quest of Merlin*, which foreshadows the drama of Guenevere's love affair, *The Marriage of Guenevere* (1891), and *The Birth of Galahad* (1898), in which we learn that the mother of the future Grail quester is none other than Guenevere herself. Of the other two groups of works, only the 1896 *Taliesin: A Masque*, which deals with Percival and Taliesin, was completed, although fragments of the others exist.

During the first decade of the century, Ernest Rhys (1859–1946) wrote three Arthurian dramas: *Gwenevere* (1905), *Enid* (1908), and *The Masque of the Grail* (also 1908). The plays, performed with music, are romantic and lyrical treatments of themes taken from Malory and from Welsh sources. Also taken from Malory is the 1907 *Romance of King Arthur*, by Francis Coutts (1852–1923); this work comprises a trilogy devoted to Uther, Merlin, and Launcelot.

The early decades of the century saw plays about various Arthurian characters (e.g., *Arthur: A Tragedy*, 1923, by Laurence Binyon, 1869–1943), but during the teens and 1920s the Tristan legend was particularly popular as a subject for drama, poetry, and fiction alike. "Michael Field" (the collective pseudonym of Katharine H. Bradley, 1846–1914, and Edith E. Cooper, 1862–1913) treated the legend in *The Tragedy of Pardon* (1911) and "Tristan de Leonois" in *The Accuser* (1911). Martha Kinross's 1913 *Tristram and Isoult* condensed the story of the lovers. Arthur Symons (1865–1945), in his 1917 *Tristan and Iseult*, presents the love potion, Tristan and Iseult's confrontation by Mark, and the story of the two Iseults. *The Famous Tragedy of the Queen of Cornwall* (1923), by Thomas Hardy (1840–1928), concentrates on the death of Tristram, who survives the crisis of the black-or-white sail and is later killed by Mark, after which Iseult commits suicide. In his 1927 play *Tristan and Isolt*, John Masefield (1878–1967) presents in condensed form the full story of Tristan's life and offers a sympathetic view of King Mark.

Most of the Arthurian plays written before World War II were romantic in tone, lyrically and fondly evoking a distant past. With the outbreak of the war, sentimentality yielded to realism. Dramatists tended to reinterpret the Arthurian story, implicitly or explicitly, against the background of world events, glorifying resistance and condemning violence. Notable examples, both from 1942, are the radio plays entitled *The Saviours*, by "Clemence Dane" (pseudonym of Winifred Ashton, 1888–1965), and *The Destroyers*, by Archibald MacLeish. Christopher Fry, in *Thor, with Angels* (1948), and *The Island of the Mighty* (1973), by John Arden and Margaretta D'Arcy, have continued the realistic tendency in Arthurian drama. In 1990, David Freeman wrote and directed a dramatic adaptation of Malory's work. His *Morte Darthur*, presented on two successive evenings (running a total of seven hours) and in two different places, was poorly received.

Arthurian drama has become something of a rarity. The number of plays, impressive at and after the turn of the century, has diminished steadily since 1930; the number of distinguished Arthurian plays is small indeed. Why this should be so is unclear. When modern authors treat the Arthurian legend, they turn more to poetry than to drama, and more to fiction than to either.

TĎE TWENTIETĎ CENTURY: POETRY

Among twentieth-century poets drawn to the Arthurian legend, either to retell or re-create it or to draw on its store of familiar and potent images and events, are Edna St. Vincent Millay ("Elaine," 1921; "Tristan," 1954), T.S. Eliot, John Masefield, and Charles Williams. Other familiar names include Edgar Lee Masters (two poems in *Songs and Satires*, 1916), Vachel Lindsay

("Galahad, Knight Who Perished" and "King Arthur's Men Have Come Again," 1923), Eugene Field (poems on the Grail and on Camelot), G.K. Chesterton ("The Grave of Arthur," 1930), and, more recently, Margaret Atwood (see below). Many other poets, though less well known, have made significant contributions to modern Arthurian literature; competent, though not in every case distinguished, they deserve note for historical or thematic reasons. Examples are Rhys Carpenter's *The Tragedy of Ettare: A Poem* (a 1912 poetic drama divided into acts and scenes, and told through dialogue); Frank Kendon's underrated *Tristram* (1934), which depicts the entire tragic story from Tristram's trip to Ireland on Mark's behalf through the drinking of the "innocent poison / philtre of love," to the lovers' "double death"; and Martyn Skinner's poems *Merlin; or, The Return of Arthur* (1951) and *The Return of Arthur: A Poem of the Future* (1966), which offer an unusual subject and perspective: they are among the few works actually to represent the return of Arthur in the time of greatest need, identified here as the year 2000.

Many poets have composed long individual compositions; others, in numbers great enough to demonstrate the broad appeal of the approach, have been drawn to the idea of sequences and cycles of short Arthurian poems. A partial list of cycles and sequences includes Ernest Rhys's *Lays of the Round Table* (1905), Masefield's *Midsummer Night and Other Tales in Verse* (1928), Margaret Atwood's *Avalon Revisited* (1963), John D'Arcy Badger's *The Arthuriad* (1972), John Heath-Stubbs's fine heroic poem in twelve parts, *Artorius* (1973), Ellen Cooney's cycle of seventy-seven poems entitled *The Quest for the Holy Grail* (1981), Alan Lupack's *The Dream of Camelot* (1990), and Wendy Mnookin's *Guenever Speaks* (1991).

Four poets stand out either for the excellence or for the originality of their treatments: Edwin Arlington Robinson, T.S. Eliot, Charles Williams, and David Jones.

EDWIN ARLINGTON ROBINSON   Among the finest achievements of twentieth-century Arthurian poetry, the three long narratives by the American Edwin Arlington Robinson (1869–1935) share an emphasis on fatality, and each deals with ill-fated love: Merlin and Vivian, Lancelot and Guenevere, and Tristram and Isolt. *Merlin* (1917) is a meditation on the fate of the Arthurian world but also emphasizes the necessity for Merlin to leave Vivian and return to Arthur's side. The destructive effect of illicit love is stressed in *Lancelot* (1920), where the victims of the passion include Gawaine, whose friendship with Lancelot is ruined, and Arthur, who is threatened with madness.

Tristram (1927) is the most original and, by many assessments, the best of Robinson's three Arthurian poems. Both the beginning and the end present Isolt of Brittany, as she waits for Tristram. In between, Robinson relates major events of the traditional story but with original additions and modifications. The poem deals with loss, separation, and death. Tristram is banished, but Mark suffers as much as he. Robinson explains Tristram's attachment to Isolt of Brittany as perceptively and as beautifully as any poet has ever done: "sorrow's witchcraft," he tells us, turned sorrow into pity and then into "the pale wine of love that is not love." Both Isolts know that the outcome of their drama will be death, and finally Tristram is betrayed by Andred; before his death, he expresses not displeasure with Andred but gratitude that "it was not Mark." At the end, Mark meditates on the lovers' drama and on fate, which made the two "for an end like this."

In all three poems, Robinson excels in the exploration of character and in the effective use of recurrent images (which, in *Tristram*, include the sun, the open sea, a passing ship) to depict and crystallize his protagonists' reactions. The result is a powerful exploration of the kind of love that binds and at the same time destroys.

T.S. ELIOT While Robinson was examining and reinterpreting dramas involving Arthurian couples, T.S. Eliot (1888–1965) was using Arthurian themes and motifs in a radically different way. Dense and complex, *The Waste Land* (1922) is one of the pivotal poems of the twentieth century. It uses Arthurian imagery (as well as references to the Bible and the Upanishads, Augustine, Dante, the Tiresias legend, and other sources) to indict the modern world and the human condition. A central theme of the poem is the decay of cities, among them Jerusalem, Athens, Alexandria, Vienna, and London.

Eliot took a number of his images from Jessie Weston's *From Ritual to Romance* (1920), including the notion of the Fisher King, whose wound rendered his land sterile. The poem introduces images of desolation (endless arid plains, cracked earth, "no water but only rock / Rock and no water and the sandy road," "dry sterile thunder without rain") that culminate in the evocation of the Perilous Chapel ("the empty chapel, only the wind's home"), whose ruin traditionally provided a test of the Grail knight by bringing him to the brink of despair. Here, however, there is no Grail knight and no quest: it is the ruin of the chapel, its emptiness and desolation, that Eliot finds significant.

The poem offers some hope in the Fisher King's question, "Shall I at least set my lands in order?" and in the concluding line: "Shantih shantih shantih," which Eliot himself glossed as "The Peace which passeth understanding." Yet remedy for the wasteland's ills is at best a remote hope, and the enduring images of the poem are those related to decay and sterility. Eliot insisted that the work was largely a reaction to his own personal difficulties, and not, as readers and critics have consistently taken it, a work of social and philosophical criticism. *The Waste Land* is in any event one of the most original and, with the exception of Tennyson's, most influential uses of Arthurian material by a modern poet. It is not, of course, an Arthurian poem in the same way that Tennyson's and others' are, but it makes prominent use of Arthurian themes as a metaphor (in Eliot's term, an "objective correlative") to support and illustrate insights of major import.

CHARLES WILLIAMS   The work of the Englishman Charles Williams (1886–1945) commands respect as one of the most distinguished poetic interpretations of the Arthurian legend in the twentieth century. (His Grail novel, *War in Heaven*, is mentioned on pp. 183–84.) Williams composed two collections of poems on Arthurian subjects, but in a sense both *Taliessin Through Logres* (1938) and *The Region of the Summer Stars* (1944) belong to the same large cycle, which was probably still not in a finished state at his death. The poems are complex and difficult and for that reason less known than they deserve to be; it is best to read them with the help of a commentary, such as C.S. Lewis's *Williams and the Arthuriad* (published with Williams's own *The Figure of Arthur* in a volume entitled *Arthurian Torso*) or the concise but helpful discussion by Taylor and Brewer (pp. 245–61). Lewis indicates the order in which the poems are to be read, which is not the order in which they stand in the text.

The poems constitute not a narrative but a series of separate texts depicting moments in the Arthurian drama. The subject of the cycle as a whole is the rise and fall of Arthur's realm. Williams is interested primarily in the mythic aspects of the legend, and the principal vehicle of that myth is the Grail. The poems are concerned more with the Grail Quest than with other traditional subjects, such as the establishment of Arthur's power and the love of Lancelot and Guinevere.

The main voice is that of Taliessin the bard, but other voices heard in the poem include those of Palomides and Bors. Taliessin not only describes the events taking place around him but attempts to shape them. He aspires to transplant in Logres the kind of grace, joy, and controlled passion he found in Byzantium. His aspirations are not fully realized. As early as Arthur's coronation, Merlin (and we) begin to foresee the downfall of the King's realm. By his incest with Morgause (which represents self-love in Williams's system), Arthur himself sows the seed of that downfall. Yet the tragedy is ameliorated by a sense that the Grail fellowship is not destroyed but simply transmuted into another dimension. The concluding poem of the cycle, "Taliessin at Lancelot's Mass," relates that "all the dead lords of the Table were drawn from their graves to the Mass"; they are present in spirit, and the poem and cycle conclude with an expression of ineffable joy.

All is at last resolved, and Williams's vision is realized. That vision concerns the working out of a divine plan involving Galahad and, in order for him to be born, the necessary substitution of Elayne for Guinevere in Lancelot's bed. The idea of substitution is central to Williams's cycle, a major "thesis" of which is the notion of mutual responsibility, the obligation we have to share burdens and unite in mutual support and effort. The development and expression of that idea require the unfolding of an extraordinary poetic and symbolic universe and also a symbolic "anatomy," in which the human body and the relation of its parts to one another are associated both with Williams's geography and especially with his ideal of harmony and peace. The cycle also explores a number of related themes, such as the function of poetry and the place of the poet in his society.

Williams's Arthuriad demands patience, attention, and the reader's collaboration. Unassisted readings of the cycle are not easy and not always satisfactory. But the persevering reader who brings to the text the necessary effort and attention will be richly rewarded by an understanding of, and participation in, a powerful poetic and mystic vision and an extraordinarily complex and subtle literary creation. *Taliessin Through Logres* and *The Region of the Summer Stars* stand as one of the three or four finest achievements in modern poetry using Arthurian material as theme. In the view of some readers, Williams's cycle may be second to none.

DAVID JONES Like Williams, the Welsh poet and artist David Jones (1895–1974) is concerned primarily with myth, and his rich and fascinating texts present a daunting difficulty that may keep some readers from a poet well worth knowing. Some find Jones's work self-conscious and intentionally obscure (despite extensive annotations); for others, his poetry offers a highly original illustration of *anamnesis*, which, he tells us in a note in *The Anathémata*, involves recalling and reanimating the past. Myth elucidates the present, but the experiences of the present can lead us back to myth. Jones believed that we respond even to myths that we do not understand rationally, such response being presumably implied in the very definition of myth.

Arthur and the Grail are central to Jones's mythology. Yet the elements of Arthurian story that preoccupied him were only indirectly, and often negatively, related to romance, love, or the glory of the quest; he was more often concerned with the martial aspects of Malory's work (one of his main sources, along with the *Mabinogi*) and with the powerful wasteland symbol. *In Parenthesis* (1937) treats Jones's experiences in the trenches of World War I, combining the analogies of the battlefields to the wasteland and of the comradeship of soldiers to the fellowship of knights. The parallels Jones establishes are less ennobling than haunting, involving a sense of horror, misery, and apocalyptic finality.

Arthurian imagery also supports the mythic structure of Jones's 1952 *The Anathémata*, subtitled "fragments of an attempted writing." The Arthurian influence is suggested by the titles of some of the sections ("The Lady of the Pool," "Mabinog's Liturgy," and "Sherthursdaye and Venus Day") and by recurring references to material from the *Mabinogi*, to local legends, to Arthurian characters and motifs, and to the King himself, the "quondam king, *rexquefuturus*." "Sherthursdaye" refers to a vision in which Christ appeared to Galahad (in Malory), and this evocation of Christ and the Grail knight together, as well as a later symbolic equivalence of Peredur and Christ, brings the two central myths of British culture into convergence. The result is to provide, in Christian belief, hope for a restoration of the wasteland.

Jones, Eliot, and Williams reinvigorated the Arthurian legend by developing its mythic value and appeal. None of the three retold or even reinterpreted the legend *per se*; instead, they used it, freely fashioned to their own ends, as myth, as symbol, as image.

THE TWENTIETH CENTURY: FICTION

Raymond Thompson notes (p. 169) that over two hundred Arthurian novels and short stories had been published in English between 1884 and the writing of his 1985 book. Nor has the flood of titles abated since then; remarkably, almost eighty Arthurian novels in English appeared between 1990 and the end of 1995. The discussions that follow will give a notion of the kinds of fictional treatments the Arthurian legend has enjoyed (or endured) and a slightly fuller treatment of some major texts.

Modern Arthurian fiction is notable for its diversity and originality. This desire for originality, while in some cases refreshing and rejuvenating the Arthurian legend, can be perilous, for the "orthodox" Arthurian story, especially as crystallized in Malory and retellings of his works, exerts a heavy weight of authority. Authors who remain faithful to that story simply compose one more retelling; authors who depart too far from it risk rejection by those who bring to their reading traditional expectations about King Arthur and Arthurian themes and characters. The challenge presented by these opposing forces—the need for originality and the traditional authority of the legend—explains why modern Arthurian material includes some fine reinterpretations of that legend but also, at the hands of less capable authors, a large number of works that are self-conscious, quirky, and mediocre or worse.

Authors often acknowledge the problems of dealing with the legendary material and discuss the relation of legend to history or pseudo-history. Certain writers seek as much historical accuracy as possible, research their sources thoroughly, and indulge as much in reconstruction as in invention; they are both scholars and writers of fiction. Others, less interested in such a reconstruction, emphasize the purely imaginative aspects of their creation. Almost all of them express a concern for "truth."

The statements of four authors will illustrate some of the approaches to Arthurian fiction. In an author's note to *Sword at Sunset*, Rosemary Sutcliff explains that she has retained certain features of the traditional story "because they have the atmosphere of truth"; she notes also that she has consolidated various characters into three (Bedwyr, Cei, and Gwalchmai) because those three are the earliest of Arthur's named companions. In contrast, Victor Canning, in the foreword to *The Crimson Chalice*, freely admits his departures from the accepted legend, "largely because I do not think it bears much relation to truth. What the truth was, nobody knows."

The middle ground is held by writers like Parke Godwin, who was seeking what he described as the "interface" between legend and truth. The truth of the legend is an inevitable preoccupation of authors of Arthurian fiction, but their understanding of that problem differs: for some, it involves the relation of legend to historical accuracy; for others, the legend contains and provides its own truth and can comfortably accommodate innovation. Thomas Berger is, however, almost alone in urging a systematic disregard for "such meager historical information as is known" about Arthur, insisting that "the legend should never be fouled by material reality" (quoted in Lupack, p. 84).

Many of the twentieth-century authors drawn to the Arthurian legend have, with varying degrees of success, made fundamental changes in the "orthodox" story. Of course, some "facts" of the Arthurian story have varied from text to text since the very beginning—does Arthur commit incest with Morgawse or Anna? is Mordred his nephew or his illegitimate son?—and many of the major writers, from Chrétien to Spenser to Tennyson, also introduced radical innovations or reinterpretations into the legend. Yet some writers go considerably farther, as witness Richard Hovey's drama *The Birth of Galahad*, which makes Guenevere the mother of Galahad. In Canning's *The Crimson Chalice*, Arthur's parents are not Uther and Igraine (or Ygerne) but Baradoc and Tia. Vera Chapman creates a daughter, Ursulet, for Arthur *(King Arthur's Daughter)*. Sutcliff's *Sword at Sunset* tells us that Bedwyr, not Lancelot, is the lover of Guenhumara (Guinevere). Her substitution of Bedwyr for Lancelot reflects a scholarly concern for accuracy and a respect for the integrity of the Arthurian legend: Lancelot was, after all, "a later French importation." Mary Stewart makes much the same point in *The Last Enchantment*, pointing out in her notes that "Bedwyr, whose name is linked with Arthur's long before 'Lancelot' ever appears, takes the Lancelot role."

Such changes, again, have a decided cost. For readers, no less than for writers, the notion of the legend's "integrity" connotes two different things. To some, it means an understanding and accommodation of the latest historical and archaeological evidence, and it involves a concern for what the Arthurian "fact" may have been, what the Arthurian age was like, and the way the legend grew by progressive accretions. For others, a particular version of the legend is likely to be so firmly established that any substantial departure, even if made in the name of truth and accuracy, will produce a shock.

Readers who otherwise admire and appreciate the works of Sutcliff and Stewart may not easily accept Bedwyr as the Queen's lover but will perhaps conclude instead that the author has simply given Bedwyr the role that properly belongs to Lancelot. Many readers "know" that Guinevere's lover is Lancelot, and the danger is that they will see the substitution of Bedwyr for him, not as restoring the "real" Arthurian story, but as tampering with it. Making such a change convincingly requires all the skill of the most effective writers.

RETELLINGS   First, however, we must consider a group of authors who are generally less concerned with narrative innovation than with fidelity to their source. They may even resist change, except insofar as their art usually requires condensation and their individual purpose and intended audience may lead them to excise some kinds of material.

Retellings of Arthurian stories, most often based on the works of Malory, are among the most common of Arthurian fictional texts. They are modernized versions, often abridged or simplified. Most are intended for the general reading public or the young reader, and the alterations their authors make in their sources most often consist of omissions: many retellings are bowdlerized to alter or remove awkward scenes that might embarrass the reader or compromise the portrayal of a noble and illustrious King Arthur. The most common alterations are in passages that deal with Arthur's conception out of wedlock, his incest, or even the details of Lancelot's and Guinevere's adulterous love.

The best-known retellings of Arthurian material are by the Americans Sidney Lanier—*A Boy's King Arthur* (1880)—and Howard Pyle (1853–1911)—*The Story of King Arthur and His Knights* (1903), *The Story of the Champions of the Round Table* (1905), *The Story of Sir Launcelot and His Companions* (1907), and *The Story of the Grail and the Passing of Arthur* (1910). Among other retellings are adaptations for children by Andrew Lang, Roger Lancelyn Green, Antonia Fraser, and Dorothy Senior.

John Steinbeck's *The Acts of King Arthur and His Noble Knights*, written in 1958–59 but published only in 1976, is an unusual case: it started out as a retelling of Malory and became something entirely different, with changes of detail and emphasis. In the course of the work, Steinbeck increasingly underlines the futility and disillusionment of much chivalric activity, as many knightly efforts are doomed to failure, while many of the successes are hollow and unsatisfying. The book also has a premature ending, as Steinbeck, perhaps because his work was taking an unanticipated turn, simply stopped writing after "The Noble Tale of Sir Lancelot of the Lake," when Lancelot and Guinevere kiss.

Retellings naturally vary greatly in terms of quality and effectiveness, and the works of Rosemary Sutcliff (1920–92) are among the best of them. In addition to two important Arthurian novels for adults, this English writer produced four for young readers: *Tristan and Iseult* (1971), *The Light Beyond the Forest: Quest for the Holy Grail* (1979), *The Sword and the Circle* (1981), and *The Road to Camlann* (1981). Sutcliff simplifies but never falsifies, and she writes for young readers, but never down to them. If retellings require less inventiveness than other novels, they surely require no less skill, and in skilled hands they can become important works of art.

Although "retellings" is an obvious and useful category of Arthurian fiction, no category is entirely clearcut. Many of the novels to be discussed below are retellings to some extent, and, as noted, Steinbeck's novel began as a retelling and soon ceased to be one. For certain other works, we may hesitate between historical fiction and fantasy or between fantasy and science fiction. Any categories we may establish will be problematic. Raymond Thompson's division into retellings, realistic fiction, historical fiction, science fiction and science fantasy, and fantasy is reasonable but not unambiguous. Division into subject matter (e.g., the entire Arthurian story, the Grail Quest, Tristan and

Iseut, Arthurian prehistory) is feasible within limits, as would be a division based on focus (works emphasizing Arthur himself, Merlin, Guinevere, or other characters) or on time frames (Dark Ages, High Middle Ages, present day, and future). The discussion to follow combines a number of these categories, making most prominent use of the last two.

THE DARK AGES While some authors bring the Arthurian legend into the present or occasionally, in the case of science fiction, into the future, most Arthurian fiction places its subjects either in the Dark Ages (the Arthurian period of the fifth and sixth centuries) or in the High Middle Ages. In the popular mind, the latter probably predominates, in part because of the influence of T.H. White and in part because filmmakers, especially in the United States, have generally preferred to locate Arthur in a period of opulent castles and colorful tourneys. Nevertheless, several of the best Arthurian novels, especially since 1960, have been set in post-Roman Britain. Those novels include the works of Gillian Bradshaw, Rosemary Sutcliff, Parke Godwin, Marion Zimmer Bradley, Mary Stewart, and Thomas Berger, and some less successful but nonetheless interesting novels, such as those of Victor Canning, Sharan Newman, Kathleen Herbert, and Stephen R. Lawhead. The diversity of these works is impressive, and they include novels that concentrate on Arthur (sometimes told in the first person), on the women around him, or on Merlin.

The American-born Gillian Bradshaw is one of a number of authors of Arthurian trilogies. Hers begins with the 1980 *Hawk of May*, which traces the efforts of Gwalchmai (Gawain) to win the trust of Arthur, and continues through *Kingdom of Summer* (1981) and *In Winter's Shadow* (1982), which follow the story through the ruin of Arthur's world. Gwalchmai represents the forces of Light, in a struggle with the forces of Darkness incarnated in Morgawse.

Stephen R. Lawhead composed a trilogy of fantasy novels set in post-Roman Britain and drawing heavily on early Welsh tradition: *Taliesin* (1987; Taliesin is here the father of Merlin), *Merlin* (1988), and *Arthur* (1989). To that trilogy he then added *Pendragon* (1994), in which Merlin retells some of Arthur's youthful adventures.

The Crimson Chalice is the title given both to British novelist Victor Canning's trilogy and to the first novel in it. In addition to that 1976 novel, the trilogy includes *The Circle of the Gods* (1977) and *The Immortal Wound* (1978). Canning makes Arturo something of a renegade or outlaw, who imposes his authority through force. This Arturo is not the son of

Uther and Ygerne, but of Baradoc and Tia; his second wife, Gwennifer, has a number of love affairs, while he has no children. Retaining a number of traditional characters (e.g., Merlin, Lancelot) and motifs of the legend, Canning has nonetheless transformed it to the point that readers will inevitably be impressed by the originality of his handling of the story—but may scarcely recognize it as the Arthurian legend.

Kathleen Herbert's trilogy consists of *Queen of the Lightning* (1983), *Ghost in the Sunlight* (1986), and *Bride of the Spear* (1988). These novels retell stories from the *Mabinogi*, from Chrétien de Troyes, and from other sources, resetting them in the Dark Ages.

fIRST-pERSON ARThURIAN NOVELS   First-person Arthurian narratives are not numerous, but the approach is appealing, because it permits the "humanizing" of characters who are historically remote. It is a risky point of view because of the difficulty of presenting the complexity and subjectivity of an individual character without at the same time diluting the richness and the epic quality of the legend. Several authors have permitted Arthur to tell his own story; they have succeeded to varying degrees—least in W. Barnard Faraday's 1930 *Pendragon*, much better in the cases of Rosemary Sutcliff and Parke Godwin. Both Merlin in Mary Stewart's novels and Guinevere in Persia Woolley's trilogy (the latter to be discussed below) have also had an opportunity to speak in their own voice.

Rosemary Sutcliff wrote some of the best modern Arthurian fiction. Her work is structurally taut and stylistically pleasing, and her narratives depart often from Malory and other sources in an effort to join historical accuracy with fictional art. In addition to her four retellings, she published two notable Arthurian novels. *The Lantern Bearers* (1959) is the pre-Arthurian story of the struggle between Vortigern and Ambrosius. The better-known work, *Sword at Sunset* (1963), allows Artos (Arthur) to tell his own story and thereby humanizes him to a greater degree than in most novels. In addition to the facts of his life and career, such as his seduction by his half-sister Ygerna or his political and military activities, the novel gives us an extended portrait of the man himself, and it is not always flattering: Artos is courageous and compassionate but far from perfect. The reader learns, for example, that Artos married Guenhumara (Guinevere) reluctantly and generally neglected her thereafter, albeit for "business reasons": the demands of leadership. The emphasis is almost as much on Guenhumara as on Artos, and on the difficulty of her life and the loneliness that finally led to her affair with Bedwyr.

In 1990, Sutcliff published *The Shining Company*. Although not directly Arthurian, the novel is based on the *Gododdin* and recounts the efforts of an army led by Mynyddog against the Angles. Unequal to Arthur, Mynyddog fails, but he and his warriors die a noble death in their cause.

Parke Godwin is the American author of an Arthurian trilogy consisting of *Firelord* (1980), *Beloved Exile* (1984), and *The Last Rainbow* (1985). The last of these is a pre-Arthurian novel (involving Ambrosius Aurelianus rather than Arthur), and *Beloved Exile* is post-Arthurian, dealing with Guinevere's life after the death of Arthur. Like Sutcliff's *Sword at Sunset* and Faraday's *Pendragon*, Godwin's *Firelord* has Arthur tell us his own story. Set in the Dark Ages, the novel presents Arthur lying at Avalon after the battle of Camlann ("where nobody won but the crows"), looking back on his life and dictating his memories and reflections to one Brother Coel. This method permits him to offer personal views and insights into events and his own character. One result is a persuasive recreation of the political and military complexities of his period. Even more important is our insight into Arthur himself: complex, pragmatic, fallible, compassionate, capable of humor even (or especially) at his own expense. As his narration informs and entertains us, it also provides a summing up and a catharsis for Arthur; and having begun by railing at his fate, he ends by commenting: "And so this place the monks call Avalon, the scratch of Coel's stylus, the smell of apple blossoms, the hum of bees beyond the casement, the quiet end to the clangorous song . . . this isn't at all a bad way to go" (p. 386).

Mary Stewart's Merlin trilogy has been among the most popular and successful of Arthurian novels. (The trilogy was later transformed into a tetralogy by the addition of *The Wicked Day* [1984], which presents Mordred as an intelligent, lucid, and finally sympathetic character caught up in the events leading to the fall of Camelot.) The Merlin novels are *The Crystal Cave* (1970), *The Hollow Hills* (1973), and *The Last Enchantment* (1979). The first volume recounts the early history of Merlin, who is here the illegitimate son of Ambrosius Aurelianus and thus the nephew of Uther Pendragon, and the events leading up to the conception of Arthur. *The Hollow Hills* presents Merlin's role in Arthur's education and his winning of the throne; as *The Crystal Cave* concluded with the conception of Arthur, this novel ends with the conception of Mordred, the son of Arthur and Morgause. The third volume depicts Merlin's poisoning by Morgause, his love for Nimue, and his disappearance. Stewart uses the first-person approach with unusual effectiveness; despite the emphasis on magic, Merlin is a surprisingly "human" character, appealing and plausible.

ARTђURIAN WOCOEN Women have provided the focus of works by Marion Zimmer Bradley, Sharan Newman, and Persia Woolley (as well as Vera Chapman, to be discussed on p. 180). Bradley's influential *The Mists of Avalon* (American, 1982) traces all the major events of the traditional Arthurian story through the eyes of Igraine, Viviane, Morgaine, Gwenhwyfar, Morgause, and others. She offers interesting and sometimes original characterizations of the men; Uther, for example, has a reputation as a womanizer but is sensitive and caring. Yet it is the female characters whom the reader comes to know. Morgaine and Igraine are particularly vivid; the latter is a woman of strong and independent mind, disinclined to accept easily the marriage to Gorlois, in which she had no say. The author introduces some innovations into the usual story: Merlin announces to her very early that she will give birth to the Great King, and she and Uther fall in love long before Merlin's stratagem permits the king to enter her palace and sleep with her. In addition to the focus on Arthurian women, Bradley emphasizes the unsettling effect of a society poised between Druidic and Christian ideologies.

The Guinevere trilogy published by American author Sharan Newman includes *Guinevere* (1981), *The Chessboard Queen* (1984), and *Guinevere Evermore* (1985). The first of these tells Guinevere's story up through her marriage night; the second concentrates on her love for Lancelot; and the last pursues the narrative beyond Arthur's final departure with the Lady of the Lake, to the deaths of Lancelot and Guinevere, telling us that the Queen was then buried at Glastonbury—but with Lancelot rather than with Arthur. If the trilogy, especially in its earlier portions, suffers from excessive sentimentality, it is nonetheless effective in depicting the development of an innocent young girl who is forced to confront the realities of a new social order and the demands of her public and royal existence.

Persia Woolley's Arthurian trilogy—*Child of the Northern Spring* (1987), *Queen of the Summer Stars* (1990), and *Guinevere: The Legend in Autumn* (1991)—concerns "Guinevere, Celtic Princess of Rheged and only child of King Leodegrance." The trilogy tells of her betrothal to Arthur and of the political and religious turmoil in which Arthur's world and hers are embroiled; it then follows many events of their life and society, concluding with the destruction of the Round Table.

TђOCOAS BERGER Unlike any of the preceding novels is American writer Thomas Berger's *Arthur Rex* (1978). One of the most entertaining modern treatments of the Arthurian legend, yet at the same time one of the most mature and solid, *Arthur Rex* is written in a mock archaic style, with abundant and often brilliant use of irony and wit. It offers memorable and vivid, if not always flattering, characterizations of Arthurian knights and ladies. One of the finest of such characterizations is that of Uther, a "great hairy brute" (p. 12) who "did rarely bathe within a twelvemonth, and disdained all scents as being appropriate only to vile sodomites" (p. 80); "one learned to keep upwind of Uther Pendragon." Arthur himself is a naive, simple youth who, the moment he learns that he is to be king, demonstrates a gift for pomposity by immediately adopting the royal "we": King Ryons tells him, "Thou art not only a boy, thou art a pompous ass of a boy!" (p. 42). Lancelot and Guinevere are lovers who appear to have little liking for each other, and she in particular is haughty, mocking, and often self-righteous.

By taking a fresh and often ironic look at the conventions of Arthurian romance, Berger shows many of them to be illogical or silly. In some cases, such as the Grail Quest, those conventions are worse than illogical: Arthur, on first hearing of the quest, points out that if only the pure and sinless can see the Sangreal, and if only Christ was free of sin, then it is surely blasphemous for knights to seek it.

Following Malory in general and supplementing him with material drawn from other sources, such as *Sir Gawain and the Green Knight*, Berger offers accounts of most of the familiar events of Arthurian legend, from Arthur's conception to the return of Excalibur to the Lady of the Lake and the King's departure for Avalon. The novel traces the defeat of Arthur's idealistic vision by human failings or, as the King notes before dying from the wound inflicted by Mordred, "the triumph of perfect evil over imperfect virtue" (p. 483). Berger concludes by remarking (p. 499) that King Arthur "was never historical, but everything he did was true."

ANTI-ROMANTIC NOVELS The majority of the novelists discussed thus far attempt, to a greater or lesser extent, to offer realistic depictions of life in post-Roman Britain. Yet that realism, which often includes a reflection of the less pleasant aspects of existence during the period, is generally tempered by the conception of Arthur and many of those around him as decent and even idealistic people who are trying to bring stability and order to their world. Not all writers share that vision. Some novels, such as *The Bear of Britain* (1944) by Edward Frankland (English, 1884–1958) and *The Green Man* (1966) by Henry Treece (English, 1912–66), depict Arthur as virtually the only honorable figure in a world characterized by brutality and ignorance. In such a context, the King may retain his dignity, but his hopes and ambitions stand no chance of realization.

Peter Vansittart's *Lancelot: A Novel* (1978) goes farther yet in presenting a negative view of the Arthurian world. Here, even Arthur's own character and stature are diminished. His only skills are military. He trusts no one, and he uses a force of secret police to perpetuate his regime. Vansittart's character entirely lacks Arthur's traditional compassion and vision, and he is not an appealing figure.

It is not difficult to understand why authors might wish to offer a realistic palliative to the more idealized popular notion of the Arthurian world as a misty golden age, and novels like those of Frankland and Treece have at least the potential to depict Arthur as a tragic figure struggling against hopeless odds. Yet Vansittart's novel is the cynical depiction of an Arthurian age incapable of even one "brief, shining hour." It is an original portrait of the King and by no means without interest as a minority view; the difficulty is simply that many readers will not be inclined to accept an Arthur without principle or vision.

THE MIDDLE AGES   A number of novels prior to 1960 were set in the High Middle Ages; that number diminished sharply thereafter, as the post-Roman era attracted the attention of Arthurian novelists increasingly concerned with historical accuracy. Many of the earlier "medieval" novels tended to concentrate more on other Arthurian characters than on the King himself. Examples include Warwick Deeping's *Uther and Igraine* (1903), Clemence Housman's *The Life of Sir Aglovale de Galis* (1905), John Erskine's *Galahad* (1926) and *Tristan and Isolde: Restoring Palamede* (1932), and Hannah Closs's *Tristan* (1940).

Among later novels set in the Middle Ages are works by Vera Chapman, Jim Hunter, Richard Monaco, Phyllis Ann Karr, Peter Dickinson, and T.H. White. Chapman is the British author of a "Three Damosels" trilogy consisting of *The Green Knight* (1975), *The King's Damosel* (1976), and *King Arthur's Daughter* (1976). The first is a reworking of *Sir Gawain and the Green Knight*, predicated on Chapman's presumption that "the story told in the romance seems on the face of it unfinished." The second novel continues the story of Lynett, and the third presents Arthur's daughter and her attempts to succeed her father on the throne.

Hunter's *Perceval and the Presence of God* (American, 1978) has Perceval narrate the story of his aspirations, his failure to achieve the Grail, and his profound doubts about himself and his destiny. American novelist Monaco published a Parsival trilogy—*Parsival* (1977), *The Grail War* (1979), and *The Final Quest* (1980)—set in a somewhat indeterminate medieval context (with castles, drawbridges, and plate armor but with occasional anachronistic references). The trilogy draws material from Wolfram von Eschenbach's master-piece and portrays Parsival's coming of age and his Grail adventures and their aftermath. The books depict an age of brutality and bloodshed, rape, and cannibalism. The world of this novel is a wasteland without a hero to restore it.

In her 1982 "Arthurian murder mystery" *Idylls of the Queen*, the American novelist Phyllis Ann Karr focuses on a single major episode from Malory: the poisoning of a knight by an apple given him by Guinevere. The novel presents Kay as a clever and incisive thinker who succeeds in clearing the Queen, but the fact that others receive the credit implicitly criticizes some traditional values and themes of Arthurian romance, suggesting that intelligence is of less worth than prowess or magic.

Peter Dickinson concentrates on the character of Merlin, both in *The Weathermonger* (British, 1968), for younger readers, and in *Merlin Dreams* (1988), in which the enchanter sleeps beneath a stone, awakening occasionally to recall an event from his former life.

T.H. WHITE   The Englishman White (1905–64) is the author of the most famous and influential twentieth-century version of the Arthurian story. His main source was Malory, although he gave free rein to his imagination and created themes and episodes that have now (partly through the adaptations of his work for the Lerner and Loewe musical *Camelot* and for Walt Disney's *The Sword in the Stone*) become a standard part of the story for many Arthurian enthusiasts.

White wrote five Arthurian volumes. Four of them were eventually published together in 1958 as *The Once and Future King*: *The Sword in the Stone* (1938), *The Queen of Air and Darkness* (1939; originally entitled *The Witch in the Wood*), *The Ill-Made Knight* (1940), and *The Candle in the Wind* (1958). *The Book of Merlyn*, written in 1940–41, was not published until 1977. White's works are set in the High Middle Ages but with some striking anachronisms involving in particular the presence of Saxons and Normans.

Although the subject of the first volume is ostensibly a serious one—the education of the young Arthur—the tone is light and the method pure fantasy, as Merlyn transforms Arthur into various animals (fish, ant, goose, and badger) in order that the future king might learn lessons about war, work, and freedom. The volume ends soon after Arthur draws the sword from the anvil. The tone quickly changes as we enter the second volume and watch the King confront problems of war and politics. There is still comedy, in the episodes dealing with Pellinore and his unending chase of the Questing Beast, for example, but the comedy is juxtaposed with scenes of cruelty, especially to animals, and with the increasing complexities of royal life. Here, too, Merlyn, who lives backward and has therefore already experienced the future, begins to hint darkly at catastrophes awaiting Arthur and—in the person of a certain Austrian tyrant and his storm troopers—us. This section ends with the seduction of Arthur by Morgause and the conception of Mordred.

The Ill-Made Knight is Lancelot, who considers himself to have monkeylike features. White traces his increasing attraction to, and eventual adultery with, Guenever, although he first sleeps with the Grail princess Elaine. The adultery is discovered in *The Candle in the Wind*, which also reveals Mordred's parentage and recounts a number of feuds, especially that of Gawaine and Lancelot. The final scene, at Salisbury, presents an aged and tired Arthur trying to figure out where his grand design went wrong, why his effort to establish the rule of law instead of force has failed. His spirits are finally buoyed by his realization that the dream and legend are alive, even though the institutions have crumbled.

The Book of Merlyn, originally intended to be the concluding section of the whole, is bitter, misanthropic, and unsubtly didactic. It, too, takes place at Salisbury, and Merlyn again transforms the King into animals, to give additional lessons about war. Instead of suggesting, as in his first volume, that we can learn something from the beasts, White here concludes simply that humans are fundamentally inferior to them. It is proposed, in fact, that the designation *Homo sapiens* be altered to *Homo ferox*, "since man is the most ferocious of the animals" (although Merlyn's owl Archimedes suggests *stultus*, "stupid," rather than *ferox*).

This volume is clearly marked by White's hatred of war, as well as of people, and some readers also find in it further biographical reflections, such as guilt at his own pacifism in time of war. Except for a melancholy epilogue concerning the deaths of Arthur, Guenever, and Lancelot, and a brief disquisition on the legend of Arthur's return, the final volume contributes little of narrative value to White's Arthuriad, but it is on the other hand a logical conclusion to an antiwar social commentary that comes more and more to use the legend of Arthur as a convenient structure and pretext. Most readers, however, choose to ignore the fifth book and read the others as an often charming, sometimes brooding, and ultimately tragic account of the Once and Future King.

FiCTiON SET iN ThE PRESENT ANÓ FUTURE   Many authors have updated the Arthurian legend to modern times and occasionally even to the future. Such updating can take several forms. First, there are incidental uses of Arthurian objects, most often the Grail, in works that are not fundamentally Arthurian in character, or only marginally so. Second, there can be an actual extension of parts of the legend, in which Arthurian characters return or where a Grail quest occurs in the modern world. Most productively, there are instances in which the legend provides a parallel to, a reflection of, or a structure for the twentieth-century events of a narrative.

An additional group, constituting "backdating" rather than updating, consists of novels in which a character out of the modern world returns to the Arthurian period. An obvious if not entirely successful example of this kind of work, of which the prototype is Mark Twain's *Connecticut Yankee*, is *The Man Who Went Back* (1940), by English novelist Warwick Deeping. Here, the victim of an automobile accident finds himself in the Arthurian world and becomes a warrior. The Scottish author Naomi Mitchison, in her 1955 *To the Chapel Perilous*, has modern journalists sent into the Arthurian world, where they try to distinguish fact from the fictions and legends that have grown up around the King. The world of advertising and the Arthurian world are juxtaposed in J.B. Priestley's *The Thirty-first of June* (British, 1962). Unlike any of these, although related to them, is James Branch Cabell's *Jurgen* (American, 1919); in this novel, celebrated in its time and the subject of an obscenity trial, an aging man meets Guinevere, Helen, and other famous women from the past.

Objects and motifs borrowed from the Arthurian legend provide the focus of a number of modern novels. Most often, the object is the Grail, or something thought to be the Grail, and the novels dealing with it are most often thrillers. Examples of such works include Michael Delving's *Die Like a Man* (1970), recounting the consequences of a bookdealer's purchasing a wooden object reputed to be the Grail, and British author Jonathan Gash's *The Grail Tree* (1979), in which the motive for murder is the desire to possess, not the object thought by some to be the Grail, but rather the silver casket that contains it. Certain of these novels are successful enough in their own terms; Gash's is probably the best of them. Yet they are clearly not Arthurian literature, and they are of passing interest here only because they dramatize the extent to which Arthurian or Grail lore permeates our culture and provides a ready and appealing stock of motifs.

In contrast to these incidental uses of the Grail, its survival is central to the novels of the Welsh writer Arthur Machen. His *The Great Return* (1915) involves the modern reappearance of the Grail, accompanied by strange and marvelous events, in a Welsh village. Machen's *The Secret Glory* (1922), in which the hero becomes the Keeper of the Grail and is eventually martyred, offers criticism of modern society for its inability to comprehend or accommodate sensitivity and morality. The English author Charles Williams, whose Arthurian poetry was discussed above, also wrote *War in Heaven* (1930), a novel that portrays the struggle between good and evil for possession of the Grail in present-day England.

Not the Grail, but Arthur's sword, is the object of a quest in Sanders Anne Laubenthal's *Excalibur* (American, 1973). A Welsh archaeologist, during an excavation in Mobile, Alabama, finds Excalibur, which had been brought to the New World by his twelfth-century ancestor Madoc (himself a descendant of Arthur). There ensues a struggle between the modern characters and the surviving Morgan and Morgause.

In early Arthurian romance, chivalry had been something of a sport as well as an activity with moral and social utility. Both the notion of sport and that of quest, which demands of the quester the highest discipline and inspires the noblest endeavors, make it inevitable that some novelists should choose the athletic arena as the setting of works that use Arthurian themes. Two who do so are American authors Babs H. Deal and Bernard Malamud. The more obviously "Arthurian" of the two (though the less successful novel) is Deal's *The Grail: A Novel* (1963). The subject is American football, and the quest for the Grail (i.e., a perfect season) is led by college coach Arthur Hill and by his quarterback Lance Hebert. The quest, however, is doomed because Lance falls in love with Arthur's wife, whose name, predictably, is Jennie.

Both better and better-known than Deal's novel, Bernard Malamud's 1952 *The Natural* recasts elements of the Perceval story in the story of a gifted baseball player. The hero, Roy, is a naive rural man (= Perceval) who has a wondrous bat (sword) and comes to the aid of a team (the New York Knights, managed, appropriately, by Pop Fisher) whose play prior to his arrival is reminiscent of the impotence of the wasteland inhabitants. The parallels with Arthurian romance are subtle and inexact, although effective, because they serve the novelist's purpose instead of shaping it. It is in characterization that Malamud makes best use of the Perceval story. Roy is an accurate and effective reflection of Perceval: his only desire early in his career is for the glory that comes with success. When he reveals his ambition to be known as "the best there ever was in the game" and is asked "is that all?" he can only reply, with a perplexity that Perceval would have understood and shared: "What more is there?"

The survival of Arthurian characters provides the subject matter of a number of works (including Laubenthal's *Excalibur*, discussed above). Both Merlin's magic and his traditional longevity or immortality make his return a tempting theme, and he is at the center of several fictional works, including C.S. Lewis's *That Hideous Strength* (1945), Susan Cooper's *The Dark Is Rising* series, and Roger Zelazny's story "The Last Defender of Camelot."

Lewis (1898–1963) depicts the struggle of a small group of people against technocrats known as the National Institute of Coordinated Experiments (NICE), who are intent on dehumanizing and dominating the world. The struggle, led by a man (with a wounded foot) who is revealed as the latest in a continuous line of Pendragons or Fisher Kings, eventually succeeds because Merlin is awakened from his sleep and joins forces with those who oppose NICE.

Susan Cooper's series—*Over Sea, Under Stone* (British-American, 1965), *The Dark Is Rising* (1973), *Greenwitch* (1974), *The Grey King* (1975), and *Silver on the Tree* (1977)—depicts the struggle of the forces of Good or Light, upheld by a line of people known as the "Old Ones," against those of Evil (the Dark). The struggle involves the quest for talismans of power; among those talismans is the Grail, which is found by three children. They are offered the protection and aid of Merlin, in the form of Professor Merriman Lyon, and Bran (the son of Arthur and Guinevere) also plays the role of protector.

In Zelazny's short story (American, 1979), Merlin, Morgan, and Lancelot all survive to the present. The "last defender of Camelot" is Lancelot, who forms an alliance with Morgan to oppose a well-intentioned but wrong-headed Merlin and to defeat his plan to use force and magic to impose good on the modern world.

Arthur, too, was supposed to return from Avalon, where he is sleeping. Surprisingly, novelists have treated his return less frequently than Merlin's and that of other Arthurian characters. His survival and measures taken to permit his return, but not the return itself, are depicted in Andre Norton's *Merlin's Mirror* (American, 1975), a science-fiction novel that attributes Merlin's and Nimue's powers to extraterrestrial sources. At the end of the novel, Merlin seals Arthur in a chamber where he will remain until future space travelers are able to heal him, at which time "on the day appointed he shall stand before the beacon and welcome those of his fathering."

Among the novels in which Arthur's predicted return does occur are three by American authors: Peter David's 1987 *Knight Life*, Donald Barthelme's *The King* (1990), and Dennis Lee Anderson's 1995 *Arthur, King*. David's entertaining but slight novel recounts Arthur's reappearance after centuries of sleep and his successful campaign, as Arthur Penn (shortened from Pendragon), to be elected mayor of New York City—his first step toward the presidency. Morgan and Merlin have also survived; the former opposes Arthur at every turn, while the magician, an eight-year-old boy, is his adviser and defender.

Barthelme (1931–89) depicts an Arthur who does not really return: he never left. His life, as Kay notes, has run on "a few centuries beyond the normal span," and he finds himself in England during the blitz. The novel—wildly humorous and parodic, yet serious at the same time—juxtaposes Arthurian chivalry to modern warfare, emphasizing the brutality of the latter but in some cases the vanity or silliness of the former. The Holy Grail is the ultimate bomb, which Arthur finally decides not to use.

Anderson's novel takes place during the same period as Barthelme's, but in this case the London blitz is the idea of Mordred, magically transposed into the modern world; he also promotes plans to bomb Coventry and assassinate Churchill. Arthur's return permits him to oppose Mordred, prevent the assassination, and eventually, with the woman (Jenny) he has come to love, go back to his own age.

Since a feeling of its "pastness" is a traditional and natural aspect of Arthurian legend, updating that legend to the present offers certain challenges—of style, perspective, and tone—that novelists have met with varying degrees of success. Updating the Arthurian story to the *future* is far more problematic still. The attempts to do so include Andre Norton's *Merlin's Mirror*, mentioned above; her *Witch World*, a 1963 "science fantasy" in which sitting in the Perilous Seat permits the hero access to the alternative world of the title; a 1952 short story entitled "Lance," by Vladimir Nabokov (1899–1977), who brings past and future into conjunction by developing the parallel of Lancelot crossing the Sword Bridge with Lancelot Boke's experiences as a pioneer of space travel; and novels by Fred Saberhagen: *Dominion* (American, 1982), a horror story in which Merlin is transported to Chicago, and *Merlin's Bones* (1995), involving time travel from Dark-Age Britain to the twenty-first century and back.

The finest example of Arthurian science fiction may well be C.J. Cherryh's *Port Eternity* (American, 1982). It deals with Dela Kirn, a woman fascinated by Tennyson's *Idylls of the King*. She is the owner of a spacecraft called the *Maid of Astolat*, operated by her servants, who are "made people" (i.e., cloned beings) to whom she gives such Arthurian names as Gawain, Percivale, Lancelot, Modred, and Elaine. When the ship is stranded in an alien dimension, the made people begin to act out their Arthurian personas and to cast others, and especially Modred, in the roles of their Arthurian counterparts.

ThE ARThURIAN LEGEND AS LITERARY STRUCTURE   *Port Eternity* is one of a number of works in which the characters' concern for matters Arthurian leads to a duplication or a reliving of certain patterns of the legend. A further example of this phenomenon is *A Glastonbury Romance* (1932), by English-born John Cowper Powys; in this work, the characters who participate in a Glastonbury festival find themselves recreating the Arthur-Guinevere-Lancelot triangle.

The Tristan story is a recurrent motif in the 1939 novel *Finnegans Wake*, by James Joyce (1882–1941). Joyce wove aspects of the legend through portions of his work, emphasizing especially the parallel of the situation of both Arthur and Mark to that of his protagonist H.C. Earwicker: all are cuckolded by younger men. The most prominent "Arthurian" passage is a long dream, some sixteen pages in length, concerning Earwicker's cuckoldry. Specifically, he dreams of the honeymoon of Tristan and Isolde and of what they will be doing while he (Mark, Earwicker) remains powerless to do anything.

Other novelists who use the Tristan story as structure include Mary Ellen Chase (American, 1887–1973) in *Dawn in Lyonesse* (1938), Sir Arthur Quiller-Couch (1863–1944) in *Castle Dor* (1961; completed by Daphne du Maurier), Maria Kuncewicz in her *Tristan* (1974; first published in Polish in 1967 as *Tristan 1946*), A.S. Byatt in *Possession* (English, 1990), John Updike in *Brazil* (American, 1994), and Rosamond Smith (pseudonym of Joyce Carol Oates) in *You Can't Catch Me* (1995).

In Chase's novel, the reading of the Tristan story leads the narrator to an understanding of the similar situation in which she finds herself. *Castle Dor*, set in Cornwall, involves a modern duplication of most of the events of the legend, and *Tristan* traces the characters' fascination with the Tristan story and the extensive parallels that develop between their lives and that story. Byatt's novel offers parallels to Arthurian characters, especially to Elaine the Maid of Astolat, to whom the heroine compares herself, but also to Tristan and Iseut, whose passion parallels that of the lovers Christabel and Randolph. Updike uses the Tristan story, loosely paralleled by his characters, to explore racial and sexual problems in the modern world; his characters, a poor black boy and a rich white girl, flee together and experience love and pain before he is tragically killed. The novel by Smith offers a distant and imprecise reflection of events from the Tristan story; Smith's character Tristram Heade endeavors to free a young woman from an unhappy marriage.

Special cases in which a novel set in the present has events reshaped to reflect Arthurian plots include Walker Percy's *Lancelot* (American, 1978), David Lodge's *Small World* (English, 1984), Anthony Powell's *The Fisher King* (English, 1986), *The Lyre of Orpheus* (1988) by the Canadian Robertson Davies (1913–95), Paul Griffiths's *The Lay of Sir Tristram* (English, 1991), and Irish-born Iris Murdoch's *The Green Knight* (1993). Obviously, this approach has proved attractive to major novelists.

Percy's protagonist, Lancelot Lamar, is a liberal southern lawyer, once robust and promising, now alcoholic, bitter, and impotent. His wife furthers her ambitions as an actress by sleeping with her director; calling himself "The Knight of the Unholy Grail," Lancelot embarks on a quest to prove his wife's infidelity by filming it. He commits multiple murders and is incarcerated in a mental hospital, from which he tells his story.

Percy's Hollywood is a wasteland as desolate as T.S. Eliot's, a wasteland that Lancelot bitterly condemns but to which he also contributes. This ingenious if self-conscious novel is at the same time a symbolic story about illusion and reality, a critique of modern society in general and of certain aspects of southern society in particular, and a psychological study of the self-deception and cynical disillusionment of a character who concludes that "there is no answer. There is no question. There is no unholy grail just as there was no Holy Grail" (p. 275).

Small World, David Lodge's brilliant comic tale, is, however, an academic novel, and some of the humor will be most appealing to professors familiar with the literary conferences and lecture trips that obsess Lodge's characters and provide a structure for their lives. Although the characters frequently discuss Arthurian matters, including Jessie Weston's theory of Grail origins, the reader only gradually becomes aware that *Small World* is itself a "Grail novel." One of the central characters is the patriarch of the literary establishment, the elderly and impotent Arthur Kingfisher. His infirmity is cured during a New York meeting of the Modern Language Association, when a character named Persse asks the proper question. A certain amount of the humor derives from inside jokes concerning the academic literary establishment, but the novel nonetheless offers entertaining reading and makes fascinating and unusually effective use of its Arthurian framework.

Anthony Powell's Fisher King figure, Saul Henchman, is impotent and in constant pain, the result of a war wound suffered long before. The plot, which unfolds in the constricted setting of a cruise ship, concerns the dissolution of a relationship between Henchman and a beautiful woman who had forsaken a career to be his companion. The primary appeal of the novel is its characterization and style, but the Arthurian element contributes an additional dimension that enriches the reader's appreciation of Powell's ship of fools.

The novels by Davies and Griffiths both deal, in different ways, with the composition of operas. Davies's *The Lyre of Orpheus* informs us that the money from a deceased man's estate is to be used to complete an Arthurian opera, *Arthur of Britain, or The Magnanimous Cuckold* (ostensibly by E.T.A.

Hoffmann); in the process, the deceased's nephew (named Arthur) finds himself reenacting the Arthurian triangle with his wife and their best friend.

Griffiths, in *The Lay of Sir Tristram*, intertwines Wagner's composition of *Tristan und Isolde* both with his own composition of the novel we are reading and also with the events of the Tristan story itself. This novel is not so much a retelling of the love story as it is the record of the novelist's and composer's efforts to choose from among the numerous possibilities offered by the traditional accounts and to piece together, fitfully and hesitantly, a creation suitable for publication or presentation.

Finally, Iris Murdoch places her *The Green Knight* in contemporary London, where the lives of a group of people are transformed by an encounter with a stranger; the resulting narrative carries echoes of a number of Arthurian texts, especially *Sir Gawain and the Green Knight*.

CONCLUSION

The preceding pages omit much. Numerous authors and titles—many dozens if not hundreds of them—merit inclusion but are victims of the need to avoid a simple inventory approach to Arthurian literature. A good many of the regrettable omissions are texts that simply do not fall into any of the categories above. For example, Francis Coutts's *The Romance of King Arthur* (1907), already mentioned, is a generic hybrid, a composite work consisting of two plays framed by two poems. Similarly, Jane Yolen, in *Merlin's Booke* (American, 1986), offers thirteen "stories and poems about the arch-mage"; her work is "not a novel, but a series of stories" connected only by the presence of Merlin, who is a different character in each.

English author Joy Chant's 1983 *The High Kings* is not so much a hybrid as it is an original form. Chant's aim is to retell stories from British history "in the way they might have been told in the last days of Britain." Each chapter is preceded by a brief description of some aspect of Celtic life (e.g., Marriage Customs and Status of Women, Religion, The Druids). Her chapters themselves are interrelated narratives leading up to and including the life and accomplishments of Arthur. Chant allows her storytellers to elaborate on traditional accounts by adding such imaginative details as the circumstances of the death of Gorlas, Igerna's husband: in an attempt to conceal Arthur's birth, the women attending Igerna burned the afterbirth; in the ashes was an egg, and from that egg hatched a worm that grew into a dragon and killed Gorlas.

Another work that defies easy categorization is Nicholas Seare's *Rude Tales and Glorious* (1983), a series of stories about Arthurian characters and events told by an emaciated old man who happens to be Launcelot, reduced to beggary but kept alive for centuries by an enchantment. Although subtitled "A Retelling of the Arthurian Tales," it is far from a retelling in the manner of Lanier or even Steinbeck. Seare's narratives, emphasizing the humorous and most often bawdy aspects of Arthuriana, include details concerning the Sword in the Stone (a trick involving a hollow rock with Merlin concealed inside), Persival's impressive sexual endowment, and a Grail quest in which all the knights are embarrassed to ask what a grail is because each assumes that he is the only one who does not already know.

Omissions from the discussions of French and German literature are generally of the same kinds: hybrid forms, minor texts, and tangentially Arthurian works. Modern literatures other than English, French, and German have thus far been excluded entirely, since modern Arthurian texts are less common in most other languages, except during the sixteenth century, which gave us a number of original Arthurian works and many translations and redactions of medieval material in Italian, Spanish, Russian, Irish, and Dutch.

Nonetheless, even the countries in which modern authors have not frequently reinterpreted the Arthurian legend have preserved his name and aspects of the legend. Sometimes this was accomplished through the oral transmission of folktales, more often through the publication and dissemination of chapbooks and broadsides (individual printed sheets or small brochures, devoted to almost any subject or form, but to the ballad in particular). Broadsides flourished well into the eighteenth century, and even into the twentieth in Spain, Portugal, and Brazil. Among the traditionally popular subjects were chivalric ballads and tales; in fact, the only three extant Spanish ballads on Arthurian subjects are known only through broadsides. Typical of chapbook composition is the work of Antonio da Silva (Portuguese, eighteenth century), whose surviving chapbooks combine material borrowed from a variety of sources, from the Prose *Tristan* to Cervantes. Considering that broadsides and chapbooks were inexpensive and, by intent, disposable items, we can reasonably assume that a remarkable amount of material, Arthurian and other, has been lost forever.

Even though texts in English, French, and German account for well over ninety percent of modern Arthurian literature, the contributions of other countries and other literatures should be recognized, and a small sampling of titles will demonstrate the geographical and linguistic diversity of those contributions.

The seventeenth and eighteenth centuries saw three reworkings of the medieval Hebrew *Artushof,* itself perhaps based on the German *Wigalois.* These modern Hebrew-letter redactions, published in Amsterdam, Prague, and Frankfurt, vary somewhat in both form and content and provide important evidence concerning the adaptation of texts to different milieux and audiences.

Tablante de Ricamonte sampo nang magasauang si Jofre at ni Bruniesen ("Tablante de Ricamonte Together with the Couple Jofre and Bruniesen") is a nineteenth-century Tagalog translation, somewhat condensed, of the Spanish *Tablante de Ricamonte.*

Among twentieth-century treatments of Arthur are works in Polish, Breton, Italian, Dutch, and Japanese. The first is Maria Kuncewiczowa's *Tristan 1946,* the English version of which, published under the name Kuncewicz, is discussed above. Xavier de Langlais wrote, in both Breton and French, a *Romant ar roue Arzhur* ("Romance of King Arthur," 1956–75) and *Tristan hag Izold* ("Tristan and Isolde"), a 1958 Breton account of the Tristan legend. In Italian, we have Umberto Eco's 1988 *Il pendolo di Foucault* (*Foucault's Pendulum* in English), a difficult and complex novel in which the central characters pursue the secrets contained within Arthurian images and themes. Among Dutch novels are *Het zwevende schaakbord* ("The Floating Chessboard," a 1923 adaptation of the Middle Dutch *Walewein*) by Louis Couperus (1863–1923) and Jaap ter Haar's *Koning Arthur* ("King Arthur," 1967), an original and effective retelling of the Arthurian story. From Japan, we have the 1905 *Kairo-kō, A Dirge,* by Natsume Sōseki (1867–1916); it combines Arthurian themes adapted principally from Malory and Tennyson with oriental tones and textures to produce a fascinating treatment of Elaine's love for Lancelot and her tragic death.

The list of modern Arthurian texts could be prolonged by the addition of hundreds of titles, drawn from numerous countries and languages, and the diversity of their treatments of Arthur would be almost as impressive as the very number of works cited; yet their inclusion here would serve only to confirm what the preceding pages have amply demonstrated: the appeal of Arthur is enduring and virtually universal, and its primary expression is literary. The result, as D.S. Brewer has pointed out (Brewer, p. 1), is "perhaps the largest single body of imaginative literature that the world has known."

NOTES

For English and American literature, the following notes give at least one reference for each author to whom we devote more than two or three sentences. Owing to the large number of such names, they are listed in alphabetical order, rather than the order in which they appear within the chapter.

(References are to the appropriate section of the Bibliography.)
French Literature

    Bowden, pp. 60–66.

    Brinkley, pp. 213–15.

    Dakyns, passim.

    Lacy et al., art. "French Arthurian Literature" (by Norris J. Lacy); "French Chivalric Romances, Eighteenth and Nineteenth Centuries" and "French Epic, Nineteenth Century" (by Patricia A. Ward); "Second Empire, French Arthurian Material During" and "Symbolist Arthurian Material" (by Janine R. Dakyns).

    Guillaume Apollinaire

        Forsyth, pp. 26–36.

    Jean Cocteau

        Lacy et al., art. "Cocteau, Jean" (by Norris J. Lacy).

    Julien Gracq

        Lacy et al., art. "Gracq, Julien" (by Robert Baudry).

    Robert Pinget

        Henkels, pp. 36–53.

    Edgar Quinet

        Crossley, esp. pp. 71–74, 95–99.

German Literature

    Lacy et al., art. "German Arthurian Literature (Modern)" (by Richard W. Kempel); "*Tristan*, Modern German Versions of Gottfried's" (by M.S. Batts).

    Müller (1), pp. 435–59.

    Weiss, passim.

    Hans Sachs

        Sobel, pp. 223–55.

English and American Literature

    General

        Lacy et al., art. "English and American Arthurian Material (Modern)" (by Raymond H. Thompson).

Thomas Berger
    Taylor and Brewer, pp. 298–300.
    Thompson, pp. 155–61.
Richard Blackmore
    Merriman, pp. 64–67.
Marion Zimmer Bradley
    Thompson, pp. 132–38, 176–78.
Gillian Bradshaw
    Thompson, pp. 105–13.
James Branch Cabell
    Thompson, pp. 150–52, 159–61.
Victor Canning
    Thompson, pp. 44–46, 55–56.
Joy Chant
    Thompson, pp. 54–55.
C.J. Cherryh
    Thompson, pp. 79–83.
Susan Cooper
    Thompson, pp. 100–04, 109–13.
Robertson Davies
    Lacy, et al., art. "Davies, Robertson" (by Ruth E. Hamilton).
Babs H. Deal
    Thompson, pp. 24–26.
John Dryden
    Brinkley, pp. 142–46, 174–76.
Umberto Eco
    Lacy, et al., art. "Eco, Umberto" (by Norris J. Lacy).
T.S. Eliot
    Taylor and Brewer, pp. 235–39.
John Erskine
    Thompson, pp. 58–59.
Henry Fielding
    Merriman, pp. 77–78.
Parke Godwin
    Godwin, pp. 24–25.
    Thompson, pp. 128–32, 135–39.
Paul Griffiths
    Lacy, et al., art. "Griffiths, Paul" (by Norris J. Lacy).

Richard Hovey
> Linneman, pp. 78–93.

David Jones
> Taylor and Brewer, pp. 235–39.

Phyllis Ann Karr
> Thompson, pp. 123–24, 136–38.

Sanders Anne Laubenthal
> Thompson, pp. 96–98, 175–76.

C.S. Lewis
> Starr, pp. 181–87.
> Thompson, pp. 95–98.

David Lodge
> Lacy et al., art. "Lodge, David" (by Constance B. Hieatt and Raymond H. Thompson).

Bernard Malamud
> Lacy et al., art. "Malamud, Bernard" (by Norris J. Lacy).

Richard Monaco
> Thompson, pp. 145–48, 159–61.

William Morris
> Taylor and Brewer, pp. 135–49.

Andre Norton
> Thompson, pp. 77–78, 112–13, 117–18.

Thomas Love Peacock
> Taylor and Brewer, pp. 54–60.

Walker Percy
> Müller (2), pp. 375–84.
> Thompson, pp. 28–31.

Anthony Powell
> Lacy, et al., art. "Powell, Anthony" (by Daniel Nastali).

John Cowper Powys
> Thompson, pp. 27–31, 56–57.

Edwin Arlington Robinson
> Starr, pp. 21–39, 72–83.
> Taylor and Brewer, pp. 179–93.

Edmund Spenser
> Brinkley, pp. 151–64.
> Lacy et al., art. "Spenser, Edmund" (by L.R. Galyon).

Lewis, pp. 355–93.

Merriman, pp. 39–44.

John Steinbeck

Taylor and Brewer, pp. 296–98.

Thompson, pp. 11–13, 142–44, 159–61, 171–72.

Mary Stewart

Thompson, pp. 50–52, 55–57.

Rosemary Sutcliff

Thompson, pp. 14–17, 46–49, 55–57, 173–78.

Alfred Tennyson

Lacy et al., art. "Tennyson, Alfred Lord" (by David Staines).

Rosenberg, passim.

Staines, passim.

Taylor and Brewer, pp. 23–33, 67–75.

Mark Twain

Taylor and Brewer, pp. 169–74.

Thompson, pp. 139–42.

Peter Vansittart

Thompson, pp. 42–43, 173–74.

T.H. White

Starr, pp. 109–10, 115–31.

Taylor and Brewer, pp. 290–95.

Thompson, pp. 126–28, 135–38.

Charles Williams

Göller, passim.

Lacy et al., art. "Williams, Charles" (by K.H. Göller).

Starr, pp. 166–78; Taylor and Brewer, pp. 245–61.

Conclusion

Broadsides

Lacy et al., art. "Broadsides" and "Broadsides (Spanish)" (by Julia Kurtz).

Natsume Sōseki

Lacy et al., art. "Sōseki, Natsume" (by Toshiyuki Takamura).

John William Waterhouse, The Lady of Shalott *(1888). By permission of Tate Gallery, London.*

ChAPTER IV

ARThUR in the ARTS

The visual and the performing arts have brought vitality and variety to the Arthurian tradition. Throughout the legend's evolution, imagery appeared concurrently with, or even before, the written record. Ephemeral expressions—pageants, music and dance, fragile stage designs—leave less substantial evidence, but enduring habits of interpretation suggest that as long as the legend has been told, it has been sung, drawn, and dramatized. The range of media is vast, reflecting changing taste, audience, and modes of expression. But the persistence of Arthurian subjects in the arts, from the earliest crude carving to the latest Hollywood spectacle, confirms that the appeal of the legend extends beyond the literary texts. By giving the Arthurian saga form, voice, color, and motion, each new interpretation positions it in space as well as time and makes the myth material.

One factor unites this body of works spanning nearly a thousand years and involving a remarkable diversity of media. The most consistent and enduring force in the Arthurian tradition is its literary evolution. Rarely do Arthurian subjects appear in the arts in a time when Arthurian texts are neglected. As is typical in western culture, the prominence of the "book" and the story it conveys provides an audience with the familiarity needed to understand a nonverbal expression. But in times of the legend's greatest popularity—the Middle Ages, the Victorian era, the present—the story becomes so familiar and so much a part of the cultural consciousness that the arts can transcend mere illustration of text. Artistic interpretations both depend upon and contribute to the ongoing tradition.

When the arts exhibit interpretative independence, their expressive power derives as much from the characteristics of the chosen medium as from the information taken from the literary text; the artistic modes reflect contemporary aesthetic conventions as well as specific subject matter. No stylistic motif in the arts can be labeled "Arthurian." To express Arthurian subjects, the arts draw upon more than textual association. The meaning of the subject is shaped by the form and function of the object on which or through which it is conveyed. A fourteenth-century French tapestry and a twentieth-century film may both depict Arthur as king. But the static form of the tapestry demands that an image be iconic, while the dynamic nature of the film associates that image with narrativity. The tapestry, created for a great room in a manor, had a limited audience by design; the film, playing in theaters and on home video, reaches as wide an audience as possible. Add to these basic differences the contrasts in size, scale, color, quality, and even the contemporary symbols of masculine authority or beauty—the power of the arts to interpret the legend thus reveals its true range. While the content may be based in literature, the form and function are bound in the medium, requiring the student of the legend's manifestations in the arts to ask not only what is depicted, but when, how, and why.

TᏏE ᎷᎥᎠᎠᏞᎬ ᎪᏀᎬᏚ

We will never know the full extent of the Arthurian legend's influence on medieval art. The surviving material legacy is far from complete. Objects have been damaged or destroyed: textiles can be ruined through wear or careless storage; gold and silver threads in tapestries were pulled for reuse; precious metal sculptures were melted in times of financial need; restoration and redecoration have reduced the authenticity of murals and stained glass. Sometimes, when tastes changed, objects were simply discarded. Manuscripts were disbound, and the decorative pages were sold as individual paintings. Only a random sample remains, saved by coincidence and circumstance.

Written records suggest that the surviving objects are a small fraction of the original production. Wealthy households kept inventories, with descriptions of the works including subject and material. Commission orders and work receipts provide further evidence. Literary descriptions of decorated chambers and fine possessions were based on actual prototypes. Most telling is the diversity of the surviving objects. Every medium—rich or modest, for public display or private use—contributed to the interpretation of the legend.

Arthurian imagery evolved in response to the growth of the literature. For four centuries (ca. 1100–1500), the legend enjoyed generous patronage and pan-European popularity, reflecting the courtly and political ideals of an aristocratic audience. But subtle differences distinguished the artistic tradition from the literary. Arthurian visual imagery reached a small, restricted audience. Except for occasional church decoration, works featuring the subject were commissioned by the wealthy laity for their personal enjoyment. Stories written for an aristocratic patron could be overheard and then retold to a broader segment of the public, but objects made for his or her use were rarely seen by the general populace.

Subject selection depended upon easy recognition, hence the many battles, feasts, and rituals portrayed, all popular motifs in secular medieval art. Stories that could be summarized in a single scene—Lancelot crossing the sword bridge, the appearance of the Grail at the Round Table, Mark spying on Tristan and Iseut—occurred repeatedly. Character identity posed other problems. There was no singular, consistent code in the arts equivalent to naming in literature. Physical appearance varied. Arthur was sometimes bearded, sometimes clean-shaven; he was portrayed with and without his crown. Heraldry helps in some depictions, but artists often took broad liberties. In a fourteenth-century French manuscript (Oxford, Bodleian Library Douce 215, f. 14), Lancelot's shield and surcoat, and even his horse's trappings, bear the lover's sign of the heart.

The oral tradition also influenced the arts. On the north-portal archivolt of Modena Cathedral (1100–40) in Italy, Arthurian iconography appears independently of any known literary source. Perhaps the story came with the arrival of Breton minstrels passing through en route to the Holy Land. The crude Perros Relief, carved on a nave pier in St. Efflam's Church in Brittany (ca. 1100), has a stronger connection to local saints' lore than the legend. But oral dissemination must remain a matter of speculation. In contrast, certain literary subjects were rapidly absorbed, then taken over, by the arts. Around 1310, Jacques de Longuyon's *Les Voeux du paon* ("The Vows of the Peacock") listed *les neuf preux*, the Nine Worthies, great men of "history" to be admired and emulated: three pagans (Hector, Caesar, Alexander), three Jews (Joshua, David, Judas Maccabeus), and three Christians (Arthur, Charlemagne, Godefroy de Bouillon). The subject was ideal for illustration. Whether presenting all nine heroes or just the three Christians, depictions can be found in every medium, including engravings, woodcuts, manuscript miniatures (Paris, Bibliothèque Nationale f. fr. 12559), windows (Lüneburg), frescoes and murals (Sion, Switzerland; Dronninglund, Jutland; La Manta, Piedmont), embroideries (Wienhausen), woodcuts (Metz), and statuary (Innsbruck). The inventories of Jean, duc de Berry (1340–1416), indicate that he owned a *nef de table* (a boat-shaped container, used for table service) and a number of enamels featuring the subject. He also had them carved on a fireplace in his palace at Bourges. Best known to the modern world is the

*Tapestry, King Arthur (Five Worthies with attendant figures; detail),
Netherlandish, fifteenth century. The Metropolitan Museum of Art,
The Cloisters Collection, Munsey Fund, 1932 (32.130.3a).*

portrayal of Arthur as the Christian worthy on a tapestry in the Cloisters Collection of the Metropolitan Museum of Art (New York). But it is rare that an iconography is so strong and consistent in so many media. In medieval art, form and function were as integral as content.

MANUSCRIPTS

This ideal balance of form and content can be seen in the illuminated manuscripts of the Middle Ages. As the dominant secular legend of the era, the Arthurian story was widely illustrated, and the number of the books that survive is impressive. For richness and variety, the medium is unparalleled. Decorations range from modest borders and tinted drawings to elaborate figurative initials and, in the most lavish examples, full-page miniature paintings. France—particularly Paris—and Flanders were the leading centers for manuscript production, with lesser but active centers in England, Germany, Holland, Italy, and Spain. The favored texts for illumination included the Vulgate Cycle (of which some one hundred eighty manuscripts exist), especially the *Queste del saint Graal*, but even chronicles and tournament books included Arthurian images along with historical references.

Surviving manuscripts suggest that the first Arthurian texts were not illustrated. The earliest known Arthurian miniature, from around 1180, is found in a Flemish manuscript of Geoffrey's *Historia Regum Britanniae* (Douai 880): an embellished initial illustrating Arthur's combat with the giant of Mont-Saint-Michel. More elaborate texts begin to appear in France in the thirteenth century. The oldest of those (Rennes 225) dates from the 1220s and features part of the Vulgate Cycle, enriched with fifty-seven historiated initials (that is, large initials within which a scene is painted). Some images are drawn from the text, as in a scene of Uther's men departing for battle (1 fol. 137), while others (1 fol. 1) derive from standard manuscript motifs, such as the "inspirational" image in which Christ delivers the book to the author. The manuscript was made in a Parisian workshop known to service the French court, producing fine psalters and books of hours. It is easy to imagine that this work, like a private devotional book, was intended for an elite patron to enjoy at leisure and in solitude.

During the late thirteenth century, books produced in Flanders and Picardy surpassed the Parisian standard. The most commonly illuminated text was the Vulgate Cycle. The Prose *Lancelot* in New York's Pierpont Morgan Library (MS 805; ca. 1315) is an excellent example from northern France, with one hundred thirty-six historiated initials and thirty-nine miniatures. Designed in horizontal bands (called registers) of two scenes each,

"*Aramont Becomes Uther's Vassal, They Leave for Battle with Claudas,*" from *Vulgate* Lancelot *Proper. Rennes MS 255, fol. 137. Bibliothèque Municipale, Rennes.*

Historiated E: quintain and jousting practice. MS 805, fol. 34v. The Pierpont Morgan Library, New York.

the miniatures provide a running narrative sequence of Lancelot's adventures. The lavish gold-leaf background and vivid jewel-toned palette are typical of deluxe manuscripts of the era. A three-volume Flemish *Lancelot* (London, British Library Add. 10292–94), featuring six hundred fifty miniatures, stands as the most elaborate example of the time.

The preference in England was for historical imagery that associated Arthur with other monarchs and celebrated his sovereignty. In the *Flores Historicum* (Manchester, Chetham's Library 6712; ca. 1230–50), Matthew Paris depicted Arthur's coronation, while the *Chronicle of Pierre de Langtoft* (London, British Library Royal 20 A II; ca. 1207) portrayed him as the lord of twelve kingdoms. In Germany, subjects also reveal a parallel national bias, with manuscripts of Gottfried's *Tristan* and Wolfram's *Parzival* popular in the thirteenth century through the fifteenth. In Holland, Arthurian iconography appeared in historical texts, such as the *Spiegel Historiael* (The Hague xx; ca. 1325). In Spain, Norman scribes collaborated with Spanish illuminators, producing a hybrid style seen in the Prose *Tristan* (Paris, Bibliothèque Nationale fr. 750; ca. 1278).

The glittering Gothic elegance associated with Arthur's court is the legacy of late-medieval illumination. Sophisticated miniatures reflected the stylish life of the late fourteenth- and fifteenth-century aristocrats, patrons of the enduring romance tradition. The fashions and habits of privilege portrayed in the illuminations seem as important as the narrative. In a Burgundian manuscript of *Guiron le Courtois* (Oxford, Bodleian Library Douce 383; ca. 1475–1500), seventeen surviving folios portray Arthur as a perfect fifteenth-century prince. He dresses in velvets and furs, and he receives his courtiers—graceful fashion plates with feather-trimmed hats and greyhounds—in a grand hall with a glazed-tile floor, a carved and vaulted ceiling, and walls hung with golden tapestries. The lavish borders surrounding each miniature feature acanthus leaves, arms, additional miniatures in rondels, and symbols of earthly luxury: roses, peacocks, and strawberries. Also notable for its vision of contemporary elegance is the *Chroniques de Hainaut* of 1468, a Flemish manuscript illuminated by Guillaume Vrelant (Brussels, Bibliothèque Royale 9243). Seven of the sixty illuminations have Arthurian subjects, including the wedding of Arthur and Guinevere. The chapel, with its star-painted ceiling and the guests in their robes of shining velvet, suggests the Gothic material world at its most elite. In other illuminations, genre details—an old woman warming her feet at a fire, armorers working at a forge—reveal the more complex structure of society and the interest in close observation typical of Flemish art. The world portrayed in these miniatures marks the intersection of cultural ideals and the legendary tradition, and, like the legend, the perfected image in art offers an enhanced reflection of reality.

SCULPTURE AND DECORATIVE ARTS

Sculpture provided a public medium for Arthurian imagery. Figurative carving was regarded throughout the Middle Ages as an integral part of architectural design, and the vast sculptural programs on important buildings, such as churches, are commonly thought to have served as "bibles for the poor," explaining the scripture in pictures for those who could not read the words. These sacred ensembles sometimes included secular subjects, perhaps as moral exemplars, and it is in this context that Arthurian imagery mixed with ecclesiastical art. But the diverse placement of these images—above doors, on columns, on furniture—defies an explanatory pattern, suggesting instead that the images appeared because the story was popular. Through sculpture, the legend became even more accessible.

The Perros Relief, about 1100, is the earliest known example of Arthurian sculpture, predating the literary tradition. The Modena archivolt also seems to reflect the influence of oral transmission. The decoration on this northern Italian cathedral, begun in 1099, is regarded as one of the masterworks of Romanesque sculpture. The north portal, the Porta della Pescheria, was probably carved late in the program (between 1120 and 1140) by an anonymous sculptor now known as the "Arthur Master." On the semicircular band of stone above the doorway, knights converge upon a fortress where a woman is held captive. Inscriptions identify the figures: the woman is Winlogee (perhaps Guinevere), her captor Mardoc. On the right, Carrado rides out to defend the castle, attacked by Galvaginus or Galvagin (Gawain) and Che (Kay). Three other knights, led by Artus de Bretania, charge from the left. The narrative most likely depicts a tale of abduction, in which the giant Carrado imprisons Arthur's queen in his stronghold, the Dolorous Tower, and the early date, before the written romances, is evidence of the legend's range.

By the end of the twelfth century, subject selection clearly reflected the romance tradition. A capital in the Cathedral of Saint-Pierre in Caen, France, depicts Lancelot crossing the sword bridge (from Chrétien's romance) and Gawain's night in the Perilous Bed. While the two knights may be regarded as models of devotion and courage, the subjects also held popular and secular appeal. In England, carvings on misericords (hinged seats in choirstalls) featured a variety of imagery drawn from romance, fable, popu-

Abduction of Winlogee (Guinevere?), Cathedral of Modena, Italy, archivolt of Porta della Pescheria. Photograph by Norris J. Lacy.

lar legend, and daily life. The profane subjects—the meeting of Tristan and Iseut (Chester and Lincoln Cathedrals, fourteenth century), Yvain charging a castle (Chester and Lincoln; New College, Oxford, late fifteenth century)—seem to defy their location near the altar, but until the seats were lifted, these carvings on the brackets below remained hidden.

Lay sculpture also appeared, though less often. The most common location was the municipal center or town hall. While romance subjects can be found—for example, the tryst of Tristan and Iseut on a corbel of the town hall of Bruges, Belgium (ca. 1385; removed to a museum in the nineteenth century)—the subject of the Nine Worthies predominated. In German countries, freestanding sculptures of notable citizens began to appear in the thirteenth century (Naumberg Cathedral), and the Nine Worthies offered an allegorical form of this tradition. The figures were generally arranged in a ring or a row, like guardians of local civic authority. The painted stone statue of Arthur in the Hall of the Hanseatic League, the Rathaus, Cologne (ca. 1325), is an early example, while the magnificent ensemble of bronze heroes in the Hofkirche, Innsbruck, Austria (after 1519), celebrates the power of both church and state by gracing the tomb of Maximilian, the Holy Roman Emperor.

In contrast to the wide audience for public sculpture, the decorative arts were reserved for the elite. As the romance tradition developed, the same aristocratic patrons who commissioned illuminated manuscripts purchased fine objects featuring Arthurian motifs for their tables and their private chambers. These included combs, mirrors, goblets, jewelry boxes, mirror cases, and tablet cases, made of rare and luxurious materials like ivory or gold. Many of these objects have been lost, but surviving examples reveal richness and variety in function and form.

Parisian workshops crafted fine ivory items for women's dressing tables during the fourteenth century. The iconography on these combs, mirror cases, and especially caskets (small boxes to hold jewelry) reflected feminine aristocratic taste. Favored scenes included Tristan and Iseut's tryst, Lancelot crossing the sword bridge, and Gawain's night on the Perilous Bed, all celebrating the male ardor and devotion inspired by courtly love. Excellent examples are in the collections of the Metropolitan Museum, New York; the Walters Gallery, Baltimore; the Victoria and Albert Museum, London; the Bargello, Florence; and Cracow Cathedral, Poland. Grail imagery occasionally appeared—Galahad at the Castle of the Maidens, the youth of Perceval—but the scarcity of examples suggests that when a woman reached for her comb or her jewels she preferred to be reminded of matters of the heart rather than of the soul.

Only a few decorative metal objects have survived the centuries, but the inventories suggest that losses are great. Subjects used for the ivories appeared on jewelry; for example, Tristan and Iseut's tryst embellishes a fourteenth-century Catalan pendant. Other subjects were more evocative and complex, relating perhaps to the object's function. An early fifteenth-century presentation tray (used to offer gifts, particularly after the birth of a child), now in the collection of the Louvre, Paris, includes Lancelot and Tristan among a circle of legendary lovers: Paris, Samson, Troilus, Achilles. In a verdant meadow, each kneels before a vision of Venus. The meaning of the iconography of the Louvre Tray may be in praise of men who sacrifice their lives to love, but given the fact that the image of the Virgin was the common iconography for this type of object, the message may instead be a warning to those who shun sacred love in worship of the profane.

The most extravagant object to survive the centuries is the Burghley Nef. During the late Middle Ages and the Renaissance, ship models known as *nefs* were made of gold and silver, embellished with jewels. Their function varied. In churches, they served as reliquaries and incense boats; in wealthy homes, they graced the table, to hold salt or drink. The Burghley Nef, now in the collection of the Victoria and Albert Museum in London, bears a Parisian hallmark dated to 1527–28. The ship, three-masted and well armed,

Burghley Nef. Courtesy of Victoria and Albert Museum, London.

is mounted on the back of a mermaid. The hull is a nautilus shell, and the silver-gilt riggings rise to fourteen inches. A couple sits at a chessboard before the mast, but they hold hands rather than compete at the game. The Burghley Nef depicts the voyage of Tristan and Iseut to Cornwall, and it is easy to imagine this handsome creation as the centerpiece of a prince's table.

Many myths surround the Winchester Round Table, now hanging on the great hall of Winchester Castle in England. Only the top survives, eighteen feet in diameter. Made of oak, it is divided into twenty-four green and white sections, each labeled with the name of a knight. A portrait of a king appears in Arthur's place, and a rose adorns the center of the table. From the late Middle Ages, the table was accepted as the authentic original. Even Caxton promoted this belief in his introduction to Malory's *Le Morte Darthur*. It was, in fact, crafted sometime in the mid-fourteenth century, when "Round Table" tournaments were popular as aristocratic entertainment. Some scholars connect it with the reign of Edward III, while others believe it to be older. Although the precise date of construction cannot be ascertained, it was made during the thirteenth or fourteenth century, and the surface painting was commissioned by Henry VIII in 1522. Henry had his likeness imposed upon Arthur's, and the rose was the emblem of the Tudor family. These layers of

The Round Table, Winchester Castle. A British Tourist Authority photograph.

meaning, and the appropriation of Arthurian authority, typified the use of the legend as monarchical propaganda.

INTERIOR ÒECORATION

To current standards of taste, trained by modernism to equate austerity with elegance, the finest interiors of the Middle Ages would seem excessively decorated. The grand chambers for receiving guests and dining were daring in their mix of form, color, and texture. The halls were hung with tapestries or painted with scenic and figurative views. Ceilings were vaulted and beamed and sometimes painted to resemble the heavens. Floor tiles, mosaics, and painted glass added to the complexity of the design. There was nothing neutral about this setting; it was meant to impress, to dazzle the eye, and to enhance the viewer's enjoyment through the richness of the visual experience. Sadly, no complete and authentic interior featuring Arthurian designs survives to this day. As tastes and domestic habits changed, interior schemes were altered and even destroyed. Knowledge of them is based on scant and often ill-preserved remains, contemporary descriptions, and images in illuminations. But these are sufficient to suggest the role played by Arthurian imagery in medieval design, a role that might have transformed the hall of a country estate into its owner's private Camelot.

Although the Arthurian story seems to have been favored for secular interiors, the few remaining floors that feature the imagery are found in ecclesiastical settings. The nave of the Norman cathedral in Otranto, Italy (1165), includes a crowned figure of Arthur, positioned near Cain and Abel, in a mosaic depiction of the history of the world. Identified by the inscription "Rex Arturus," he rides a goat and holds a scepter. A giant cat looms nearby, rearing to confront him. The meaning of the image is now lost, but a clue to its origin could be the Chapalu, or Palug's Cat (see Glossary). Like the Modena Archivolt, this mosaic establishes an early development in Italy, in advance of the literary tradition.

Chertsey Abbey, near Windsor, England, had a magnificent tile pavement illustrating scenes from Thomas d'Angleterre's Anglo-Norman version of *Tristan*. Only fragments remain, and most of the surviving tiles are now in the British Museum, London. The late thirteenth-century date (ca. 1270) may indicate a royal commission, for at that time the abbey enjoyed the generous patronage of the Plantagenets. Made of dark-red clay, approximately nine and one half inches in diameter, each tile features a narrative design in a rondel set in a foliate square. This design was stamped into the wet surface before firing, the resulting impression filled with white clay.

Thirty-five scenes of Tristan's story, from his birth to his death, survive. Additional tiles represent the adventures of Richard the Lion-Hearted and unidentified battles. Other pavements of this type existed, including one at the Abbey of Halesowen near Birmingham, where some of these tile molds were reused, but in its original state the Chertsey Abbey program was the most extensive and the most magnificent.

Painted chambers constitute the greatest loss to medieval interior decoration. Few survive, and those that do have been damaged, faded, or obscured by bad restoration. Clues to what did exist are found in documents. Dover Castle at one time had rooms called "Arthur's Hall" and "Guinevere's Chamber" (ca. 1250). Even the romance tradition gives evidence of splendid decoration. According to the Vulgate *Lancelot*, when Lancelot was held captive by Morgan le Fay he passed his time by painting his history, complete with incriminating inscriptions. The scene of Arthur discovering this visual confession became a popular subject for manuscript illumination (e.g., Paris, Bibliothèque Nationale f. fr. 112, vol. 2, fol. 193; ca. 1470). In addition to narrative scenes, a procession of Arthur, his knights, and their ladies was a favored motif, as described in Boccaccio's *Amorosa visione*.

A set of poorly preserved murals (mid-fourteenth century) survives at the château of Saint-Floret in the French Auvergne. After the fashion for painted chambers waned, the room became a threshing floor, and the walls are scarred with marks from hay forks. The remaining images suggest a complex scheme, including scenes from the Prose *Tristan* and *Meliadus*. The Tristan saga also provided the subject of elaborate ceiling paintings (ca. 1380) in the Palazzo Chiaramonte in Palermo, Italy. The Nine Worthies reigned, with Tristan also a popular subject. In the Summer House at the Schloss Runkelstein in the Tyrol (late fourteenth or early fifteenth century), the Nine Worthies motif is combined with representations of the Round Table knights and romance vignettes from *Tristan* (after Gottfried von Strassburg) and *Wigalois* (after Wirnt von Grafenberg). The Ducal Palace in Mantua hosts an incomplete program attributed to Antonio Pisanello (ca. 1395–1455). Preparatory drawings remain on three walls, but only one was painted. The subject, Bohort's visit to Brangoire's castle, derives from the French Vulgate *Lancelot*. These scattered sites offer a glimpse into a splendid tradition that spanned England and the Continent, in which rival families competed in lavish visual display.

Arthurian imagery makes a late entrance in the art of stained glass. While Caxton's publication of *Le Morte Darthur* exerted some influence in the late fifteenth century, Arthur's iconography began to be included in monarchical ensembles in public buildings by the middle of that century in England. (Concerning the Tudor use of Arthurian imagery, see Conclusion.) Examples of this type, positioning Arthur with William the Conqueror and Richard the Lion-Hearted (rather than with the Christian Worthies), can be seen in the windows at All Souls Chapel Library at Oxford (1441–47), St. Mary's Hall, Coventry (1450s), and the east window of York Minster. A fifteenth-century window from a church in Langport (near Glastonbury) shifts the iconography to sacred imagery, depicting Joseph of Arimathea, with cruets containing drops of the blood and sweat of Christ. Continental examples vary, including both the popular Nine Worthies motif (Rathaus at Lüneburg) and Grail imagery (a single window in a small church in Tréhorenteuc in Brittany). These random survivals again are only a suggestion of the craftsmanship in this glorious but fragile medium.

TEXTILES

Textiles are the rarest of all Arthurian artifacts. This is due in part to the inherent weakness of the medium. Natural fibers suffer through exposure to light and damp. Insects nest in the threads and consume them for food. Damage from improper handling also led to losses in the textile arts. Large works were often trimmed to fit new locations or cut into strips for moving and storage. Storing soiled fabrics often resulted in rot, but poor cleaning methods were equally damaging. As with interior decoration, when tastes changed textiles were remodeled or discarded; in time of financial stress, gold and silver threads were picked out of fabrics to be reused or sold. The practical, daily use of these works—covering walls, tables, and beds—led to wear and ruin. Yet the way that textiles were used in the Middle Ages reveals the deep interaction of Arthurian story and the domestic lives of privileged society.

The handsome tapestries that hung in grand halls were practical and symbolic as well as ornamental. Thick hangings of wool and linen provided insulation in cold chambers. They were a prized diplomatic gift; they were also taken as spoils of war and regarded as a valued investment. King Charles VI of France owned over one hundred fifty tapestries. According to a fifteenth-century inventory, several had Arthurian subjects, including the Grail Quest, the story of Yvain, and the ubiquitous Nine Worthies. The finest surviving example of the medium is the King Arthur tapestry in the Metropolitan Museum, New York (the Cloisters Collection). Once part of a Nine Worthies program, the large panel, approximately fourteen by ten feet, presents Arthur enthroned and crowned, attended by cardinals and bishops. His arms feature traditional heraldry: three crowns representing England, Scotland, and Brittany against an azure background. From the early fifteenth century and formerly identified as the work of the Parisian master Nicolas Bataille, it is now thought to be Netherlandish.

The widespread use of Arthurian motifs in embroidery in decorative textiles and clothing is described in both literary and historical documents, but there is scant material evidence. Most of the needlework (wall-hangings and tablecloths) that does survive is German, dating from the fourteenth century. Tristan's saga provided the most popular subject, as seen in the three Wienhausen embroideries (ca. 1310), which depict a running narrative in bands of pictures and text alternating with heraldic shields. Other examples

Scenes from the Tristan legend, Sicilian wall-hanging, fourteenth century. Courtesy of Victoria and Albert Museum, London.

of Tristan motifs can be found in the collections in Lüneburg (fragments of white linen embroidered in white, green, and yellow), Erfurt (a linen table-cloth embroidered in red and blue, ca. 1370), and the Victoria and Albert Museum, London (fragments stitched together, related to the Erfurt textile in style and motif). In Sicily, needleworkers decorated padded linen quilts with Tristan imagery, but the text worked with the figures draws from several sources (*Tavola Ritonda*, the *Cuento de Tristán de Leonís*, and the Stanzaic *Le Morte Arthur*). Heraldic devices featured on two of the quilts (in the Victoria and Albert Museum, London, and the Bargello, Florence) suggest that they were made for the wedding of Piero de Luigi Guicciardini and Laodamia Acciaiuoli in 1395. As an intimate gift, these quilts offered a poignant message for newlyweds, perhaps defining the contrast between romantic love and arranged marriage. Whether impressing guests in public rooms or prompting reflection on false and true love in the most private chambers, owners of these textiles used the legend to enhance their lives.

TRANSITION AND DECLINE

In the mid-fifteenth century, the Arthurian legend attained its zenith as the favored secular subject for aristocratic patronage. At the same time, advances in print technology brought the illustrated legend to a wider audience. Block books, with pages incorporating text and simple illustration cut into a single block of wood, began to appear in the 1430s, providing a less expensive alternative to the hand-painted manuscript. Further advances came in the 1450s with Johann Gutenberg's design for a movable-type press, separating the production of a picture from the text. Illustrated books were transformed from unique to multiple objects; as they gained greater circulation, they lost their exclusive status. In addition to books, single sheets with printing on one side only, featuring a poem or ballad, appeared. These "broadsides," the first form of popular literature marketed on a mass scale, were simple to print and sold for a few pennies. They often featured an image of a knight or a battle, generally stock images used for more than one text. Although it is difficult to date the first appearance of the legend as a subject for woodcut illustration, several sets of images of the Nine Worthies survive in Paris, Bern, and Hamburg (ca. 1465). The figures are for the most part rough and crudely cut, but some were enhanced with watercolor, a practice commonly used for religious broadsides.

In 1484, a *Tristan*, drawn from Eilhart von Oberge's poem, was printed in Augsburg by Anton Sorg. Containing fifty-nine modest woodcuts, it is the oldest surviving example of the legend in print. Four years later, Jean Dupré published a French *Lancelot* (1488) with remarkable illustrations. Each of the two volumes opens with a large and intricately crafted woodcut, framed with a border of foliage and birds. The first represents the Round Table with an empty Perilous Seat; the second shows the seat occupied by Galahad, with small peripheral scenes presenting his knighting and his prayers before the Grail. This latter was used again in 1508 by Antoine Vérard to illustrate a *Tristan*. Vérard became infamous for appropriating and reusing imagery almost at random. He simply bought or borrowed blocks whenever available and incorporated them in his books

Woodcut, "King Arthur and His Knights," from Tristan de Leonnoys
(Paris: Antoine Vérard, 1506).

with little regard for integrity of style or subject. This, however, was common practice in the early printed books, and Vérard made an important contribution in the number and variety of Arthurian subjects he published, including several *Tristans* (1489, 1494, 1499, 1506), two *Lancelots*, a *Merlin*, a *Prophécies de Merlin*, and a *Guiron*.

In 1498, Wynkyn de Worde published the first illustrated Malory. Born in Alsace, he worked as William Caxton's foreman in Bruges. He moved with Caxton to London and inherited the printing practice at Caxton's death in 1491. Using Caxton's text for the *Morte* of 1485, Wynkyn embellished each chapter heading with a small woodcut illustration. The blocks were crudely cut and of uneven quality, but the images reveal links to Flemish painting in their landscape settings and formal composition. Wynkyn reissued the Malory in 1529 and, like Vérard, reused his blocks in other, unrelated works.

Other factors contributed to the decline of the legend in aristocratic patronage. In the sixteenth century, many of the courts of Europe adopted the new humanistic beliefs and classical taste preferred in Italian intellectual circles. Renaissance ideals, however, came late to England, and Arthurian imagery continued to provide monarchical imagery through the early seventeenth century. But little evidence remains, for the legend was used in pageant design, producing ephemeral works including banners, sets, and costumes, rather than lasting monuments. When Henry VIII faced Francis I on the Field of the Cloth of Gold (1520), his banner featured Arthur as conqueror of the world. During Elizabeth I's reign, court spectacles, including tilts, tournaments, and plays, used Arthurian themes. When George Clifford, third Earl of Cumberland, became the Queen's Champion in 1580, he rode in the Accession Day pageant as the Knight of Pendragon Castle. Nicholas Hilliard painted his portrait in character to commemorate the event. The Stuart court continued this interest in Arthurian theatricals under the patronage of Henry, Prince of Wales. One example, the masque *Prince Henry's Barriers* (written by Ben Jonson in 1610), had sets and costumes designed by architect Inigo Jones. Only a few drawings survive, revealing that Jones incorporated the new Renaissance aesthetic into his fantastic vision of Arthur's realm. With Henry's death in 1612, the popularity of the subject diminished, and England joined the rest of Europe, adopting classical tastes and subjects. The Arthurian legend, waning as a popular subject in the visual arts for more than a century, retreated into neglect and obscurity.

THE GOTHIC REVIVAL

A change in taste returned the Arthurian legend to the arts in eighteenth-century England. The Gothic Revival, sparking interest in a romanticized vision of the medieval past, began with the construction of "garden follies," small pleasure buildings constructed on the grounds of country homes, allowing their owners to escape into the Middle Ages on a flight of fantasy. Some of these sham castles, mock ruins, and imaginative grottoes had Arthurian themes. William Kent, master carpenter to Queen Caroline, wife of George II, built two such follies on the grounds of Richmond Castle: the Hermitage (1732), a rustic retreat housing a pantheon of British "Worthies," and Merlin's Cave (1735), a thatched, pseudo-Gothic cottage inhabited by six life-sized wax figures, including Merlin, his secretary, and Queen Elizabeth I. Neither has survived.

Garden follies were commissioned and enjoyed by a select audience, distinguished by wealth and position. The return of Arthurian imagery to the general public was a slower process, trailing behind the recovery of the literature. During the eighteenth century, Arthurian subjects were rare in the popular arts. One of the first modern painters to depict a scene from the legend was John Hamilton Mortimer (ca. 1741–79). *The Discovery of Prince Arthur's Tomb by the Inscription on the Leaden Cross* (ca. 1767) reflects the reconstructive interest of the Gothic Revival, basing the narrative on history and archaeology rather than on the saga itself. Unfortunately, the painting is lost, but its subject is preserved through drawings and an engraving. A few years later, Thomas Jones painted *The Bard* (1774), portraying Merlin on a windswept landscape with a megalithic formation (apparently Stonehenge). Subjects from *The Faerie Queene* also enjoyed a modest revival through the turn of the century in the works of Mortimer, Henry Fuseli (1741–1825), Benjamin West (1738–1820), and Charles Eastlake (1793–1865), but a full return of the legend to the arts would not come until the Victorian era.

THE ARTHURIAN REVIVAL

Widespread resurgence of Arthurian imagery in the popular arts depended upon the general public's reacquaintance with the legend. The republication of Malory's *Le Morte Darthur* in the early nineteenth century began that process, but it was not until the middle of the century that Tennyson's reworking of the legend created a fluent and receptive audience in English speaking countries. Tennyson's early Arthurian poems, most notably "The Lady

John Hamilton Mortimer, The Discovery of Prince Arthur's Tomb by the Inscription on the Leaden Cross *(ca. 1767). The National Galleries of Scotland.*

of Shalott," "Sir Galahad," and "Morte d'Arthur" (1842), established currency for the legend, while his *Idylls of the King* (1859–86) gave the Victorian public its own Arthuriad. This in turn drew wider attention to Malory's *Morte,* made even more accessible through modernized versions, as well as the works of other aspiring Arthurian writers. The resulting revival flourished in England and America throughout the nineteenth century and well into the twentieth, and its effect on the popular arts is evident still today.

PAINTING

After centuries of neglect, the Arthurian legend reappeared in British art by official mandate. In 1848, at the request of Prince Albert and a gov-

ernment commission, painter William Dyce (1806–64) began the design
and execution of a program of seven frescoes with Arthurian themes in the
Robing Room in the House of Lords at the new Westminster Palace. The
chamber was small but significant. It was there that the reigning king or
queen donned the robes of state in preparation for presiding over the annual
opening of the parliamentary session. The scenes from the legend, depicting
contemporary British values as traditional Arthurian virtues, offered a model
of monarchy, intended to instruct and inspire the current sovereign to emulate the Once and Future King.

To prepare for this project, Dyce studied the history and archaeology of
ancient Britain, but he rejected a historical approach for an allegorical interpretation. Using the 1817 Southey edition of Malory, Dyce selected key characters and subjects to create a pantheon of Arthurian heroes to personify what
he described as "the moral qualities which make up the ancient idea of chivalric
greatness." Each of Dyce's designs was reviewed by Prince Albert and a gov-
ernmental board for sound aesthetics and appropriate content. Only one design was rejected. Although the reasons for refusing the subject *Piety: The
Knights of the Round Table Departing on the Quest of the Holy Grail* were not
recorded, the tragic content of seeing Arthur bid his knights a sad farewell
probably did not suit the uplifting purpose of the Robing Room decoration.
But the visual elements in the design, presented in a highly finished watercolor of 1849 (National Gallery of Scotland, Edinburgh), set a tone of dignity
and grandeur for the portrayal of the legend.

As the work proceeded, Dyce revised the legend to express modern
ideals as national mythology. In *Religion: The Vision of Sir Galahad and His
Company* (1851), he suppressed Catholic mysticism with Protestant enthusiasm. *Generosity: King Arthur Unhorsed, Spared by Lancelot* (1852) celebrated
fair play and respect for authority. Both *Courtesy: Sir Tristram Harping to La
Belle Isolde* (1852) and *Mercy: Sir Gawaine Swearing to Be Merciful and Never
Be Against Ladies* (1854) demonstrated manly behavior toward women, while
Hospitality: The Admission of Sir Tristram to the Fellowship of the Round Table
(1864; finished by C.W. Cope) showed the nobility of mutual respect. The
original plan offered two more subjects, *Courage: The Combat Between King
Arthur and the Five Northern Kings* and *Fidelity: Sir Lancelot Rescuing Queen
Guenevere from King Meliagaunce,* but these were abandoned after the artist's
death. Throughout the ensemble, Dyce's massive yet graceful figures with
their grand gestures (based on Renaissance prototypes) conveyed the noble
message of the legend. As the first full portrayal of the Arthurian story in
British art since the Middle Ages, Dyce's frescoes set important precedents.

He created physical identities for his characters: an older yet still powerful Arthur; a dark, brooding Lancelot; a fair, athletic Galahad. He used a classical rather than a medieval aesthetic, merging two traditions into one. Above all, guided by the scrutiny of the Prince and his commission, Dyce expurgated the legend to reflect modern rather than medieval ideals.

William Holman Hunt, The Lady of Shalott *(1886–1905). Wadsworth Athenaeum, Hartford. The Ella Gallup Sumner and Mary Catlin Sumner Collection Fund.*

Before Dyce finished the "official" version of the visual legend, an alternative interpretation appeared. In 1848, seven young idealistic men formed the Pre-Raphaelite Brotherhood. This small, private society sought to reform the prevailing standards of art. They swore to "sympathize with what is direct and serious and heartfelt in previous art." They criticized all that was "conventional and self-parading and learned by rote" in current art practice, and they sought "genuine ideas to express." They found many of their ideas in Arthurian legend, and although the Brotherhood lasted only until 1853, their influence and the association of Pre-Raphaelite aesthetic and the Arthurian legend continued well into the twentieth century.

Their earliest works were based on Tennyson's poetry. In 1849, Frederic G. Stephens (1828–1907) undertook the subject *Mort d'Arthur* (Tate Gallery, London) but did not complete it. In the following year, William Holman Hunt (1827–1910) made a drawing after Tennyson's "Lady of Shalott" (National Gallery of Victoria, Melbourne). A former student of Dyce, Hunt would return to this subject repeatedly, painting a monumental version at the end of his career. This late *Lady of Shalott* (1886–1905; Wadsworth Athenaeum, Hartford) visually glossed Tennyson's description with mythological parallels to chivalric virtues (Hercules in the Garden of Hesperides) and biblical salvation (the Virgin Mary praying over her Child). Even Hunt realized that his iconography was dense and unfamiliar; when the work was first exhibited, he published a pamphlet to explain it. Although the art of the Pre-Raphaelite Brotherhood and their associates differed in style, interpretation, and critical success, they shared a fascination with the past. Enchanted by a romantic view of the Middle Ages, their works often exhibited personal identification with the subjects they selected.

Nowhere is this more evident than in the work of Dante Gabriel Rossetti (1828–82). He was the first in the Pre-Raphaelite circle to break away from Tennyson's poetry, painting *Arthur's Tomb* (1854–55; Tate Gallery, London), a subject loosely based on Malory (Book 21, Chapter 9). Like so many of Rossetti's subjects, *Arthur's Tomb* celebrates the lovers rather than the heroes of the legend. Undeterred by the years or by Guinevere's retreat into convent life, Lancelot begs for one last kiss. Rossetti's passionate sentiments stood in strong contrast to Dyce's high-minded allegories. Similarly, Rossetti's crowded composition, with his stiff, archaic figures and excess of iconographic detail, marked a deliberate but nonhistorical association with medieval prototypes, as opposed to Dyce's

Dante Gabriel Rossetti, Arthur's Tomb *(1854–55). By permission of Tate Gallery, London.*

classical aesthetic. The first artist to portray openly the illicit love triangle, Rossetti shifted the message of the Arthurian world from public virtue to private tragedy.

In 1857, Rossetti gathered a group of friends to decorate the upper gallery of the new debating hall of the Oxford Union. Eager for a commission to rival Dyce's at Westminster, Rossetti agreed to oversee the painting of ten murals without remuneration beyond travel expense, materials, and lodging. Choosing subjects from Malory, Rossetti and his friends threw themselves into the work with enormous but short-lived enthusiasm. Continuing his identification with Lancelot, Rossetti took subjects that featured the passionate knight: *Launcelot's Vision of the Sangreal* and *Launcelot in the Queen's Chamber.* He also took another Grail subject, *How Sir Percival, Sir Bors, and Sir Galahad Saw the Sangreal,* and he assigned to the others *King Arthur Obtains the Sword of Excalibur* (J. Hungerford Pollen), *The Jealousy of Sir Palomedes at the Sight of Sir Tristram and the Lady Yseult* (William Morris), *Sir Pelleas Leaving Lady Ettare* (Valentine Prinsep), *Sir Gawaine Meets the Three Ladies at the Well* (J. Rodham Spencer Stanhope), *Merlin and Nimue* (Edward Burne-Jones), and *Arthur in the Death Barge* (Arthur Hughes). Before the year was out, Rossetti left the project, one mural incomplete, the others not even started. Studies do exist, and Rossetti returned to the subjects in highly finished watercolors in the following years. With Rossetti gone, the other artists left as well, some leaving their works to be finished by artists, William Riviere and his son Briton, hired by the Union. Within a few months of completion, the murals began to flake and fade; inexperienced in wall decoration, Rossetti and his team had painted on damp brick walls, prepared only with whitewash. Despite several restorations and a recent conservation project, the murals can be seen today only with special lighting. But the project served to strengthen the association of the Pre-Raphaelites and the legend and to popularize Malory's saga for its romance and tragedy. It also drew the young artists Edward Burne-Jones (1833–98) and William Morris (1834–96) into the Pre-Raphaelite circle. Both had a longstanding fascination with the legend and embraced Arthurian subjects. Morris, soon to turn his attention to domestic interior design, completed only one painting in his career, the sorrowful portrait of *Guenevere* (sometimes identified as *La Belle Iseult*; Tate Gallery, London) of 1858, but Burne-Jones painted subjects from the legend throughout his career.

Unlike Morris and Rossetti, Burne-Jones openly admired the poetry of Tennyson. Shortly after leaving the Oxford Union, he met the poet, and his graceful pen-and-ink drawing of *Sir Galahad* (1859; Fogg Art Museum, Cambridge) recalls the narrative details of Tennyson's 1842 poem. In the

Dante Gabriel Rossetti, How Sir Galahad, Sir Bors and Sir Percival Were Fed with the Sanct Grael *(1864). By permission of Tate Gallery, London.*

years that followed, Burne-Jones returned to the subject of his Oxford mural, *Merlin and Nimue*. Out of his five known renditions of the subject (between 1857 and 1884), *The Beguiling of Merlin* (1875–77; Lady Lever Art Gallery, Port Sunlight) is the most striking. Drawing upon several text sources, including Tennyson's *Idyll* "Vivien" (1859) and a fifteenth-century English translation of the Vulgate *Merlin* republished by the Early English Text Society (1865), Burne-Jones presented Nimue as a *femme fatale*, murmuring spells over the enchanted wizard, a victim of seduction as much as of magic. In the last decades of his life, Burne-Jones portrayed scenes from the legend in oil paint and watercolor, in tapestry designs and cartoons for stained glass. He filled personal sketchbooks with Arthurian vignettes and heraldry. He even designed costumes and sets for J.C. Comyns Carr's play *King Arthur* (1895).

The Grail legend and its chaste hero remained Burne-Jones's favorite subject, but his last and most memorable painting depicted *The Sleep of Arthur in Avalon* (1881–98; Museo de Arte de Ponce, Puerto Rico). He began the work on commission, but the painting progressed so slowly and grew to such a grand scale (9 feet 3 inches by 21 feet 2 inches) that his patron and longtime friend George Howard freed him from his obligation. Burne-Jones continued to work on the painting for his own pleasure. He worked on it the day before he died, and he never regarded it as finished. Intended to be neither shown nor sold, it was a personal testament of artistic ideals through an Arthurian metaphor, a painting of a place that no mortal could ever see and no poet could describe.

As the Arthurian legend gained broad popularity in Victorian England, the two modes of visual interpretation—Dyce's instructive personification and the rich, highly detailed Pre-Raphaelite aesthetic—merged in portrayals of favorite characters from Tennyson. The bright boy-knight of the 1842 "Sir Galahad" enchanted artists and audiences alike throughout the era, and George Frederick Watts's (1817–1904) depiction of him as a fair, androgynous adolescent (1862; Fogg Art Museum) became a symbol for innocent youth. The work was so popular that Watts made several replicas for patrons, and reproductions were used as prizes for promising young men in some public schools. The image of Elaine, destroyed by her tragic love for Lancelot, served as a counterpart for feminine innocence. Portraits of her as a pensive girl on the brink of womanhood or on her death barge en route to Camelot were painted by a wide range of artists, from Pre-Raphaelite associates Arthur Hughes (1830–1915) and Henry Wallis (1830–1916) to academy regulars Edward Corbould (1815–1905) and Sophie Anderson

Edward Burne-Jones, The Beguiling of Merlin *(1875–77). Board of Trustees of the National Museums and Galleries on Merseyside (Walker Art Gallery/Lady Lever Art Gallery).*

THE·HIGH·HISTORY·
OF·THE·HOLY·GRAAL·

Edward Burne-Jones, The Grail. *Frontispiece for* The High History of the Holy Grail
[Perlesvaus], *trans. Sebastian Evans.*

(1823–1903). Innocence had an appeal, but so did danger, seen in the portrayals of the legend's temptresses *Vivien* (1863; Manchester City Gallery) and *Morgan-le-Fay* (1864; Birmingham City Gallery and Museum) by Frederick Sandys (1829–1904).

Images of Arthur's death and passing served as an icon of the legend throughout the Revival, seen in the work of Joseph Noel Paton (1821–1901), Frank Dicksee (1853–1928), and James Archer (1823–1904), who painted the subject at least four times. "The Lady of Shalott" endured to evoke the legend's mystery and romance. John William Waterhouse (1849–1917) painted a series of three works on the subject, presenting the Lady lamenting at her loom (1915; Art Gallery of Ontario, Toronto), caught in the spell (1894; Leeds City Art Galleries), and on her fated journey to Camelot (1888; Tate Gallery, London). In each, Waterhouse combined Pre-Raphaelite intensity with a new naturalistic setting, a response to the innovative views of light and color seen in the French art movements Naturalism and Impressionism.

There was a modest response to the British Arthurian Revival in America. For the most part, in emulation of the better-known Victorian works, Tennyson's poetry provided the subjects and Pre-Raphaelite art provided the style, as seen in John La Farge's (1835–1910) *The Lady of Shalott*

Arthur Hughes, Sir Galahad *(1870). Board of Trustees of the National Museums and Galleries on Merseyside (Walker Art Gallery, Liverpool).*

James Archer, Morte d'Arthur *(1861). Copyright Manchester City Art Gallery.*

(ca. 1862; New Britain Museum of American Art) and Toby Edward Rosenthal's (1848–1917) *Elaine* (1874; Art Institute of Chicago), but exceptions may be found in the moody landscapes of Albert Pinkham Ryder (1847–1917) that feature small Arthurian vignettes. Edwin Austin Abbey (1852–1911) painted the most notable American ensemble of Arthurian subjects. In the 1890s, the architectural firm of McKim, Mead, and White hired the anglophile artist to paint fifteen murals depicting the Grail Quest for the Delivery Room of the new Boston Public Library. Abbey used a combination of sources, including Tennyson's "The Holy Grail," the works of Chrétien de Troyes and his continuators, Wolfram von Eschenbach's *Parzival,* and Malory's *Le Morte Darthur,* to produce the most extensive and synthetic pictorial telling of the saga in the modern era. Unlike his British counterparts, Abbey was concerned with historical accuracy, setting the legend in the twelfth century and employing what he called a "Celtic Style." Although the strong, graceful figures and clear, balanced compositions recall the work of Dyce, Abbey emphasized narrative rather than allegory for his interpretation.

A profound shift in the content of painting in the twentieth century, moving the artist's attention from representative imagery to purely formal concerns, led to a waning of Arthurian imagery. Painters influenced by the European symbolists, such as Jean Delville, continued to create visual narratives from the legend, but as seen in the works of Edward Reginald Frampton (1872–1923), Sidney Meteyard (1868–1947), and Frank Cadogan Cowper (1877–1958), Arthurian subjects gained their vitality from a strange and often erotic energy. The Welsh artist David Jones—his poetry is discussed in Chapter III—presents the rare example in his enduring attachment to the legend in modern art. Arthurian subjects appear in his highly charged, expressionist works as early as the 1930s and remain a staple in his repertoire throughout his career. Strongly influenced by Matisse, Jones's works are nonnarrative, but lyrically figurative, a modernist response to the traditional subject matter. A few contemporary artists, most notably Anselm Keifer (born 1945), use the legend as a departure point for introspective expression, but for the most part the pictorial version of the late twentieth-century legend is the realm of film and the design of mass-produced products, including games, comics, and computer graphics, rather than painting.

SCULPTURE

Compared with the wealth of carved Arthurian imagery in the medieval era, the amount of work in this medium in the modern revival is modest. This is partly due to the reduced importance of sculpture as architectural decoration in the nineteenth and twentieth centuries. However, one of the most important sets of carvings in the Victorian era was used to embellish an interior. In 1866, the British government commissioned H.H. Armstead (1828–75) to design and carve eighteen bas-relief oak panels, to finish the ensemble in the Robing Room at Westminster Palace. Armstead's panels, installed by 1870, tell the tales of Galahad's Grail Quest and Arthur's defeat and passing in concise narrative sequence.

Arthurian subjects typically appeared in single freestanding form, featuring a character from the legend. Pre-Raphaelite Thomas Woolner (1825–92) sculpted *Elaine* and *Guinevere* in marble in the 1870s, but both works are simply serene figures of beautiful women, classicized forms in medieval dress. More charming is the work of William Goscombe John (1860–1952), who cast a playful Merlin instructing a rambunctious infant Arthur in bronze in 1902 (National Museum of Wales, Cardiff). American-born William Reynolds-Stephens (1862–1943) spent most of his life and career in Britain. His experiments with unorthodox materials produced an extraordinary depiction of *Guinevere's Redeeming* (1907; Nottingham Castle Museum and Art Gallery). Combining bronze, ivory, and enamel, this severely dressed queen has a stark, white face. Her hands clasped in prayer, she rises as a penitent above images of her former identities as lover and queen, cast in medallions on the statue's plinth. George Frampton (1860–1928) also combined materials to give an eerie beauty to his portrait busts of *La Beale Isoude* and *Enid the Fair*. The intense expression and strange aesthetic of both Reynolds-Stephens's and Frampton's styles ally them with the European Symbolist movement.

In the twentieth century, Arthurian iconography offered poignant subjects for commemorative statues. Young men who fell in the Boer War and in World War I were remembered through the image of the ideal knight Sir Galahad, still eager, still ready to serve his quest and country. These memorials appeared in England, America, and Canada. A typical example is Ernest W. Keyser's statue of *Sir Galahad* (1905) on Wellington Street in Ottawa. With his sword clasped in his right hand and his eyes turned heavenward, this depiction of Galahad embodies resolute youth. It was built in commemoration of a local war hero, whose last words—"If I lose myself, I save myself," drawn from Tennyson's "The Holy Grail"—are carved on the statue's rocky base.

DECORATIVE ARTS

In modern times, as in the Middle Ages, the production of decorative arts with Arthurian subjects responded to audience demand. But in contrast to the earlier era, diversity rather than exclusivity reigned. Images from the legend appeared in all media and at all levels of value, ranging from expensive, commissioned designs to cheap, mass-produced goods. The variety of known objects frustrates attempts to map patterns of development, with one notable exception. During the Victorian era and well into the twentieth century, Arthurian subjects in decorative arts were associated with the reformist aesthetic of the Arts and Crafts movement.

The principles of the movement were first articulated and enacted by William Morris (whose Arthurian poetry is discussed in Chapter III). A critic of modern industrial production, he offered an alternative: the return to individual designs, quality materials, and hand-craftsmanship. The companies he founded (Morris, Marshall, and Faulkner in 1861; Morris and Company in 1875; Merton Abbey Tapestry Works in 1881) were artists' collectives. Morris would secure the commission, match a designer with the project (often serving as the designer himself), and hire the skilled craftsmen to make the goods. Although Morris's designs in tile, textile, and glass featured Arthurian themes only occasionally, those examples, particularly in stained glass and tapestry, combined with Morris's own interest, forged a link between the legend and the Arts and Crafts movement that had wide and enduring influence.

In 1862, Walter Dunlop commissioned a set of thirteen stained-glass panels from Morris, Marshall, and Faulkner. Morris chose the subject—the romantic tragedy of Tristram and Iseult, derived from Malory—and hired his friends to produce the designs. The artists included Dante Gabriel Rossetti, Edward Burne-Jones, Arthur Hughes, Valentine Prinsep, and Ford Madox Brown. All were members of the Pre-Raphaelite circle, and all but Brown had worked on the Oxford Union Murals project. As an ensemble, the panels retold the tale of ill-fated love, from Tristram's birth to his death at the hands of Mark. Each scene, a simple dramatic vignette, had a line of text inscribed below. Morris rounded out the narrative with two portrait panels, featuring King Arthur and Sir Lancelot in one and Guinevere and Iseult in the other. The panels, originally installed in Dunlop's music room in his house at Harden Grange near Bingely, Yorkshire (now in the City Art Gallery, Bradford), mark the most unified collaboration of Pre-Raphaelite design, in both narrative and aesthetic.

One other Arthurian stained-glass project is associated with Morris. In 1886, Burne-Jones designed four panels depicting the Quest for the Holy Grail. He followed the form set in the Tristram windows, using a continuous narrative and pairing image with text. Burne-Jones created unity within his design with a river that flows through all the panels. The first three present the separate encounters of Gawaine, Lancelot, and Galahad with an angel bearing the Grail, and the last depicts the holy vessel on the altar in the Grail Chapel, where Galahad would be welcomed as King of Sarras. Morris made the windows according to Burne-Jones's design, and although the artist planned them for his own home in Rottingdean, he gave them as a gift to his neighbor Lady Leighton-Warren. They are now in the collection of the Victoria and Albert Museum in London.

Morris's influence on stained-glass design extended into the twentieth century. An American example can be seen at the Princeton University Chapel (1925–28). Designed by Charles J. Connick (1875–1945), the program of glass panels celebrates four Christian epics: the works of Bunyan, Milton, Dante, and Malory. Thirty-six panels portray Arthurian characters and key subjects, including Arthur receiving Excalibur, Galahad achieving the Grail, and Arthur's fatal wounding at the hands of Mordred.

As May Moneth Floreth and Floryssheth.
Princeton University Chapel window, the Malory window; Charles J. Connick, artist.
Reproduced from Richard Stillwell, The Chapel of Princeton University. © 1971 by
Princeton University Press. Reprinted by permission of Princeton University Press. Additional
permission from the Charles J. Connick Stained Glass Foundation, Ltd., Newtonville, Mass.

Let Every Man of Worship Florysshe his Herte in this World.
Princeton University Chapel window, the Malory window; Charles J. Connick, artist.
Reproduced from Richard Stillwell, The Chapel of Princeton University. © *1971 by*
Princeton University Press. Reprinted by permission of Princeton University Press. Additional
permission from the Charles J. Connick Stained Glass Foundation, Ltd., Newtonville, Mass.

Fyrst Vnto God and Next Vnto the Joye.
Princeton University Chapel window, the Malory window; Charles J. Connick, artist.
Reproduced from Richard Stillwell, The Chapel of Princeton University. *© 1971 by*
Princeton University Press. Reprinted by permission of Princeton University Press. Additional
permission from the Charles J. Connick Stained Glass Foundation, Ltd., Newtonville, Mass.

Of Them That He Promysed his Feythe Vnto.
Princeton University Chapel window, the Malory window; Charles J. Connick, artist.
Reproduced from Richard Stillwell, The Chapel of Princeton University. *© 1971 by*
Princeton University Press. Reprinted by permission of Princeton University Press. Additional
permission from the Charles J. Connick Stained Glass Foundation, Ltd., Newtonville, Mass.

Connick kept Morris's formula for pairing image with text but divided his vertical panels into three scenes, emulating the smaller, more contained medieval design prototype. Stained-glass war memorials also appeared in England, the United States, and Canada, but the largest twentieth-century ensemble of Arthurian panels was designed by Veronica Whall (1887–1967) for King Arthur's Hall of Chivalry, a meeting hall for the society of "The Fellowship of the Round Table" in Tintagel. The ensemble of seventy-three windows includes narrative, allegorical, and heraldic images and represents Whall's clear dedication to the principles of Art and Crafts design.

A set of tapestries featuring Arthurian images was produced by the Royal Windsor Tapestry Manufactory in 1879, after the designs of Herbert Bone. But the best-known and most influential example was the product of Morris's Merton Abbey Tapestry Works. In 1891, Australian mining magnate W.K. D'Arcy commissioned a set of six pictorial hangings to cover the walls, with six smaller decorative panels of foliage and scrollwork below them. Designed by Burne-Jones, they trace the saga of the Grail Quest from the Grail Maiden's first appearance in Arthur's hall to Galahad's attainment of the sacred vessel. Installed in D'Arcy's Middlesex estate, Stanmore Hall, the tapestries transformed a modern dining room into a medieval chamber where a Victorian industrialist could offer his guests a trip back in time along with their dinner. The tapestries, finished in 1894 (now in the collection of the Duke of Westminster), were copied twice: for Laurence Hodson (1895–96, now in the collection of Birmingham City Galleries) and for D'Arcy's partner George McCulloch (1898–99, Private Collection).

Although the influence of the Arts and Crafts movement has waned, Arthurian themes enjoy a random and unpredictable presence in contemporary decorative arts. The sources and media vary widely, from mass-produced souvenirs sold at theme hotels like the Excalibur Hotel in Las Vegas or the Medieval Times restaurant chain across the United States, to limited-edition tableware, such as the strong, sparely decorated dinner set named "Camelot" by jewelry designer Robert Lee Morris. Morris also produced a line of jewelry named after the characters in Marion Zimmer Bradley's *The Mists of Avalon* (1990). Outstanding among contemporary decorative designs is the elegant glass sculpture *Excalibur*, a cut-crystal stone with a sterling silver blade embellished with an eighteen-carat-gold hilt, designed for and produced by Steuben Glass of New York. A subject for collector's plates, commemorative coins, and figurines, Arthurian imagery also is found in the commercial world of collectibles.

James Houston, Excalibur *(1963). By permission of Steuben, New York.*

BOOK ILLUSTRATION

Of all the visual arts, book illustration has played the greatest role in bringing the Arthurian legend to the widest audience. For generations, from the Victorian period to the present, a child's first introduction to the legend was through a storybook with pictures. Though illustration emerged slowly during the Arthurian Revival, trailing a decade or two behind painting in popularity, illustrated books for children continue to be published, as the twentieth century draws to a close.

The first Arthurian images appeared in Victorian anthologies. *The Book of British Ballads*, edited and published by Samuel Carter Hall in 1842 and illustrated by a team of artists, featured two Arthurian poems, "King Arthur's Death" and "Lancelot du Lake," both adapted from Thomas Percy's *Relics of Ancient English Poetry* (1765). A similar project, undertaken to produce the first illustrated collection of the early poems by Alfred Tennyson, had farther-reaching influence. In 1855, Tennyson and his publisher, Edward Moxon, selected a group of artists to provide the designs for *Poems* (1857, known as the Moxon Tennyson). The six Arthurian illustrations were assigned to three artists: Pre-Raphaelites Dante Gabriel Rossetti ("The Palace of Art," "The Lady of Shalott," and "Sir Galahad") and William Holman Hunt ("The Lady of Shalott") and the academy and government favorite Daniel Maclise ("Arthur Obtains the Sword Excalibur" and Arthur in the Death Barge for "Morte d'Arthur"). The interpretations linked the images to medieval prototypes in varying degrees. Rossetti's dense, claustrophobic compositions and lean, attenuated figures suggested an arcane style to Victorian viewers, while Hunt's grander figure type recalled models from Botticelli. Maclise conformed to the conventions of history painting as seen

Dante Gabriel Rossetti, drawing for "The Palace of Art," from the Moxon Tennyson (1857). Courtesy of Kenneth Spencer Research Library, University of Kansas.

Daniel Maclise, "Arthur Obtains the Sword Excalibur." From the Moxon Tennyson (1857). Courtesy of Kenneth Spencer Research Library, University of Kansas.

in Dyce's work at Westminster: sparse compositions, heroic figures and gestures, and restrained emotion. The book met with mixed critical success, and Tennyson was disappointed with the results, but the fine production and serious approach to illustration influenced book design for the next half-century.

Equally influential were the designs of French illustrator Gustave Doré (1832–83), who provided thirty-six drawings for the first four poems of Tennyson's *Idylls of the King*. The project (1867–68) was a joint venture between Moxon and the Parisian firm Hachette. Issued in separate folio editions, the works appeared in England and France simultaneously. (The French edition was translated by Francisque Michel.) Doré's drawings, transferred to steel plates by English engravers, focused upon the most dramatic moments of the poems—Uther finding the crown of the dead brothers, Elaine's journey to Camelot—in a richly romantic interpretation. The emphasis on moody landscape reveals Doré's link to his own national traditions, while the dense forests, fantasy castles, and crumbling ruins featured in them appealed to English taste. Although Doré read Tennyson's poems only in translation, he fully understood the balance of reality, idealism, and the supernatural with which the poet infused the legend. As with the Moxon Tennyson, Doré's illustrations failed to please the poet, but public reception was positive, and Doré's dark, mysterious aesthetic became linked in some circles with the legend, surviving even today in the illustration of fantasy literature.

The most extensive illustrated publication of the Victorian era proved to be both the most influential and the most notorious. In 1893, publisher John Dent hired Aubrey Beardsley (1872–98), a precocious but inexperienced artist, to provide drawings for a two-volume edition of Malory's *Le Morte Darthur*. Dent formulated his plan in a rivalry with William Morris's Kelmscott Press. Morris founded his firm to produce high-quality hand-printed books. After publishing his own *Defence of Guenevere* (1892), Morris planned an illustrated Malory in collaboration with Burne-Jones, but it was never realized. Dent had hoped to cut the market from under Morris by saving on production costs (using line block rather than hand printing), less expensive paper, and an artist who worked for a minimal fee.

Beardsley provided nearly five hundred black-and-white drawings for Dent's publication: chapter headings, decorative initials, borders, and full- and double-page illustrations. The style varies throughout the production. Beardsley's early designs reveal his admiration for the work of Burne-Jones, while the later ones chart his progressive evolution into the aesthetics of Art Nouveau. The quality varies as well, and some of the images drawn late in the project were carelessly conceived or even redundant, documenting the artist's admitted impatience with the size of the commission and the limited time he was granted to complete it. Although

Gustave Doré, "Uther Finds the Crown" *from Tennyson's* Idylls of the King *(1859).*
Courtesy of The Newberry Library, Chicago.

some of the full-page illustrations, such as the "Lady of the Lake Instructing Arthur about Excalibur," conform to standards typical of the Arthurian
Revival, others subvert that standard through nudity, androgyny, and violence. More often than not, Beardsley stripped the heroes of their strength

and nobility, presenting them reclining, sleeping, or dominated by women. He even challenged the mode of representing the knight as an athlete in armor, as seen in the broad-hipped form of Bedivere as he returns Excalibur to the Lady of the Lake. In the end, Beardsley made a mockery out of Dent's sham medievalism, but his bizarre and some-

Aubrey Beardsley, "How Sir Bedivere Cast the Sword Excalibur into the Water," from the Dent Le Morte D'Arthur *(1893-94). Courtesy of Kenneth Spencer Research Library, University of Kansas.*

Aubrey Beardsley, "How Sir Tristram Drank of the Love Drink," from the Dent Le Morte
D'Arthur *(1897). Courtesy of Kenneth Spencer Research Library, University of Kansas.*

times erotic imagery took the illustration of the legend into the twentieth
century.

In the years before World War I, English illustrators continued to dominate the field of Arthurian illustration. The finest of these were women, working
in the Pre-Raphaelite style. Jesse Marion King's (1875–1949) exquisite black-

and-white drawings for *The Defence of Guenevere and Other Poems* (1904) appear, in their fresh innocence, as opposite to Beardsley's designs, but her energetic, descriptive lines reveal his influence. In *Tennyson's "Idylls of the King"* (1912), Eleanor Fortiscue Brickdale (1871–1945) offered a set of miniature paintings in the Pre-Raphaelite style. Through meticulous narrative detail and sensitive interpretation, Brickdale's work conveys the poignant intimacy appropriate to the private experience of reading an illustrated book. Florence Harrison's *Tennyson's "Guinevere" and Other Poems* (1911) presented a variety of illustrations, ranging from elegant chapter headings in the style of King to full-page black-and-white images and glowing color reproductions that suggest the influence both of Beardsley and of the Pre-Raphaelites. While Harrison contributed nothing new to the illustrator's repertoire, her slender anthology evoked a nostalgic atmosphere, linking the styles of the nineteenth century with the emerging interpretation of the twentieth.

Illustrated children's books appeared late in the nineteenth century, and a lively market rapidly developed in England and America. The preferred narrative was taken from Malory's *Morte*, abridged or revised for younger readers. As early as 1881, the American Sidney Lanier published *The Boy's King Arthur*, one of the most enduring examples of Arthurian juvenilia; it enjoyed many editions, as well as several illustrators, on both sides of the Atlantic.

The invention of photomechanical color reproduction in the 1890s offered an inexpensive means to include color pictures in illustrated books. This process was rapidly applied to children's publications, where a selection of color plates could be included in a volume more heavily illustrated in black-and-white. Walter Crane (1845–1915), well known for his "toy-books" of the 1870s and a fine illustrated edition of Spenser's *Faerie Queene* (1894–97), designed the imagery for *King Arthur's Knights* (1911) and *The Knights of the Round Table* (1915), stories retold for children by Henry Gilbert. Both books featured reproductions after Crane's watercolors and drawings, a selection of subjects that would appeal to young readers, including "Arthur Draws the Sword from the Stone," "Beaumains Wins the Fight at the Ford," and "Sir Galahad Brought to King Arthur's Court." Each image is dominated by a brave boy-knight, ready for adventure, certain to spark the reader's imagination and sense of identification. A similar approach can be seen in Arthur Rackham's (1867–1939) *The Romance of King Arthur and His Knights of the Round Table* (1917), abridged from Malory by Alfred W. Pollard. Like Crane, Rackham draws his readers into a special world, but Rackham emphasizes fantasy over adventure.

In America, generations of Arthurian enthusiasts first encountered the legend through the illustrated books of Howard Pyle (1853–1911). His four volumes—*The Story of King Arthur and His Knights* (1903), *The Story of the Champions of the Round Table* (1905), *The Story of Sir Launcelot and His*

Walter Crane, "Sir Galahad Brought to King Arthur's Court," from Arthurian stories retold by Henry Gilbert (1911, 1915). Courtesy of The Newberry Library, Chicago.

Companions (1907), and *The Story of the Grail and the Passing of Arthur* (1910)—enjoyed many editions and became the standard American version of the legend. Pyle's books are richly decorated with full- and half-page black-and-white drawings, initials, and ornamental images at the head and tail of each chapter. Many of his full-page images are portraits, presenting stern knights and sloe-eyed damsels, showing the young reader a world of masculine adventure and feminine mystery. N.C. Wyeth (1882–1945) studied with Pyle. He became a prominent magazine and book illustrator, but he is best remembered for his version of Lanier's *The Boy's King Arthur* (1920). Unlike Pyle, Wyeth clearly preferred action, and most of his images depict fierce knights in combat. The wealth of color printing in this volume heightens its spirit and energy and, like Pyle's volume, it endures as an American standard. Many other illustrators joined Pyle and Wyeth through the rest of the century. Edmund Dulac's images for John Erskine's texts ran serially in *American Weekly* (1940); Alexander Dobkin provided new pictures for Mary Macleod's *King Arthur and His Knights* (1950); Juan Wijngaard illustrated Selina Hasting's *Sir Gawain and the Loathly Lady* (1985); and Trina Schart Hyman's designs accompanied Margaret Hodges's *The Kitchen Knight* (1990). Although Pyle's and Wyeth's interpretations may echo in some of the works, the styles and results vary widely, depending more on the artist's vision than on a particular convention or prototype.

COMICS, POSTAGE STAMPS

In the decades after World War I, Arthur found a new realm in comic books. In the strips of colorful images and sparse text, the King, characters from the legend, and even a continuation of the saga in modern terms reached even broader audiences. The most enduring of these illustrated serials is *Prince Valiant*, created by Harold ("Hal") Foster in 1937 (currently illustrated by John Cullen Murphy). The adventures of this knight of King Arthur's court has been a regular feature of the Sunday comic pages for over three thousand episodes. The tale's longevity has allowed the hero "Val" to grow from a young knight, eager to please his sovereign, to a married man with children. Unchanging are Val's distinctive bowl haircut and the old but still effective king he serves. More current strips feature Arthurian characters as superheroes. The *Camelot 3000* series, created by Mike W. Barr and Brian Bolland (twelve issues, D.C. Comics, 1982–85), transforms the Round Table knights into mutants, musclemen, and even transsexuals. The simple "pulp" illustration style and the emphasis on action and physique link *Camelot 3000* with contemporary comic sagas featuring martial-arts specialists as

Yvonne Gilbert, Arthur and Merlin stamp (1985).

much as with the tradition of the legend.

The connection between comics and the legend has been recently ac-knowledged as an American symbol: Prince Valiant is among the characters honored in the U.S. Postal Service Cartoon Series (1995; designed by Carl Herrman). Ten years earlier, the British Post Office also used the legend as imagery for stamps. A set of four, designed by Yvonne Gilbert (and depicting Merlin and King Arthur, the Lady of the Lake, Lancelot and Guinevere, and Galahad), celebrated the quincentenary of Caxton's publication of Malory's *Morte*. These two examples of philatelic illustration—and there are others—reveal a national divergence in the interpretation and reception of the legend. Gilbert's nostalgic imagery looks back to the storybook pictures of the early twentieth century, while Foster's clean-cut American knight looks forward to the animated and cinematic image of Arthur and his knights that prevails in contemporary popular entertainment.

phorography

In the Victorian era, when photography was still a relatively new me-dium, photographic images of the legend were rare. Henry Peach Robinson (1830–1901) positioned a model in a boat in front of a natural backdrop, arranged her hair in what he called "PR fashion" (Pre-Raphaelite), and shot a picture of the *Lady of Shalott*. His albumen print of 1861 is the earliest known photograph of an Arthurian scene, but the work of Julia Margaret Cameron (1815–79) has overshadowed his pioneering contribution.

Henry Peach Robinson, photograph, The Lady of Shalott *(1860-61).*
Courtesy The Royal Photographic Society, Bath, England.

In 1874, Tennyson invited his neighbor Cameron, an innovative portrait photographer with ties to the Pre-Raphaelite circle, to provide illustrations for a new edition of *Idylls of the King.* Cameron accepted immediately and proceeded with enthusiasm. Her models included friends and relatives—her husband posed for Merlin—but she sometimes corralled strangers from the street simply because they fit her conception of the characters. Cameron's photographs were copied as wood-engraved designs for publication, but she was disappointed with the results and reprinted the images directly from her large-scale glass negatives. She selected twelve illustrations to publish as a photographic suite in 1874; three other volumes followed. The volumes met with limited popular success, but critics generally praised them, and Tennyson found them closer to his vision than any other set of illustrations. The photographs taken by Robinson and Cameron brought the legend to life for contemporary audiences. Although they seem stiff and stagelike today, they represent the first step toward cinematic interpretations as the dominant visual medium for the modern legend (see below).

MUSIC AND DANCE

Arthurian music began even before the appearance of the first romances. Before 1150, the troubadours composed songs that referred to many Arthurian characters. Arthur, Gawain, and others are mentioned, but Tristan, with twenty-seven occurrences, was the most popular of all: as the model of the lover consumed by his passion, he set a standard against which all others could be measured.

From the late Middle Ages onward, folksongs in English, Gaelic, and other languages featured Arthurian subjects. As with the troubadour lyrics mentioned above, these songs often made passing references to characters from Arthurian legend and sometimes used them as the butt of satire or comedy. Yet the very presence of Arthurian names—Arthur himself, Merlin, Lancelot, and others—in folksongs gives evidence of the persistent popularity of the legend.

Until the nineteenth century, however, more substantial musical compositions inspired by Arthurian themes were rare; the earliest significant example is *King Arthur, or the British Worthy* (1691), a masque or semiopera

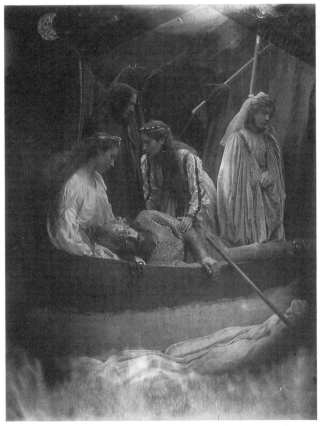

Julia Margaret Cameron, photograph, So Like a Shattered Column Lay the King, *from Tennyson (1875). Courtesy of The J. Paul Getty Museum, Santa Monica, California.*

composed by Henry Purcell (1659–95) on a text by John Dryden, with dances arranged by Josiah Priest. The value of this work lies mainly in the music, as scholars generally agree that Dryden's genius is not much in evidence. Although *King Arthur* is occasionally revived and usually receives reserved praise, some critics have condemned the work as extravagant and derivative.

In 1733, Thomas Arne (1710–78) presented a burlesque entitled *The Opera of Operas, or Tom Thumb the Great*, with libretto by Eliza Haywood after Henry Fielding. Later the same year, the work was reduced in scope and presented again, with new music composed by John Frederick Lampe (1703–51).

Merlin is the subject of several musical works or masques from the eighteenth century. Examples are the vocal portion of a 1734 "entertainment call'd Merlin; or, the devil of Stone-Henge," by Lewis Theobald (1688–1744) and a "dramatic opera" entitled *Merlin: or the British Inchanter*, dating from 1736 and reputedly written by William Giffard. Aaron Hill is the author of a 1760 masque entitled *Merlin in Love, or: Youth Against Magic*. This composition, which includes recitatives and twenty-five airs, has Merlin using his magic to steal Columbine from Harlequin; at the end the lovers are reunited, and Columbine uses Merlin's wand to transform him into an ass. Such works generally have no association with Arthurian legend beyond the presence of Merlin, described by Hill as "a conjurer, with his wand, long beard, and trailing robe."

OPERA

During the nineteenth and twentieth centuries, well over forty operas were devoted to Arthurian subjects, by composers major and minor. A number of Arthurian operas, now little more than footnotes in music history, are rarely or never performed. This group includes works by such composers as Isaac Albéniz, Joseph Parry, Amadeo Vives, Augusta Holmes, Thomas S. Cooke, Colin McAlpin, Paul Dessau, M.W.C. Vogrich, L.A. Bourgault-Ducoudray, Frederick Corder, and numerous others. Most of the operas deal with Arthur or the Arthurian story in general; several treat Merlin, while others (e.g., the 1916 *Lanzelot und Elaine*, by Walter Bergh, with libretto by Walter Couvoisier) focus on Lancelot and one, by H.T. Pringuer, takes as its subject *Guinevere, or Love Laughs at Law*. Composers have given us also masques, "entertainments," and operettas, including several that are based on Walter Scott's *The Bridal of Triermain*. Settings of Scott's work include J.L. Ellerton's 1831 *The Bridal of Triermain* and Thomas Simpson Cooke's 1834 entertainment (sometimes identified as an opera) *King Arthur and the Knights of the Round Table.* Scott's text would also provide the subject and the title of an 1886 composition by Frederick Corder, for soloists, chorus, and orchestra.

In addition to such works, most of them of limited interest, a number of opera projects were abandoned or left incomplete. We have only fragments of the music for an Arthurian opera planned by Sir Arthur Sullivan. Isaac Albéniz (1860–1909) planned a *King Arthur* opera trilogy, but only the first of the operas (*Merlin*, 1900, published 1906; libretto by F.B. Money-Coutts) was completed, and it was never performed; *Lancelot* was left uncompleted, and *Guinevere* was not composed.

Even less remains from one of the most intriguing Arthurian projects: the proposed opera by Claude Debussy (1862–1918). Because he objected to Wagner's treatment of the Tristan legend, Debussy eagerly accepted an invitation to write an opera or "lyrical drama" on the subject *Le Roman de Tristan*, with libretto by Gabriel Mourey (1865–1943), who adapted it from Joseph Bédier. Their collaboration was announced in 1907, but the opera scarcely progressed beyond the planning stage, and there now exists only a twelve-measure sample of the music.

In other cases, we have a complete libretto but no music. In 1816–17, Carl Franz Van der Velde (1749–1824) wrote a libretto entitled *Der Zaubermantel* ("The Magic Mantle"), in which Arthur is presented as an ineffectual and long-suffering husband. Owing, perhaps, both to the unflattering portrait of Arthur and to the librettist's social views (including an obvious disdain for the aristocracy), the text never found a composer.

RICHARD WAGNER
The great name in Arthurian opera is Richard Wagner (1813–83). During his youth, Wagner was more interested in poetry and drama than in music. He spent his early years moving (Leipzig to Dresden to Magdeburg to Riga to Paris and back to Dresden, all before the age of thirty), developing his talents and his awakening musical vocation, and generally meeting with professional frustration. This period of his life ended with *Tannhäuser* (1845) and *Lohengrin* (1848, performed 1850). The next phase was even more dramatic. He met with increasing musical success, but his involvement in the 1848 revolution (an effort to promote a unified Germany) resulted in a lengthy exile in Zurich, during which he composed most of *Tristan und Isolde.* Throughout this period, and in fact for much of his life, his ambition and his romantic entanglements made him enemies and created jealousies; he was hounded by financial problems until King Ludwig of Bavaria

offered his continued patronage. The final period of his life consisted of productive but often troubled years, especially in Munich and Bayreuth, during which he composed *Die Meistersinger von Nürnberg*, *Der Ring des Nibelungen*, and *Parsifal*. He died in 1883.

The traditional term "opera" is scarcely applicable to Wagner's compositions after 1845, including his two greatest works treating Arthurian subjects, *Tristan und Isolde* and *Parsifal*. The composer himself considered them "musical dramas" rather than operas. To him, the drama was paramount; melody and all other aspects of the presentation existed to support the drama. One result was that Wagner often used singers orchestrally and the orchestra melodically. Moreover, he abandoned the distinction between recitative and aria, creating what he called "endless melody," an uninterrupted development from the Prelude to the end of an act; into this development are woven striking leitmotifs (reminiscences in the form of repeated musical phrases that are associated with particular themes, characters, or dramatic moments). In the process, he revolutionized opera.

Three of Wagner's works are of interest here. *Lohengrin*, the last of his true operas in the conventional Romantic sense of the word, is the least significant for its treatment of Arthurian themes. Lohengrin, the son of Parsifal, is a Grail guardian, and although a Grail theme recurs through the work, Lohengrin's role is explained only late in the opera, when, ignoring the requirement that a Grail knight's identity remain secret, he reveals his ancestry and the fact that he has been sent by the Grail.

Tristan und Isolde (three acts; first presented 1865) is one of Wagner's greatest operas. Condensing the work of Gottfried in order to concentrate on the core of the drama, Wagner illustrates the destructive power of passion. The work begins with Tristan's mission to Ireland to bring back Isolde as a bride for Mark; Wagner includes the love potion, the betrayal of the lovers by Melot (a single adversary, replacing the traditional group of enemies, who mortally wounds Tristan), and Tristan's departure for Brittany. Mark learns of the love potion and forgives Tristan and Isolde; he brings Isolde to find her lover, but Tristan dies as she arrives, and she quickly follows him in death.

In *Tristan und Isolde*, the Prelude is built on a short theme that represents both longing and suffering. This theme recurs in various forms through the opera, recalling and frequently foreshadowing the events of the unfolding tragedy. Beginning with the Prelude, Wagner resists resolutions, permitting dissonances to resolve only into other dissonances. The Prelude leads directly, without cadence, into the beginning of the action, postponing resolution until the final notes of the act. The same is true of the other acts. The result of this instability or tonal ambiguity is a constant expectancy and a level of tension that allow no release, musical or emotional, until the end.

The magnificent "Liebestod" that concludes the opera is one of the most beautiful and moving love songs in opera. A short theme recurs again and again through a prolonged series of rising modulations; at the same time, a great crescendo, born almost at the beginning of the song, builds to an intense peak just prior to Isolde's death, which is followed by a brief and serene conclusion—a resolution at long last—including an echo of the longing theme heard at the beginning of the Prelude. Tristan and Isolde are united in love and death, and the very first notes of the opera are finally given a conclusion.

Parsifal, Wagner's *Bühnenweihfestspiel*, or "sacred festival stage play," is in many ways the culmination of all his work. He had completed the text much earlier but began the music in 1878, finally producing the opera in 1882, a year before his death. The drama is heavily dependent on the music. It is a work of religious and mystic ritual, and the ritual and music are intimately linked, to the frequent disadvantage of the text. In *Tristan und Isolde*, at least after the first act, the lyrics often cease to be intelligible, either because characters simultaneously sing different words or because vowel sounds are extended until their sense is lost and the musical tones supplant verbal meaning. More accurately, in light of Wagner's theory of *Gesamtkunstwerk* (literally, "total work of art"), the music and words are united in a single unit. In *Parsifal*, the theory holds, but in practice the tendencies expressed in the earlier opera are carried nearly to their logical conclusion: the libretto is unusually short, and yet a performance of the opera lasts more than four hours. Music, ritual, and pageantry fill the stage, as long scenes of baptism, anointment, beguilement, and gatherings of the Grail fellowship are supported by extended musical expositions, often without any dialogue at all.

Wagner set out to compose a work that would be not only a great musical drama but also a work of mythic or allegorical dimensions. In so doing, he condensed Wolfram von Eschenbach's work, as he had condensed Gottfried's for *Tristan und Isolde*. The wounded Amfortas, who represents suffering humanity, can be cured only by a "guileless fool" or "pure fool," Parsifal, whose simplicity is more a matter of purity and sinlessness than of stupidity. Resisting the blandishments of Kundry, Parsifal recovers the sacred spear with which Amfortas had been wounded. He joins the Grail fellowship, becomes its head, and, through his examples and sacrifices, brings about Kundry's baptism.

Like *Tristan und Isolde*, *Parsifal* is an extremely chromatic opera. The tonal center seems to shift constantly, providing few moments of rest or resolution. Amid the shifts and deceptive cadences, the few passages that offer a sense of stability are related to the Grail or the Grail fellowship. Wagner uses the familiar Dresden "Amen" as the Grail motif, repeated frequently to provide momentary sensations of peace or tranquility; however, an unsettling effect is created by his use of this motif to lead not to a true resolution but into a newly chromatic development.

Parsifal has often been criticized for pretention and excessive sentimentality. Yet, although it is uneven, the best passages offer music of unparalleled beauty and majesty. One of the clearest examples of Wagner's undiminished power is the sublime lyricism of the "Good Friday music" (or *Karfreitagszauber*, "Good Friday Spell"), which depicts Parsifal's reawakening and his understanding that the beauty of nature is linked to the spiritual redemption of humankind. If the mysticism of the revelation—that nature is reborn from dew representing the tears of repentant sinners—is overly romanticized, the music itself is unsurpassed.

OPERA AFTER WAGNER

Following Wagner, several German composers wrote Arthurian operas, although in some cases their sources were not medieval but modern. An influential literary composition was Karl Immermann's play *Merlin* (1832), which served as the inspiration for Karl Goldmark's (Austro-Hungarian, 1830–1915) opera *Merlin* (1886, revised 1904) and Felix August Bernhard Draeseke's (German, 1835–1913) opera of the same title (1903–05, first performed 1913).

Ernest Chausson (1855–99), to whom we also owe the tone poem *Viviane*, was the French composer and librettist of *Le Roi Arthus*, written in emulation of Wagner's *Tristan und Isolde* and described by one critic, with understatement, as "somewhat Wagnerian." Written in 1895 but not performed until 1903, it deals with Lancelot's love for Guinevere (a parallel to that of Tristan and Isolde) and with Mordred's betrayal of Arthur.

Opera composers continue to draw on Arthurian subjects. Recent examples include Richard Blackford's *Gawain and the Green Knight* (1978–79) and two Tristan operas: New Zealand composer Gillian Whitehead's *Tristan and Isolt* (first performance 1978) and Timothy Porter's *Trystan and Essylt* (1980). A children's opera on the theme of the Loathly Lady, *Gawain and Ragnell*, was composed by Richard Blackford (1984); and Iain Hamilton's *Lancelot*, concerning the love of Lancelot and Guinevere, was presented in 1985. In 1991, Sir Harrison Birtwistle's operatic version of *Sir Gawain and the Green Knight* (with libretto by David Harsent) premiered at Covent Garden and received generally favorable reviews.

BALLET

Arthurian ballets were popular in France since the seventeenth century, and the most common subject was Merlin. Of the modern ballets inspired by Arthurian themes, however, the most popular subject, doubtless because of the possibilities offered by a love that is both fated and fatal, is Tristan. Ballets devoted to Tristan include Leonid Massin's *Mad Tristan* (1944), Herbert Ross's *Tristan* (1958), and the *Tristan* created in Berlin in 1965 by Boris Blacher and Tatjana Gsovsky. Arthurian subjects other than the story of Tristan and Iseut attracted French choreographer Maurice Béjart (*Les Vainqueurs*, "The Conquerors," 1969), John Neumeier (*König Artus*, 1982), and English choreographer Frederick Ashton (*The Lady of Shalott* [1931] and *Picnic at Tintagel* [1952]).

ChORAL AND INSTRUMENTAL MUSIC

Throughout most of the nineteenth century, Arthurian music was dominated by opera, and the twentieth century has continued to cultivate that form. Since late in the last century, however, composers of nonoperatic works have regularly treated Arthurian themes, in a variety of choral and instrumental forms. Beginning with such works as Ernest Chausson's 1882 symphonic poem *Viviane* and Anton Averkamp's symphonic ballad *Elaine and Lancelot* (1901) and continuing to the present, the appeal of Arthuriana has proved pervasive. Early in the present century, French composer Olivier Messiaen's Opus 1 (unpublished; for piano) was Arthurian: it was *La Dame de Shalott*, composed in 1917, when he was nine.

The number of Arthurian compositions is impressive, and few generalizations can be made beyond the fact that the stories of Merlin and Vivian and of Tristan and Iseut appear more popular than those of Lancelot and Guinevere, Arthur himself, or the Grail. The following paragraphs will try only to give an idea of the diversity and the continuing attraction of composers to Arthurian themes.

Henry Hadley (1871–1937), a prominent American conductor, composed *Merlin and Vivian: A Lyric Drama* around 1903 (it was published in 1970); this work, for chorus, soloists, and orchestra, takes as its text an unimpressive poem by Ethel Watts Mumford. In three parts (set in the "fairy isle" of Avalon, in Arthur's court, and in Castle Joyousguard), it depicts the entrapment of Merlin by Vivian, who, acting under orders from

Morgan-le-Fay, offers the magician a potion that saps his strength and imprisons him forever.

One of the most ambitious Arthurian projects in recent music is Rutland Boughton's (English, 1878–1960) cycle of choral dramas or oratorios (which are sometimes considered operas). Only the earlier parts of the cycle were ever presented, and the music remains unpublished. Composed over almost thirty-five years (1911–45), the work consists of five parts: *The Birth of Arthur*, *The Round Table*, *The Lily Maid* (Elaine and Lancelot), *Galahad*, and *Avalon*. Boughton also wrote choral music on Arthurian subjects: *Chapel in Lyonesse* (1905, for three voices, piano, and strings) and *King Arthur Had Three Sons*. Boughton also composed *The Queen of Cornwall*, an opera, which has occasionally been revived and presented, based on Thomas Hardy's play of the same title.

Arnold Bax (English, 1883–1953) was the composer of *Tintagel: A Symphonic Poem* (first performed 1917). This work, beginning with fanfare motifs, moves into a development featuring a quotation from *Tristan* that is then elaborated and finally restated in the conclusion.

Brian Hooker, in 1915, devoted an oratorio to the subject of *Morven and the Grail* (music by Horatio Parker). A better-known oratorio—it is occasionally performed or recorded today—is Swiss composer Frank Martin's *Le Vin herbé* ("The Potion," completed 1940), inspired by Joseph Bédier's reconstruction of the Tristan story. Using a choir of twelve, a small string orchestra, and piano, the composition relates the story of the two lovers; the title refers to the magic potion that first united them in a passionate and eventually fatal love. The year of Martin's work, 1940, also saw the first performance of another oratorio, or choral symphonic poem, American composer Elinor Remick Warren's *The Passing of King Arthur*. Composed for soloists, chorus, and orchestra, it is based on the final sections of Tennyson's *Idylls of the King* and is characterized by an interplay of thematic motifs associated with Arthur, Excalibur, the three queens, and other characters and events.

Other compositions throughout the century include orchestral works, by Guy Ropartz (*La Chasse du Prince Arthur*, symphonic studies, 1912); incidental music to plays or films, by Sir Arthur Sullivan (incidental music for J. Comyns Carr's *King Arthur*, 1895), Edward Elgar (incidental music to a play by Laurence Binyon, 1923), Paul Ladmirault (music for the *Tristan et Iseut* of Bédier and Artus, 1929), Benjamin Britten (incidental music for *The Sword in the Stone*, a 1938 radio play adapted from T.H. White's work by Marianne Helwig), Georges Auric (music for Cocteau's 1943 film *L'Eternel Retour*); works for piano and orchestra, by Hans Werner Henze (*Tristan:*

Prelude für klavier tonbänder und orchester, 1973); and compositions for other instruments, such as Niek Scheps's 1984 composition *The Grail*, for harp and piano, inspired by Chrétien and Wolfram von Eschenbach.

Many compositions use Arthurian themes or allusions as part of a larger mythology. For example, *Mor-Bihan*, a 1994 oratorio with French text by Patrick Jackson-Röhrer and music by Christophe Guyard, celebrates the history and legends of the Gulf of Morbihan in Brittany. It concludes by evoking Viviane and Brocéliande, the quest for the "celestial Grail," and the "mystical ecstasy" of Arthur.

MUSICALS

Several stage or film musicals have been based on Arthurian subjects. The best known is *Camelot*, the 1960 Broadway play based on T.H. White's *The Once and Future King*. The music is by Frederick Loewe, the libretto by Alan Jay Lerner. The early portions of the play are dominated by a light musical-comedy tone that, for some tastes, trivializes Camelot and the Arthurian legend; toward the end, however, the emphasis shifts to the tragedy of an aging and almost despairing Arthur and to the love of Lancelot and Guinevere, which has caused Camelot to crumble. A film version of the play appeared in 1967. White's work was also the source of a radio play, *The Sword in the Stone*, by Marianne Helwig with music by Benjamin Britten, broadcast in London in 1938; lost during the war, the music was rediscovered and rebroadcast in 1952.

Mark Twain's *A Connecticut Yankee in King Arthur's Court* inspired two musical interpretations. The first, *A Connecticut Yankee*, was the work (ca. 1927) of Richard Rodgers and Lorenz Hart. The second, a 1949 movie starring Bing Crosby (see below), is a slight musical version with little to commend it.

Of more serious intent is *Merlin oder das wüste Land* ("Merlin or the Waste Land," 1984), a "semimusical" production of Tankred Dorst's drama of the same title (see above), in which Merlin's hope of reforming the world is frustrated. Other musicals have featured Merlin as well; an example is a 1983 "Magical Musical" entitled *Merlin*, with music by Elmer Bernstein.

POPULAR MUSIC

In the imprecise category of "popular music," Arthurian themes have proven generally unproductive, being limited for the most part to incidental references to an Arthurian character, motif, or place, especially Merlin, Avalon, and the Holy Grail. There are however several notable exceptions to this tendency. One is Rick Wakeman's 1975 *The Myths and Legends of*

King Arthur and the Knights of the Round Table (A&M Records). The seven sections of this ambitious composition treat Arthur (including the sword in the anvil), Lady of the Lake, Guinevere, Sir Lancelot and the Black Knight, Merlin the Magician, Sir Galahad, and the Last Battle. The composition, with words and music by Wakeman, uses band, orchestra, choir, synthesizer, rhythm section, and narrations; it effectively mixes and juxtaposes varied styles, from the most traditional choral harmonies to the sounds and rhythms of early rock musicals. That portions of it sound seriously dated after two decades does not detract from its position as one of the most significant Arthurian efforts in popular music.

Other Arthurian compositions include *King Arthur, Poem for Piano*, by Mikhael (Edelweiss, 1989); among the nine parts of this work are "Guinevere's Theme," "Way to Avalon," and "The Holy Grail." The following year gave us a six-part *Excalibur* by Medwyn Goodall (New World, 1990), followed in 1991 by Alan Stivell's *The Mist of Avalon* (Dreyfus).

Although these pages are intended to give an indication of the quantity and diversity of music treating Arthuriana within the last two centuries, much has been omitted, particularly in the area of opera. Even so, the number of composers, musical forms, and media provides impressive evidence of the musical potential of the Arthurian legends, and if some compositions are naturally mediocre or worse, others have more durable appeal, and a number of them, Wagner's works in particular, are immortal works of art.

fILm

BRITISh AND AMERICAN fILm

Arthurian subjects have provided material for the movies since Edwin Porter's *Parsifal* in 1904. There have been dozens of Arthurian films, and many have achieved reasonable box-office success. However, no more than a handful have won wide critical praise, and that fact dramatically illustrates the problems inherent in the filmic interpretation of a legend as extensive and rich as that of Arthur.

Following Porter's innovation, an American film on *Lancelot and Elaine* appeared in 1910. That in turn was followed by the first of three versions of Mark Twain's *A Connecticut Yankee in King Arthur's Court*. The 1921 silent film, starring Harry Myers, was entitled simply *A Connecticut Yankee*, as was the second (Fox, 1931), a spoof of Arthurian days, starring Will Rogers, Maureen O'Sullivan, and Myrna Loy and directed by David Butler. The third, *A Connecticut Yankee in King Arthur's Court*, was a 1949 musical version of the 1931 film, starring Bing Crosby and Rhonda Fleming (and Sir Cedric Hardwicke as a doddering but likable Arthur) and directed by Tay Garnett for Paramount.

British cinema indulged in comedy in the 1942 film *King Arthur Was a Gentleman*, directed by Marcel Varnel and starring Arthur Askey; the subject is a soldier who, thinking that he possesses Arthur's sword, becomes a hero.

Many films, especially from the United States, have taken great liberties with the legend in an effort to bring to the screen a sense of the swashbuckling adventures and the love intrigues of the Arthurian world. One of the first is *The Adventures of Sir Galahad*, a fifteen-part serial directed by Spencer Bennett (Columbia, 1949). This was soon followed by *Knights of the Round Table* (MGM, 1953, directed by Richard Thorpe), which cast Robert Taylor as Lancelot and Ava Gardner as Guinevere, in a film that, though colorful, quickly becomes more tedious than moving. It is notable, however, for its departure from tradition, as it has Lancelot return to defeat Mordred.

The Black Knight (Warwick, 1954) was directed by Tay Garnett (who had also directed the 1949 *Connecticut Yankee*); this film, memorable only for the unintentional comedy some viewers find in it, pits a swordmaker (played by Alan Ladd) against King Mark. The same year saw the release of *Prince Valiant* (Fox), directed by Henry Hathaway and based on the Hal Foster comic strip.

The following decade gave us *Sword of Lancelot* (Emblem, 1962; British title *Lancelot and Guenevere*), directed by Cornel Wilde. It concentrates on Lancelot's desire for Guenevere and the frustration of that desire when, after Arthur's death, she enters a convent. *Siege of the Saxons* (1963, directed by Nathan Juran) traces a Saxon plot to overthrow Arthur. More ambitious and artistically successful than either of these is Bruce Baillie's lyrical film *To Parsifal* (1963). Transposing the Grail myth into a technological world, Baillie treats it indirectly (the notion of a wounded Fisher King being evoked, for example, by a fish cut with a knife). The film, divided into two sections representing sterility and regeneration, features music from Wagner's *Parsifal*.

Walt Disney's *The Sword in the Stone* dates from the same year (1963). Directed by Wolfgang Reitherman, this film, offering examples of outstanding animation, is based on the first volume of T.H. White's *The Once and Future King*. Large portions depict the young Arthur's early education by Merlin; for the most part, the Arthurian legend simply provides a framework for long, fanciful action sequences, as Merlin transforms Arthur into a fish, a squirrel, and a bird. The final climactic scenes show the youth drawing the sword from the anvil and reluctantly accepting the crown.

Disney also used the Arthurian legend in various cartoons and in an amusing 1979 comedy unfortunately titled *Unidentified Flying Oddball* (British title *The Spaceman and King Arthur*). This film, directed by Russ Mayberry and starring Dennis Dugan, is an updating of *A Connecticut Yankee*, in which an astronaut and his robot land at Arthur's court.

Camelot, directed by Joshua Logan (Warner, 1967), is a film version of the Lerner and Loewe musical, itself based on T.H. White's *The Once and Future King*. Starring Richard Harris and Vanessa Redgrave, *Camelot* is a pleasant diversion and a colorful if unsubstantial evocation of a Camelot of the High Middle Ages. The lavish film begins slowly but eventually creates a degree of drama by concentrating on the tragic effects of Lancelot's and Guinevere's love. Although not a distinguished film, it is redeemed at the end by an effective depiction of Arthur's grief for the collapse of his realm, a grief lightened by his final realization that the ideal will be remembered even though the reality has failed.

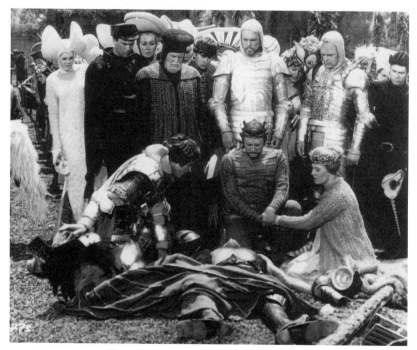

From the film Camelot, *Joshua Logan (1967).*

The 1975 film *King Arthur: The Young Warlord* (Heritage Enterprises; directed by Peter Hayers, Patrick Jackson, and Peter Sasdy, with music by Elmer Bernstein) resists the temptation to update Arthur to the High Middle Ages. Instead, it attempts (effectively in a brief prologue and ploddingly thereafter) to depict the conditions of life and the political fragmentation in post-Roman Britain. It concentrates on Arthur's dream of unification and on the obstacles, such as the ruthlessness and ambition of various tribal chieftains, opposing that dream. In an effort to balance the emphasis on politics and wars, it also includes a treatment of Arthur's love interest—in Rowena, not Guinevere.

The story of Sir Gawain and the Green Knight has been brought to the screen twice, with Stephen Weeks directing both times. The first, *Gawain and the Green Knight* (1972), was hardly memorable, and the 1982 remake, entitled *Sword of the Valiant* (a Golan-Globus film featuring Miles O'Keeffe as Gawain and Sean Connery as the Green Knight), was no improvement. Only the opening sequence and, to a much lesser extent, the last one will identify this story as *Sir Gawain and the Green Knight*. The events at Bercilak's castle, including the temptations of Gawain, have been omitted, and to the skeletal story of the beheading game is added a riddle that Gawain must solve if he is to save his head. The events that flesh out the story include a sequence (similar to the story of Chrétien de Troyes's Yvain) involving Gawain's killing of a land's defender and his subsequent protection by a maiden (Linet) with a magic ring capable of rendering its wearer invisible. Unlike the situation in *Yvain*, however, Gawain falls in love not with his victim's widow but with Linet.

The year 1979 saw a lifeless and rarely seen adaptation of the Tristan and Iseut story; *Lovespell* was directed by Tom Donovan and starred Richard Burton (as Mark), Kate Mulgrew, and Nicholas Clay. Critics generally condemned the screenplay, the direction, and the very conception and adaptation of the tale.

For some tastes, the most successful of the Arthurian films in English is *Excalibur* (C.L.C., 1981); others criticize it for attempting, with uneven results, to do too much. Director John Boorman has tried to tell the full Arthurian story, from Uther's reign to Arthur's death; as a result, the screenplay, by Boorman and Rospo Pallenberg, takes some liberties with its putative source (Malory) and necessarily deals perfunctorily, and occasionally confusingly, with a good many characters and sequences. Nonetheless, *Excalibur* is notable for the spectacular cinematography by Alex Thompson and the effective use of music by Carl Orff and Wagner, along with original compositions by Trevor Jones.

From the film Excalibur, *John Boorman (1981).*

From the film Monty Python and the Holy Grail, *Terry Gilliam and Terry Jones (1975).*

In a class by itself, *Monty Python and the Holy Grail* (1975; directed by Terry Gilliam and Terry Jones) may best be described as inspired silliness. The comedians known collectively as Monty Python use the Grail Quest as a thin pretext for extended humorous sketches, including such absurdities as the attack of the Killer Rabbit. The film demonstrates an acquaintance (mostly through Malory) with Arthurian conventions and characters but develops them in a decidedly original way, as a framework for physical comedy, puns, anachronisms, and parodies of film conventions. The result, a masterpiece of cinematic humor, is a striking indication of the adaptability of Arthurian themes.

Four American efforts, none of them an actual retelling of the Arthurian story, suggest the cinematic possibilities of films in which the Arthurian element serves as a structuring device. *Knightriders*, a 1981 film by George Romero, involves a troupe that recreates Arthurian jousts on motorcycles at fairs and festivals. The characters adopt Arthurian personas and find themselves prey both to tensions within the group and to attacks from without. *The Natural* (1984), a screen version of Malamud's novel (see p. 184), directed by Barry Levinson and provided with a new ending, offers effective and in some cases subtle echoes of the Perceval/Parzival story. *The Fisher King* (1991, director, Terry Gilliam, screenplay by Richard LaGravenese) is a story of mutual redemption in which a "Fisher King"

From the film Knightriders, *George A. Romero (1981).*

figure, while being saved himself, saves the man who caused his wife's death. The Fisher King story is intricately and sometimes explicitly woven into the film, as is the quest for a Grail that ironically turns out to be a simple trophy.

Whereas the Arthurian inspiration of *The Fisher King* is undeniable, *Indiana Jones and the Last Crusade* is a film that Arthurian purists might well dismiss as marginal or trivial. The Grail appears to be a mere pretext for swashbuckling adventures, and the film is indeed intended solely for mass entertainment. Nonetheless, the Grail lore included in it is sufficiently prominent that Arthurians should perhaps not neglect it entirely. In addition, the notion of a Nazi quest for the Grail has historical antecedents that also provide the background of Pierre Benoit's novel *Montsalvat* (see p. 144).

Closer to a retelling, though a partial and strikingly unsuccessful one, is *First Knight* (1995, directed by Jerry Zucker). This disappointing film concentrates squarely on the Lancelot-Guinevere-Arthur triangle but replaces adultery by a single kiss that would have destroyed the realm were it not for Arthur's magnanimity. Missing are other traditional elements of the story, such as the Grail and the character of Merlin. Missing also are the basic spirit and appeal of the Arthurian legend.

The 1990s have also given us several other films, of widely disparate approach and quality. *Outside Time* (1991, directed by Sion Humphreys), is a four-part dramatization, for television, of stories from the *Mabinogi*. Paul Hunt's 1992 *Merlin* (British title *October 32*) is a slight effort about the reincarnation of Merlin's daughter and Mordred's son. Richard Kurti, in 1994, gave us *Seaview Knights*, concerning a man who believes he is Arthur, come to save England. During the same year, *Guinevere* (directed by Jud Taylor) presented a nontraditional queen to television viewers. Finally, in 1995, Canadian director Robert Tinnell directed *Kids of the Round Table*, a film for younger audiences; in this effort, the eleven-year-old hero discovers Excalibur and enlists the aid of Merlin to thwart an attempted robbery.

FRENCH FILM

The French have made several outstanding films on Arthurian subjects, beginning with Jean Cocteau's 1943 *L'Eternel Retour*, an ingenious transposition of the Tristan and Iseut story (directed by Jean Delannoy, featuring Jean Marais and Madeleine Sologne) into the twentieth century. In his original retelling of the lovers' story, *Tristan et Iseult* (1972), Yvan Lagrange uses little dialogue but creates a powerful effect with a combination of electronic music and arresting visual images.

From the film Lancelot du Lac, *Robert Bresson (1974).*

The most controversial of the French Arthurian films is Robert Bresson's *Lancelot du Lac* (1974), whose admirers and detractors are equally passionate. This film explores the conflict within Lancelot, torn between his love for Guinevere and his obligation to Arthur. Bresson's directorial style is best described as elliptical: he frequently evokes the power and confusion of battle, not, as most directors do, by a fast montage of combat scenes or by a wide-angle shot, but simply by showing two swords striking each other or by focusing on a warhorse's rump or legs. Such ellipsis and Bresson's eccentric camera angles strike some viewers as sterile and self-conscious, while others see the film as an original and powerful retelling of the Lancelot story. *Lancelot du Lac* won the 1974 International Critics' Prize.

Eric Rohmer directed *Perceval le Gallois* (1978), in which Chrétien de Troyes's last romance is faithfully brought to the screen, with Fabrice Luchini as Perceval. This beautifully stylized film uses obviously artificial two-dimensional props (trees and buildings) to create an effect similar to that of a medieval miniature. The characters provide both dialogue and narration, occasionally announcing, as though in the author's voice, the direction the story is to take. *Perceval le Gallois* includes all the major events of the Perceval story from Chrétien de Troyes, but only the initial adventures of Gauvain;

From the film Perceval le Gallois, *Eric Rohmer (1978).*

Rohmer adds to Chrétien's text a concluding sequence in Latin, depicting the stations of the Cross and the Crucifixion. The film raises a serious question about whether an entirely faithful transposition from literary text to screen can ever be successful; this is a question that a good many film lovers, but by no means all, answer emphatically in the affirmative.

In 1990, Denis Llorca released his *Chevaliers de la Table Ronde* ("Knights of the Round Table"), a four-hour film of his eleven-hour theatrical presentation (1986) concerning events ranging from Merlin's birth and the founding of the Round Table to Galahad's final triumph. The critical and popular reception of the film was unenthusiastic.

GERMAN FILM

Veith von Fürstenberg made *Feuer und Schwert—Die Legende von Tristan und Isolde* ("Fire and Sword—The Legend of Tristan and Isolde") in 1981. He reinterprets some aspects of the legend; for example, he has Isolde carefully plan the love-potion scene, rather than cause the lovers to drink the potion by mistake.

The Parzival/Parsifal story has been filmed twice by German directors but from different sources and with widely different results. In 1980, Richard Blank directed a television movie of Wolfram's *Parzival.* Two years later, Hans-Jürgen Syberberg, who had used Wagnerian music and reminiscences in his *Hitler,* also made a remarkable four-hour film of *Parsifal.* This work, the last film in the cycle he called *Der Gral*, is an original exploration of Wagner's opera in which two actors, one male and one female, play the role of Parsifal and in which the production emphasizes the inevitable artifice of opera by using puppets at times, by choosing not to disguise the stage machinery, and by sometimes using as a set an enormous model of the composer's death mask. The soundtrack is an excellent recording made by the Monte Carlo Philharmonic, conducted by Armin Jordan.

RADIO AND TELEVISION

The 1930s saw the production of a number of Arthurian radio dramas in Britain, including a 1931 adaptation of *Sir Gawain and the Green Knight* by William Ford Manley. Other examples from the period include Stanley Baird Reed's series of nine programs collectively entitled *Merlin, Maestro of Magic* (1932) and David Taylor's *King Arthur and the Knights of the Round Table* (1933). At the end of the following decade, Ben Aycrigg presented Arthurian dramas entitled *In the Days of King Arthur* (1948), *Merlin the Magician* (1950), and *The Pursuit of Morgan le Fay* (1950). In 1953, the BBC Third Programme broadcast J.R.R. Tolkien's translation of *Sir Gawain and the Green Knight*, along with a talk by the translator. From periods when radio drama was taken seriously, these and similar efforts presented Arthurian (or, in some cases, mock Arthurian) themes to large numbers of listeners.

Arthurian themes have been used frequently in television, not only in the television films discussed above but also in a number of series and in a television version of Roger Zelazny's story "The Last Defender of Camelot" (1979). In the latter case, Lancelot and Morgan collaborate against Merlin in a modernized drama filmed as a segment of *Twilight Zone*. The story that is familiar from *A Connecticut Yankee in King Arthur's Court* has been updated several times, though never very effectively, on television. For example, the American series *McGyver* presented a two-part adaptation of the story in 1991–92.

Like the *Twilight Zone* presentation mentioned above, several television series from Britain and the United States have modernized aspects of the Arthurian story. A British series, *Raven*, evokes the "cave legend," according to which Arthur and his knights are sleeping in a cave and will one day rise again to save Britain; the series deals with a fictional conservation effort to save the cave. The 1970s BBC production of *The Changes* concentrates on Merlin's powers; and the magician was also the subject of an American television series entitled *Mr. Merlin*, in which the title character is reincarnated as a garage owner in California.

Three series, all British, resisted the temptation to update the legend for popular audiences. The first, dating from the 1950s, was *The Adventures of Sir Lancelot*, in which Lancelot performs various feats not based on the original legends. The other two series, from the 1970s, held more documentary and dramatic value. *Arthur of the Britons* offered a depiction of life in the Dark Ages, while the BBC's *The Legend of King Arthur* offered twelve episodes based on the traditional Arthurian story.

In addition, BBC1 offered in 1991 a telecast of six thirty-minute episodes of *Merlin and the Crystal Cave*, based on Mary Stewart's *The Crystal Cave*. This project, which depicts the childhood, youth, and maturity of Merlin, makes a more serious effort than do most television projects to offer an accurate evocation of the Arthurian period.

Finally, television has seen several animated series. Two of them were seen in 1992: *King Arthur and the Knights of Justice* concerns, not a Connecticut Yankee, but a Connecticut football team transported back to Arthurian times; and the Family Channel's *The Legend of Prince Valiant* featured characters drawn from Hal Foster's comic strip.

CONCLUSION

The present chapter is far from exhaustive. A full treatment of Arthur in the arts would require many times the space given the subject here—entire books have been devoted to it—and would involve the discussion of many hundreds of additional paintings and book illustrations, of composers of operas and other musical compositions, and of additional creators of commemorative plates, jewelry, comic strips, political cartoons, and virtually every other imaginable form. No secular legend has provided as much inspiration to painters, illustrators, composers, and filmmakers through the centuries as has the story of King Arthur and his court. The appeal of the legend has by no means run its course. The number and variety of artistic interpretations of the legend at the end of the twentieth century confirm the conclusions suggested by the number of recent novels, stories, and other literary treatments: the Arthurian legend, even after fifteen hundred years, is in full flower, and that flowering could as easily and as accurately be termed an explosion.

NOTES

(References are to the appropriate section of the Bibliography)
General
    Lacy et al., art. "Visual Arts, Arthurian Legend in" (by Debra N. Mancoff).
    Whitaker, passim.
Medieval Manuscripts
    Branner, passim.
    Lacy et al., art. "Manuscripts, Arthurian Illuminated" (sections by M. Alison
        Stones, Marilyn Stokstad, Muriel A. Whitaker, Lilian Armstrong).
    Loomis, pp. 86–144.
    Meiss, passim.
    Stokstad, pp. 285–88, 327–30.
    Whitaker, pp. 25–85.
Sculpture and Decorative Arts
    Fox-Friedman, passim.
    Stokstad, pp. 315–26.
    Whitaker, pp. 86–120.
Interior Decoration
    Lacy et al., art. "Murals (Medieval)" (by Marilyn Stokstad),
    Nickel, pp. 280–83.
    Whitaker, pp. 121–36.
Textiles
    Lacy, et al., art. "Tapestry" (by Marilyn Stokstad).
    Loomis, pp. 27–30, 38–40.
    Souchal, pp. 34–38.
Gothic Revival
    Mancoff (1990), pp. 3–64.
Painting (Modern)
    Christian, pp. 33–62.
    Faxon, pp. 13–39.
    Mancoff (1990), pp. 65–249.
    Mancoff (1995), passim.
    Tate Gallery, passim.
    Whitaker, pp. 317–31.
    Wildman, Stephen, passim.
Decorative Arts
    Banham and Harris, passim.
    Baumstark and Koch, "Die Gralswelt König Ludwig II" (by Michael Petzet).

Baumstark and Koch, "Das Viktorianische und der Gral" (by Debra N. Mancoff).

Book Illustration (Modern)

Casteras, 13–39.

Lacy et al., art. "Book Illustration (American)" and "Book Illustration (British)" (by Muriel A. Whitaker).

Mancoff (1990), pp. 250–74.

Muir, passim.

Photography

Gernsheim, esp. pp. 80–81, 178–79.

Music, Modern

Mancoff (1992), "Edward A. MacDowell and the Arthurian Twilight" (by Joe K. Law) and "Rutland Boughton's Arthurian Cycle" (by Michael Hurd).

Müller (1), pp. 366–74; (2), pp. 319–42; (3), pp. 438–43.

Richard Wagner

Baumstark and Koch, "Richard Wagner und der Gral," (by Oswald Georg Bauer).

Lacy et al., art. "Wagner, Richard" (by Frederick L. Toner).

Müller (4) pp. 479–502.

Newman, I, pp. 169–278 (*Tristan und Isolde*); II, pp. 635–724 (*Parsifal*).

Film

Harty, passim.

Lacy et al., art. "Films" (by Alice Grellner and Raymond Thompson).

Mancoff (1992), "The Body of the Hero in Robert Bresson's *Lancelot du Lac*" (by Julie F. Codell) and "Wagner, Spielberg, and the Issue of Jewish Appropriation" (by Martin B. Shichtman).

chapter v

Conclusion

The legend of King Arthur is our most pervasive and enduring secular myth. Out of a few facts, not all of them certain, grew a story elaborated in impressive detail and dimension, and it is apparent that the evolution of that story is not yet finished. The Arthurian Revival of the nineteenth century and the second one during the twentieth (especially since mid-century) both confirm the durability of the legend and offer remarkable examples of its potential for constant renewal and reinterpretation.

The revival also holds mysteries: Why this extraordinary appeal? Why now? And why mainly in English-speaking countries and more North American than British? Some answers, at least to the first of these questions, are obvious, even though they will only partially resolve the mystery. This legend attracts us by its combination of high seriousness and good fun. Accounts of Arthur traditionally incorporate a clear sense of moral direction and include an evocation of a past "golden age" when the world seemed to work as it was supposed to work, or at least, if it did not, Arthur had both the vision and the power to put it right. Yet those same accounts, by emphasizing action and love, fantasy and magic, have a basic narrative appeal. Arthurian literature is escapist literature in the best sense of the term; it consists simply, as Caxton noted in his preface to Malory, of "many joyous and playsaunt hystoryes."

To the notions of Arthurian glory and fantasy, we must add the attraction of thoroughly human emotions, relationships, and conflicts; the Arthurian legend (to quote Caxton again) explores "noble chyvalrye, curtosye, humanyte, frendlynesse, hardynesse, love, frendshyp, cowardyse, murdre, hate, vertue, and synne." Of particular interest to most readers are the romantic tragedies (the impossible loves of Tristan and Iseut and of Lancelot and Guinevere) and the greatest human tragedy, the ruin of Arthur's dream, brought about by forces that separate him from his wife and require him to go to war against his best friend and thereby destroy the Round Table.

Writers and readers alike are touched by this cruel irony of the Arthurian story: the fact that Arthur's honor and the system he instituted require him to undertake action that will undo that very system. Thus, the king who legendarily created a great civilization built on honor, justice, and high moral purpose can only accept the inevitability of its fate with sadness and resignation and lucidly set about implementing it. With the belief in Arthur's survival and predicted return, his story possesses a messianic dimension, but in a great many accounts the messiah is also profoundly human: at the end, as T.H. White poignantly observed, "he was only a man who had meant well."

An important fact favoring the popular appeal of the Arthurian legend is its essential versatility and "movability." We can, and often do, mold it to our own preferences, fantasies, or ideological concerns. We remake it in whatever image we wish, updating it to the High Middle Ages, the present, or even the future, or moving it back to the Dark Ages. Arthur could be adapted to political purposes: the Tudors and Stuarts used their supposed Arthurian lineage to solidify support for their thrones (see Merriman, Chapters 2–3), whereas in nineteenth-century France Arthur sometimes became the vehicle for attacks on unpopular political figures, and in the twentieth the Camelot legend was appropriated as a metaphor for an American presidency. Writers can treat Arthur in pseudo-history, historical fiction, romance, fantasy, or science fiction; the legend can support epic, tragedy, or melodrama; and it can be used as political or religious tract, psychological investigation, or feminist fiction.

Ultimately, the best explanation of the appeal of Arthur may lie in our very inability to explain it adequately. Arthur is not just legend and certainly not just a historical or pseudo-historical figure: his story, as suggested above, is myth. And it is in the nature of myth that, to a significant degree, our response to it occurs on an unconscious level: we remain aware of its power but unable to account rationally for it.

But if we cannot fully explain the Arthurian phenomenon, we can document it, and the preceding chapters have provided much of that documentation. What they may not have indicated as fully as they might is the extent to which the legend has flourished in folklore and permeated popular culture.

The most common beliefs about Arthur, discussed in Chapter I, concern predictions of his survival and return. Since the twelfth century, that theme has figured prominently in legends concerning the King. Transported to Avalon to be treated for his wounds, he is thought to be sleeping in a cave, inside a hill or under the sea, and when he is needed he will return. This belief was widely accepted well into the nineteenth century and, sporadically, into our own. A number of sites from Scotland to Cadbury to Sicily have been identified as the place where Arthur sleeps. There is also a competing belief, particularly in Somerset, that Arthur, having survived, was instead transformed into a raven.

Many other places have been associated with Arthur and Arthurian characters. The birthplaces of Merlin, Tristan, and others have been identified at locations throughout Britain and Brittany. Several hundred topographical features bear Arthurian names: Arthur's Seat, Arthur's Bed, Arthur's Chair, Arthur's Table; Merlin's Tree, Merlin's Rock, Merlin's Bridge, Merlin's Cave; the Tristan Stone; and so on.

The grip of Arthurian legend on the popular mind has led some enthusiasts to re-create aspects of the legend or of Arthurian themes. Beginning in the thirteenth century and continuing well beyond the Middle Ages, "Round Tables" proved to be popular events, as Arthurian devotees dressed in the appropriate costume to join in feasts, jousts, and dancing in imitation of the King and his knights. In some cases, the participants assumed the names and arms of Arthur's knights, and more elaborate Round Tables might even include a real castle built for the occasion.

Later expressions of the same spirit include "Merlin's Cave," described by Merriman (p. 79) as "an architectural whim . . . a queer combination of 'Gothic' windows and thatched roofs, including among its interior furnishings wax figures of Merlin and his scribe." Built at Richmond in 1735, Merlin's Cave immediately generated considerable controversy but also became the object of enthusiastic popular interest.

If the twentieth century does not have a Merlin's Cave, it has its own kind of Round Tables in clubs and societies and in such organizations as the Society for Creative Anachronism, which hold tourneys and other medievalized festivities. Arthur also flourishes in popular culture through comic strips, films and animated cartoons, toys and computer games. And the vogue of things Arthurian is dramatized, if trivialized, by the names of commercial enterprises everywhere: if Las Vegas is alone in boasting an Excalibur Hotel, almost every city offers other examples, such as King Arthur's Pub, Pendragon Jewelry, Camelot Cleaners, and the like.

What the future may hold for Arthur cannot easily be predicted. His popularity has waxed and waned in various places and times and for various reasons and will doubtless continue to do so. Yet the fundamental durability of a legend born almost fifteen centuries ago and still flourishing cannot ultimately be in doubt. The vitality of that legend in the twentieth century is extraordinary: more scholars than ever are examining Arthurian literature, art, and history; and writers, artists, and filmmakers are creating new Arthurian materials as actively as scholars are interpreting those that already exist.

It may well be that the present pace and the intensity of interest in Arthuriana cannot continue forever unabated; indeed, there can be no assurance that a future generation will not see King Arthur largely as the seventeenth century did: as material for nursery rhymes and fairy tales or as the object of minor antiquarian interest. Yet even should that happen, the legend will surely survive, as it has done until now, and we may safely take Arthur's designation as once *and future* king to be not only a hope, but also a prediction.

An Arthurian Glossary

ACCOLON Lover of Morgan le Fay. He appears first in a continuation of Robert de Boron's *Merlin* by an unknown hand, and Malory takes up his story. Morgan steals Excalibur and gives it to him, leaving a nonmagical replica to deceive Arthur, but the King recovers his sword and overthrows Accolon in combat.

AGNED Mountain or hill that was the scene of Arthur's eleventh victory over the Saxons, according to the *Historia Brittonum*. Its location is unknown. In a different context, Geoffrey of Monmouth identifies it with the Dolorous Mountain and says the Castle of Maidens stood on it. He seems to have Edinburgh's Castle Rock in mind. This is probably fancy, and there is no reason to think that the author of the *Historia* battle list also means Edinburgh.

One guess is that "Agned" is a product of scribal contraction and corruption, and that the name was correctly *Andegavum*, meaning Angers in Gaul, now France. There is rising ground hereabout, and a battle during the 460s resulted in the defeat of Saxon settlers along the Loire by Roman and Frankish troops. Britons were active in northwest Gaul at that time, as allies or auxiliaries of what was left of the Empire. Some reason exists for thinking that they took part in the battle, or, at any rate, that their descendants claimed they did.

Several manuscripts give "Breguoin" instead of "Agned," or in addition to it. Breguoin is probably Bremenium, the Roman fort of High Rochester in Northumberland. In Welsh poetry, it becomes Brewyn. Verses in praise of the Cumbrian king Urien refer to a battle fought during the late sixth century in the "cells of Brewyn," meaning the derelict rooms of the fort. Legend may have transferred this battle to Arthur.

AGRAVAIN Son of Lot and Morgause and brother of Gawain in the Vulgate Cycle and Malory. Supported by Mordred, he plays a leading part in the public exposure of the love affair between Lancelot and Guinevere. Lancelot kills him.

ALAIN Called Alain le Gros. The second Grail keeper, a son of Bron. He is one of the group by whom the Grail is conveyed to the remote West and given a resting place in the Vales of Avaron or Avalon, that is, central Somerset, the future location of Glastonbury Abbey. A "Fisher King" like Bron, Alain builds the castle of Corbenic. Although he is stated at first to be celibate, *Perlesvaus* and other texts make him the father of Perceval. They defy chronology, since they put the reign of Arthur only two generations from Joseph of Arimathea.

AMBROSIUS AURELIANUS The only fifth-century Briton whom Gildas names, and one of the few at any time whom he singles out for praise. Described as a Roman, a word probably implying a pro-imperial stance, Ambrosius was the son of important parents who died in the Saxon devastation. Perhaps in the 460s, after the Saxons in Britain had ceased raiding and withdrawn into their settlements, he launched a counteroffensive that led to a phase of fluctuating warfare. This rose to a climax in a British triumph at the siege of Mount Badon, about the year 500, which more or less stabilized the situation.

To judge from Gildas, if Ambrosius held any national status it was as a war leader only, possibly in the service of a high king whom Gildas ignores or knows nothing about. Confusingly, the *Historia Brittonum* gives him no such military role, offering instead a brief reference to Vortigern's being afraid of him and a much longer legend of his showing paranormal gifts as a boy before the same king, confounding the royal magicians. Later, the *Historia* refers to Ambrosius in a passing phrase as a king paramount over other rulers, but this too looks like legend, partly because it conflicts with Gildas, partly because in Welsh tradition Ambrosius is called "Emrys gwledig." The word *gwledig*, "land-holder" or "prince," implies in the post-Roman context a regional power only, founded on military command. Indeed, the *Historia Brittonum* almost admits as much by quoting the "Emrys gwledig" designation and saying that after the magical performance (said to have taken place in a hill-fort called Dinas Emrys to this day), Vortigern made Ambrosius overlord of Wales. Historically, however, a southern territory appears more likely. Notes appended to the *Historia* say he fought an opponent named Vitalinus at Wallop in Hampshire, seemingly in 437. If so, he can hardly have lived long enough to command throughout the Saxon war up to Badon itself.

It has been suggested that he had a hand in the pioneer British colonization of western Armorica, the first step toward its conversion into Brittany, but serious evidence is lacking. History goes no farther with him. Arthur is often linked with him as a relative or partner, perhaps a junior partner. This idea is found in William of Malmesbury but, although plausible, is not on record earlier. Geoffrey of Monmouth presents "King Aurelius Ambrosius" as Arthur's uncle and transfers the youthful wonder-working to Merlin.

AMESBURY Town in Wiltshire near the eastern edge of Salisbury Plain, not far from Stonehenge. In the Middle Ages, it had a monastery and a convent. Malory says Guinevere retired to the convent to end her days. Reputedly, a British religious community did exist here in early times, but if so the pagan Saxon conquest blotted it out and there was no continuity. The old form of the name, *Ambres-byrig*, may go back to a connection with Ambrosius Aurelianus. A late Welsh triad testifies to a belief that he founded the original British monastery. It is more likely, although still a matter of conjecture, that he stationed troops here and that the place was named after him as being the camp of Ambrosius's men, the *Ambrosiani*. Geoffrey of Monmouth calls the monastery's founder Ambrius, not Ambrosius, but his knowledge of the area is confused.

AMR Son of Arthur, cryptically alleged, in an appendix to the *Historia Brittonum*, to have been slain by him (see *Ercing*). The name is sometimes given as Anir. The Welsh romance *Geraint* mentions an Ambar son of Arthur, doubtless the same person, who is one of four squires attending the royal bedchamber. He is not even named first of the four. His unimportance suggests illegitimacy.

ANDRET Mark's nephew and cousin of Tristan, to whom he is hostile.

ANEIRIN North British bard, one of several named in the *Historia Brittonum*. He probably flourished in the sixth century and the early seventh. His chief composition is the *Gododdin*, a series of laments for the nobles who fell at Catraeth—probably Catterick in Yorkshire—in an ill-fated expedition against the Angles, about the year 600. Aneirin says that he accompanied the army himself and survived because of his fine songs. Passages have been added to the text, but his authentic work is a valuable specimen of old Welsh poetry, showing the sort of milieu in which the Arthur saga began to take shape. An allusion to Arthur himself, if it is not one of the additions, is the earliest known mention of him by name.

ANfORTAS In Wolfram's *Parzival*, the hero's uncle, the Grail King. Having failed in his sacred obligations, he has been stricken with a spear wound that can be healed only when Parzival questions him about it. Meanwhile, he is in constant pain, kept alive by the presence of the Grail. When Parzival first comes to the Grail Castle, he asks no questions and the visit is a failure. On a second visit, Parzival has learned compassion and does ask, and Anfortas is cured. Wagner spells the name "Amfortas" and makes the causes and nature of his sufferings more complex.

ANGLES, see *Saxons*

ANGUISĐ King of Ireland, the father of Iseut, Tristan's beloved. He demands tribute from Cornwall and sends his brother-in-law, Morholt, to enforce the demand in combat with a Cornish champion. Tristan accepts the challenge and kills Morholt. Anguish is the Irish Angus or Aengus. In the latter part of the fifth century, a King Angus ruled in Munster, a part of Ireland from which emigrants had been crossing to Wales and southwest England and founding colonies. Irish attempts to assert local dominance may underlie the tribute story.

ANIR, see *Amr*

ANNA Arthur's sister in Geoffrey of Monmouth. She is the second child born to Uther and Ygerna. Geoffrey's statements about her are inconsistent. First, he says that Uther gave her in marriage to King Lot of Lodonesia, that is, Lothian in Scotland. Elsewhere, he says that Lot's queen was a sister of Aurelius Ambrosius, Gawain and Mordred being their sons, and that Arthur's sister married King Budicius of Brittany.

These statements can be harmonized up to a point by supposing that Budicius's wife was another sister of Arthur who is not named and that Lot married twice, his first wife being Aurelius's sister and his second being Anna. In that case, Gawain and Mordred would be Anna's stepsons and Arthur's stepnephews. Geoffrey speaks of Lot as "mature in age" when he weds Anna, at a time when she is scarcely out of childhood herself, so that he might have had a previous wife. Even these guesses, however, lead to impossibilities with the ages of Gawain and Budicius's son Hoel. Geoffrey may have revised the text and not noticed the contradictions he was creating.

Most romancers do not recognize Anna or any other sister of Arthur. They make him the only child of his parents. Anna's place in the scheme of relationships is taken by his half-sister Morgause, a daughter of Ygerna by her first husband, the duke of Cornwall. It is Morgause who marries Lot.

ANNALES CAMBRIAE "Annals of Wales." A tenth-century Latin chronicle with two allusions to Arthur, which follows the *Historia Brittonum* in the chief manuscript. It consists of a table of 533 years beginning with a Year 1 best taken as A.D. 447. Events are written in beside some of the year listings. The chronicle is a compilation from previous ones, and most of its early entries are posted from an Irish source. The first that refers to anything British is at Year 72, probably 518. It notes "the battle of Badon, in which Arthur carried the cross of Our Lord Jesus Christ for three days and three nights on his shoulders, and the Britons were victors." Twenty-one years farther on is "the strife of Camlann, in which Arthur and Medraut fell." This is the earliest known reference to the fatal battle. Medraut is the original Mordred.

The Badon entry concurs with the earlier *Historia Brittonum*, although not with the even earlier Gildas, in crediting this success to Arthur. Despite its legendary air, it can be rationalized. "Shoulders" may mistranslate a Welsh word for "shield," and the cross could be an emblem, or one of the many reputed pieces of the True Cross. The date, however, seems incompatible with Gildas, who wrote when the battle was within living memory. As for Camlann, while the Welsh had a strong and sad tradition about it, an Arthur still an active warrior in 539 cannot be reconciled with other clues to his *floruit*. The Camlann entry may reflect a fictitious extension of his career far into the sixth century, which can be observed also in some of the Welsh saints' lives.

It has been urged that, although the Arthur items appear in a tenth-century chronicle, they are copied from a much older text and are therefore historically trustworthy. This argument cannot be sustained, and, as a sidelight on reliability, it is worth noting that the entry before Badon records that a bishop who died was three hundred and fifty years old. Nevertheless, since everyone in the *Annales* outside the Arthur entries did exist, his inclusion tells in favor of his reality, or at least the reality of a person whose exploits went into the making of the Arthurian saga.

ANNWFN (ANNWN) In Welsh legend, an otherworld region sometimes pictured as underground. Annwfn is a survival from pre-Christian Celtic mythology. Its inhabitants are immortals—fairy folk or demons according to one's point of view. Some are deities only slightly disguised. Humans can enter, bodily or in spirit, but Annwfn is properly neither heaven nor hell in a Christian sense.

Its ruler is Gwyn ap Nudd, that is, Gwyn son of Nodons, a British god who had a temple at Lydney in the Forest of Dean. Gwyn can appear among mortals, and he does. He is at Arthur's court in *Culhwch and Olwen*, where it is said that God has given him power over Annwfn's demons "lest this world be destroyed." Folklore makes him a leader of the Wild Hunt, careering through the clouds summoning human shades, accompanied by the red-eared hounds of Annwfn and sometimes by the undying Arthur himself.

Annwfn can be reached by various points of access, among them Lundy Island and Glastonbury Tor. Legend relates that Collen, a wandering Welsh saint, entered Gwyn's palace inside the Tor and tried to banish him by scattering holy water.

The so-called Book of Taliesin includes an obscure Welsh poem called *The Spoils of Annwfn*. Not Taliesin's authentic work, it probably dates from the tenth century. It tells of a raid in which Arthur and his men voyage over the otherworld's waters in quest of a talismanic cauldron. Their expedition is perilous and only seven return. The poem is pagan in substance and has been thought to foreshadow the Grail Quest. A noteworthy feature is that the cauldron is in the custody of nine maidens. They recall actual groups of nine priestesses that existed in pre-Christian Celtic society. Geoffrey of Monmouth, in his poetic *Vita Merlini*, speaks of Morgan le Fay as heading a sisterhood of nine on the Isle of Apples, otherwise Avalon, with which Annwfn is sometimes more or less identified.

ᴀʀɢᴀɴᴛᴇ In Layamon's *Brut*, the queen of Avalon who will heal Arthur's wounds. She is doubtless the same as Morgan le Fay.

ᴀʀᴛᕼᴜʀ King of Britain and central figure of the Arthurian legend, created, as such, by Geoffrey of Monmouth. While Geoffrey follows a normal medieval practice by depicting Arthur in terms of his own time, he places the reign during the Roman Empire's last phase in western Europe, not long after Britain's *de facto* separation from it, which occurred historically about 410. Whether through knowledge or accident, Geoffrey makes Arthur a British version of a kind of messiah who haunted the imagination of Late Roman antiquity—the *Restitutor Orbis* or World Restorer, the ruler who would bind up the wounds of internal war, crush the barbarians, defeat external enemies, and reestablish peace and prosperity. The collapsing fifth-century Empire never found its Restorer, but in Geoffrey's flight of fancy a recently Roman Britain does. His conception of Arthur's reign as a golden age founded on a rescue from strife and disintegration persists right through to Malory, even though romancers lose sight of the real troubles of the period.

Geoffrey's *Historia Regum Britanniae*, from about 1136–38, portrays Britain as suffering from misfortunes familiar in the Roman world generally—plots and corruption in high places, unprincipled bids for power, barbarian onslaughts. The usurper Vortigern invites the heathen Saxons to settle in Britain as auxiliary troops, just as hard-pressed emperors opened the door to other barbarians. Vortigern's Saxons get out of hand. After a spell of near-anarchy, Uther becomes king. With Merlin's aid, he wins access to Ygerna, the duchess of Cornwall, and begets Arthur, making the lady his queen soon afterward so that their son counts as legitimate.

Arthur succeeds him while still young and soon proves himself a capable leader. He routs the Saxons and confines them to a small area. He then subdues the Picts, Scots, and Irish. He marries Guinevere and during a long spell of peace founds an order of knighthood, enrolling men of note from all countries. Britain rises to a degree of wealth and culture unparalleled abroad. Arthur conquers most of Gaul and holds court magnificently at Caerleon. A Roman demand for tribute provokes him to march into Gaul again, leaving his nephew Mordred in charge at home, jointly with the Queen. While Arthur is embroiled on the Continent, Mordred revolts. Arthur has to return to Britain to fight him, and gains the victory, but is grievously wounded and "carried off to the Isle of Avalon for his wounds to be attended to." Geoffrey pursues him no farther, leaving his end in doubt. He gives a date here, 542, but this is in conflict with the rest and may be due to a misguided emendation. While Geoffrey is not very responsible in such matters, he regards Arthur's story as basically belonging to the fifth century. This is made clear by family relationships and by several calibrations with known history, such as a repeated reference to the emperor Leo, who reigned from 457 to 474, as contemporary with Arthur.

For the antecedents of Geoffrey's conception, it is necessary to look first at the "Celtic fringe" comprising Wales, Cornwall, and Brittany. The peoples of these countries were all descended from fifth-century Britons, themselves a Celtic people, newly independent but retaining a certain amount of the Roman legacy. Their Roman-ness faded, but their descendants, especially in Wales, built up a saga of Arthur as a heroic warrior-prince flourishing in the post-Roman period before the Celts succumbed to the Saxons, a doom long deferred partly because of him. Fragments of the saga survive in Welsh poetry, in the tale *Culhwch and Olwen*, and in the triads, all of which show that before Geoffrey's time Arthur had become preeminent in story and numerous other heroes of the Welsh had been attached to his entourage. While Geoffrey doubtless drew general inspiration from the saga, about one-fifth of his Arthur narrative is based more specifically on two Latin texts of Welsh provenance, giving Arthur a quasi-historical status. The ninth-century *Historia Brittonum* lists twelve battles supposedly won by him as war leader against the Saxons. The tenth-century *Annales Cambriae* repeat one of his battles, Badon (certainly real, though no early evidence links his name with it), and add Camlann, where he fell.

These texts prove that Geoffrey is using earlier tradition, and not merely inventing, when he makes Arthur lead the Britons against their re-bellious Saxon settlers. As a matter of history, furthermore, the Saxons did settle, in something like the way Geoffrey romanticizes, and did rebel. The Arthur story echoes reality here. Alone among Rome's provincial peoples, the Britons became autonomous before the barbarians moved in and fought back when they did, with temporary success. The Saxons finally overran what is now England, but the phase of resistance bred legends of resistance leaders, handed down by the Britons' Welsh descendants. One of these lead-ers, Ambrosius, was certainly real. Arthur was another and may have been real. However wildly Geoffrey exaggerates, he is enlarging the image of a hero who fits into a recognized historical picture. Although he inflates a counterattack into a sort of revolution, the counterattack did happen.

The difficulty is to get any farther. No Welsh allusion to Arthur can be proved close enough to his time to inspire much confidence. Several of the battles are plausible singly, yet they spread his career over an incredibly long period. The Welsh matter suggests an early layer of legend rather than history. While Arthur has never been convincingly explained away altogether (as a Celtic god, for instance), the Celtic fringe supplies only two pieces of positive evidence for him that skeptics have allowed to be significant.

One is his name. "Arthur" is the Welsh form of the Roman *Artorius*, convincing as the name of a Briton born in the fifth century or not much later (although such a person might still have been a poetic invention). The other item arises from a fact that looks purely mythical. For a long time, Arthur was widely believed to be still alive. He was in the Isle of Avalon, or he was asleep in a cave. Some day, the Bretons maintained, echoed by the Cornish and Welsh, he would return. The cave legend has lingered on into modern times as a folktale. Much the same tale is told of other kings and heroes, and there is not a single established instance, at least in Europe, of the sleeper in the cave being imaginary. Always he seems to be an actual, historical figure. Therefore, by analogy, Arthur is.

Further light may be shed by looking in other places. Four-fifths of Geoffrey's account of Arthur has no specific Welsh foundation. He dates a large part of it, dealing with the warfare in Gaul, by the aforementioned allusions to the emperor Leo, and there are signs that he is using some record of a "king of the Britons" who did lead an army over to Gaul during Leo's reign. Continental sources call this king Riothamus, which is a latinization of a term that could mean "high king." A Breton text apparently refers to him and calls him Arthur. This man may at least in part be Arthur's historical original. However, he cannot cover the whole of Arthur's reputed lifespan—no one could—and the legendary King may be a composite character, as, for example, Merlin is.

Geoffrey's *Historia* supplied the framework for medieval Arthurian romance, together with some of the characters, but it was far from being the sole inspiration. Stories told by others, such as Breton minstrels, flowed in. Wace's verse paraphrase of Geoffrey adds features that become part of the scheme, notably the Round Table, and Chrétien de Troyes marks a trend away from Arthur himself and toward the knights and ladies around him. The King, for most romancers, is mainly a magnificent chairman, and his court is a point of departure for the adventures of Lancelot, Gawain, and their colleagues. His martial activity is toned down, his concern for justice and noble conduct is stressed. He is wise, kind, magnanimous, and active when action is required, yet he grows more symbolic, an embodiment of Christian and chivalric ideals. Occasional weakness and even wrongdoing never destroy his essential dignity.

Persisting through many presentations of him, from the far-off Welsh to some modern ones, is the perennial dream of a golden age. In this case, it has the added quality that Arthur still lives and will return, so that the golden age will be reinstated. The appeal to the imagination has the power to outlast literal belief.

ASTOLAT, see *Escalot*

AURELIUS AMBROSIUS Arthur's uncle in Geoffrey of Monmouth. He and his brother Uther are sons of King Constantine. As boys they live at the court of Brittany, out of reach of the usurper Vortigern. When they grow up, they return to Britain and overthrow him, and Aurelius becomes king. He captures and executes the Saxon chief Hengist and with Merlin's aid sets up Stonehenge as a monument over the mass grave of four hundred and sixty nobles whom Hengist had massacred. Soon after, a vengeful son of Vortigern murders him by means of a Saxon poisoner, and Uther succeeds to the throne.

Geoffrey takes a hint for this character from the British war leader Ambrosius Aurelianus, whom Gildas mentions. The supposed kingship is based on a few words in the *Historia Brittonum*. So far as Geoffrey can be said to date the reign, he seems to make it short and to put the whole of it in the 430s, whereas Gildas implies that Ambrosius was still active many years later.

AVALON (AVALLACh)   Enchanted island where, according to Geoffrey of Monmouth, Arthur's sword was forged and where he was conveyed after his last battle for his wounds to be attended to. Calling it *Insula Avallonis* in Latin, Geoffrey interprets the name as "isle of apples," the apples doubtless being paradisal or magical fruit. A question arises from the fact that the Welsh called the island *Ynys Avallach* and supposed it to take its name from Avallach, its overlord. Geoffrey's *Insula Avallonis* does not precisely latinize Avallach and has been influenced by Avallon, the name of a town in Burgundy. But the town's name, which is Gaulish, certainly does mean "apple place," and for this reason and others it may be judged that Geoffrey knows what he is talking about, in the absence of proof that he does not.

He touches on Avalon at more length in his poetical *Vita Merlini* than in his *Historia*. He describes it as an island over western waters with the agreeable qualities of the Fortunate Isles of classical myth. It is ruled by Morgen (that is, Morgan le Fay), a well-disposed enchantress and healer heading a sisterhood of nine. There is an echo here of the nine otherworld maidens in *The Spoils of Annwfn* and of real island-dwelling groups of Celtic priestesses, of a kind noted by the Roman author Pomponius Mela in the first century A.D. Morgen has Arthur placed on a golden bed and undertakes to heal his wounds if he entrusts himself to her care for a long treatment.

Avalon has sometimes been interpreted as an abode of departed spirits. But the point of Arthur's residence is, precisely, that he is not a departed spirit. He is magically alive and awaiting the hour of his return. Wace and Layamon refer to this as a Breton belief, and romancers who consider his present state usually accept the same version, although they move the island about irresponsibly, to the Mediterranean and even farther afield.

The only challenge to this mythical view of Avalon came in 1191 at Glastonbury, with its ancient monastery in a Somerset hill cluster, once almost encircled by water. A pre-Christian eeriness that clung to the highest of its hills, the Tor, helped to sustain a claim by the monks that Glastonbury was the true Avalon, Arthur's last earthly destination. They said so because they had found what they asserted to be his grave, with an inscribed cross bearing his name and the island's. The equation passed into some of the Grail literature that drew on legends of Glastonbury's Christian antiquity.

Avalon thus has two meanings: as Glastonbury, and as the otherworldly isle. Malory hesitates between them. In both cases, it is Arthur's last destination, but at Glastonbury it is his resting place in death, whereas the island is the scene of his retreat from the world, his healing, and his immortality.

BADON Named as the location of Arthur's climactic battle against the Saxons. According to Gildas, a victory over them at the "siege of Mount Badon" brought a spell of comparative peace. His words have been construed in various ways, but the date seems to have been somewhere about 500. Archaeology is in fair agreement. The Anglo-Saxon advance did halt for some decades, apart from small inroads near the Hampshire coast.

Badon was almost certainly in southern England, and the "mount" may have been a reoccupied Iron Age hill-fort. Hills near Bath (Geoffrey of Monmouth's choice), Badbury Rings in Dorset, and Liddington Castle in Wiltshire, which has a village of Badbury close by, have been proposed as candidates. The Liddington hill-fort is perhaps the best. Its earthwork defenses are known to have been refurbished at about the right time.

Although Badon was a real battle, Arthur's connection with it presents a problem. Gildas does not name the Britons' commander. Arthur is first named in this role by the *Historia Brittonum* in the ninth century, and then by the *Annales Cambriae* in the tenth. Both allusions have legendary touches making them suspect and raise difficulties because other, more plausibly Arthurian, battles are likely to have occurred forty or fifty years earlier. Bardic tradition may have come to introduce Arthur here because Badon was the major result of the war effort with which he was associated, or because of the presence of warriors fighting under his name, "Arthur's men" (see *Llongborth*). Actually, however, the early Welsh do not show much interest in Badon or stress it for Arthur's glorification. It is absent from the triads.

BALIN AND BALAN Brothers who help Arthur in his early struggles to establish his power. Balin, a violent character, beheads the Lady of the Lake in an act of family vengeance. Later, he kills a knight named Garlon. This happens in Pellam's castle, and Pellam, who is Garlon's brother, tries to avenge him. Balin snatches up a lance and wounds Pellam with it. The lance is the one with which the soldier Longinus pierced the side of Christ. Felled by this "Dolorous Stroke," Pellam lies wounded for many years, to be healed only by the Grail achiever Galahad, and the land round about becomes waste.

Balin is doomed for his sacrilegious use of the Holy Lance. Through a misunderstanding, he and Balan kill each other. They are buried together. Merlin takes Balin's sword and implants it in a block of marble, where it remains till Galahad proves his vocation as Grail achiever by extracting it. The brothers appear first in the *Suite du Merlin* and later in Malory.

BAN Lancelot's father, named first in the Vulgate *Lancelot*. He is the wise king of Benoic in western France. When Lancelot is still an infant, Ban suffers defeat by his enemy, Claudas of Berry, and dies. This is the reason for Lancelot's being taken away and reared by the Lady of the Lake.

Malory makes Ban an ally of Arthur in his early warfare against unruly vassals. Lancelot becomes lord of Benoic himself. Malory claims that "Benwick," as he spells it, is the name of a city, either Bayonne or Beaune. Since the place can be reached by sea from Cardiff, Beaune, which is in Burgundy, seems to be ruled out.

BASSAS RIVER, the scene of Arthur's sixth battle, according to the *Historia Brittonum*. It cannot now be identified. The name, like some others in the battle list, may have been effaced from the map by conquerors speaking Anglo-Saxon, although in fact the old British river names frequently survived, if in distorted form.

BEDIVERE (BEDEVERE, BEDWYR) In Welsh matter prior to Geoffrey of Monmouth, the warrior Bedwyr is one of Arthur's two principal companions, next in importance to Cai. He is mentioned in poetry, in *Culhwch and Olwen*, in the life of St. Cadoc, and in the triads, being described as handsome, brave, and skillful with a spear. Geoffrey effects his transition to medieval knighthood, with his name spelled in the more familiar way, and makes him Arthur's cupbearer and governor of Normandy. Bedivere goes with Arthur and Kay, that is, Cai, on an expedition against a giant on Mont-Saint-Michel. He falls fighting the Romans and is buried at Bayeux, a city that Geoffrey says was founded by his grandfather, a man of the same name.

Romancers generally reduce Bedivere, although in England he has a memorable role as the last knight to remain with the dying King. He throws Excalibur into the water, watches Arthur's mysterious departure, and retires to a hermitage near Glastonbury. Several modern novelists, trying to recreate Arthur's Britain with more regard for early tradition, have restored him to his former importance.

BEDWYR, see *Bedivere*

BERCILAK In *Sir Gawain and the Green Knight*, the lord of a castle where Gawain stays before his encounter with the Green Knight. When the encounter takes place, it turns out that the Knight is Bercilak himself, magically transformed by Morgan le Fay. Gawain is spared because of his honorable conduct during a series of tests at the castle, which the Knight, in his character of Bercilak, knew all about.

BESTE GLATISSANT, see *Questing Beast*

BLAISE Merlin's secretary, to whom, according to Robert de Boron and subsequent authors, he dictated the history of the Grail and other matters. "Blaise" is a variant of "Bleheris," the name of a twelfth-century Welsh storyteller whom the romancers fictionalize.

BLEEDING LANCE Magical or sacred object in the Grail ceremonies. Blood drips from its point. When the Grail is given a Christian meaning, this weapon becomes the Holy Lance, which in the hands of the Roman soldier Longinus pierced the side of Christ on the Cross. The blood is Christ's and drips perpetually into the Grail. In the Vulgate Cycle, and later, the lance is also the weapon that gave the Grail keeper his wound. Sometimes, however, it is also credited with the power of healing.

BOHORT, see *Bors*

BORRE, see *Llacheu*

BORS (BOHORT) Cousin of Lancelot. One of the more successful Grail seekers, although impeded by a past act of unchastity, he accompanies Perceval and Galahad to Sarras. After Galahad attains the supreme vision and dies, Bors returns to Britain and is welcomed at Camelot, where he reports what has happened.

He vainly warns Lancelot of the scheme of Agravain and Mordred to trap him with Guinevere and sides with him in the dispute that splits the Round Table. When Arthur has passed away, Bors enters the religious life—according to Malory, joining his cousin for a time in a retreat near Glastonbury but dying in the Holy Land as a crusader.

BRAN Ruler of ancient Britain in Welsh mythology and a prototype of the Fisher King who keeps the Grail. In his origin, he is a Celtic god. More or less humanized, although gigantic, he is called "the Blessed," a Christian epithet that may be an adaptation of a pagan one. In the *Mabinogion*, Bran leads an army to Ireland and is wounded in battle by a poisoned spear. He tells his surviving followers to cut off his head and return with it to Wales. They do so, and it keeps them in a state of enchanted bliss for many years. At last, the spell is snapped. They go to London, still in compliance with Bran's last wishes, and bury the head on Tower Hill, where it acts as a talisman against foreign plagues and invasions. After several centuries, Arthur digs it up, saying that Britain should not rely on such protection. In the triads, this act is one of the three "Wicked Uncoverings" or "Unfortunate Disclosures."

"Bran" means The Raven. An Irish hero of the same name, who voyages to an otherworld over the western ocean, is doubtless a form of the same deity. The Grail character Bron may derive from Bran, and the Grail motif of the spear wound echoes Bran's wounding. Bran, moreover, possesses a wonderworking vessel, a cauldron that restores life to the dead, and after he is wounded the land becomes barren, like the wasteland of Grail romance.

Perhaps because of the Grail connection, perhaps also because of the epithet "blessed," late Welsh legend humanizes Bran completely and gives him a setting in history. He becomes the father of the British patriot Caratacus, goes to Rome with him, is converted by St. Paul, and returns to Britain as a missionary. This is antiquarian and has no Arthurian relevance.

BRANGΑENE (BRANGWΑIN) Iseut's maid, who attends her on her voyage to Britain to marry Mark. Brangaene brings a love potion in preparation for this event, but Iseut and her male escort, Tristan, drink it by mistake on the way over and become lovers. Iseut persuades Brangaene to take her place on the wedding night, so that the woman whom Mark assumes (with the lights out) to be his bride will be a virgin, as Iseut ostensibly is but actually, after her commitment to Tristan, is not. The ruse succeeds. Iseut then becomes afraid that Brangaene will betray what has happened, and plans to have her killed, but relents.

BREGUOIN, see *Agned*

BROCÉLIΑNϽE Forest in Brittany where strange adventures occur in French romances, notably Chrétien de Troyes's *Yvain*. One of its best-known features is a magical spring, which causes a rainstorm when water taken from it is poured over a nearby stone. In the Vulgate *Merlin*, Brocéliande is the scene of Merlin's entrapment by Viviane.

It was a real forest, and Breton popular legend made it a place of enchantments. Wace went there in the hope of seeing fairy folk, but he returned disappointed. A remnant of the forest, westward of Rennes, is today called Paimpont and still has Arthurian associations.

BRON (hEBRON) Husband of Joseph of Arimathea's sister. He catches a symbolic fish, which he places on the Grail table beside the sacred vessel, and is called the Rich Fisher. Instructed in the secret words concerning the Grail, he takes it to Britain. His twelfth son, Alain, and a follower named Petrus have already gone to the Vales of Avaron or Avalon (central Somerset) to prepare a place for it. Bron, as Fisher King, lives on in Britain for many years till enabled by Perceval to die a peaceful death.

Ultimately, he may well be the same as Bran the Blessed. The Grail story gives him a role unknown to the legends of Bran. However, it has points of contact with them, and the Grail theme in a more general sense has others. Welsh antiquarian speculation seems to accept tacitly that the two are the same by connecting Bran with an early Christian mission to Britain.

BRUTUS According to a confused Welsh legend in the *Historia Brittonum*, Brutus (or Britto) was a great-grandson of the Trojan Aeneas, hero of Vergil's epic the *Aeneid*. In the twelfth century B.C., he led a party of migrant Trojans to Britain, then called Albion, and they took possession. Geoffrey of Monmouth vastly elaborates the story, telling how the island was renamed Britain after Brutus, and its new people were called Britons. He traces a long succession of kings, including Arthur. Since Britain's legendary monarchy starts with Brutus, various works based directly or indirectly on Geoffrey use his name as their title, the chief being Wace's *Roman de Brut*, Layamon's *Brut*, and a number of Welsh chronicles.

BUELT Old regional division of Wales. Its name survives in Builth Wells. The list of "marvels" attached to the *Historia Brittonum* mentions a pile of stones in Buelt, with a stone on top bearing a dog's footprint. This was Arthur's dog Cabal. During the hunting of the boar Trwyth (a tale told in *Culhwch and Olwen*), he put his foot on the stone and marked it. Arthur built up the heap with that one on top and called it Carn Cabal, Cabal's Cairn. The "marvelous" thing, the list's compiler explains, is that the paw-printed stone cannot be removed for more than a day, because it always reappears on the heap.

Modern maps give the name Carn Cabal, in the form Corngafallt, to a wooded ridge near Rhayader. There are piles of stones near the highest part of it, but none has been found with the sort of paw-shaped depression that might have inspired the legend. It is doubtful whether the hill now called Corngafallt is the place intended. The story of the boar hunt in *Culhwch and Olwen* does not bring Arthur and his huntsmen to this part of Wales.

CABAL (CAFALL) Arthur's dog. He is said to have left his footprint on a stone in the Welsh regional division of Buelt. Confusion may be suspected here, because in other instances of this footprint legend, as at Carn March Arthur in Gwynedd, the animal is not Arthur's dog but his horse. Furthermore, "Cabal," derived from the Latin word *caballus*, does actually mean "horse."

CADBURY-CAMELOT Cadbury Castle, an Iron Age hill-fort above the village of South Cadbury in Somerset. There was never a castle on the site, in the medieval sense. The fortified hill is itself the "castle," dating, as such, from the last centuries B.C. It has four lines of earthwork defenses (now largely overgrown with woods but exposed to view on the eastern side) encircling an eighteen-acre enclosure, which rises to a plateau where a village stood till the Romans captured the hill and removed its inhabitants.

Cadbury's Arthurian interest arises out of its later history and folklore. It is the locale of one version of Arthur's cave legend, according to which a pair of gates in the hillside opens once a year and he can be seen sleeping within. Arthurian ghost stories are also told. In 1542, John Leland referred to the hill as Camelot, stating this as local belief rather than conjecture. While the Camelot of romance is a medieval fantasy, an "original Camelot" might be admitted in the sense of a headquarters or temporary capital belonging to an original Arthur.

Excavation in 1966–70 revealed serious possibilities. Deserted in the post-Roman decades, the Cadbury hill-fort was reoccupied and refortified on a massive scale during the 460s or after, but probably not much later than 500. Embedded in its topmost earth bank is a dry-stone wall sixteen feet thick, which was bound with a framework of timber beams. The total perimeter was nearly three-quarters of a mile. A gatehouse guarded the entrance to the enclosure, and a hall stood on the summit plateau. The excavation of other hill-forts has shown reoccupation in roughly the same period, but nothing like the Cadbury stone-and-timber defensive system has been found anywhere else in England or Wales, and a few similar fortifications in Scotland are markedly smaller and have no gatehouses. Leland's accurate picking-out of the most appropriate hill throughout Britain makes it unlikely that he was merely guessing. Some sort of local tradition is probable.

In view of the amount of manpower and labor required, Cadbury has been held to imply a king—perhaps a "high king"—with resources unparalleled, so far as present knowledge goes, in the Britain of his time. Owing to the shortage of records, nothing more can be inferred with any certainty.

CADOC Founder of the monastery of Llancarfan in Glamorgan, where several Lives of Welsh saints were written introducing Arthur. The Llancarfan material tends to be unfriendly, treating him as a foreigner who enters Wales but whose home is in southwest England, so far as he is located at all.

Arthur figures in the Life of St. Cadoc himself. First, he becomes involved in the elopement of the saint's mother, whom he lusts after, but finally, under pressure, helps in her escape with her lover. Cadoc is the result. Long afterward, Cadoc, as abbot of Llancarfan, grants sanctuary for seven years to a man who has killed three of Arthur's soldiers. A dispute ensues in which Arthur is overawed by a miracle and concedes Cadoc's right to give sanctuary for such a long period.

This second story raises important chronological issues. It calls Arthur king of Britain, implying a political unity that could not have existed much after the mid-fifth century. But by making him contemporary not only with St. Cadoc as abbot but with St. David, it places him far on in the sixth, later even than the reputed date of the battle of Camlann. Cadoc's Life witnesses to the spreading of Arthur's career in Welsh legend and the historical difficulties created thereby.

CADWY (CATO, CADOR) Welsh and Breton sources refer to Cadwy as a prince of Dumnonia, Britain's southwest peninsula. In the legendary Life of St. Carannog, he reigns jointly with Arthur at Dindraithov, usually taken to be Dunster in Somerset. Since Cadwy is named first (as Cato), the story may echo a supposed phase of Arthur's career when he was a junior chief only. Cadwy's father's name is given as Geraint. This is one of several facts pointing to a Geraint in Arthur's time, who came to be confused with the later hero Geraint son of Erbin.

Geoffrey of Monmouth modifies Cadwy's name to Cador and makes him duke of Cornwall after Gorlois, being, by inference, a younger brother. Guinevere is brought up in his household. Cador is one of Arthur's best commanders, a loyal, genial man who has an honored function in the great ceremony at Caerleon. Before departing to Avalon, Arthur hands over the crown to Cador's son Constantine. Nothing has been said about the death of Cador himself. The assumption may be that he was too old to restore order after the civil war and Saxon resurgence.

CAERLEON Small town in the Welsh county of Gwent, beside the River Usk. It has remains of a Roman legionary fort and an amphitheater. The Welsh name means "City [originally "Fort"] of the Legion," and Caerleon has been claimed as the scene of Arthur's ninth battle in the

Historia Brittonum, but in that context the place meant is almost certainly Chester.

Geoffrey of Monmouth calls Caerleon the "City of the Legions"—plural—and gives a lavish account of Arthur holding court there. It supplies the essential hint for the romantic portrayal of Camelot. Camelot, however, does not supersede Caerleon, which continues to be named as an Arthurian center, if a lesser one. Geoffrey may have conferred that status on it as being the nearest place to his native Monmouth with impressive remains of ancient buildings. Besides making Caerleon a sort of Arthurian capital, he makes it the location of the convent to which Guinevere retired.

For many years, prior to excavation, the amphitheater was buried under a mound of accumulated soil. This conformed to the oval shape of the structure it hid and was claimed locally as the real Round Table. The neighborhood has a version of the cave legend, telling of an underground chamber in a wood, where a thousand of Arthur's soldiers lie sleeping till Wales shall need them.

CAI, see *Kay*

CALEDONIAN WOOD Forest known in early Welsh as Coit Celidon, reputedly the scene of Arthur's seventh battle (*see* CELIDON). Caledonia is an old name for Scotland. Classical geographers locate the people called Caledonii north of the Clyde-Forth line, but the Welsh applied the name to forested country much nearer the Border.

CALIBURN In Geoffrey of Monmouth, the name of Arthur's sword. Romancers modify it into the better-known "Excalibur." Geoffrey says that the sword was forged in the Isle of Avalon, here almost certainly an enchanted otherworld place, not Glastonbury. Arthur wielded Caliburn when he quelled the Saxons at Bath and again in single combat with the Roman governor Frollo outside Paris. He bore it in battle with the Roman army of Lucius, waving it as he encouraged his troops and slaying many of the enemy, whose armor gave them no protection.

The weapon's name was doubtless suggested by the Latin *chalybs*, "steel," which, like the English word "steel" itself, could be used poetically to mean a sword. There may be an echo of the Welsh name Caledfwlch given to Arthur's sword in *Culhwch and Olwen*, which in turn echoes Caladbolg, the name of a sword famous in Irish legend (See also *Excalibur*).

CAMEL (CAMBULA) Cornish river, the scene of Arthur's last battle in Geoffrey of Monmouth. In choosing this location, he is thinking of the

Camlann of Welsh tradition. Local legend, making the story more specific, points to Slaughter Bridge, where the river flows along a small valley about a mile above Camelford. The Tudor writer John Leland tells how Arthur and Mordred met on the bridge, in a hand-to-hand combat fatal to both. He speaks also of fragments of armor and other military gear being dug up in nearby meadows. A battle was actually fought here, but it was fought in 823 between the West Saxons and Cornish. Relics of it such as Leland describes, found before Geoffrey's time, may have reinforced the name of the river when he was making his geographical choice. But the quarrel between Arthur and Mordred, if not the final clash, does seem to have been associated with Cornwall before Geoffrey.

CAMELOT In romance, Arthur's capital, to use an anachronistic term. The name refers primarily to the castle, but the castle stands within or beside a town. Camelot is a word of unknown derivation. It may have been suggested by the Roman *Camulodunum*, Colchester. *Camulodunum*, however, means "Fort of Camulos," an ancient British war god, and hardly seems relevant. Nor would a town in Essex, almost on the Saxon shore, have been a likely one for even imagination to pick on. Camel occurs as a village name near Cadbury Castle in Somerset. Its relation with Cadbury's Arthurian lore is uncertain. Archaeology has shown that this is more than a mere fantasy inspired by the place-name.

Perhaps the most significant fact is that Camelot is a personal capital, not a national or permanent one. It is Arthur's own center. No previous overlord is mentioned, and his successor, Constantine, does not take it over. Indeed, Camelot is said to have been destroyed by Mark after Arthur and Lancelot were gone. The Italian poet Fazio degli Uberti, in the fourteenth century, professes to have seen the ruins. Its individual, nonpolitical character is one of the reasons for entertaining Cadbury's claim to be the original Camelot so far as anything ever was, that is, a headquarters created by a particular king and not an enduring seat of government.

Although foreshadowed by Geoffrey of Monmouth's account of Caerleon, Camelot is first named in Chrétien's *Lancelot* and becomes prominent only in the Vulgate Cycle. Descriptions by thirteenth-century romancers speak of a surrounding plain, a river, a forest. Camelot has a religious quality. Knights are baptized there, and it is the point of departure for the Grail Quest. Its location, however, remains vague. Eventually Malory more or less equates it with Winchester, the capital of King Alfred's Wessex and long a rival of London in importance. He may have been influenced by

Winchester's "Round Table," made in the thirteenth century or thereabout but by Malory's time widely believed to be the original. This equation ignores Camelot's purely Arthurian character, and it is interesting, if surprising, that Malory's own editor, Caxton, rejects it. Caxton in his preface opts for a Welsh Camelot, thinking perhaps of the Roman ruins at Caerwent.

Other speculations have pointed to Camelford in Cornwall, down the River Camel from the place where Geoffrey locates Arthur's last battle. But no medieval romancer would have pictured Arthur's principal home so far west and in the domain of Mark. Camelot is a medieval dream-city, focal to the romancers' chivalric Utopia, and not to be pinned down geographically. While Cadbury has a serious claim to be its prototype, neither Cadbury nor any other place can claim to be more.

CAMLANN (CAMLAN) In Welsh literature, Arthur's last battle, in which he fought Medraut (otherwise Mordred). Not mentioned in the *Historia Brittonum*, it appears first in the tenth-century *Annales Cambriae*, where the entry for a year that is probably 539 records "the strife of Camlann in which Arthur and Medraut fell." It is not stated that Medraut was a villain or even that the two were opposed. The triads make Camlann one of the "Three Futile Battles," a tragic and bloody clash arising partly or wholly out of a feud, with Medraut as the aggressor. This conflict sounds like a quarrel of equals rather than the struggle of a ruler against a rebellious deputy. Geoffrey of Monmouth, who introduces the latter theme, identifies Camlann with the River Cambula or Camel in Cornwall. There are signs that he is trying to combine the Welsh version of Arthur's end with a separate story of his betrayal and a quite different demise. Romancers keep the treason as Geoffrey defines it but drop Camlann and locate the final battle near Salisbury.

The name is derived from the British *Camboglanna*, "crooked bank," or less probably *Cambolanda*, "crooked enclosure." While Geoffrey is doubtless right in taking it to mean a river, certainty is impossible. The Camlann entry in the *Annales* cannot have been copied, as some have thought, from a trustworthy sixth-century record, because the British word would not have become the Welsh "Camlann" directly; it would have passed through a transitional form over a long period. The entry may be correct, but it is too remote from the asserted event to be reliable. Also, the year 539 is too late to reconcile with other indications of Arthur's *floruit*.

One of the forts on Hadrian's Wall was called Camboglanna. But the known story of the Arthur-Medraut quarrel is set in Cornwall. Geoffrey is at least looking in the right direction. It could have been transferred from an earlier locale, but not necessarily all the way from northern Britain. There are two Camlans in Merioneth, and the Somerset River Cam, near Cadbury-Camelot, is another candidate.

While Camlann probably happened, it has defied definition as a localized battle with a real Arthur in it. The Welsh testimony could be preserved, despite the date problem, by supposing that the Arthur of legend is a composite figure and that a "Camlann Arthur" was drawn into a saga with earlier origins (See also *Llongborth*).

CARADOC OF LLANCARFAN Monk in the Glamorgan community founded by St. Cadoc. One of several of its members whose writings introduce Arthur, he produced, about 1130, a Life of Gildas with several features of importance for the early growth of Arthurian legend. He also wrote on Welsh history. Geoffrey of Monmouth, in an appendix to his own work, acknowledges Caradoc's claim to be a continuator of the story.

CARANNOG Early Welsh saint. His legendary Life says that he had a floating altar that drifted down the Bristol Channel to Somerset, near a royal residence belonging to Cato (otherwise Cadwy) and Arthur, who here seems to be a junior prince. When Carannog arrived, the altar was nowhere to be seen. He found Arthur in vain pursuit of a giant serpent. Arthur promised to tell him where the altar was if he would subdue the serpent. Carannog summoned it and banished it from the country, whereupon Arthur produced the altar, which he had appropriated himself and tried to use as a table, only to find that it threw off everything he put on it. He made Carannog a gift of land.

CARBONEK, see *Corbenic*

CARDUEL (KARDOIL) In French romance, a place where Arthur holds court. It is basically Carlisle, but the geography is vague.

CARLISLE City of Cumbria, of Roman origin, that survived for some time after the separation of Britain from the Empire. The first syllable of its old name, *Luguvallum*, suggests a connection with the god Lugh. In the course of time, the name was shortened and the Welsh *caer*, "city," was prefixed.

During the later sixth century, the kingdom of Rheged, centered in this area, produced several bards who commemorated the warriors of the north. Thanks to this heroic poetry and saga, which lost touch with any clear dating, Carlisle figures in stories of Arthur. French romancers call it Carduel or Kardoil. Under its own name, it figures in English tales with Gawain as hero. It is also the place where, in Malory, Lancelot rescues Guinevere when she is about to be burned at the stake.

CARMARTHEN Town in southwest Wales, said to be Merlin's birthplace, and named after him. Actually, it is the other way about. "Myrddin," the original Welsh form of his name, is apparently derived from the old name of the town, *Moridunum* as the Romans made it.

CASTLE DORE Earthwork fort near Fowey in Cornwall, associated with the Tristan romance. As at Cadbury-Camelot, the name does not imply a medieval castle. The fortification dates from about the third century B.C. and protected an Iron Age village until the Roman period. After a long phase of abandonment, the enclosure may have been brought into use again some time after the end of Britain's Roman connection. If so, it is possible that one of the occupants was Kynvawr, who ruled over Dumnonia, the southwest peninsula of Britain including Cornwall, during the first half of the sixth century.

The Latin form of his name is Cunomorus. A monument that was once near Castle Dore but now stands just outside Fowey calls him so and shows that he had a son named Drustanus (Tristan). A ninth-century text identifies Cunomorus with Mark, and several places in the area figure in the Tristan romance. Opinions differ as to whether the legend is rooted in traditions about these two historical characters or whether it merely came to be relocated here through the invention of a Mark-Cunomorus equation that was in fact spurious.

CASTLE OF MAIDENS Geoffrey of Monmouth speaks of a Castle of Maidens on Mount Agned, or the Dolorous Mountain, by which he is thought to mean the hill overlooking Edinburgh with the real castle on top. The founder, he says, was Ebraucus, a king contemporary with David in Israel. Ebraucus had twenty wives, twenty sons, and thirty daughters, but the castle had nothing to do with his family. Geoffrey may be thinking of a story about a Pictish king sending his daughters to Edinburgh for safety in time of war.

The Castle of Maidens reappears in romance, sometimes presided over by Morgan le Fay. Another location for it is in the neighborhood of Gloucester. Its nature varies. It may be an abode of temptation, where the resident girls try to seduce visiting knights. It may be a prison with kidnapped inmates, as in a tale where Galahad comes as rescuer. It may be simply one of the places where the Arthurian aristocracy gathers. The Castle of Maidens is the scene of a tournament at which Dinadan causes trouble by ridiculing Tristan when that knight falls off his horse. There is no known connection with an Iron Age fort in Dorset called Maiden Castle.

cath palug, see *Palug's Cat*

cauldron   Large round cooking vessel, of prime importance in ancient Celtic society. Some were highly valued and used for ritual purposes, to judge from the decorations on a famous specimen, made of silver, that was found at Gundestrup in Denmark. Cauldrons with magical properties figure in Welsh mythology and Arthurian exploits.

A cauldron of inspiration belonging to the enchantress Ceridwen plays a major part in the birth legend of the bard Taliesin. In *The Spoils of Annwfn*, Arthur and his followers undertake a perilous raid on the otherworld in quest of a cauldron, rimmed with pearls, that is tended by nine maidens who warm it with their breath and that "will not boil the food of a coward." In the *Mabinogion* tale of *Branwen*, the giant Bran has a cauldron of regeneration. Dead warriors who are cast into it emerge alive, although without the power of speech. In *Culhwch and Olwen*, Arthur's men go to Ireland to obtain the cauldron of Diwrnach, which is filled with treasure.

The nine cauldron-tending maidens are derived from sisterhoods of Celtic priestesses, and the same motif reappears in Geoffrey of Monmouth's *Vita Merlini*, where Morgen is the chief of nine sister enchantresses on the Isle of Avalon. There are doubtless echoes in the imagery of the Grail, which like the cauldron is a wonderworking vessel carried and attended by maidens, while the theme of a quest for a vessel by Arthur's warriors of course recurs. Furthermore, the Grail's property as a source of bodily nourishment recalls Irish tales introducing cauldrons of plenty, although Britain offers no exact parallels for these.

cave legend   One of the forms that Arthur's immortality takes is the belief that he lies asleep in a cave. He may have his knights with him, or a royal treasure, or both. While at least two actual caves bear his name, the typical story is that the cave is a mysterious place that can be found and entered only under special conditions.

The earliest recorded version is the one told of Cadbury Castle in Somerset, Cadbury-Camelot, where it is part of a larger body of local folklore. Here the cave has gates that open once a year giving a glimpse of the sleeping King inside. There are several Welsh versions, and others in north-ern England and Scotland, the total being about fifteen. Sometimes, the cave harbors knights or treasure without Arthur, who is presumably in a different retreat. One of the best-known legends, because of an account of it by Walter Scott, is that of the Eildon Hills near Melrose. Possibly owing to Norman influence, Arthur and his knights are also said to be inside Mount Etna in Sicily.

A recurrent theme is that someone is taken into the cave by a stranger, who may be Merlin, or the Scottish poet Thomas the Rhymer. The visitor is subjected to a test, which differs from one locale to another, but, if passed, will bring him good fortune or cause some great event, even Arthur's awak-ening. He may, for instance, be shown a sword and a horn, and forced to decide whether to draw the sword or blow the horn. He always fails the test and is expelled from the cave and never finds it again.

Both the principal versions of Arthur's survival, the cave legend itself and the belief that he is alive in the Isle of Avalon, seem to derive from a myth of the British Celts recorded by Plutarch, about a banished god whom Plutarch identifies with the Greek Cronus, lord of a lost golden age. The Britons said that he was asleep in a cave, on an island across the western sea.

Sooner or later, it is assumed, Arthur and his knights will wake up, and he will reign once more, as a champion of the Welsh or as the restorer of his own golden age. Other national heroes of Europe also lie asleep in caves, Arthur's legend being perhaps the prototype. In some of the Welsh instances, it is doubtful whether the sleeper is Arthur or Owen Lawgoch, a medieval Welsh patriot. Despite the mythical background of the motif, the sleeping hero is normally a historical person, and that fact has been cited as evidence for Arthur himself being historical.

CEI, see *Kay*

CELIDON Arthur's seventh battle in the *Historia Brittonum* takes place in Coit Celidon, the forest of Celidon. This is the same as the Caledonian Wood. It covered most of Dumfries and Selkirkshire and extended over the high country around the upper Clyde and Tweed. Since the northern Angles did not enter this region at any time credible for Arthur, the likeliest implica-tion is that he was fighting Picts in alliance with them. Bede mentions an Anglo-Pictish alliance in the first phase of warfare, around the middle of the fifth century. None is recorded at any relevant time afterward. Hence, this battle, if authentic, points to an early date for Arthur, raising a problem over his association with the later battles of Badon and Camlann.

Celidon is the scene of the wanderings of Lailoken or, in Welsh tradition, Myrddin, the original, or part-original, of Merlin. This is the reason for a belief that Merlin was buried at Drumelzier on the Upper Tweed.

CELLI WIG, see *Kelliwic*

CHAPALU, see *Palug's Cat*

CHESTER   Roman town on the Dee. Nearby was an army base called *Devana Castra*, the "Deeside Camp." Later, the town became simply *Chester*, "The Camp." In the *Annales Cambriae*, it is *Cair Legion*, the City of the Legion, being therefore apparently the scene of Arthur's ninth battle in the list in the *Historia Brittonum*.

Chester is a long way from the early settlements of Angles and Saxons. It has been argued that Arthur could not have fought them here and that the Welsh author of the battle list wrongly included a battle fought at Chester in the seventh century, making it a victory, which, from the Welsh viewpoint, it was not. But Gildas attests raiding right across to the Irish Sea in the mid-fifth-century Anglo-Saxon revolt, and an action at Chester could fit in there. It follows that both the most securely locatable Arthurian battles, those fought in the forest of Celidon and the City of the Legion, favor an early date for Arthur.

CITY OF THE LEGION   In the *Historia Brittonum*, the scene of Arthur's ninth battle. Geoffrey of Monmouth portrays him holding court, although not fighting a battle, at a "City of the Legions," with details showing that he means Caerleon in southeast Wales. But in the older *Annales Cambriae*, which are in the same manuscript with the best copy of the *Historia*, the City of the Legion is Chester. This is almost certainly the place meant in the battle list.

CLAUDAS   Enemy of Lancelot's father, Ban. Their conflict is the reason for Lancelot's being taken away as a child by the Lady of the Lake.

CLIGÉS   Hero of a romance by Chrétien de Troyes, although an account of his parents takes up one-third of the poem. He is a nephew of Gawain. On the death of his father, he is rightful heir to the throne of Constantinople, but a kinsman, Alis, usurps it. Cligés falls in love with Fénice, Alis's bride. Although she loves Cligés, she explicitly rejects Iseut's solution of such a problem. Cligés distinguishes himself at Arthur's court. Eventually, Fénice escapes by pretending death, like Juliet. They live together and, after Alis's death, marry.

CONSTANS Eldest son of the Breton prince Constantine, according to Geoffrey of Monmouth. Constantine comes to Britain after its severance from Rome and is crowned king. Constans enters a monastery. When his father is killed, the scheming Vortigern persuades him to renounce his monastic vows and sets him up as a puppet ruler. Presently, Vortigern contrives his assassination and seizes power openly himself. Constans appears in later narratives that embroider Geoffrey's account. The Vulgate *Merlin* calls him simply "the Monk," Moine.

CONSTANTINE (1) Prince of Brittany, Arthur's grandfather, according to Geoffrey of Monmouth. Invited to Britain to organize defense against marauding barbarians, after the island's abandonment by Rome, he routs the invaders and the Britons award him the crown. He has three sons: Constans, who becomes a monk; Aurelius Ambrosius; and Uther, the eventual Pendragon, father of Arthur. After a ten-year reign, Constantine falls to an assassin. A dispute over the succession is checked by Vortigern, who for his own ends persuades Constans to leave the monastery and become king.

Geoffrey took a hint—no more than a hint—from the career of a soldier named Constantine who was proclaimed emperor in Britain in 407 and had a son Constans who left a monastery to join him. He called himself Constantine III. His actual reign in Britain was brief. He tried to make his claim good on the Continent and met his death overseas, together with his son.

CONSTANTINE (2) Arthur's successor, a cousin. The son of Cador, duke of Cornwall, he appears first in Geoffrey of Monmouth. After the fatal battle with Mordred, Arthur hands over the crown to him and departs to Avalon. Constantine's father seems to be still alive, but would have been old by this time, and apart from him Constantine is Arthur's nearest surviving male relative. The new king has to fight against resurgent Saxons and two sons of Mordred, one of whom holds London, the other Winchester. Defeated, they seek sanctuary in churches, but Constantine slays them there without mercy. Four years afterward, he is struck down by divine vengeance for the sacrilege and is buried in the royal cemetery inside Stonehenge.

He figures briefly in several subsequent works, with variations on the succession theme. More than one writer has Arthur tell him, before departure, about the imminent voyage to Avalon and expected return. Later versions prefer Girflet or Bedivere as the companion of the King's passing. In Malory, Constantine is merely chosen as successor after an interregnum.

Geoffrey developed the character from a real British king called Constantine who reigned during the first half of the sixth century and is denounced by Gildas for murdering two princes in a monastic church. By then, however, Britain had broken up into small kingdoms, and Constantine was ruler of Dumnonia only, comprising Cornwall, Devon, Somerset, and some, but not much, territory beyond. His enlargement into Arthur's cousin and successor reflects the belief, current before Geoffrey and perhaps factually based, that Arthur's home country was in this region.

CORBENIC (CARBONEK) Town with a castle where the Grail is kept. During Arthur's reign, the overlord of this elusive place is Pelles. Corbenic may be derived from *cor benoit*, "blessed body," meaning the body of Christ, which Joseph of Arimathea took from the Cross, abiding as a mysterious presence in the Grail. Another suggestion is that Corbenic echoes Corbeny, a place in France with a Benedictine abbey, but there is no obvious link between the abbey and the Grail story.

CULHWCH Hero of the early Welsh tale *Culhwch and Olwen*. He is under a curse and cannot marry unless he wins Olwen, the daughter of Ysbaddaden, the chief giant. Olwen is willing, but Ysbaddaden, too, is under a curse and destined to die when his daughter weds. He therefore tries to delay the marriage by demanding that the suitor perform a long series of seemingly impossible tasks. Arthur and his men come to Culhwch's aid, the giant is foiled, and the spells expire.

DAGONET In the French Vulgate *Lancelot*, a foolish knight. Malory makes him Arthur's court fool, and Tennyson follows him in this and expands the character.

DINADAN Companion of the hero in the Prose *Tristan*. He is a good-natured but satirical figure, treating the chivalric code with amused skepticism. Deploring the knights' extreme readiness for combat, he remarks that cowardice has the advantage of keeping one alive. He cannot understand, either, why the knights go to so much trouble and suffer such pangs in seeking the favors of haughty ladies, when equally attractive women are easily available. Yet he is a brave fighter when need arises and a loyal friend to Tristan, whose death is a bitter blow to him.

Dinadan does not voice a recognized point of view. Others regard him as a licensed humorist, sound at heart whose quirks are not to be taken too seriously. In Malory, he composes a song lampooning Mark.

DINAS EMRYS Welsh hill-fort on the southern fringe of Snowdonia. Reputedly, this is the scene of the confrontation of Vortigern and a boy-prophet who is identified in the *Historia Brittonum* as Ambrosius but whom Geoffrey of Monmouth converts into the young Merlin. Brought to the site as a human sacrifice, to enable the king to build a stronghold, he reveals a subterranean pool that has been undermining the foundations and has two dragons in it, one red, one white. They fight, and after an initial defeat the red drives the white one back. The seer interprets them as symbolizing the Britons and Saxons.

The *Historia Brittonum* says that Vortigern fled and left the place in Ambrosius's hands, hence its name, "Emrys's Fort," *Emrys* being the Welsh form of Ambrosius. Subsequent legend, following Geoffrey in making out the boy to be Merlin, says that he lingered for a while and hid a golden cauldron, full of treasure, that will be found only by a destined person. According to another legend, recorded late but possibly old, a son of the emperor Maximus, named Owen (i.e., Eugenius), fought a giant in the valley below.

Excavation has shown that Dinas Emrys was used in the early Christian era, that there actually was a pool—an artificial one—and that a fifth-century occupant maintained a Christian and prosperous household. Some tradition of this last fact may have inspired the legendary connection with Ambrosius, who was a British leader of importance at about the right time, however fabulous his youthful overawing of Vortigern.

DOLOROUS GARD Original name of Lancelot's castle. It is under an evil enchantment that he ends. Inside, he finds a tomb with his own name on it and realizes that this is destined to be his home and last resting place. He settles his household in the castle and renames it Joyous Gard (q.v.). After his tragic rift with Arthur, bringing the doom of the Round Table, it reverts to its old name.

DOLOROUS MOUNTAIN Hill in Scotland. Geoffrey of Monmouth identifies it with Agned and probably means the hill above Edinburgh with the castle on it. However, Chrétien de Troyes locates the Dolorous Mountain near Melrose, perhaps because the valley of Wedale was sometimes called Wodale, a name that could be construed as "Woe-dale." (See also *Guinnion*).

DOLOROUS STROKE Blow with which Balin wounds Pellam, using the Holy Lance. In the *Suite du Merlin*, it is the reason for the wasteland becoming so, this being a divine judgment for Balin's sacrilege in employing the lance as a weapon. Malory adapts the story.

ÒRUST Pictish royal name, with such variants as Drostan and, in Latin, Drustanus. Welsh adapts it into Drystan and sometimes Tristan (q.v.). Hence, it has been argued that the nucleus of the Tristan legend is Pictish, the familiar location in southwest Britain being due to a literary transfer. Since an eighth-century Pictish king was called Drust son of Talorc, and Tristan, in the triads, is Drystan son of Tallwch, a reminiscence of the king certainly seems to have found its way into the legend. This is all the more likely because of an early tale in which Drust is revealed as the rescuer of a noblewoman from robbers, under circumstances echoed when Tristan is recognized at the Irish court.

However, a long-distance importation by storytellers is not the only reason why this name could have appeared in a Cornish-centered romance. Northern names were adopted in southern Britain and borne by real persons. This one is carved on the Tristan Stone, a monolith that stands just outside Fowey in Cornwall but was formerly closer to Castle Dore, a reputed residence of King Mark. The inscription, dating from the early sixth century, reads DRUSTANUS HIC IACIT CUNOMORI FILIUS, "Drustanus lies here, the son of Cunomorus." It has been contended that the man commemorated is *the* Tristan and that the story has historical roots around Castle Dore, whatever details it may have absorbed from Pictland or anywhere else. On the other hand, the story may have come to be located here partly or wholly because of the inscription.

ÒUBGLAS The *Historia Brittonum* says that Arthur fought four of his battles against the Saxons—the second, third, fourth, and fifth—by a "river that is called Dubglas and is in the district Linnuis." *Dubglas* means "blue-black" and appears on the map, with variants meaning "black stream," in quite a number of versions (Douglas, Divelish, Dawlish, for example) and also, Englished, as Blackwater. The "district Linnuis" seems a more promising clue. It is probably Lindsey, the central and northern portion of Lincolnshire. That name goes back to *Lindum*, that is, Lincoln. Such an identification would accord with the likely location of the River Glein, the scene of Arthur's previous battle, and with the distribution of early Anglian settlements.

The trouble is that Lindsey now has no river with the right name in any form. West of Loch Lomond in Scotland there is a river called Douglas Water, and the classical geographer Ptolemy mentions another Lindum hereabout, implying the possibility of another Linnuis with a Dubglas in it. The enemy would have had to be Picts. While Bede's mention of an Anglo-Pictish alliance would allow this to be the case, it is hard to imagine a real Arthur waging a whole campaign in such a remote part of the country.

ECTOR (ÞECTOR) In Malory, Kay's father, to whom Merlin entrusts the child Arthur for his upbringing. After the episode of the Sword in the Stone, Ector reveals to Arthur that he is his foster-father only.

ELAINE (TÞE NAME) Equivalent to Helen, in Welsh *Elen*, the name of a princess of Britain in Welsh legends about the last phase of Roman rule. There are indications of a belief that Vortigern married one of her daughters. Several Arthurian writers introduce women so named, including a sister of Gawain and a daughter of Pellinore. The four following Elaines are those generally recognized.

ELAINE (1) Daughter of Ygerna by her first husband, the duke of Cornwall, hence a sister of Morgan and Morgause and a half-sister of Arthur. She marries Nentres, king of Galot. Malory gives these family particulars.

ELAINE (2) King Ban's wife, the mother of Lancelot in the Vulgate.

ELAINE (3) Daughter of Pelles, the lord of the Grail Castle, Corbenic. Sometimes anonymous, but named in Malory. She bears the Grail when it is brought in to be seen from a distance. Pelles regards her as the destined mother of the knight who will carry on the line of Joseph of Arimathea and attain the full vision. When Lancelot visits Corbenic, Pelles leads him to think that his beloved Guinevere is in a castle nearby. Sending Elaine to this castle, Pelles contrives by a magic potion to make Lancelot suppose her to be Guinevere. Lancelot goes to bed with her and begets Galahad, discovering the trick too late. Thus, ironically, the adulterous passion that debars Lancelot from success in the Grail Quest produces the pure knight who does succeed.

Elaine truly loves Lancelot. When she comes to court, the Queen is jealous and dismisses Lancelot with a violence that drives him out of his mind. After long wandering, he comes to Corbenic again and is cured by the Grail.

ELAINE (4) Called Elaine le Blank, the White, by Malory. Tennyson's Lady of Shalott (*See also* Escalot).

ENIÓ (ENIÓE) Long-suffering wife of a husband who loves her but is deludedly cruel, Erec in Chrétien de Troyes, Geraint in the Welsh prose tale named after him.

ERCING In early Welsh geography, a region extending over much of the present Herefordshire. Derived from the Roman *Ariconium*, the name survives in the modern Archenfield. Among the "marvels" listed at the end of the *Historia Brittonum* is a mound in Ercing said to be the grave of Arthur's son Amr, whom Arthur himself slew in some unrecorded tragedy and buried here. Its "marvelous" property is that it changes in size, varying from six feet long to fifteen. Near it is a spring. The spring is Gamber Head, the source of the Gamber. There used to be a mound fairly close to it, perhaps truly a burial mound, but this no longer exists.

EREC Hero of a romance by Chrétien de Troyes. He marries Enide. Presently, he is reproached for being too fondly attached to her and neglecting his duties. She speaks of this, and Erec sees the justice of the criticism but is disturbed by the way she puts it, wrongly scenting disloyalty. He treats her harshly and drags her off on a series of adventures that restore his reputation and strengthen their love through mutual respect. (See also *Geraint*).

ESCALOT In the Vulgate *Mort Artu*, the home of an unnamed maiden who falls hopelessly in love with Lancelot and dies of grief. Her body is floated on a barge down a nearby river to Camelot. Malory calls her Elaine and her home Astolat, and has the barge go down the Thames to Westminster. It might be inferred that he pictures Astolat as upstream. Confusingly, however, he makes it out to be Guildford, which is on a tributary, the Wey, not navigable in the Middle Ages. Quite aware that it was not, he says that Elaine's father and brother conveyed the body ten miles or more to the Thames. This geographical difficulty is self-inflicted. His story requires that Astolat must be on the road from London to Winchester.

Tennyson adapts the older place-name in his first poem on the theme, "The Lady of Shalott." He follows the Vulgate in leaving the lady nameless and locating her home on a river above Camelot. However, in his *Idylls of the King*, she is, as in Malory, Elaine, the "lily maid of Astolat," another echo of Malory, who calls her "le Blank," the White.

ESSYLLT, see *Iseut (1)*

ETTARD, see *Pelleas*

EVALAC Pagan king in the *Estoire del saint Graal* who is converted and adopts the name Mordrain. Galahad cures him of blindness. "Evalac" suggests "Avallach" (see *Avalon*), but the connection, if any, is not clear.

EXCALIBUR   Arthur's sword in romance. The name is a modification of Geoffrey of Monmouth's "Caliburn" (q.v.), which echoes the Latin *chalybs*, "steel." Excalibur is sometimes identified with the sword that Arthur draws from the stone but usually not. According to one account, it belonged to Gawain first. In the most familiar story, Arthur breaks the sword drawn from the stone, and Merlin arranges for him to receive Excalibur, a magical, otherworldly weapon, as a replacement. They go together to meet the Lady of the Lake and row out in a boat to where a hand has risen from the water, grasping Excalibur. The sword is in a scabbard, and Merlin tells Arthur that the scabbard is more precious, because so long as he carries it he cannot lose blood. Its eventual disappearance is due to the scheming of Morgan.

When Arthur lies wounded after his last battle, he commands a surviving knight, Girflet or Bedivere, to cast Excalibur into the water. After twice disobeying, he does. Again, a hand rises above the water. It catches the sword and draws it below. At least five places claim to be the scene of this incident, notably Pomparles Bridge near Glastonbury and Dozmary Pool on Bodmin Moor. Tennyson locates it at Loe Pool in southern Cornwall. There is archaeological evidence for a custom that the tale may reflect. A warrior's sword was peculiarly his own, and sometimes, after his death, it would be dropped into a pool, perhaps weighted down and even damaged to discourage any attempt at retrieval by someone else.

When Richard I visited Tancred of Sicily in 1191, he presented him with a sword that he claimed was Arthur's. It is not clear where it came from, but he was doubtless aware of the reported finding of Arthur's grave at Glastonbury, and he may have used this to "sell" another relic. He would not have felt any inconsistency in producing the sword, because the story of its casting-away was not yet embodied in any literary version.

FISHER KING   Title of the Grail keeper. In Chrétien de Troyes, it occurs but is not explained. Robert de Boron makes it originate with a symbolic fish caught and placed on the Grail table by Bron, Joseph of Arimathea's brother-in-law, who is therefore known as the Rich Fisher. Bron becomes explicitly the Fisher King when he is lord of the Grail Castle in Britain. His son Alain is another who is called so, and another, in a different account, is Pelles. The Fisher King is sometimes identified with the Grail King, sometimes not. Where they are distinct characters, the Grail King, in Arthur's time, is maimed and behind the scenes. Where they are the same, the Fisher King himself is wounded or sick. Indeed, he may be so even if there is a wounded Grail King, too. His cure depends on the asking of a question.

GAHERIS (GAHERET) Son of Lot and Morgause and younger brother of Gawain. Romancers do not always distinguish him from Gareth. Where they are two persons, it may be a case of a single character being split. In Malory, when Gareth marries Lyones, Gaheris marries her sister Lynet. Gaheris kills his mother, Morgause, when he catches her with Lamorak, son of Pellinore. Gaheris is killed himself, together with Gareth, in the fight that breaks out when Lancelot saves Guinevere from burning.

GALAHAD Lancelot's son by Elaine of Corbenic. Her father, the Grail keeper Pelles, arranges their sexual encounter by a magical deception, so that the knight destined to succeed in the Quest shall be born of the stock of Joseph of Arimathea. When Galahad is old enough for knighthood, he comes to Arthur's court and is revealed as the Grail achiever by several signs. He can sit in the Perilous Seat at the Round Table and draw out a sword from a block of marble where Merlin fixed it long before.

Galahad is foreshadowed in the *Perlesvaus*, but he is named first in the Vulgate Cycle. He is handsome, and skillful in combat, but his chief quality is chastity, which is here made vital for the full experience of the Grail—one consequence being that Lancelot, despite his noble qualities, is doomed to fail in the Quest and succeed only by proxy through his son. After many adventures, Galahad attains the vision in Sarras, and dies.

His name is taken from "Galaad," or Gilead, in the Vulgate Bible (Genesis 31:48). This, in terms of medieval interpretation, makes him a type of Christ. He represents an attempt to fuse chivalry with religion. The only earlier figure from whom a hint may have been taken is the Welsh soldier-saint Illtud.

GALEHAUT (GALAHALT) Not to be confused with Galahad. A character first developed in a long episode of the Vulgate *Lancelot*, he is overlord of the Lointaines (Faraway) Isles, perhaps the Scillies, and of Surluse, a district in Lyonesse. He arranges the first tryst between Lancelot, who is a close friend of his, and Guinevere. She aids him in his own love affair with the Lady of Malehaut. According to the Vulgate *Mort Artu*, Galehaut was buried in Lancelot's castle Joyous Gard, and Lancelot was buried in the same tomb.

Dante's best-known Arthurian allusion, the story of Paolo and Francesca (*Inferno* 5.121–38), treats Galehaut as a pander.

GANIEDA Merlin's sister in Geoffrey of Monmouth's *Vita Merlini*; she joins him on his wanderings and becomes a prophet herself. In earlier Welsh poetry, she appears as Gwenddydd, but her role is less important.

GARETH Lot's youngest son, known as Gareth of Orkney, much loved by his brother Gawain. In Malory, he has the nickname Beaumains, which is construed by those friendly to him as implying large-handedness or generosity. His chief adventure is a much-frustrated but successful amour with the lady Lyones, whom he eventually marries. Lancelot accidentally kills him while rescuing Guinevere from the stake at Carlisle. For this act, Gawain vows vengeance, the first definite step toward the breakup of the Round Table. Gawain prevents any reconciliation between Lancelot and Arthur till it is too late.

GAWAIN (GAUVAIN, GALVANUS, ETC.) One of Arthur's principal knights—in medieval English eyes, the chief of them all. He is often identified with a warrior called Gwalchmei (q.v.) in Welsh but is far more important. A peculiar quality of his, that his strength increases till noon and then declines, hints that he has a background in solar myth, but if so he is fully humanized. Tales of him were current on the Continent before Geoffrey of Monmouth.

Gawain's father is Lot. There are uncertainties about his mother, but the romancers' final consensus makes her Morgause, Arthur's half-sister. Mordred is either Gawain's brother or his half-brother. Gawain's undoubted brothers are Gaheris, Agravain, and Gareth, and in the *Didot-Perceval* he has a sister, Elaine. As early as 1125, William of Malmesbury speaks of him as a nephew of Arthur and asserts that his tomb was found on the coast of Pembrokeshire in the reign of William the Conqueror. He says also that Gawain fought against a brother of Hengist, the Saxon leader, and that he was attacked by enemies on a ship and thrown overboard, or according to another account was killed at a banquet. An obscure St. Govan, who has a chapel near the southernmost point of the same county, has been confused with him.

Apart from the relationship with Arthur, William seems to be drawing on a tradition that fades out, connecting Gawain and his famous uncle with the struggle against the first major wave of Saxons, around the middle of the fifth century, to judge from such fairly credible evidence as there is. Geoffrey of Monmouth and his successors have nothing to correspond. Geoffrey says that Gawain was educated at Rome in the papal household, fought bravely for Arthur, and met his death in Mordred's rebellion.

Romancers and poets portray him variously. Sometimes, especially in English works, he is courteous and heroic and passes alarming tests, above all the one imposed on him in *Sir Gawain and the Green Knight*.

Sometimes, however, he is made slightly comic. Sometimes, he is altogether less admirable, a womanizer, a cheat, and a violent, vengeful person. He comes close to the Grail, but inconclusively, because of his sins and shortcomings, and he draws his brothers into a murderous vendetta against Pellinore, who had slain Lot in battle while Gawain was still a child, and Pellinore's son Lamorak. His enmity toward Lancelot fatally prolongs the dispute that disrupts the Round Table. Wounded by Lancelot, he dies at Dover. Caxton's preface to Malory assures the reader that Gawain's skull can still be seen in Dover Castle.

GEOFFREY OF MONMOUTH   Author responsible for the main framework of the Arthurian legend and for the figure of Arthur as a quasi-historical king of Britain. Born at Monmouth in southeast Wales, of Welsh or possibly Breton extraction, he was a teacher at Oxford between 1129 and 1151. His three surviving works are in Latin. The first is entitled *Prophetiae Merlini* ("Prophecies of Merlin"). Here, Geoffrey took up Welsh poetic predictions of a Celtic recovery ascribed to the northern bard Myrddin. Modifying this name as Merlin, he added many more prophecies, most of them probably of his own invention. About 1136–38, he produced a *Historia Regum Britanniae* ("History of the Kings of Britain") and incorporated the "prophecies" into it. Toward 1150, he wrote a long narrative poem, *Vita Merlini* ("Life of Merlin"), enlarging on Welsh traditions about the original prophet.

All three works mention Arthur, allusively or directly, and the *Historia*, which is by far the most important, deals with him at great length. Geoffrey's chief aim is to glorify the Celtic Britons of old, ancestors of the Welsh, showing how they rose to greatness but were finally dispossessed by the Saxons, ancestors of the English, through treachery and their own decadence. He begins by expanding a Welsh legend tracing the Britons' origins to a company of wandering Trojans led by Brutus. After narrating a long series of fictitious reigns, Geoffrey carries the story through the Roman period, reducing the conquest to a vague protectorate. The break with Rome leaves Britain independent again, but the usurping king Vortigern invites the heathen Saxons into the island as auxiliary troops, and they come in growing numbers, get out of hand, and ravage the country. During this time of trouble, Geoffrey introduces Merlin, creating him by combining two or three figures from earlier legend. Vortigern is ousted, and after some years Arthur becomes king.

His reign is the climax of the *Historia*. First, he crushes the Saxons and other barbarians. His early triumphs, and marriage to Guinevere, are followed by a long spell of peace and prosperity, during which he founds a famous order of knighthood. Having conquered most of Gaul, still shakily in Roman hands, he holds court magnificently at Caerleon. A Roman demand for tribute and the return of his conquests provokes another overseas war. Arthur, although victorious, is betrayed by the rebellion of his nephew Mordred, whom he left in charge at home. Forced to return and fight the traitor, he is gravely wounded and carried off to the Isle of Avalon. The Britons gradually succumb to the Saxons, who regain the upper hand and bring over allies. The *Historia* ends in 689, with a British remnant surviving in their island only as Welsh, although Merlin's prophecies portend an eventual change of fortunes.

Wherever Geoffrey can be checked, as in his account of the Roman period, it is plain that he is a writer of fiction and can never be trusted for historical facts. Like many medieval authors, he updates, making Arthur's court thoroughly twelfth-century. From Julius Caesar onward, however, he is nearly always using real history or what purports to be so, not merely inventing, and some of his sources can be identified—for instance, Gildas, the *Historia Brittonum*, and Bede, besides Roman writers. On the face of it, he is usually expanding and fictionalizing fairly meager data. His own preface claims that the *Historia* is a translation from a much ampler source, an "ancient book in the British language" (meaning possibly Welsh but more likely Breton) given him by Walter, the archdeacon of Oxford. No copy exists, and the claim is incredible as it stands. But Geoffrey's story of Arthur—by contrast, say, with his story of Vortigern—can be accounted for only fractionally from the sources mentioned, a fact suggesting that the rest of it does take hints from lost material of some kind. To judge from apparent echoes of fifth-century events in Gaul, the missing source may have been continental. There are possible traces of the use of such a source in another text, the preface to the Breton *Legend of St. Goeznovius*.

Geoffrey's poetical *Vita Merlini* is an attempt to resolve a difficulty arising out of the *Historia*. Having learned more about Myrddin, the northern character who was the primary ingredient in the enchanter's making, he has realized that the account of Merlin in the *Historia* does not square with this further knowledge. His attempted harmony of the data is ingenious but unsuccessful. One interesting passage is a description of Avalon and Arthur's voyage thither.

Geoffrey's works were not the sole inspiration of Arthurian romance, but they gave the King an appearance of authenticity and provided some of the major characters and a frame into which their adventures could be fitted. Many medieval chroniclers accepted the *Historia* as factual, at least to some extent. Finally, disbelief set in. Spenser, however, paraphrases much of the book in *The Faerie Queene*, and *King Lear* and other dramas are based on episodes in it.

GERAINT (GEREINT) Character drawn from Welsh historical tradition. Geraint is originally the Celtic Gerontios or Gerontius. A British general so named held a command under the imperial pretender Constantine III, in 407–11. Both names, Constantine and Gerontius or Geraint, are afterward borne by the Dumnonian royalty of southwest Britain. The latter survives in Cornish place-names, such as Gerrans.

One Gerontius from this region was reputedly the father of Cadwy. A prince of the same name fought the Saxons toward the year 500 in a battle that was commemorated by a poem. A tenth-century rehandling of this poem locates the battle at Llongborth, probably Portchester in Hampshire, and converts the leader's name into its Welsh form, Geraint. It also refers to "Arthur's men" as taking part in the action. The poem's heading betrays a confusion by identifying the prince with one of his later namesakes, Geraint son of Erbin, who lived about the end of the sixth century and is probably mentioned in *Gododdin*. This confusion between men of the same name persists in Arthurian storytelling, where Geraint is called the son of Erbin but lives in Arthur's time.

The Welsh romance *Geraint* tells much the same tale as Chrétien de Troyes's *Erec et Enide*. Both probably derive from a common source. Geraint is the central figure instead of Erec, but his wife is still Enid. The Welsh author gives a stronger motive than Chrétien for his ill-treatment of her, wording the speech of Enid that provokes it so as to make Geraint suspect outright infidelity, if not very plausibly.

GIFLET, see *Girflet*

GILDAS Monk of northern origin, who flourished during the first half of the sixth century and wrote *De Excidio Britanniae* ("Concerning the Ruin of Britain"), commonly although not unanimously dated to the 530s or 540s. The greater part of this tract is a denunciation of British rulers and ecclesiastics in his own time. He preludes it, however, with a sketch of what he supposes to be Britain's history from the first century A.D. onward. He is not professing to write history as such; he is making a long-term survey of the misconduct of his countrymen, which has brought the Saxon invasion upon them.

His book is a testimony not to Arthur but to a situation that laid the groundwork for Arthur's emergence as a legendary deliverer, although a temporary one. The Saxons, Gildas says, were invited into the country as auxiliary troops to fight the Picts. The invitation came from a ruling council in concert with a *superbus tyrannus*, which in this context means something like "preeminent ruler," and looks like Gildas's rendering of a British title meaning "high king." The *superbus tyrannus* is assumed by Bede and most later authors to be the person elsewhere styled Vortigern.

Gildas relates how Saxons poured into Britain, made excessive demands for supplies, and when these were not met revolted and ravaged the country, raiding as far as the western sea. They withdrew at last to their authorized settlements, and a British counterattack began, led by Ambrosius Aurelianus. After a phase of fluctuating warfare, the Britons won a victory at the siege of Mount Badon, somewhere about the year 500, which stabilized the position. Gildas goes on to complain that his contemporaries have forgotten the marvelous deliverance and are relapsing into conduct that augurs ill for the future.

He has an odd reluctance to name people before his own time—Ambrosius is his only named Briton in the fifth century—and he does not name the British commander at Badon. Later, Arthur comes to be credited with this triumph. Gildas sheds no light on the claim, or on the origins of the Arthurian legend, beyond his picture of a disaster-and-rescue train of events that would have produced heroes with at least some factual basis. From the end of Roman rule till near his own time, the broad pattern is all he can be trusted for.

Gildas passes into Welsh legend himself. He is at Arthur's court in *Culhwch and Olwen*. A Life of him by Caradoc of Llancarfan, written about 1130, says that he had a brother, Hueil, whom Arthur executed as a rebel and pirate. Gildas was grief-stricken. Eventually, Arthur sought his pardon and they were reconciled. Some time afterward, Caradoc adds, Gildas lived in the Glastonbury community. King Melwas of Somerset carried off Guinevere and kept her at Glastonbury. Arthur tried to recover her, without success, and Gildas and the abbot settled the affair by mediation. William of Malmesbury, too, connects Gildas with Glastonbury, and a passage in *De Excidio* may suggest that he at least knew the place. Caradoc's story of Melwas and the abduction of Guinevere may derive from an older tale, and it becomes a recurrent theme of romance, although with variations that wander far from the original.

GIRFLET (GIFLET)   Knight who figures in French romances by Chrétien de Troyes and others. In the Vulgate *Mort Artu*, after the last battle, he accompanies the wounded King and twice disobeys his command to throw Excalibur into a nearby lake but finally does so. A hand rises from the water, catches the sword, and vanishes with it. In England, this episode is transferred to Bedivere.

GLASTONBURY   Small town in Somerset with a ruined abbey. Glastonbury has a long history and has inspired much legend and speculation. It lies in a cluster of hills surrounded by low and level country. The hill cluster was once almost an island. Two Celtic "lake villages" in the neighborhood, which flourished around the beginning of the Christian era, were centers of some importance with overseas trade. The highest of the hills, Glastonbury Tor, seems to have figured in early myth and perhaps ritual, being regarded as a point of entry to Annwfn, the otherworld. This was one of several pre-Christian aspects that aided Glastonbury's identification as the true Isle of Avalon, Arthur's last earthly destination, although the asserted finding of his grave was the operative cause.

A Celtic establishment of some kind existed on the Tor in the sixth century, very possibly before. Its nature is uncertain, but it is likely to have been religious rather than secular, a monastery or settlement of Christian hermits. On the abbey site, there was certainly an early Christian community, in an unknown relationship to whatever was on the higher ground. This one may really have originated a little later, though still before the Saxon occupation of Somerset. However, extreme claims were made in the Middle Ages about its antiquity. They focused on the "Old Church," a small building that stood till 1184, when a fire destroyed most of the abbey. Legend could grow around it freely because there was no authentic record of its foundation.

William of Malmesbury notes, without commitment, a claim that the Old Church was built by disciples of Christ himself. Glastonbury, under the name Avalon, came to be involved with the Grail story in Robert de Boron and *Perlesvaus*, and during the first half of the thirteenth century Joseph of Arimathea was named both as the disciple who brought the Grail to Britain and as the founder of Christian Glastonbury. His two roles are never clearly combined in medieval literature, and Glastonbury's account of him, although often assumed to be a mere borrowing from Grail romance, is incompatible with it. The problem of sources here is unresolved.

Arthur is first connected with Glastonbury about 1130 by Caradoc of

Llancarfan. His Life of Gildas includes an early version of the abduction of Guinevere. Melwas, king of Somerset, is stated to have carried her off and kept her at Glastonbury. Arthur came to get her back with troops from Cornwall and Devon, but the marshy terrain made the place difficult of access, and the dispute was settled by negotiation.

Arthur's reputed grave was found in 1190 or early 1191. Its whereabouts had long been a mystery, as William of Malmesbury attests. A Welsh or Breton bard, it is said, divulged the long-kept secret to Henry II, telling him that Arthur was buried in the monks' graveyard at Glastonbury between two "pyramids" or memorial pillars. Excavation brought to light an inscribed cross with Arthur's name on it and a coffin made of a hollowed-out log, with the bones of a tall man inside, and smaller bones taken to be Guinevere's. Modern reexcavation of the site has shown that the monks did find an early burial. The claim that it was Arthur's depends on the inscribed cross. This has vanished, but its appearance is preserved in a later drawing. Most historians have taken the view that it was faked to establish the grave as Arthur's in order to enhance the prestige of the abbey and attract funds needed for rebuilding after the fire of 1184. However, there is no evidence that the monks did exploit the grave to attract funds, and peculiarities in the inscription suggest that the cross was not a twelfth-century forgery, whatever it may actually have been.

Malory introduces Glastonbury toward the end of his work. Lancelot and other survivors retire from the world to live as hermits in a small valley between two hills nearby. The allusion is probably to the valley between the Tor and the adjacent Chalice Hill, where the much-earlier *Perlesvaus* indicates a tradition of a religious settlement during Arthur's time. This may have some relationship to the actual early community on the Tor.

Glastonbury's legend of the Holy Thorn is postmedieval. It relates that Joseph of Arimathea, on arrival, drove his staff into the ground, and it became a tree that blossomed at Christmas. The Glastonbury Thorn is a real tree, a kind of hawthorn. The earliest known specimen grew on one of the hills. Puritans destroyed it, but descendants of it are widespread, and it does blossom in December or early January. The tale of its growing from Joseph's staff cannot be traced back farther than the eighteenth century. However, it has been claimed that the un-English Thorn is a type of tree native to Palestine or Syria—Joseph's country, more or less—and that the first specimen may have been conveyed to this northern home by a returning medieval pilgrim.

GLEIN Arthur's warfare against the Saxons, as sketched in the *Historia Brittonum*, opens with a battle "at the mouth of the river that is called Glein." The word "mouth" (*ostium*) may refer, as in modern English, to the place where this river flowed into a lake or sea, but Welsh usage allows that the author may have been thinking of a confluence with a larger river, as, to this day, in the place-name Monmouth. *Glein* is of Celtic British origin and means "pure" or "clear." Two rivers still bear the name, in the form *Glen*. One is in southern Lincolnshire, the other in Northumberland. If the Glein of the battle list is either of these, the former is more likely, because of known early Anglian settlement in that area but not in Northumberland. Its "mouth" would be its confluence with the Welland.

"Glen" in the sense of "valley" is a different word, irrelevant here.

GLEWLWYD Gatekeeper of Arthur's court, who raises objections when Culhwch seeks admission. A Welsh poem makes him someone else's gatekeeper, with Arthur himself seeking admission and finding him obstructive. It may be supposed that as storytellers made Arthur more and more prominent they annexed the gatekeeper to him as they annexed many other characters. The Glewlwyd of *Culhwch and Olwen* speaks of his wide-ranging and fanciful travels, sometimes in Arthur's company.

GODODDIN Early Welsh poem, or rather series of poems, ascribed to the northern bard Aneirin. Obliquely, through laments for the fallen, the poet tells the story of an expedition of Britons from Manau Guotodin around Edinburgh, to dislodge the Angles from a strong point called Catraeth, probably the Roman fort at Catterick in Yorkshire. Nearly all were killed. *Gododdin* dates from about 600. Much information on the Celtic society of the north can be extracted from it.

A couple of lines praise the warrior Gwawrddur as "glutting black ravens on the wall of the fort, though he was not Arthur." "Glutting ravens" is a poetic phrase for "slaying enemies," and the sense seems to be that Gwawrddur was a great fighter even though admittedly not the greatest, the Arthur proverbial for martial prowess. On the face of it, this is the first known reference to Arthur by name. Unfortunately, *Gododdin* underwent interpolation after Aneirin's time, and the allusion may have been added. If genuinely his, it is close enough to Arthur's *floruit*, even on the earliest dating for this, to carry weight as evidence for his reality. It is not evidence for anything more of a specific nature. It does not imply that he was one of the northern men himself, or contemporary with them.

GORLOIS   Duke of Cornwall just before Arthur's birth. Geoffrey of
Monmouth tells how King Uther desired Gorlois's wife, Ygerna. A quarrel
resulted, and the royal and ducal troops fought each other in Cornwall.
Gorlois immured his wife in the castle of Tintagel, on a promontory almost
cut off from the mainland, easily guarded. Merlin, however, transformed
Uther into an exact likeness of Gorlois. Disguised as the lord of the castle,
he was able to pass its guards and spend a night with Ygerna. Arthur was
begotten. Meanwhile, the real Gorlois fell in battle, so that Uther could
return to his normal shape, marry Ygerna, and make Arthur his heir. Romancers repeat the story with slight variations. Malory opens his work with
it but leaves the duke unnamed.

Gorlois's successor as duke of Cornwall is Cador, seemingly a brother,
since Gorlois and Ygerna have no male offspring, and Cador's son
Constantine is spoken of as Arthur's cousin.

GORRE   In Chrétien's *Lancelot*, a country to which Meleagant, the
son of its king, carries off Guinevere. Lancelot goes to rescue her. A known
antecedent of the story is an episode in the Life of Gildas by Caradoc (see
Gildas; Melwas). There, Arthur's queen is taken to Glastonbury in Somerset.
Various indications in *Lancelot*, such as a reference to Bath, suggest that
Lancelot's adventures take place in the same general area, and Gorre has
"otherworld" characteristics that may be a legacy of mythic beliefs about
Glastonbury. Arthur seems to have no jurisdiction over it.

Malory introduces the "land of Gore" and, confusingly, makes it out
to be the domain of the northerner Urien.

GRAIL (GRAAL)   Wonderworking vessel in the care of a mysterious
"king" or keeper. The goal of a quest by Arthur's knights, it has antecedents
in pagan fertility myths, in talismans related to these, and in the idea of a
rapport between the land and a sacred person through whom it flourishes or
fails. But the Grail comes to be explained as a Christian thing, and while it
never sheds the strange imagery surrounding it, there is a shift in its attributed powers from physical to spiritual life-giving.

The Old French word *graal* meant a large dish or serving vessel.
Chrétien de Troyes, in his *Conte del Graal*, tells of Perceval visiting the
wounded Fisher King's castle and seeing a procession of young people carrying curious objects. Last is a maiden bearing a jeweled, resplendent graal.
It later transpires that this is a special and sacred one with a supernatural
power of nourishment, making it possible to sustain life with a single mass
wafer daily placed in it. The inspiration for such a notion doubtless lies in

Celtic myths about cauldrons of plenty and kindred vessels. When Perceval first sees the procession, he asks no questions. It turns out that he should have asked, and that if he had, the Fisher King would have been healed.

Subsequent authors take up this theme of a special graal or Grail, with a medley of developments. The wound that more or less paralyzes the lord of the castle is said to be sexual in nature and related to the fact that the land round about is barren and accursed. If the knight who sees the Grail asks the right question—as a rule, rather puzzlingly, "Who is served from the Grail?"—the wound will heal and the wasteland will revive. The Grail has female attendants and is often accompanied by other "hallows," principally a lance with blood dripping from its point. Sometimes, there are two keepers, the Fisher King and a separate Grail King who is out of sight, but the wound motif is recurrent. The substratum of magical beliefs about fertility, physical vigor, and the wellsprings of life is obvious. However, the stories are highly various, and the vessel itself has several guises.

Robert de Boron and his successors Christianize it in plain terms, absorbing the pre-Christian elements, after a fashion, into a greater myth. Although the object's history never becomes a mere holy-relic legend, it is now the "Holy" Grail or Sangrail and declared to be the vessel of the Last Supper, the dish or chalice in which Christ instituted the eucharist. Thus, it is involved with the doctrine of his Real Presence in the sacrament of the altar, received in communion, and with nourishment for the soul rather than the body and spiritual rather than physical life, a pursuance of Chrétien's hint with a radical shift of emphasis.

The Grail is stated to have passed, after the Last Supper, into the possession of Joseph of Arimathea. He used it to collect drops of the sacred blood. The risen Christ taught him "secret words" that were the key to mystical knowledge that the Grail could impart. Kept by Joseph and a host of companions, the vessel was a token of divine friendship, a source of visions and spiritual discernment. It was placed on a special table commemorating the table of the Last Supper. Through the agency of the group led by Joseph, it came to Britain—initially, to the Vales of Avalon, the future site of Glastonbury, then to a succession of Grail keepers in a hidden, elusive castle, the one visited by Perceval.

Thus, the Arthurian Grail Quest is made out to be the second phase of a train of events initiated much earlier. In Arthur's time, it becomes known that contact with the vanished Grail is to be restored, although the reestablishment of this link with God is an uncertain enterprise. The Vulgate *Queste del saint Graal*, introducing Galahad as the Grail seeker who succeeds, is the most highly developed version and the basis of Malory's. The Grail makes a phantasmal appearance in Arthur's hall, inspiring many of the knights to ride out and seek the reality. Even here, it has not lost its pre-Christian power of bodily nourishment, since each knight is miraculously fed with the food of his choice. The Quest itself may derive from another Celtic myth, dimly surviving in Arthur's quest for a cauldron in *The Spoils of Annwfn*. Other pre-Christian elements reappear, but the Grail is now associated with Christian marvels, such as apparitions of Christ. More is involved than merely locating or seeing it. The Quest's ultimate goal is a penetration of its mysteries. From the outset, various signs point to Galahad as the destined Grail achiever, but some of the other questing knights have partial glimpses. Success is through divine election rather than effort, and only the pure Galahad is worthy of the supreme vision. He attains this in Sarras, where the Grail has gone, and dies in ecstasy.

The vision seems to be the same imagined by Dante at the close of the *Paradiso*, a mystical experience of the Godhead—of the Trinity, and the human manifestation of its Second Person in Christ. It is a face-to-face awareness of the source of eternal life and beatitude. Dante's vision is granted through the intercession of Mary, and it may be significant that she is a constant presence in the Grail romance *Perlesvaus*, while in the *Queste* itself Galahad's crowning moment comes during "the Mass of the Glorious Mother of God."

The Grail stories have no consistency. *Parzival*, for instance, diverges sharply both from Chrétien's prototype and from other Christian versions, its Grail being a stone of celestial origin. The church never recognized the Grail, partly perhaps because of its un-Christian features, including the prominence of women in the ritual, and partly because of its stress on a private and suspect mysticism aloof from the Christian community. Hence, the mystique never settles into a standard or orthodox form. The chronicles of Glastonbury, although they claim Joseph as the founder, neglect the Grail. The romancers themselves sometimes give the impression that the Quest was adverse to the Round Table, drawing away its best members and indirectly causing a moral decline. Tennyson carries this idea farther.

GREEN KNIGHT, see *Bercilak*

GUINEVERE (GUENEVERE, GANDUMARA, GUENIEVRE, ETC.) Arthur's wife (see also *Gwenhwyfar*). Giraldus Cambrensis says the inscribed cross in the royal grave at Glastonbury called her his second wife. The statement cannot be checked, because the surviving drawing of the cross shows only one side of it, and any reference to Guinevere was presumably on the other. Nothing is known about the first wife.

Geoffrey of Monmouth makes Guinevere a beautiful lady of Roman ancestry, brought up in the household of Duke Cador of Cornwall. He says little more about her until the last phase of Arthur's reign, when she betrays the King by becoming the paramour of his would-be supplanter Mordred but flees to Caerleon while the two are at war and enters a convent. The theme of involvement with a man other than her husband, either willingly when he is her lover or unwillingly when he abducts her, recurs with variations. When carried off, she has to be rescued. The archivolt in Modena Cathedral, possibly pre-Geoffrey, shows Arthur doing this, and he does it again in Caradoc's Life of Gildas, where King Melwas of Somerset is the culprit. Later, the abduction theme is combined with the love theme when the rescuer is not Guinevere's husband but Lancelot, with whom her connection is an ardent but stormy one.

The background of these adventures may be an authentic tradition of ancient Celtic queenship. A Celtic queen was her consort's equal and could take lovers without being condemned. If stories of such relationships reached medieval writers, the altered social setting would have prevented a proper understanding. The free and equal woman could only have been imagined as a headstrong, unfaithful woman, and that is what Guinevere becomes.

In the romances, her father is Leodegan, said to have been a previous owner of the Round Table, which she brings to Arthur as a dowry. She has a double called the False Guinevere, who is a daughter of Leodegan by a different mother. The False Guinevere temporarily lures Arthur away from the court. This episode, together with his encounters with Morgause and other women, gives Guinevere's conduct an excuse that it may not originally have needed. While the Welsh are always censorious of her (in Wales, till quite recent times, it was a reflection on a girl's virtue to call her a Guinevere), it is doubtless a half-sympathy that leads continental romancers to break sharply with Geoffrey, portraying the Queen as scornfully rejecting the lustful Mordred and erring instead with the magnificent Lancelot.

That famous amour is already established in the work of Chrétien de Troyes. Writers who take it up have to face the problem of the King's attitude to it. Arthur, it has been remarked, is rare among literary characters as having an unfaithful wife without losing dignity. He does his best to turn a blind eye till Agravain makes the affair a public scandal. Arthur tries to execute Guinevere, but Lancelot saves her. The consequent disputes and rival partisanships are the beginning of the end.

Malory's Queen is a richer character than his precursors foreshadow. She is generous, passionate, tragic. Childless and married to Arthur, whom she respects but can never love, she loves Lancelot, whom she can never marry. Their adulterous partnership is jealous, occasionally cruel, yet long-enduring and impossible to break off. The convent where she retires when all is lost is at Amesbury, and Lancelot visits her there. Guinevere dismisses him with a splendid and penitent farewell, acknowledging that their actions have ruined the noblest fellowship in the world. "She was a true lover," Malory says, "and therefore she had a good end." Those who accept that Arthur died, and was buried at Glastonbury, add that Guinevere was buried there with him.

GUINNION   The *Historia Brittonum* says that Arthur won his eighth battle in a fort called by this name, perhaps by defeating a Saxon garrison. A Roman or possibly Iron Age fort may be meant. There is no good identification. The claim of Stow in Selkirkshire rests on a medieval belief that its church, St. Mary of Wedale, possessed fragments of an image of the Virgin Mary that Arthur carried into the battle. The *Historia* mentions such an image but gives no hint as to what became of it. An attempt has been made to fault the Guinnion passage on the ground that Marian devotion was not known so early in Britain. However, it was well established in Mediterranean countries by the middle of the fifth century, and there are traces of it in Britain not much later.

GWALCHMEI   Hero of Welsh legend who appears in the triads, *Culhwch and Olwen*, and elsewhere. His name is often explained as "Hawk of May," but only the "hawk" part of it is certain. He is a brave warrior and a courteous, eloquent person. He comes to be regarded as Arthur's nephew, a son of the King's sister, and to be equated with the more conspicuous Gawain (q.v.).

GWENHWYFAR   Arthur's wife in the early Welsh tradition. Her name means "White Phantom" and becomes the familiar Guinevere (q.v.) in non-Welsh literature. Several of the triads mention her. The triad of the "Three Unrestrained Ravagings" says that Mordred struck her during a raid on Arthur's court, and this was one of the causes of the quarrel leading up to the battle of Camlann. Despite her husband's implied loyalty to her, Gwenhwyfar's reputation is dubious. The triad of the "Three Faithless Wives" adds her as a fourth "more faithless than those three."

A curious triad speaks of Arthur's "Three Great Queens," all named Gwenhwyfar. Characters in Celtic mythology sometimes appear in several guises, and even the Vulgate Cycle has two Guineveres, a true and a false. The Welsh trio may be derived from ancient portrayals of such deities as the Great Mother in triple form. Some would interpret Gwenhwyfar's name as "White Goddess."

GWYÒRE   Son of Arthur in *Culhwch and Olwen*, killed during the hunting of Twrch Trwyth (q.v.). To judge from his insignificance, and the fact that neither Arthur nor anyone else seems to care much about his death, he is illegitimate, as Amr and Llacheu apparently are.

GWYN AP NUÒÒ, see *Annwfn*

ÞEBRON, see *Bron*

ÞECTOR, see *Ector*

ÞISTORIA BRITTONUCO   "History of the Britons." A Latin compilation that underlies parts of Geoffrey of Monmouth's work. It dates in its present form from the early ninth century. According to a preface, it is the work of Nennius (q.v.), a cleric at Bangor in North Wales. The authenticity of the preface is uncertain, and some medieval copies ascribe the book, impossibly, to Gildas. Today, Nennius is commonly cited as the person responsible, although the extent of his share, if any, in the work of compiling is subject to debate.

The *Historia* is a medley of Welsh legends and traditions together with a little genuine history. Some of its materials are much older than the ninth century. It includes early versions of several themes taken up by Geoffrey, notably the colonization of ancient Britain by migrating Trojans. During the fifth century A.D., the *Historia* introduces Vortigern as the ruler of Britain and tells of his fatal invitation to Hengist and Horsa to settle in Thanet, with the uncontrollable Saxon influx following.

Important for later legend is an episode in which Vortigern tries to build a fortress in Wales. The building materials keep vanishing, and his magicians tell him that he must find a "child without a father," kill him, and sprinkle his blood on the foundations. A boy is found whose mother claims to have conceived without intercourse, and he is brought to the site. He turns out to be a seer, revealing what the magicians do not know, that there is a subterranean pool with two serpents in it, a red and a white. These are duly discovered, fighting, and the boy explains that they symbolize the Britons and Saxons. The awestruck Vortigern spares him. He turns out to be Ambrosius, that is, the historical British leader Ambrosius Aurelianus, here depicted as having had paranormal gifts in his youth. When Geoffrey elaborates the tale, he converts the seer into the young Merlin, who makes his debut in this episode.

A later chapter of the *Historia* gives a list of twelve battles won by Arthur against the Saxons and, to judge from the geography, Picts allied with them. It refers to him as the *dux bellorum*, or war leader, organizing campaigns in concert with regional kings. The battle sites, so far as they are identifiable, are widely spread. The list culminates in the ascription to Arthur of the major victory of Badon, which Gildas attests much earlier but without naming the British commander. On that occasion, it is claimed, Arthur slew nine hundred and sixty of the enemy single-handed, a statement that gives the Badon sentence a legendary air, making it less plausible than the rest.

This list is thought to be a Latin paraphrase of a lost Welsh poem in Arthur's praise. Other instances of Welsh martial panegyric prove that such a poem need not have been contemporary with its subject or anything like it. Indeed, a poem in Welsh could not have been composed as early as Arthur's apparent *floruit*, because the Welsh language did not then exist. The historical value of the battle list therefore remains uncertain. A point of interest is that Arthur is said to have carried an image of the Virgin Mary into battle and to have won by celestial aid. There is a contrast here with the Welsh monastic tradition shown in the saints' lives, which tend to be hostile to him.

Appended to the *Historia*, and perhaps a few decades later, is a catalogue of *Mirabilia*, or "marvels," that is, strange phenomena. Two of these, in the Welsh regional divisions of Buelt and Ercing, introduce Arthur.

HOEL (1)   King of Brittany in Geoffrey of Monmouth. Geoffrey makes him a nephew of Arthur. This is impossible, because he is commanding an army when his supposed mother, Arthur's sister, can hardly be much more than fifteen and Hoel therefore cannot be out of infancy. Perhaps Geoffrey has confused the family details by a careless revision. Hoel plays a distinguished part in Arthur's wars. When the King has to leave Gaul because of Mordred's rebellion, he leaves Hoel in charge of his continental realms. Geoffrey calls him Hoel the Great and mentions a Breton son and great-grandson of the same name.

HOEL (2)   King of Brittany in romance, the father or grandfather of the Breton Iseut whom Tristan marries. Chronology suggests that he might be the same as Hoel (1).

IDER, see *Yder*

IGERNE, IGRAINE, see *Ygerna*

ILLTUD   First of the great saints of Wales, founder of the monastery of Llantwit Major in Glamorgan, toward the end of the fifth century. It rose to high importance, both in public service and in the continuance of learning. Reputedly, Gildas was a pupil at the school. If so, his Latin style suggests a significant survival of Roman-type education.

Illtud is said to have been a soldier before he embraced the religious life and to have visited the court of Arthur, who was his cousin. A church dedicated to him on Caldey Island has a stained-glass window portraying him as an Arthurian knight. The combination of saint and warrior may possibly have supplied a hint for the character of Galahad.

More interesting as history is the statement that Illtud was given land for a monastic foundation by a local ruler named Marcianus, arguably the father of Mark, in the Tristan story.

ISEUT (1) (ISOLT, ESSYLLT, ISEULT, ISOLDE, YSEULT)   Heroine of one of the most famous love stories in literature, perhaps the first to portray a mutual passion that is a law unto itself, overriding all others and not condemned for that. In terms of medieval values, this anarchic quality is more conspicuous in the conduct of Iseut, as an unfaithful wife, than in that of her lover. While the best-known versions depict the passion as imposed on this particular couple by magic, it is treated as something humanly real, not alien to normal psychology.

Iseut's lover is Tristan. The couple are mentioned in the triads as Drystan and Essyllt, and Essyllt is the original Welsh form, but the development of the theme is due to continental romancers. Iseut is the daughter of King Anguish of Ireland. She is skilled in the arts of healing and makes Tristan's acquaintance when she is treating a wound given him in combat by Morholt, her uncle. Tristan obtains Iseut as a wife for his own uncle, King Mark of Cornwall. Her maid Brangaene accompanies them on the voyage over, bringing a love potion for the bridal pair, but Tristan and Iseut accidentally drink it and are doomed to perpetual love themselves.

Iseut marries Mark as planned. Tristan, however, is at the court and they spend time together whenever they can. The triangular situation passes through many episodes. Mark is never quite certain what is happening or what he should do, and Iseut shows herself to be crafty, dissembling, and ruthless when necessary. Lancelot is friendly to the lovers and receives them at Joyous Gard as his guests. A phase of exile and despair induces Tristan to marry a Breton princess, also named Iseut. Even then, his Irish beloved is willing to come over and heal him when he is wounded, but she arrives too late.

It has been suggested (as also, and more strongly, in the case of Guinevere) that the romancers are dealing with traditions of Celtic queenship that, in the Middle Ages, are no longer comprehensible. A Celtic queen was her husband's equal, in some ways his superior, and could take lovers as a king could take concubines. Transplanted into the context of medieval wifely duty, the story becomes different and Iseut becomes theoretically "bad." A feeling persists that she is excusable and her love is condoned, being blamed on the potion and sometimes extenuated by vile conduct on her husband's part. Nothing, however, can prevent it from being furtive and tragic.

ISEUT (2) Iseut "of the White Hands," daughter or granddaughter of King Hoel of Brittany. Tristan in exile is drawn to her by her name, the same as his beloved's, and marries her. His fidelity to the first Iseut deters him from consummation. Some romancers make her responsible for his death. When he is lying wounded, the other Iseut is sent for to cure him. She sails over from Cornwall, but the jealous Breton, misreporting a signal, tells him she is not aboard the ship and he dies in despair.

JOSEPH OF ARIMATHEA In the Gospels, the rich man who obtained the body of Christ from Pilate and laid it in the tomb. An apocryphal text, the *Acts of Pilate*, adds an account of his being imprisoned, and delivered by the risen Lord. Robert de Boron's *Joseph* and the *Estoire del saint Graal* expand the story. Joseph is said to have acquired the Grail, to have been taught its mysteries by Christ, and to have been miraculously sustained by it through a long imprisonment. Released by Emperor Vespasian, the narrative continues, he set off with a party of companions on divinely guided wanderings that eventually brought the Grail to Britain. Romancers disagree as to whether he came to Britain in person but give prominence to a son of his, Josephe or Josephus, who does. Joseph himself is a collateral ancestor of all the Grail keepers down to Pelles, and thus of Galahad.

Joseph is also the reputed founder of Christian Glastonbury. William of Malmesbury, writing toward 1130, records a belief that disciples of Christ built its celebrated Old Church. He does not name them, but an interpolated edition of his book, compiled at Glastonbury Abbey about 1247, claims that they were led by Joseph. They arrived in the year 63, built the church, and lived on the spot for the remnant of their days.

Joseph's two roles are never fully combined in medieval literature. The plain statement that Joseph brought the Grail to Glastonbury seems not to have been made by any writer of note before Tennyson. While Robert de Boron, and the author of *Perlesvaus*, show an acquaintance with Glastonbury and its legends, Joseph himself does not appear in any known abbey document till after his establishment as a hero of Grail romance. Hence, it is often assumed that he was first brought to Britain by romancers and then annexed by the Glastonbury monks and woven into their chronicles. But this reading of the data presents difficulties, and some prior tradition or speculation, possibly Welsh, may have drifted into England and France with the rest of the Celtic matter drawn in by the Arthurian legend, ultimately prompting both accounts of Joseph's British activities. The basic question, which neither the Grail cycle nor the Glastonbury story convincingly answers, is why anyone's imagination should have brought Joseph—a most unlikely person—to Britain at all.

JOSEPHE (JOSEPHUS) Joseph of Arimathea's son, an important character in the *Estoire del saint Graal*. He is called the First Bishop of Christendom, a title that has sometimes been construed as a hint at an antipapal and even heretical strain of thinking in Grail romance. In the *Queste del saint Graal*, he revisits this world and celebrates the mass at which Galahad attains the supreme vision. He is a figure of romance only, not found in the Bible or Christian legend.

JOYOUS GARD (JOYEUSE GARDE) Lancelot's castle, originally Dolorous Gard. He renames it on taking possession and receives Arthur and Guinevere as his guests. When he saves Guinevere from the stake at Carlisle, he brings her to Joyous Gard. Arthur besieges it, and Lancelot is persuaded to restore her to her husband, but their conflict is the beginning of the end. On Lancelot's death near Glastonbury, his body is taken to the castle for burial.

Joyous Gard is in the north of England. The French author of the Vulgate *Mort Artu*, whose geographical knowledge is slight, places it near the Humber. Malory suggests Alnwick or Bamburgh in Northumberland. Bamburgh was the capital of the old Northumbrian kingdom of the Angles. Before they occupied it, there was a British fort on the site called Din Guayrdi. Lancelot's castle may have been one result of the twelfth-century rediscovery of Welsh material, offering in this case a northern stronghold with a name sounding like the French *garde*, "defense" or "protection."

KARDOIL, see *Carduel*

KAY (KEU) Arthur's seneschal, that is, chief steward or manager of the royal household. The early Welsh call him Cai or Cei, probably the

Roman name Caius, and make him Arthur's principal follower, the second being his comrade Bedwyr or Bedivere. The two appear with their leader in the Life of St. Cadoc. A poem extols Cai as a slayer of monsters, his combat with Palug's Cat being renowned. In *Culhwch and Olwen*, he heads the list of characters at Arthur's court and has superhuman qualities, such as the ability to hold his breath under water for nine days. The tale gives him a prominent role. However, there are darker touches, such as his curmudgeonly unwillingness to admit the newcomer Culhwch to the hall and his resentment over a satirical verse that Arthur makes up, a resentment that causes him to withhold needed support.

Geoffrey of Monmouth introduces the spelling with a K and gives Kay his position of seneschal but does not make him purely a civilian. He becomes Arthur's governor of Anjou, aids him in the killing of a giant on Mont-Saint-Michel, sustains a mortal wound fighting the Romans, and is buried in a wood near Chinon, a town he founded.

Romancers (spelling the name variously) develop the worse sides of his nature, sometimes making him a mere foil to Gawain. Kay becomes a boastful, scoffing troublemaker, third-rate as a knight, and churlish toward young entrants to the court. The *Perlesvaus* has him treacherously slay Arthur's son Loholt. Malory presents him as the son of Ector, with Arthur as his foster-brother, and in the episode of the Sword in the Stone he tries to pretend that he pulled it out himself.

Near Lake Bala in Wales is a hill-fort called Caer Gai, Kay's Fort, an echo of the older, more honorable Welsh view of him.

KeLLIWIC (CeLLI WIG) Earliest place named as a residence of Arthur, in *Culhwch and Olwen* and the Welsh triads. Its most significant feature is that it is in Cornwall, a fact attesting a tradition of Arthur as outside Wales, too deeply rooted for Welsh patriotism to challenge.

Kelliwic means "woodland." The likeliest candidate is probably the earthwork fort Castle Killibury or Kelly Rounds, near Wadebridge. Callington is the favorite among other claimants. The triads make Kelliwic the scene of an aggression by Medraut, the original Mordred, who is said to have raided it with his followers and struck Guinevere. Arthur retaliated by raiding Medraut's home. Their actions were major steps in the quarrel leading up to the battle of Camlann. In this early and barbaric tale, Arthur and Medraut-Mordred sound more like feuding equals than a monarch and a younger subordinate. Their better-known relationship is due to Geoffrey of Monmouth, who combines the conflict of Welsh tradition with a separate theme of betrayal by a deputy ruler. He keeps the Cornish location of the final clash but drops Kelliwic itself.

keu, see *Kay*

lady of the lake Enchantress with otherworld affiliations, in her origins perhaps a Celtic priestess. The phrase denotes a role rather than an individual. There are several Ladies of the Lake, diversely imagined and not wholly distinguishable. The lake itself, a "fair water and broad" in Malory's words, is geographically vague.

The "Dame du Lac" of the Vulgate *Lancelot* is a fay who carries off Lancelot as an infant, rears him, and conducts him to Arthur's court when he is eighteen. Malory's Lady, from whom Arthur receives Excalibur, is mysterious. She presides over a group of "damsels of the lake." One of them, Nimue or Viviane (with many different spellings), is the well-known damsel who entraps Merlin. She is definitely human, but with magical powers, and she succeeds to the chief role after the Lady of the Excalibur episode is slain by Balin. The Lady of the Lake, whoever she may be at a given moment, is friendly to Arthur and aids him with occasional magic. Nimue is among the company who bear him off over the water after his last battle.

lailoken, see *Myrddin*

lamorak Son of Pellinore and elder brother of Perceval. He becomes Morgause's lover. Catching them together, her son Gaheris kills her but spares Lamorak because he is unarmed. Gawain contrives Lamorak's death shortly afterward.

lancelot Called *du Lac*, "of the Lake." The most famous knight of the Round Table, a paragon of chivalry but a flawed person. Early Welsh materials never mention him, or offer a fully convincing prototype, nor does Geoffrey of Monmouth. He may have Irish or Breton antecedents, mythical rather than historical. The first romancer to introduce him is Chrétien de Troyes. The Vulgate Cycle enlarges on his career at great length, and Malory perpetuates his preeminence.

Lancelot is a son of King Ban of Benoic, a domain in western France. He is carried away as an infant by the Lady of the Lake, who brings him up and, when he reaches the age of eighteen, presents him at Arthur's court. His nobility and his prowess in combat are soon recognized. Between adventures, he attends gatherings of the Round Table and takes part in tournaments, being usually the winner. His home is the northern castle of Joyous

Gard, perhaps meant to be Bamburgh, on the site of a British fort called Din Guayrdi.

Lancelot's best-known role is as the illicit lover of Guinevere. The Queen is high-handed and callous toward him, as the conventions of courtly love require, but their liaison, however tempestuous at times, is deep-rooted and enduring. It is intertwined with the Grail theme. Pelles, the Grail keeper, has a daughter, Elaine. When Lancelot is his guest, Pelles leads him to suppose that the Queen is in the neighborhood and contrives by magic that Lancelot sleeps with Elaine under the impression that she is Guinevere. Elaine becomes pregnant and bears a son, Galahad, the destined Grail knight. When Galahad grows up, he comes to the court. Many knights ride out on the Grail Quest. Lancelot does not achieve the Grail himself, because of his adulterous love, yet ironically the same sin has produced Galahad, the knight who does.

The affair with Guinevere is not a complete secret, but a tactful silence is generally observed until Agravain and Mordred force it into the open. Since the Queen's infidelity counts as treason, Arthur has to order her execution, which is attempted, in Malory's account, at Carlisle. Lancelot and his followers ride up to rescue her. A fight breaks out and a number of knights are killed, Lancelot accidentally slaying Gawain's youngest brother, Gareth. He takes Guinevere to Joyous Gard. The Round Table is now split. Lancelot restores the Queen to her husband but moves to France accompanied by many supporters and founds a rival court. Arthur follows him with an army. Efforts at peacemaking are foiled by Gawain's enmity to Lancelot over the death of his brother.

When Mordred revolts, Arthur goes back to Britain and Gawain dies, so that a reconciliation becomes feasible. But Lancelot arrives too late, when the fatal battle with Mordred has been fought and the King has gone. Lancelot takes a sad farewell of the penitent Queen and goes to live as a hermit near Glastonbury with other survivors. There he dies, making a good end. His body is taken to Joyous Gard for burial.

LEO Roman emperor named by Geoffrey of Monmouth as reigning during both of Arthur's campaigns in Gaul. He is not in Rome, and the Britons never confront him directly. It appears that he is emperor of the east, in keeping with the division of power that was normal in the later Empire. Toward the end of Arthur's career, Leo has a western colleague, Lucius, who provokes the second Gallic campaign.

The references to Leo occur in three widely separated passages. He is certainly Leo I, who reigned at Constantinople from 457 to 474, and he therefore provides a chronological fix for Arthur—that is, a clear synchronization with known history outside Britain—which, moreover, is the only one given anywhere up to Geoffrey's time. Such a dating for Arthur is consistent with other features of the story, notably his family relationships, and a tradition of it is discernible in several continental chronicles as well as Capgrave's in England. The incompatible year 542, given by Geoffrey for Arthur's passing, can be brought into agreement as a misguided emendation, on recognized lines, of a date within the same period. This remains a conjecture, but an error in dating must be assumed somewhere if the account of Arthur is to cohere at all.

LEODEGAN Father of Guinevere and the False Guinevere. He receives the Round Table in succession to Uther and passes it on to Arthur as Guinevere's dowry. He appears first in the Vulgate *Merlin*.

LINNUIS District or "region" in which, according to the *Historia Brittonum*, Arthur waged a campaign comprising his second, third, fourth, and fifth battles. It is usually taken to be Lindsey, the central and northern portion of Lincolnshire. Geoffrey of Monmouth understands it thus, because he locates an Arthurian battle at Lincoln "in the province of Lindsey." The original Latin word could have been *Lindenses*, meaning the dwellers in and around Lindum, that is, the city of Lincoln itself, and hence their territory.

However, the *Historia* also mentions a river called Dubglas, and Lincolnshire now has no river with a name anything like this. Rival suggestions have naturally been offered. There was another Lindum in Scotland, and Douglas Water, acceptable as Dubglas, is not far from its apparent site near Loch Lomond. It may also be that scribes dropped a letter and "Linnuis" should be "Lininuis," derived from *Lindinienses*, a tribe in Dorset, where there is a River Divelish. Both alternatives are doubtful because of the lack of evidence for significant numbers of enemies in those areas.

LLACHEU Son of Arthur. Welsh poems and tales mention him, but with few details, and while he may have begun as a fairly prominent character he eventually fades out. It might be inferred that he is illegitimate. One son of Arthur who appears in romance is called by names suggesting that he is the same person, such as "Loholt," and an explicit Llacheu-Loholt identification is sometimes made. In *Perlesvaus*, Loholt (here Arthur's legitimate son) is slain by Kay. In Malory, Arthur's son by Lyonors is apparently another version of Llacheu, although Malory calls him Borre.

Llacheu is certainly not the same as the sons Amr and Gwydre, and the notion that Mordred, too, was a son of Arthur raises the tally of the King's bastards to four. When Arthur passes away, his cousin Constantine succeeds him, with no hint of a closer relative who might claim to be the legitimate heir.

LLONGBORTH Scene of a battle commemorated by a Welsh poem in the Black Book of Carmarthen, belonging to the tenth century as it stands, but thought to be a rehandling of a much earlier version. Speaking in the character of an eyewitness, the poet extols the prowess of Geraint, a ruler of the West Country who led his troops on this occasion. *Llongborth* probably means "warship port," and the likeliest location is Portchester on the Hampshire coast. The *Anglo-Saxon Chronicle* records a battle hereabouts, dating it to 501 (perhaps a little too late), and archaeology attests Saxon occupation of the Roman fort. The poem sheds light on the tradition of a Geraint living more or less in Arthur's time, while its heading, by calling him Geraint son of Erbin, reveals a confusion with a later namesake that occurs elsewhere.

One stanza has an additional point of interest. It praises "Arthur's men," who took part in the action, and calls Arthur "the emperor, ruler in toil of battle." This recalls the role assigned to him in the *Historia Brittonum*, where he is a war leader fighting alongside regional kings, such as Geraint. "Emperor," the Latin *imperator*, may mean "commander-in-chief," but *imperator* was used in Ireland to refer to the high kings, and the word may have a similar sense here.

The Llongborth stanza has been taken as saying that Arthur was present in person, but the most acceptable reading rules this out. Seemingly, a force known as "Arthur's men" existed, or was supposed to have existed, independently of his presence and perhaps after his departure. It has been argued that allusions to "Arthur's men" on other occasions, misconstrued similarly as implying that he was there when he was not, may explain events in his reputed career that cause trouble with chronology.

LOATHLY LADY The magical transformation of a "Loathly Lady" is a folklore theme, probably Celtic, that appears in the *Wife of Bath's Tale* in Chaucer (his only Arthurian story) and in two other versions having Gawain as the hero. One of the latter is a ballad that calls the lady Dame Ragnell. Arthur is in jeopardy unless he can answer the question "What do women most desire?" A repellent hag supplies the answer—essentially, that women most desire to have their own way—and as a reward demands Gawain as her husband. He chivalrously complies, and she tells him that she is under a spell. She can be ugly by day and beautiful by night, or the other way round, and he must make a choice. He chooses to allow her to decide for herself, whereupon she becomes beautiful all the time. Chaucer changes the story to make it conform better to the Wife of Bath's interests.

LOGRES Approximately, the portion of the island of Britain now known as England, when it was still Celtic territory—though sometimes it seems to be a more limited area specially associated with Arthur. The name corresponds to the Welsh *Lloegyr*, which in Geoffrey of Monmouth's Latin becomes "Loegria." "England" does not appear till the ninth century and is "Angle-land," being a product of the Anglo-Saxon conquest and not properly applicable in Arthur's time, although Malory uses it.

LOHENGRIN Originally Loherangrin, in Wolfram von Eschenbach. Parzival's son, who must keep his background and identity secret. When his wife insists on questioning him, the spell is broken and he is carried off by a swan. In Wagner's opera, the point is that the supernatural powers that the Grail confers on its guardians depend on their true identity being unknown.

LOHOLT, see *Llacheu*

LOT (LOTH) Ruler of Lothian in Scotland and, in later literature, of the Orkneys as well. He is the father of Gawain and other characters, by a marriage about which the texts disagree. Geoffrey of Monmouth says that his wife was a sister of Aurelius Ambrosius and their sons were Gawain and Mordred. Elsewhere, he has Lot married to Arthur's sister Anna. This may be merely an inconsistency, but Lot is much older than Anna and could have married twice. In the romances, the lady whom Lot marries is not Arthur's full sister but his half-sister Morgause, a daughter of Ygerna by her first husband. Lot and Morgause have four sons, Gawain, Gaheris, Agravain, and Gareth. Mordred is sometimes accounted for as yet another son of Morgause, conceived in unknowing incest with Arthur.

According to Geoffrey, Lot commanded the British army toward the end of Uther's reign and was made king of Norway when Arthur conquered that country. In romance, he at first resists Arthur's authority, then ceases to resist, but later becomes estranged again. He is slain by Pellinore, and Merlin constructs a splendid tomb for him.

Lot may be the allegedly historical Leudonus, who is said to have reigned over Lothian some time in the fifth century from the hill-fort Traprain Law, on the edge of the Lammermuir Hills. Traprain Law was a flourishing settlement in Late Roman times, but occupation afterward is unproved, and if Lot-Leudonus did reign there it cannot have been much later than 450. As a literary character, Lot may owe something to the Celtic god Lugh. This god had a solar aspect that could explain an odd quality of Lot's firstborn, Gawain, who grows stronger during the morning and weaker during the afternoon, and perhaps also Gawain's link with Carlisle, a town that may have been a center of the god's cult.

LucaN   Bedivere's brother and Arthur's butler, a domestic office that does not preclude his bearing arms. In Malory, as one of the few survivors of the last battle, he helps Bedivere to carry the wounded King away, but the weight causes him to collapse and die of his own wounds.

Lucιus   Roman ruler of western Europe during the last part of Arthur's reign. In Geoffrey of Monmouth's story, he demands that Arthur should pay the tribute formerly paid to Rome by the Britons and restore various conquered lands. The King retorts with an invasion of Gaul. Lucius is defeated and killed, and Arthur sends his corpse to Rome with the message that this is the only tribute the Romans will get.

Geoffrey is unsure about Lucius's status. He first calls him Procurator of the Republic. "Procurator," a title given to deputies of the emperor in minor provinces, suggests that Lucius has something less than supreme authority, an impression confirmed by the fact that the Senate has power to give him orders. Later, Geoffrey calls him an emperor, and so do subsequent writers who take up the tale. But Geoffrey appears to have some inkling of the actual situation in the years 455–76, when the Empire was still divided between two emperors, but the western ones were greatly reduced in their powers and territories. After 476, there were no western emperors at all.

This reading is supported by Lucius's having an eastern co-emperor named Leo, whom Geoffrey mentions more than once. He is a real person, Leo I, who reigned at Constantinople from 457 to 474. While there was no emperor Lucius, the *Chronicle* of Sigebert of Gembloux, which Geoffrey may have used, gives "Lucerius" as Leo's western colleague in 469–70, a mistake but a sufficient hint.

LyNeτ, see *Gaheris*

LyoNes, see *Gareth*

LyoNesse   Country of romance and popular legend. Tristan is the son of its king. It may originally have been Leonais in Brittany, or Lothian in Scotland, Loenois in Old French. However, it comes to be identified with a tract of country that once supposedly extended Cornwall southward and westward but was overwhelmed by the sea. The legend is based on folk memories of times when, as archaeology shows, part of Mount's Bay was above water and inhabited, and the main Isles of Scilly were joined together.

The Lyonesse of romance includes a district called Surluse, which is ruled by Galehaut. Tennyson makes Lyonesse the scene of Arthur's last battle, with Excalibur cast away from a heightened version of what is now Loe Bar, on the east of Mount's Bay.

"Lyonesse" is one spelling of the name of the lady beloved by Gareth.

LYONORS In Malory, mother of Arthur's illegitimate son Borre.

MAhELOAS, see *Melwas*

MARGAWSE, see *Morgause*

MARhAUS, see *Morholt*

MARK King of Cornwall and husband of Iseut in the Tristan legend. He figures in Welsh sources as March son of Meirchyawn, that is, Marcus son of Marcianus. Both names are Roman, and the second is that of an emperor who reigned from 450 to 457, a fact suggesting that these are historical persons and that Mark's father was a governor or official named after the emperor.

Meirchyawn is associated with southern Wales. According to one view, the domain of Mark himself was in that country and was transplanted to Cornwall by storytellers when the Tristan romance was taking shape. Certainly, he came to be widely known. He is the butt of a northern Welsh tale unconnected with Tristan, and a fort on the south coast of Scotland, occupied in the sixth century, is called Mote of Mark. His Cornish location, as anything more than fiction, depends mainly on the belief, traceable as early as the ninth century, that the historical king Cunomorus or Kynvawr, who is commemorated on the Tristan Stone near Fowey and who perhaps made use of Castle Dore, is Mark under another name. However, archaeology has cast serious doubt on Castle Dore's post-Roman status.

Mark appears in the triads when Arthur tries to steal his pigs and Tristan defends them, an oddly primitive incident. Tristan is already the lover of "Essyllt" or Iseut. The tale of the tragic love triangle varies. Normally, Tristan is Mark's nephew and is sent to Ireland to bring back Iseut as a bride for him. The couple fall in love during the voyage, and the rest of the story revolves around their prolonged passion, Mark's jealousy and malice, and the end in death.

Besides his reputed residence at Castle Dore, Mark is the lord of Tintagel, the heir or heirs of Gorlois having presumably abandoned it. Iseut's infidelity means that Mark is the wronged party, yet while earlier romancers treat him with a degree of sympathy, he tends to become a villain, devious, cowardly, and malignant. Some authors make him kill Tristan treacherously with his own hands, using a poisoned spear. He is further said to have gone on reigning after the passing of Arthur and to have spitefully destroyed Camelot.

MeÒRAUT (MeÒRAWÒ)   Chieftain in Welsh tradition, whom medieval authors develop into the traitor Mordred (q.v.). The tenth-century *Annales Cambriae*, under the year 539 (probably), record the "strife of Camlann in which Arthur and Medraut fell." It is not stated here that they were opposed. However, a story summarized in the triads makes them enemies, raiding each other's households in Cornwall. Medraut is said to have assaulted Arthur's wife, this being one of the acts leading up to Camlann, regarded as an exterminatory clash between the two leaders and their followings. The conflict sounds like a feud of equals, and nothing suggests that they were related or that this was an opposition of good and evil.

Medraut's transformation into the villainous Modred or Mordred, Arthur's nephew or illegitimate son who is left in charge at home during Arthur's Gallic war and stabs the King in the back, is due to Geoffrey of Monmouth. In his *Historia*, he took up the notion of hostility and a fatal battle in Cornwall and interwove this with a separate theme of betrayal by a deputy, which may have belonged to a different conception of Arthur's downfall hinted at in his earlier-written *Prophetiae Merlini*. The "Modred" form of the name, which is Cornish or Breton, likewise indicates the annexation of non-Welsh matter.

MeLWAS (MeLeAgANT)   In Caradoc's Life of Gildas, written about 1130, Melwas is the king of the Summer Land, that is, Somerset. Caradoc says that he carried off Guinevere and kept her in his stronghold at Glastonbury when Gildas was in the neighborhood. Caradoc calls the place the Glass City, having in mind its reputed Celtic name Ynyswitrin, the Isle of Glass—"Isle" because of the marshes and lakes that once almost surrounded it. These prevented Arthur from mounting an effective attack, but Gildas and the abbot mediated, peace was made, and the lady was restored.

This is the first known linkage of Arthur with Glastonbury, and the first written version of the recurrent theme of the abduction of Guinevere. Chrétien de Troyes has two characters derived from Melwas. In his *Erec*, Maheloas is lord of an Isle of Glass with otherworld qualities. In *Lancelot*,

Meleagant abducts Guinevere, but here Lancelot, not her husband, comes to the rescue. Malory has a relocated version, giving the abductor a castle near Lambeth.

ᴏᴇRLIN Prophet and enchanter who presides over Arthur's coming into the world, establishes him as king, and during the early part of his reign is his chief adviser. Merlin as known to literature is the creation of Geoffrey of Monmouth. His name, "Merlinus" in Geoffrey's Latin, is an adaptation of "Myrddin" (q.v.), the name given in Welsh legend to a northern bard living toward the close of the sixth century, who was said to have had a gift of prophecy and to have foretold a Celtic revival. Geoffrey composed a series of *Prophetiae Merlini* and then incorporated these into his *Historia Regum Britanniae*, where he made his first attempt to give Merlin substance as a quasi-historical character.

He took from the ninth-century *Historia Brittonum* the story of the young seer, the "child without a father," who was brought to Vortigern's building site as a human sacrifice but saved himself by exhibiting powers superior to those of the king's magicians. The *Historia Brittonum* called him Ambrosius, but Geoffrey gave him the name of the poet-prophet explaining that "Ambrosius" was another name for him. In Geoffrey's narrative, he is begotten by an incubus and therefore has no human father. Discovered at his birthplace, the town afterward known as Carmarthen, he is taken to Vortigern and brings to light two subterranean dragons, which he interprets as symbolizing the Britons and Saxons. The "prophecies" follow. Geoffrey pictures him here as a youth rather than a child prodigy. Since the episode belongs to the fifth century, more than a hundred years before the Myrddin of Welsh tradition, it is clear that, at the time of writing his *Historia*, Geoffrey knew little about this person beyond his name and prophetic reputation. In ensuing passages, Merlin supervises the building of Stonehenge on Salisbury Plain, a much greater anachronism. He also contrives the magical ruse that enables Uther to lie with Ygerna and beget Arthur.

Toward 1150, Geoffrey returned to the topic in his long poem *Vita Merlini*. Here, having obviously learned more about the original Myrddin, he relates and expands the story of the sixth-century prophet, fudging dates and other details to reconcile them with his previous account in the *Historia*, but not very convincingly. Merlin's sister Ganieda, who acquires prophetic gifts herself, is a prominent character.

The *Historia* remains the basis for the portrayal of Merlin in romance. It never brings him into contact with Arthur although a passing reference

hints that a meeting may have been edited out. His larger development begins with Robert de Boron. Merlin is now said to have been begotten by a
devil with the aim of creating an evil prophet to oppose Christ. Thanks to
his mother's virtue, the scheme miscarried, and his hell-bestowed supernatural gifts were turned to good ends. Robert and his Vulgate continuators
follow Geoffrey's *Historia* by placing Merlin in the fifth century and more
or less repeat his dealings with Vortigern and Uther. But now he does more.
He causes the Round Table to be made for Uther as a successor to the table
on which Joseph of Arimathea placed the Grail. He lives on after Arthur's
birth and arranges for his fostering. He is also responsible for the Sword in
the Stone test that proves Arthur's royal right.

All this is pursued still farther by later romancers. Merlin aids Arthur
in his early struggles and obtains Excalibur for him from the Lady of the
Lake. He also prepares the way for the Grail Quest, but before it happens he
becomes enamored of Nimue (or Viviane), who learns magical secrets from
him and then entraps him in an enchanted prison. This is the version of his
end adopted by Malory. However, a late Welsh legend makes his retreat
voluntary. He is on Bardsey Island in an underground chamber or an invisible house of glass, looking after a set of magical objects called the Thirteen
Treasures of Britain, together with the true throne of the realm, on which he
will seat Arthur when the King returns.

For practical purposes, Merlin becomes the tutelary genius of the whole
Arthurian scheme of things. T.H. White's modern handling in *The Sword in
the Stone* gives him a function as Arthur's boyhood tutor. Another modern
development is the semicomic portrayal of him as an old man with a long
white beard. His youth in the Vortigern episode rules out his being much
over forty, even at the end of his recorded career.

Geoffrey created the character by combining two figures, the fifth-
century seer and the sixth-century poet-prophet. He may have incorporated
a third, a god or hero connected with Stonehenge. On the face of it, Merlin
is an accident, the result of Geoffrey's ignorance when he wrote the *Historia*.
Possibly, however, he was on the right track. There are signs that "Myrddin"
may have been a general term of pre-Christian origin, referring to divine
inspiration, and that men supposedly inspired may have been called
"Myrddin" as a sobriquet. Vaguely aware of a plurality of Myrddins, Geoffrey,
lacking the key, may have tried to unite two such persons by treating them as
literally the same individual. The sixteenth-century Welsh chronicler Elis
Gruffudd asserts that Geoffrey's first Merlin figure was reincarnated as the
later one and also as the bard Taliesin, perhaps another confused hint at

identity through inspiration. Whatever may lie in this obscure substratum, Merlin is certainly ambiguous and transitional, a Christian after his fashion, yet a sort of druid with roots in an older world.

MODRED, see *Mordred*

MODRON, see *Morgan le Fay; Owain*

MORDRAIN, see *Evalac*

MORDRED   Traitor whose rebellion brings Arthur's reign to an end. He originates as Medraut (q.v.), a character in Welsh legend—perhaps in history—who feuds with Arthur and fights him at the battle of Camlann, with results fatal to both. The Welsh do not make Medraut sinister. His villainy in the medieval literature is due to Geoffrey of Monmouth. Geoffrey gives his name the form "Modred," which is Cornish or Breton and points to an infusion from non-Welsh sources. His Modred is Arthur's nephew. Left to govern Britain jointly with Guinevere during Arthur's absence in Gaul, he persuades the Queen to live in adultery with him and seizes the crown, making a treaty with the heathen Saxons whom Arthur had crushed. Arthur returns and clashes with him by the River Camel in Cornwall. The traitor is slain and the wounded King goes away to Avalon.

Mordred continues to be a villain in romance. He has sexual designs on Guinevere, although now she rejects him, and he aids Agravain in dragging her affair with Lancelot into public view. The Vulgate Cycle augments the evil by making him out to be secretly Arthur's son by his half-sister Morgause. At the time, Arthur did not know who she was, but the incest is a fact and its product is therefore a kind of nemesis. This development is not found everywhere, and Mordred is sometimes less wicked, being allowed, for instance, to feel remorse. Romancers part company entirely with his Cornish connection and locate the final battle near Salisbury.

MORGAN LE FAY (MORGAIN LA FEE)   Basically, the Lady of Avalon. Geoffrey of Monmouth's poem *Vita Merlini* introduces her as such. Her name is there spelled "Morgen" and she presides over a sisterhood of nine, who live on her enchanted island and have marvelous powers. She receives the wounded Arthur after his last battle and undertakes to cure him if he remains on the island long enough.

Behind Geoffrey's sketch lie ancient Celtic traditions, not only of magical islands ruled by fairy women but of actual sisterhoods of healers and wonderworkers recorded in classical literature. The head of such a group might have been the priestess of a goddess and her earthly manifestation. Medieval authors, such as Giraldus Cambrensis, are quite aware of Morgan's original divinity. Comparison of the Welsh Arthurian matter with the non-Welsh reveals that she can be equated to some extent with Modron, ultimately the river goddess Matrona. Her name suggests influence from the Irish goddess Morrigan also.

Christian belief reduces and eventually blackens her. At first, she becomes a kind of good fairy, who befriends Arthur at other stages of his career besides the end. Her father is said by the Welsh to be Avallach, king of the isle in its Welsh guise, but he is an obscure figure who generally fades out. As Avalon, the Isle of Apples, the place is essentially Morgan's. With the progress of Arthurian storytelling, the former goddess is further humanized. She is made out to be Arthur's half-sister, a daughter of his mother, Ygerna, by her first marriage. Arthur's exhumation at Glastonbury, and its identification as the "real" Avalon, inspired a notion that Morgan lived and ruled there. But romance brings her to various places. Another home that she acquires is the Castle of Maidens, probably in the neighborhood of Edinburgh. Several continental romancers shift her Avalon to the Mediterranean. Sicily is one choice. Italians call her Fata Morgana and give that name to a mirage phenomenon in the Straits of Messina once ascribed to her magic.

Since medieval Christianity, unlike the earlier Celtic variety, had difficulty finding a place for a benign or neutral enchantress, Morgan tends to become more sinister, a witch taught by Merlin who applies her arts maliciously. She causes trouble at Arthur's court, showing special enmity toward Guinevere. Sometimes, she has a husband, Urien, and bears a son, Owain or Yvain. Sometimes, she is a prey to frustrated passions that lead her to try to snare a man for her own pleasure in a "Valley Without Return." But she never becomes totally evil and retains attractive qualities. She is associated with art and culture, and despite all the scheming at the court it is still Morgan, with attendant ladies, who carries away the wounded King over the water to his Avalonian place of healing.

MORGAUSE (MARGAWSE) One of Arthur's half-sisters, a daughter of Ygerna by her first husband, the duke of Cornwall. Morgause marries Lot, and their sons are Gawain, Gaheris, Agravain, and Gareth. In the Vulgate Cycle and some later versions, including Malory's, Mordred, too, is her son, begotten by Arthur himself. Arthur is unaware of their relationship when the encounter takes place, but the act is incestuous nonetheless, and the role of Mordred as his nemesis is thereby underlined. Morgause is slain by Gaheris when he finds her in bed with Lamorak.

MORHOLT (MARHAUS) Gigantic warrior, brother of the queen of Ireland. He comes to Cornwall to demand tribute on behalf of the king, his brother-in-law. Tristan meets him in single combat and slays him. The corpse is sent back to Ireland as "tribute," a gesture recalling Arthur's treatment of the body of Lucius. This is the beginning of Tristan's involvement with the Irish court and, specifically, with the Irish princess Iseut.

MYRDDIN Welsh name that Geoffrey of Monmouth latinizes as "Merlinus," that is, the more familiar "Merlin" (q.v.). Older Welsh materials give the name to a northern character who figures in the legendary Life of St. Kentigern, the patron saint of Glasgow, and is there called Lailoken. Lailoken is said to have stirred up strife leading to a tragic inter-British battle at Arfderydd (Arthuret) in Cumbria, about 575. Because of his guilt, he was driven out of his mind and wandered in the forest of Celidon, gifted or cursed with second sight. Lailoken is a "Wild Man of the Woods" with counterparts in other folklore. But when the Welsh speak of him and call him "Myrddin," they make him a more significant and dignified person, a bard who prophesies on national issues and promises a Celtic resurgence.

In his *Historia Regum Britanniae*, Geoffrey applies the name, as "Merlin," to an earlier seer, the boy-prodigy in the *Historia Brittonum* who defeats the magicians of the fifth-century king Vortigern. This looks like a plain mistake, and in his *Vita Merlini*, where he tells and expands the story of the northern prophet, Geoffrey tries to retrieve the blunder by manipulating dates and details so as to make out that his two Merlins were identical. The attempt is unconvincing, and Giraldus Cambrensis, among others, concludes simply that there were two Merlins.

Yet while Geoffrey does become confused here, he may be rationalizing a fact of which he is hazily conscious but does not understand. It is possible that in pre-Christian Celtic belief, the gift of prophecy produced a kind of shared identity among its recipients. Welsh poetry sometimes uses "Myrddin" as if it were a synonym for the prophetic muse rather than a proper noun. The key to its etymology is Merlin's association with Carmarthen. Its Welsh name does mean "Town (of) Myrddin." "Myrddin" here seems in fact to be derived from an old name of the town, which meant "the sea fort" and was latinized as *Moridunum*. Whether or not the notion of someone actually existing called Myrddin reflects a local cult of a god or demigod, a Welsh text implies a belief in some such being. It says that the first, prehistoric name of the island of Britain was "Myrddin's Precinct," pointing to a mythical figure as a prototype. There are reasons for conjecturing that he was a god of inspiration, a sort of British Apollo. If so, different persons could have been vessels of his inspiration, even incarnations of him, and a fifth-century prophet and a sixth-century prophet could both have been Myrddin's men or simply Myrddins in that sense.

It is Geoffrey's fifth-century Merlin, although poorly attested historically, who grows into the Merlin of romance. His life could have overlapped that of the original Arthur. The sixth-century Myrddin's could not.

NENNIUS Welsh cleric, reputed compiler of the *Historia Brittonum* (q.v.), which includes the list of Arthur's twelve battles. The ascription depends on a preface not found in all the manuscripts, although there is evidence for its being early. In this, Nennius introduces himself as a disciple of Elvodug, bishop of Bangor during the first decade of the ninth century, and says that he has "made a heap of all that he has found" sifting old chronicles and traditional matter. The *Historia* has an artless confusion quite consistent with that statement. This tells somewhat in the compiler's favor. Whoever he is, he has genuinely "found," not invented. He is not a literary contriver like Geoffrey of Monmouth, who exploits and expands the ancient material he uses so as to turn it into manifest fiction.

Whether or not Nennius really was the compiler, wholly or partly, his name is often used for convenience. References to Nennius are references to the *Historia Brittonum*.

NIMUE (NINIANE, VIVIANE, ETC.) One of several women known as the Damsel or Lady of the Lake. Her name varies greatly from text to text. In Malory, she is a companion of a previous Lady and succeeds her in the role. Merlin falls in love with her, and they travel together through Brittany and Cornwall, although she never consents to be his mistress. He teaches her many of his magical secrets. At last, growing tired of him, she uses one of the spells she has learned and imprisons him. He never returns to the court. Later, she employs magic more benignly to disentangle Pelleas from his involvement with Ettard, and they become lovers and eventually marry. She is one of the ladies who bear Arthur away in a boat at the end of his career.

Different versions treat the place of Merlin's imprisonment differently, as a cave or a tomb or an invisible enclosure. Tennyson adopts the last. He distinguishes Vivien, as he calls this character, from the Lady of the Lake and makes her a mere cynical seductress, whose ruin of Merlin is part of a general spite against the court.

OLWEN   In the Welsh tale *Culhwch and Olwen*, the daughter of Ysbaddaden, the chief giant. Culhwch woos her, and, after immense difficulties that Arthur helps him to overcome, weds her.

OWAIN (OWEIN)   Historically, Urien's son, a prince of Rheged in the north. "Owain" is equivalent to the Roman name Eugenius. Like his father, he fought the northern Angles during the latter part of the sixth century. Taliesin composed an elegy on his death. The so-called Giant's Grave, in a churchyard at Penrith, was long supposed to be his.

Owain became a hero of Welsh legend. Although unknown to the Arthurian saga at the date of *Culhwch and Olwen*, which never mentions him, he was drawn anachronistically into *it*, perhaps because of a brief allusion to him by Geoffrey of Monmouth. According to a triad, his mother was Modron, originally a Celtic goddess. He appears in *The Dream of Rhonabwy* and *The Lady of the Fountain*. The latter is a Welsh version of the story told by Chrétien in *Yvain*, and Yvain is simply Owain in a French guise. Several romancers including Malory are aware that he was Urien's son and say that his mother, Urien's wife, was Morgan le Fay. This is one of a number of indications, in view of the triad, that Morgan and Modron should be at least partly identified.

PADARN   Welsh saint. "Padarn" is the Roman name Paternus. His legendary Life tells how "a certain tyrant named Arthur, from foreign parts," entered his cell at Llanbadarn Fawr near Aberystwyth and tried to carry off a fine tunic, a present from the Patriarch of Jerusalem. Miraculously thwarted, Arthur had to beg the saint's forgiveness.

Geoffrey of Monmouth mentions Llanbadarn but, understandably, not this incident. It is one of several monastic legends depicting Arthur in the stock role of a proud and powerful layman who has to be taught a lesson. The word "tyrant" need not imply oppression, but it does imply an authority of doubtful legitimacy. Such tales show that the clerical approval of Arthur evinced in the *Historia Brittonum* and the *Annales Cambriae* was far from unanimous among Welsh churchmen.

PALAMEDES (PALOMIDES)   Saracen knight in the Prose *Tristan*, a loyal friend to Tristan but enamored of Iseut. Malory makes him Pellinore's successor as pursuer of the Questing Beast and in the final quarrels a supporter of Lancelot, who gives him the dukedom of Provence.

PALUG'S CAT   A monster, Cath Palug. It lived in the island of Anglesey off the northern Welsh coast, having swum ashore from the Menai

Strait as a kitten. The sons of Palug, a local resident, rescued the little creature and raised it, with disastrous results. It grew to a huge size, embarked on a career of ravaging, and devoured a hundred and eighty warriors. According to an anonymous early Welsh poem, Arthur's companion Cai fought and apparently slew it, although the end of the story is unclear.

A legend of the terrible cat as the "Chapalu" (a corruption of *Chat de Palug*) spread to France, where Arthur was said to have fought with it himself and even, in a hotly disputed version, to have been killed by it. Savoy has a mountain known as the *Dent du Chat* or Cat's Tooth. The Vulgate *Suite du Merlin* tells of another Arthurian cat fight hereabouts, and the Welsh story may have been fused with it.

Palug's Cat is described as speckled, a detail that suggests an exaggerated leopard. But the Irish tale of St. Brendan's Voyage calls a walrus a sea cat and portrays it alarmingly.

PARZIVAL Perceval (q.v.) in his German guise, in the epic of Wolfram von Eschenbach. Much of it is based on Chrétien de Troyes, but the nature of the Grail Quest is greatly altered. The Grail is not a vessel but a stone brought down from heaven, a mystical link between God and humankind. It is in France, in the custody of a sacred order of knights (Wolfram calls them Templars) headed by the Grail King, Anfortas, whose spear wound has been inflicted on him because of his failure to live up to his vocation. Parzival is his nephew, divinely chosen through the Grail's agency to deliver him, and the crucial question he must ask is one of compassion: "Uncle, why do you suffer so?" Tested and purified in his chivalric career, Parzival becomes the Grail King himself.

Wagner's *Parsifal* reduces the number of characters and the complexity of the narrative, while deepening the examination of motives and on the whole shifting the theme closer to Christianity.

PELLAM Variously spelled. One of the Grail keepers, the father of Pelles and Pellinore. Balin wounds him with the Dolorous Stroke. Known consequently as the Maimed King, he is healed after many years by his great-grandson Galahad. He appears first in the *Suite du Merlin* and later in Malory.

PELLEAS Hero of a Malory episode that marks the blackening of the character of Gawain. Pelleas is the persistent would-be lover of the lady Ettard, who will have nothing to do with him. Gawain promises to help and goes to Ettard but tells her that he has put Pelleas out of the way and succeeds in seducing her himself. Pelleas finds them sleeping together and falls into despair. Nimue, the Lady of the Lake, comforts him and casts a spell on Ettard so that she changes her mind and loves him—too late, as Nimue well knows, since he has lost interest. Pelleas and Nimue become lovers instead. Being very strong, he takes revenge on Gawain by beating him in tournaments.

PELLES According to the Vulgate and later texts, one of the Fisher Kings, lords of Corbenic and custodians of the Grail. (The name occurs earlier, in *Perlesvaus*, but there he is not identified as a Fisher King.) Pelles is of the stock of Joseph of Arimathea. His name may be derived from the Cornish *peller*, meaning a wise man or wizard, and in his origins he is perhaps the same as a Welsh mythical character called Pwyll.

Pelles is Pellam's son and Pellinore's brother. His daughter Elaine becomes, by Lancelot, the mother of Galahad. He is host to several Grail seekers at Corbenic—Gawain with discredit because Elaine distracts him, and Galahad, Perceval, and Bors more fruitfully.

PELLINORE In the French Vulgate, in Malory, and elsewhere, King of the Isles and brother of Pelles. He is the father of Lamorak and, in some accounts, Perceval. In a joust with him, Arthur breaks the sword he extracted from the stone. Excalibur is a replacement for it. Pellinore pursues the Questing Beast and kills Lot in battle. Ten years later, Lot's sons, headed by Gawain, treacherously kill Pellinore. They also kill Lamorak. This vendetta is one of the first flaws in the order of the Round Table.

Perceval's father is sometimes called Pellean or Pellehan, probably because of confusion with Pellam. Elsewhere, his family relationships are different.

PENDRAGON Title conferred on Uther, Arthur's father. Someone called Uthr Pendragon is mentioned in an early Welsh poem, although not as a relation of Arthur. Geoffrey of Monmouth, taking up the character, tells of a celestial portent with a dragon as its main feature. Merlin expounds this as applying to Uther, and the title follows. Geoffrey interprets it as "dragon's head." A likelier translation is "head dragon," meaning "foremost leader," probably in a military sense.

The Vulgate *Merlin* makes Pendragon a separate person, a brother of Uther. Uther succeeds him as king and adopts his style. Modern authors have carried this extension further, treating "Pendragon" as a more general title held by Arthur himself. C.S. Lewis *(That Hideous Strength)* even imagines a whole series of Pendragons continuing secretly to the present day, holding an office that is spiritual rather than political. Such ideas are not found in medieval literature.

PERCEVAL   Chief hero of the Grail Quest before Galahad's emergence (see also *Parzival*; *Peredur*). His adventures in Chrétien de Troyes are partly paralleled in the Welsh tale of *Peredur*, and the two characters are basically the same, but the question of origins and priority remains open. The mythical character Pryderi may hover in the background.

There are several accounts of Perceval. He is brought up in Wales by his widowed mother and knows nothing of the chivalric world, which she loathes, but he becomes fascinated with knighthood and sets off for Arthur's court to seek it. Naive, charming, and slightly absurd, he gradually matures, although he remains, except in the German *Parzival*, innocent sexually. The story, up to a point, is the story of his education. It begins badly. Warned against being too forward in asking questions, he fails to do so when confronted with the Grail mysteries, so that the Fisher King's wound is not healed and the land is doomed to desolation. Another blunder that Perceval commits is an attempt to sit in the Perilous Seat at the Round Table, the destined chair of the Grail achiever. It quickly becomes clear that the place is not for him at this point.

After his early disasters, he goes on a search for the Grail Castle. In some versions, he finds it and asks the question that cures the Fisher King. In others, his Grail pursuit draws toward its close with a voyage. *Perlesvaus* sends him across the ocean on a strange journey influenced by Irish sea romances. The Vulgate *Queste*, and Malory's adaptation of it, take him to Sarras as the companion of Galahad. He does not share the ultimate vision and stays in the distant land as a hermit, soon dying there.

His family affiliations do not always agree with his mother's widowhood. Some romancers make him a son of Alain, a relationship that puts the story, nonsensically, in the first century A.D. or the second at latest. Elsewhere, he is a son of Pellinore and brother of Lamorak, fortunately untouched by Gawain's vendetta against them.

PEREDUR   Hero of a Welsh romance resembling Chrétien's *Perceval* or *Le Conte del Graal* but not derived from it. Both may draw on a common stock of Welsh legend. Peredur is the youngest son of a northern noble. After his father and brothers meet with violent deaths, his mother brings him up in a remote and peaceful spot. At last, however, he insists on going to Arthur's court to be made a knight.

In the course of a series of adventures, he visits two elderly men who turn out to be his uncles. One of them is lame. At the house of the other, Peredur sees a bleeding lance and a severed head on a dish but recalls a warning given him by his lame uncle against asking questions and refrains from doing so. Long afterward, he learns that he should have asked about the mysterious objects and that if he had, the lame uncle would have been cured. His injury was caused by a band of witches, who also beheaded Peredur's cousin (hence the severed head). Peredur must suppress them. With Arthur's aid, he kills the witches. This is a kind of Grail story without the Grail, Peredur corresponding to the Grail hero Perceval. The secret in this case concerns the murder of a kinsman and the duty of vengeance.

"Peredur" occurs as a name in Welsh poetry, the *Annales Cambriae*, and Geoffrey of Monmouth. Where there is a clear historical reference, the person meant is a northern noble of the late sixth century. The author of the romance may have had this man in mind, but if so, the result is the same blurring of dates and places that arises from the introduction of Owain and other characters into the Arthurian milieu.

PERILOUS SEAT (SIEGE PERILOUS)   Seat at the Round Table that is left vacant. It is sometimes said to correspond to Judas's place at the table of the Last Supper. No one can safely sit here except the knight who will achieve the Grail Quest, that is, as it transpires, Galahad. In the *Didot-Perceval*, the "enchantments of Britain" are caused by Perceval ill-advisedly sitting in the empty place. This is a variant on the wasteland theme.

PETRUS, see *Bron*

PRIDWEN (PRYDWEN)   Arthur's ship, in which he and his men visit a watery otherworld in *The Spoils of Annwfn* to seek a magical cauldron. In *Culhwch and Olwen*, they also cross water to obtain a wonderful cauldron, but here the voyage is to Ireland. Geoffrey of Monmouth transfers the name to Arthur's shield, possibly because it means "Fair Face" in Welsh and the shield had a painting of the Virgin Mary on it.

QUESTING BEAST (BESTE GLATISSANT)   Literally, the yelping or barking beast. It has a serpent's head, a leopard's body, a lion's hindquarters, and a hare's feet. A noise like the baying of sixty hounds issues from its belly. Pellinore pursues it, and after his death Palamedes takes up the pursuit. Perceval is also mentioned. It usually remains uncaught, but according to one story Palamedes did catch up with it by a lake where it had stopped to drink and killed it with his lance, whereupon it sank into the water and a storm broke out.

The Questing Beast is explained as the offspring of a princess who practiced the black arts. She made sexual advances to her brother. When he repulsed her, she gave herself to the Devil, who caused the brother to be eaten alive by dogs and begat the Questing Beast on the princess. Its internal clamor of hounds was a tormenting reminder of the brother's death. The Beast carries a suggestion of chaos and evil, and its hybrid shape hints at its incestuous background, the joining-together of things that should not be joined. Arthur has a glimpse of it after his own incest with Morgause.

The Questing Beast figures in the *Suite du Merlin* and in Malory. *Perlesvaus* introduces the Questing Beast quite differently. It is a harmless creature beset and torn apart by real hounds and is interpreted as standing for Christ slain by the Jews.

RAGNELL, see *Loathly Lady*

RHONABWY In *The Dream of Rhonabwy*, a twelfth-century Welshman who has an experience of time travel. Pursuing the outlawed brother of a king of Powys, he comes to a semiderelict hall where he lies down to sleep on a yellow ox-hide. His sleep lasts for three nights and three days, during which he is conducted on a minutely detailed visit to Arthur's army preparing for battle. He meets Arthur himself, who is called "the emperor." The ox-hide that induces this vision is a survival of Celtic divinatory practices.

RIOTHAMUS (RIOTIMUS) Fifth-century "king of the Britons" whose career arguably underlies parts of Geoffrey of Monmouth's account of Arthur. In 468, during the reign of the eastern emperor Leo, he took a British army to Gaul to oppose the Visigoths and advanced into the heart of the country. Betrayed by an imperial governor, he was defeated in late 469 or early 470 and escaped into the territory of the Burgundians. While Geoffrey, in his account of Arthur's Gallic warfare, transforms this campaign as he transforms others and hugely exaggerates it, there are several indications that he has it in mind.

Riothamus, as given (with slight spelling variations) in early texts that refer to this man, appears to be a title or assumed style. It latinizes a British form, *Rigotamos*, composed of *Rig* plus a superlative suffix. The meaning is "supreme king" or "supremely royal." A modern word formed in an analogous way is "generalissimo." *Vortigern* and *Vortimer* are cognate. Riothamus perhaps had some shadowy claim to a British high-kingship in succession to Vortigern.

He doubtless had another, personal name. Geoffrey may have supposed it to be Arthur (Artorius) and identified him with the war leader Arthur of Welsh legend. There are traces of a pre-Geoffrey tradition to this effect. A Breton text apparently refers to the same man and calls him Arthur, and several medieval chronicles point in that direction.

The possibility that an Arthur-Riothamus equation goes back to early times, and even that this British high king *was* the original Arthur so far as anyone was, is raised by the archaeological findings at Cadbury-Camelot, which revealed the presence of a powerful royal occupant for whom Riothamus is the only documented candidate. Nothing is on record about his activities in Britain (under the style Riothamus, that is) before he shipped his army to Gaul. However, the trans-Channel contact suggests that his own territory was in the southwest, Arthur's reputed homeland, and he could plausibly have fought some of the battles ascribed to Arthur.

RON Arthur's spear, "long, broad in the blade, and thirsty for slaughter," according to Geoffrey of Monmouth. He arrived at this odd word by abbreviating the full name Rhongomyniad, which occurs in *Culhwch and Olwen.*

ROUND TABLE Geoffrey of Monmouth portrays King Arthur founding an order of knighthood but says nothing of an actual piece of furniture called the Round Table, giving a name to the order. Wace mentions it first, claiming a Breton source. Some sort of Celtic background is likely, in view of an ancient custom by which Celtic warriors sat in a circle around their chief. Wace explains that Arthur had the Table made thus to prevent the quarrels over precedence to which a long table would give rise, since, in a medieval banqueting hall, the end nearer the king would be more honorable. Layamon enlarges on that idea.

Later, the Round Table precedes Arthur and has a mystical meaning. It is the successor to two previous tables, that of the Last Supper and that of the Grail. Merlin causes it to be made for Uther, its shape being an image of the round world and the heavens. One seat remains vacant in memory of Judas. This is the Perilous Seat and can be safely occupied only by the knight who will achieve the Grail Quest. The Table passes from Uther to Guinevere's father and comes to Arthur with his bride as her dowry. As to its final fate, the only clue is an assertion that after Arthur's passing Mark captured Camelot and destroyed the Table.

The number of places is given variously. Sometimes, it is thirteen, in direct reminiscence of the Last Supper. With the reputed number of knights rising to a hundred forty or a hundred fifty (Malory gives both figures), and even two hundred fifty, the problem of physical practicality becomes obvious. One or two medieval artists solve it by depicting the Table not as a disk but as a ring, with gaps for servitors to pass through. The table at Winchester has twenty-four places, plus one for Arthur.

In 1344, Edward III contemplated reviving the Round Table knighthood, but after some reflection he founded the Order of the Garter instead.

SAGREMOR Knight who plays a minor role in the Grail stories. The Vulgate *Mort Artu* makes him one of the longest-surviving combatants in the final battle, but he is eventually slain by Mordred. In the Prose *Tristan*, it is Sagremor who conveys the dying Tristan's last greetings to Lancelot and others and takes his armor to Arthur. The romance *Meliador* by the chronicler Froissart gives him an otherwise unrecorded love affair.

SANGRAIL, see *Grail*

"SARMATIAN CONNECTION" Interpretation of Arthurian legends in terms of influences from eastern Europe. Auxiliary troops drawn from the Sarmatian steppe dwellers were established in Roman Britain in the second century and apparently maintained their ethnic identity for some time. Modern study of the folktales of the Ossetes, a tribe in the Caucasus reputedly of Sarmatian descent, has revealed parallels with Arthurian motifs, such as the casting away of Excalibur. It has been suggested that these are remnants of Sarmatian mythology, that the Sarmatian auxiliaries in Britain played a part in the post-Roman resistance to the barbarians, and that their mythology became, so to speak, acclimatized, originally as part of the saga of that resistance.

SARRAS Imaginary city where Galahad, Perceval, and Bors are conveyed by the ship of Solomon, and where Galahad, in the "spiritual palace," attains the supreme vision of the Grail and falls dead. The name echoes the word "Saracen" and suggests a vague East.

SAXONS General term covering the closely related peoples from across the North Sea who moved into parts of Britain during the fifth century. These were the enemies on whose temporary defeat, according to Welsh tradition, the glories of Arthur were founded. They included the Saxons proper and the Angles, plus the Jutes and minor groupings. Their takeover from the Celtic Britons, and expansion westward and northward, gradually created "England"—that is, Angle-land—with an "English" language evolved from Anglo-Saxon. Heathen and barbarous at the time of their advent, with a long record of piracy, they were christianized and to some extent civilized during the seventh century.

The Britons' Welsh descendants handed down a story that the first Saxons arrived under the leadership of the brothers Hengist and Horsa, who were encouraged to make their homes in Kent, and to bring over their followers, by the British king Vortigern. More colonists joined them, and the reinforced host got out of hand, but after many disasters was pushed back and held for several decades by Ambrosius and Arthur. This is the story that emerges confusedly from Gildas and the *Historia Brittonum*. The Arthurian legend grew from the notion of a phase of British triumph and peace during which the Saxons were confined to a fairly small area and reduced to passivity. In Geoffrey of Monmouth, their importance and menace are still clear, but in Arthurian romance they receive less and less attention, till they come to be almost forgotten.

Archaeology suggests that the Saxons began settling in Britain not much later than the beginning of the fifth century. The major bodies of migrants were probably coming over from the 420s on, as *foederati*, barbarians allotted land and supplies on the condition of their keeping order and holding off other barbarians, in this case chiefly the Picts. The Britons, although autonomous by that time, were following Roman precedents. Vortigern was apparently an actual ruler and may well have played a leading role, though the legendary account is an oversimplification. The *foederati* revolted, seemingly toward the middle of the fifth century, but after a period of anarchy and widespread raiding they withdrew to their authorized settlements. Much of their subsequent expansion may have taken place peaceably. However, the counteraction associated with Ambrosius and Arthur kept up a fluctuating warfare that contained them in parts of the country and may have temporarily regained ground here and there.

SHALOTT   Tennyson's adaptation of "Escalot," the name, in French romance, of the home of a maiden who falls in love with Lancelot. Elsewhere, she is called Elaine and her home is Astolat.

SIEGE PERILOUS, see *Perilous Seat*

SOUTH CADBURY, see *Cadbury-Camelot*

SPOILS OF ANNWFN, see *Annwfn*

STONEHENGE   Geoffrey of Monmouth refers to this megalithic structure as the Giants' Ring, *Chorea Gigantum*, with a suggestion of a round dance. He says it formerly stood on Mount Killaraus in Ireland. Giants had brought over the stones from Africa and set them up in a magic circle. The British king Aurelius Ambrosius, Arthur's uncle, wanted to build a memorial over the mass grave of several hundred nobles massacred by the Saxons. On Merlin's advice, he sent an expedition to Mount Killaraus. With the enchanter's aid, the Giants' Ring was dismantled and shipped to Britain, where Merlin reconstituted it on Salisbury Plain over the grave. Aurelius, Uther, and Arthur's successor Constantine were buried here.

This is a fantasy, although it may possibly have been inspired by some legend of a god or magician who built Stonehenge and whom Geoffrey chose to equate with Merlin. The monument was set up on its present site in stages, mostly during the third millennium B.C. Geologists have maintained that some of the smaller stones must have been quarried in the Prescelly Mountains in southwest Wales and floated up the Bristol Channel on rafts, so that Geoffrey's account of seaborne stones from the west could preserve a factual tradition. Although disputed, this ancient feat of quarrying and sea transportation continues to have its advocates.

SWORD IN THE STONE   Magical test, usually supposed to have been devised by Merlin, that shows Arthur to be the rightful king. Different versions give different accounts of it. The sword may be directly implanted in the stone, or it may pass down through an anvil. Whatever the details, Arthur alone can draw it out.

Geoffrey gives no hint of any such test. The Arthur of his *Historia* is well known to be Uther's son and successor. The motif emerges when Arthur's status becomes less clear. Robert de Boron is the first to introduce it, in his *Merlin* romance. He makes the sword symbolic of justice, and Arthur's ability to withdraw it and take possession is a sign of God's approval. Later, as with Malory, the emphasis is more on proving him the heir of the kingdom. The sword is sometimes identified with Excalibur, but in the main tradition Arthur breaks it jousting with Pellinore, and Excalibur is a replacement.

Galahad is confirmed as the predestined Grail Knight by a similar test. The origin is unknown, although other mythologies tell of a sword wedged in a tree, which the hero must pull out.

TALIESIN   Most famous of several northern bards mentioned in the *Historia Brittonum*. He is said to have traveled widely, but in the latter part of the sixth century he was at the court of Rheged, the kingdom comprising Cumbria and neighboring territories. His few surviving poems in Old Welsh extol Rheged's king Urien and Urien's son Owain, who both fought against the northern Angles.

The Book of Taliesin is a medieval compilation in which the genuine verse appears among items of later date, including *The Spoils of Annwfn*. Taliesin is the ostensible utterer of a Welsh riddling poem often construed as a list of previous incarnations. If this meaning were certain, it would raise issues about the persistence of druidic beliefs. Robert Graves put forward a cryptographic solution that would likewise point to pre-Christian myth.

Taliesin has a legendary history and is the hero of colorful legends. Mostly, these are unrelated to Arthur, but the poet is anachronistically at Arthur's court in *Culhwch and Olwen*, and Geoffrey of Monmouth brings him into his *Vita Merlini*, telling how Arthur was borne away to Avalon, the "island of apples," after his wounding at Camlann. Wace has heard Taliesin's name but gives him far too early a date. He does not appear in medieval romance. Charles Williams's Arthurian poems assign him an important role.

TINTAGEL Village on the north coast of Cornwall, from which a ravine runs down to the sea and a cove, between two rocky headlands. High on the left headland are the ruins of Tintagel Castle. Here Geoffrey of Monmouth locates the begetting of Arthur. He relates how King Uther lusted after Ygerna, the wife of Gorlois, duke of Cornwall. Gorlois immured her in the stronghold on the promontory, believing her to be inaccessible there, because the only approach was by way of a narrow, easily guarded isthmus. Uther, however, aided by Merlin's magic, passed the guards and reached the object of his desire. According to common belief, Ygerna remained at Tintagel, or returned to it, and gave birth to their son in the same place.

Nothing is said about Arthur using Tintagel after he became king, and in romance, where Mark is the overlord of Cornwall, it becomes a castle of his. Tennyson's version of the coming of Arthur retains Tintagel but more or less eliminates the scandalous matter of Uther. The infant Arthur is alleged to have been mysteriously washed ashore on the beach and caught up out of the water by Merlin. Today, a cave that runs through the base of the promontory is known as Merlin's Cave and is reputedly haunted by the enchanter's ghost.

The castle was built in the Middle Ages and has nothing to do with Geoffrey's characters. However, imported pottery and other archaeological data attest an important settlement during the fifth century or early sixth. This was first explained as a monastery, but it now seems likely that there was a princely stronghold on the headland, perhaps a regional seat of government. Excavation of a burial ground has carried the date of origin more definitely back into the fifth century. Geoffrey's choice of Tintagel was prompted by some Cornish tradition of occupancy at about the right time.

TRIAdS Summaries of Welsh bardic lore, grouped in sets of three. The "Triads of the Island of Britain" record the names and deeds of numerous characters from the period prior to the Saxon ascendancy. Most of the triads are quite brief, giving little more than tantalizing allusions to stories now lost in their entirety. A few are influenced by medieval literature, but many preserve much older material. The triadic grouping was a mnemonic device, helping a bard who had told one of the stories to call another to mind. Thus, in the triad "Three Generous Men of the Island of Britain," the first is Nudd, the second is Mordaf, the third is Rhydderch. Having told the story of Nudd, the bard could go on easily to Mordaf for an encore, and to Rhydderch for another. Taken as a whole, the series of triads is an index of Welsh heroic mythology.

Some of the characters are historical, some (including a number of animals) are mythical, and many are doubtful. Arthur's preeminence is shown partly by his occurrence in more triads than anybody else, partly by the fact that he is added to several as a fourth. At the end of the "Three Generous Men" an added line says that Arthur was more generous than the three. Arthur is one of the "Exalted Prisoners," owing, it seems, to a lost tale of his being imprisoned and rescued, perhaps in the course of early guerrilla adventures. He is one of the "Red Ravagers," so formidable that no grass grew for seven years where he trod. He is blamed for one of the "Unfortunate Disclosures," the digging up of the head of Bran on Tower Hill, resulting in the loss to Britain of its magical protection. The battle of Camlann is one of the "Futile Battles," arising from a conflict of Arthur with Medraut, the original Mordred, which is noted in other triads. But the battle of Badon is never mentioned. With the Welsh bards and their audiences, the earlier anti-Saxon struggle, even in its successful "Arthurian" phase, seems not to have been a popular subject.

Other Arthurian characters appear in the triads, notably Gwenhwyfar (Guinevere), Drystan (Tristan), and Essyllt (Iseut).

TRIbRuIT Unidentified river, on whose "strand" or shore, in the *Historia Brittonum*, Arthur's tenth battle is fought. The Welsh form of the name is *Tryfrwyd*, and the battle is mentioned in an early Welsh poem, which includes Bedwyr (Bedivere) among the combatants. A theory that the river was in Scotland is no longer thought valid.

TRISTAN (TRISTRAM) Best known as the lover of Iseut, although he has numerous adventures only remotely connected with their affair. His name is the Pictish Drust or Drostan, but it occurs in southern Britain almost if not quite as early as the supposed time of the events. The love story is a composite. Its central theme may have taken shape in Wales, where the triads call the couple Drystan and Essyllt and give them a curiously primitive setting that involves them in such matters as pig stealing. Some have detected influence from the Irish tale of Diarmaid and Grainne, from a legend about a Pictish king named Drust, and from more exotic quarters. To complete the complication, the story is planted finally in Cornwall, with details showing this location to be more than uninformed fancy. Tristan is a nephew of Mark, the Cornish king, and Iseut is Mark's wife. The name of Tristan's home territory, Lyonesse, which may once have meant Lothian in Scotland (Old French Loenois), comes to signify a land stretching southwestward from the Cornish peninsula that, according to local legend, is now sunk beneath the ocean.

The Cornish location is related to the Tristan Stone, a monument near Fowey commemorating "Drustanus, son of Cunomorus." Cunomorus is the historical ruler Kynvawr, who flourished during the first half of the sixth century. It was affirmed at least as early as the ninth that he was identical with Mark, whose full style in Latin would thus have been Marcus Cunomorus. If so, the Tristan legend has a historical basis and its Cornish setting is correct, whatever the accretions from elsewhere. This view invites the criticism that it makes Tristan not Mark's nephew but his son, with the implication that Iseut was his stepmother. Storytellers might have changed the relationship to make it less discreditable. But Tristan is still Mark's son, if the reading is correct, in the triad of the "Three Peers of Arthur's Court."

The Tristan-Iseut amour is at first only tenuously linked with the Arthurian cycle. Romancers draw it in, and prose versions make Tristan (or Tristram) a knight of the Round Table and a friend of Lancelot. A tragic birth story gives his name a spurious derivation from the French *triste*, "sad." Although assimilated to the courtly Arthurian scene, and credited with exploits like those of other knights, he is differently conceived from most of them, being more versatile, a linguist, a skillful harper and huntsman, and a good chess player. Furthermore, his abilities as a fighter, although great, never cease to be overshadowed by the love between himself and Iseut, perhaps the first literary instance of such a passion being portrayed as overriding all other concerns and justifying virtually any conduct that serves its ends.

The details of Tristan's career differ widely from one version to another. He is launched upon it by a combat with Morholt, the brother of the queen of Ireland. Morholt comes to Cornwall to demand tribute and Tristan kills him. When in Ireland himself, Tristan is revealed to be Morholt's slayer but appeases the wrath of the royal family by other deeds. Iseut is the daughter of the Irish king. She uses her healing arts to cure Tristan when he is wounded and agrees to marry his uncle Mark, but while he is escorting her to Cornwall they accidentally drink a love potion intended for Iseut and her bridegroom, and their obsessed and doomed passion results. Mark, uncertain of the situation, alternately harries them and relents. Tristan is banished and marries another Iseut in Brittany, but the bond with the Irish woman is never broken. His death is due in the verse romances to a lie told by his jealous Breton wife, but in prose ones to a cowardly assault by Mark himself. Iseut dies also, grief-stricken. The lovers are buried side by side. A vine grows from Tristan's grave and a rose from Iseut's, and the stems intertwine.

TWRCH TRWYTH Gigantic boar, actually a king transformed into a boar for his sins. In *Culhwch and Olwen*, the giant Ysbaddaden demands that Culhwch obtain a comb and a pair of scissors that Twrch Trwyth carries between his ears. Arthur and his men hunt the boar across Wales and down to Cornwall, suffering casualties, but at last getting the comb and scissors. (See also *Buelt.*)

URIEN (URBGEN) Historically, the most famous king of the northern British kingdom of Rheged, centered on Cumbria but extending beyond it. The *Historia Brittonum*, and several early poems, speak of his leadership of a north British coalition against the Angles between 570 and 590. He defeated them and besieged their army on the island of Lindisfarne but was assassinated. The bard Taliesin was at Urien's court, and some of his surviving poems extol the king's courage, prowess in war, and high-spirited generosity.

Despite the incompatibility of dates, Urien is involved in Arthurian legend. Perhaps the first hint of this is the fact that a battle he fought at Brewyn—probably the Roman fort of *Bremenium* or High Rochester—finds its way into some texts of the list of the victories of Arthur and even replaces the canonical battle of Agned. A more important influence was the glorification of Urien's son Owain, who also fought the Angles and was also praised by Taliesin. A triad makes him the son of Urien by Modron, originally a Celtic goddess. Geoffrey of Monmouth knows both father and son as northern rulers, and Owain passed into Welsh Arthurian romance bringing his father with him. The *Suite du Merlin*, followed by Malory, has Urien marry Morgan le Fay. In view of the triad where his wife is Modron, this is a reason for believing that Morgan is Modron under another name or rather a romanticized and enlarged version of her.

UTHER   Arthur's father, according to Geoffrey of Monmouth (see also *Pendragon*). He is a son of King Constantine. At the time of Vortigern's usurpation, he and his brother Aurelius Ambrosius are still children, and their guardians take them to Brittany for safety. They grow up, return to Britain, and overthrow Vortigern. Aurelius is crowned. He sends Uther on an expedition to Ireland to bring back the stones called the Giants' Ring, with a view to setting them up as a monument to four hundred and sixty British nobles slain by the Saxons. Merlin, whose idea it was, accompanies the party and uses his arts to uproot the stones and afterward to reerect them on Salisbury Plain. Hence Stonehenge.

Aurelius is poisoned by a Saxon and buried at Stonehenge himself. A celestial portent appears with a dragon in it, and through Merlin's interpretation Uther acquires his title "Pendragon." As king, he holds a banquet in London at which he is seized with ungovernable desire for Ygerna, the wife of Gorlois, duke of Cornwall. A quarrel ensues and the king's men fight the duke's. Gorlois shuts Ygerna up in Tintagel Castle while he goes to oppose the royal army. Merlin, however, magically turns Uther into a replica of Gorlois, enabling him to enter the castle unchallenged and reach Ygerna, who imagines him to be her husband. He begets Arthur. The real Gorlois has just fallen in battle, so Uther reverts to his true shape and marries Ygerna.

Romancers generally follow Geoffrey here. Tennyson, however, wishing to keep Tintagel but get rid of such a disreputable story, offers a legend of his own. The infant Arthur is mysteriously washed ashore in the cove below the castle, and Merlin takes him up out of the water.

Uther is troubled through the rest of his reign by failing health and Saxon aggression. The most important event (not in Geoffrey) is that Merlin makes the Round Table for him. After about sixteen years, he falls victim, like his brother, to Saxon poison and is likewise buried at Stonehenge, being succeeded by his young son, Arthur. Geoffrey's account of this reign has no links with history, and whereas Uther's father and both his brothers have real originals he himself is shadowy. A Welsh poem earlier than Geoffrey briefly mentions "Uthr Pendragon." But the idea of his fatherhood of Arthur may be due to a mistake. *Uthr* means "terrible" or "awe-inspiring," and the poetic phrase "Arthur the terrible" might have been misconstrued as "Arthur son of Uthr."

VIVIANE, see *Nimue*

VORTIGERN Fifth-century British king. The Welsh call him Gwrtheyrn the Thin and blame him for the settlement of the Saxons, and hence for their depredations (checked by Arthur, but only for a time) and conquest of what is now England. "Vortigern" means "over-king" and, as applied to this ruler, is probably a title or designation that corresponds to the Irish "high king" and means the real or nominal overlord of several regional ones.

The *Historia Brittonum* relates how Vortigern allowed a party of Saxons led by Hengist and Horsa to make their homes in Kent, with a view to employing them as auxiliary troops. Many more of these pagan barbarians arrived, and Hengist strengthened his hold over the king by giving him his daughter in marriage. More and more ground was lost to the heathen. Vortigern tried to build himself a fortress in Wales, but the work was halted by supernatural happenings, and the youthful Ambrosius gave the king an ominous demonstration of mantic powers. Vortigern died without honor, rebuked for his sins by the visiting Gallic bishop Germanus and hated by his people.

Geoffrey of Monmouth expands the story, making Vortigern an unscrupulous usurper, turning the young seer into Merlin, and shaping his narrative so that Arthur eventually emerges as Britain's savior after the time of trouble that Vortigern has caused.

Vortigern seems to have been a real ruler. He appears in Anglo-Saxon sources unaffected by Welsh legend, and he is commonly assumed to be the *superbus tyrannus* mentioned by Gildas, although Gildas gives the *tyrannus* only a partial responsibility for the Saxon advent. There are slight indications that Vortigern may have achieved power through an agreement with Rome. Notes at the end of the *Historia Brittonum* put the beginning of his paramountcy in 425 and the landing of his first Saxons in 428. Geoffrey picks up the point about Germanus, mentioning his visit to Britain with Lupus, another bishop, which took place in 429. He uses this to date Vortigern's main deal with Hengist and other events. While the *Historia Brittonum* dates cannot be trusted as exact, they are more plausible than a long-accepted chronology putting everything more than twenty years later. This was due to a mistake by Gildas, adopted and developed by Bede. But, however dated, the story oversimplifies a process of Saxon settlement that was more drawn-out and widespread and can hardly all have been due to this one high king.

VORTIMER Vortigern's eldest son, who is said in the *Historia Brittonum* to have broken with his father's pro-Saxon policy and fought to expel the barbarians from Kent. He won several battles but died soon after, and they returned with Vortigern's acquiescence.

Geoffrey of Monmouth says that the Britons, alarmed at the rapid influx of Saxons following Vortigern's crucial deal with Hengist, deposed him and made Vortimer king. But when he won his victories, his Saxon stepmother poisoned him and Vortigern resumed power. Here, Geoffrey supplies one of his few chronological fixes for the fifth century. He has already stated that the deal with Hengist involving Vortigern's Saxon marriage occurred during the visit to Britain of the bishops Germanus and Lupus, which began early in 429, and he implies that when Vortimer fought his battles Germanus was still in the country or had only recently left. While this dating sheds light on Geoffrey's chronological scheme, so far as he has one, it scarcely works as history. Nor can Vortimer's campaign be cogently associated with battles in Kent that are recorded later in the *Anglo-Saxon Chronicle*.

"Vortimer" is derived from a British form *Vortamorix*. *Vor* meant "over," *tamo* was a superlative suffix, *rix* meant "king." Vortimer is therefore the "over-most" or "highest" king, a designation that is cognate with others in the same period and may be thought to favor his reality, perhaps as a rival to Vortigern (whether really a son or not) who adopted a distinctive and more grandiose style.

WASTELAND Recurrent feature of the Grail stories. The basic theme is that the country around the Grail Castle in Arthur's time has become barren because of an enchantment or sacrilege. It will revive when the Grail-seeking knight asks the correct question in the castle. The state of the land is associated with the Grail keeper's wound, which is usually of a sexual nature, and may be due, as in the episode of the Dolorous Stroke, to the same event that blighted the territory. He will be healed when the question is asked.

There are variations from one version to another, and the Wasteland does not always figure at all. Such things as pagan fertility magic, and the link between the health of the land and the well-being—especially sexual—of a sacred king, clearly have their place in the evolution of Grail mythology. However, they cannot be pressed as giving a complete explanation. Stress on the Wasteland is mainly a modern phenomenon due to T.S. Eliot, who was influenced by the anthropological and religious theories of Jessie Weston.

WILD HUNT Widespread folklore theme. Departed heroes ride through the sky with supernatural companions. They draw after them the spirits of evildoers and, sometimes, unbaptized infants. The chief Welsh hunter is Gwyn ap Nudd, the lord of Annwfn. His hounds have white bodies and red ears. A spectral Arthur may also lead the hunt, and a French version of it, probably Breton-inspired, is called the *Chasse Artu*.

WILLIAM OF MALMESBURY   England's first medieval historian of stature. In his *Gesta Regum Anglorum* ("Acts of the Kings of the English"), completed about 1125, he gives a short account of Arthur mainly based on the *Historia Brittonum*, speaking of Ambrosius as king after Vortigern and of Arthur as a colleague who was the Britons' principal military leader. William refers to fantastic tales current about him and remarks that he deserves to be commemorated in true history. Elsewhere, he notes the discovery of the grave of Gawain on the Pembroke coast and adds that Arthur's grave is unknown and his return is prophesied.

In this book, William referred to Glastonbury Abbey. His information was erroneous, and when the mistake was pointed out he accepted an invitation to go to the abbey and write its history correctly. The result was the short treatise *De Antiquitate Glastoniensis Ecclesiae* ("On the Antiquity of the Church at Glastonbury"), supporting the claim of a very early foundation and mentioning several saints connected with the place. After his death, the Glastonbury monks expanded the treatise, interpolating, among much else, their story of Joseph of Arimathea.

WINCHESTER   Cathedral city in Hampshire, formerly the Roman *Venta Belgarum*, later the capital of Wessex, and long a rival of London as a place for coronations and royal burials. Geoffrey of Monmouth gives it prominence in the Britain of Arthur. For Malory, Winchester is Camelot, although this equation defies the fact that the Camelot of romance is Arthur's capital solely, not a city with a long history before and after him.

The hall of Winchester Castle houses the so-called Round Table, or rather table-top (the legs have gone), hung on the wall like a very large picture. Eighteen feet in diameter, it was made in the thirteenth or fourteenth century, probably for a type of aristocratic festival called a Round Table, in which nobles played Arthurian roles, banqueted, and jousted. If a king was responsible for it, Edward I, who held several such entertainments, may be the best candidate, although Henry III is eligible. The origin of the table was soon forgotten. Caxton believed it to be actually Arthur's.

Henry VII, the first Tudor sovereign, who tried to exploit the Arthurian mystique, accepted Malory's Camelot identification and had his first son baptized at Winchester and named Arthur, the intention being that he should reign as Arthur II. The prince died young and Henry VIII came to the throne instead. He kept up the propagandist myth for a while and in 1522 had the Winchester table painted in segments, with places allotted to the King and his principal knights. The design was repainted in the eighteenth century and is still vivid.

YDER (IDER) Young knight noted for his brave and sometimes foolhardy exploits. At Glastonbury, he was said to have slain three giants single-handed, on the hill Brent Knoll a few miles away. In the thirteenth-century romance *Yder*, he kills a bear that has wandered into Guinevere's bedroom. Arthur subsequently takes it into his head that the Queen's feelings for her rescuer go beyond gratitude, but Yder marries the lady of his heart, Guenloie, and the tension relaxes.

YGERNA (IGERNE, IGRAINE) Arthur's mother. She is the wife of the duke of Cornwall, who in Geoffrey of Monmouth (the first to tell the story) is Gorlois, but in Malory is anonymous. Merlin, by a magical device, enables the enamored King Uther to spend a night with her, and Arthur is the result. As her husband has just been killed in battle, Uther can marry her and legitimize their son. They have at least one more child, Anna.

Geoffrey mentions no children by Ygerna's first marriage and represents the dukedom of Cornwall as passing to Cador, who may be Gorlois's brother. Malory, however, names three daughters by this marriage, Morgause, Elaine, and Morgan le Fay, and makes Arthur her only offspring by Uther. The three are therefore his half-sisters, with disastrous consequences in the case of Morgause.

YSBADDADEN, see *Culhwch*

YSEULT, see *Iseut*

YVAIN Owain (q.v.) in his French guise. The adapted name is of Breton origin. Chrétien's *Yvain* tells essentially the same story that is told of Owain in the Welsh romance *The Lady of the Fountain*. Yvain wins the love of the widow of a knight he has killed. They are married, but Gawain lures him back to Arthur's court, alone. He fails to return at the promised time, goes out of his mind when his wife deserts him, and has to undertake fearful adventures to expiate his offence. He has a lion as his companion and is called the Knight with the Lion.

There are later versions, and Yvain is a respected figure in the Vulgate *Mort Artu*.

BIBLIOGRAPHY

The following bibliography goes well beyond a listing of the sources cited for each chapter. Even so, it is highly selective: we offer a small number of titles, whereas the bibliography of the International Arthurian Society (see below) records over seven hundred items each year. We have for the most part listed books rather than articles, and general or broad presentations rather than technical studies. Readers seeking further information should consult the following bibliographies.

BIBLIOGRAPHIES AND REFERENCE VOLUMES

Bibliographical Bulletin of the International Arthurian Society/Bulletin Bibliographique de la Société Internationale Arthurienne, 1 (1949)–48 (1996). Annual.

Lacy, Norris J., ed. *Medieval Arthurian Literature: A Guide to Recent Research*. New York: Garland, 1996. [Includes essays and extensive bibliographies on all medieval vernacular literatures.]

———, Geoffrey Ashe, Sandra Ness Ihle, Marianne E. Kalinke, and Raymond H. Thompson, eds. *The New Arthurian Encyclopedia*. Updated Paperback Edition. New York: Garland, 1996.

Last, Rex, ed. *The Arthurian Bibliography, 3*. Cambridge: Brewer, 1985.

———, ed. *The Arthurian Bibliography, III: Supplement 1979–1983*. Cambridge: Brewer, 1987.

Minary, Ruth, and Charles Moorman. *An Arthurian Dictionary*. 1978; Chicago: Academy Chicago, 1990.

Pickford, Cedric E., and Rex Last, eds. *The Arthurian Bibliography, I: Author Listing*. Cambridge: Brewer, 1981.

———, ———, and C.R. Barker, eds. *The Arthurian Bibliography, II: Subject Index*. Cambridge: Brewer, 1983.

Reiss, Edmund, Louise Horner Reiss, and Beverly Taylor. *Arthurian Legend and Literature: An Annotated Bibliography. I: The Middle Ages*. New York: Garland, 1984. [Volume II was never published.]

CHAPTER 1: ORIGINS

Adams, Jeremy duQuesnay. "Sidonius and Riothamus: A Glimpse of the Historical Arthur?" *Arthurian Literature* XII, ed. James P. Carley and Felicity Riddy. Woodbridge: Brewer, 1993, pp. 157–64.

Alcock, Leslie. (1) *Arthur's Britain: History and Archaeology A.D. 367–634*. London: Allen Lane/Penguin, 1971.

———. (2) *"By South Cadbury Is That Camelot . . .": Excavations at Cadbury Castle 1966–70*. London: Thames and Hudson, 1972.

———. (3) "Cadbury-Camelot: A Fifteen-Year Perspective." *Proceedings of the British Academy*, 68 (1982), 355–88.

Annales Cambriae, see "Nennius."

Ashe, Geoffrey. (1) *Avalonian Quest*. London: Methuen, 1982.

———. (2) "A Certain Very Ancient Book." *Speculum*, 56 (1981), 301–23.

———. (3) *The Discovery of King Arthur*. New York: Anchor/Doubleday, 1985.

———, ed. *The Quest for Arthur's Britain*. New York: Praeger, 1968.

Bromwich, Rachel. *Trioedd Ynys Prydein: The Welsh Triads* (with translation and notes). Cardiff: University of Wales Press, 1961; 2nd ed. 1978.

———, A.O.H. Jarman, and Brynley F. Roberts, eds. *The Arthur of the Welsh: The Arthurian Legend in Medieval Welsh Literature*. Cardiff: University of Wales Press, 1991.

Campbell, James, ed. *The Anglo-Saxons*. Oxford: Phaidon, 1982; Ithaca: Cornell University Press, 1982.

Carley, James P., ed., and David Townsend, trans. *The Chronicle of Glastonbury Abbey*. Woodbridge: Boydell and Brewer, 1985.

Chambers, E.K. *Arthur of Britain*. London: Sidgwick and Jackson, 1927.

Collingwood, R.G., and J.N.L. Myres. *Roman Britain and the English Settlements*. London: Oxford University Press, 1937.

Darrah, John. *Paganism in Arthurian Romance*. Woodbridge: Boydell, 1994.

Dumville, David. "Sub-Roman Britain: History and Legend." *History*, 62 (1977), 173–91.

Fletcher, Robert Huntington. *The Arthurian Material in the Chronicles, Especially Those of Great Britain and France*. Boston: Ginn, 1906; 2nd ed. Roger Sherman Loomis. New York: Franklin, 1966.

Fleuriot, Léon. *Les Origines de la Bretagne*. Paris: Payot, 1980.

Geoffrey of Monmouth. (1) *Historia Regum Britanniae*, ed. Neil Wright. Cambridge: Brewer, 1985.

———. (2) *The History of the Kings of Britain*, trans. Lewis Thorpe. Harmondsworth: Penguin, 1966.

————. (3) *Vita Merlini ("The Life of Merlin")*, ed. and trans. J.J. Parry. Urbana: University of Illinois Press, 1925.

Gildas. In *History from the Sources*. Vol. 7, *The Ruin of Britain*, col. and trans. Michael Winterbottom. Chichester: Phillimore, 1978.

Historia Brittonum, see "Nennius."

"Historical Arthur." Special number of *Arthuriana*, 5.3 (1995). [Articles and commentary by Geoffrey Ashe, D.R. Howlett, Antonio L. Furtado, C. Scott Littleton and Linda A. Malcor, R.W. Hanning, Dennis M. Kratz, O.J. Padel, and M.H. Keen.]

Jackson, Kenneth H. *Language and History in Early Britain*. Edinburgh: Edinburgh University Press, 1953.

Jarman, A.O.H., and Gwilym Rees Hughes, eds. *A Guide to Welsh Literature*. 2 vols. Swansea: Christopher Davies, 1976, 1979.

Lacy, Norris J., et al., eds. *The New Arthurian Encyclopedia* (see above). Updated Paperback Edition. New York: Garland, 1996.

Lapidge, Michael, and David Dumville, eds. *Gildas: New Approaches*. Woodbridge: Boydell, 1984.

Littleton, C. Scott, and Linda A. Malcor. *From Scythia to Camelot: A Radical Reassessment of the Legends of King Arthur, the Knights of the Round Table, and the Holy Grail*. New York: Garland, 1994.

Loomis, Roger Sherman, ed. *Arthurian Literature in the Middle Ages: A Collaborative History*. Oxford: Clarendon, 1959; 2nd ed. 1961.

Morris, John. *The Age of Arthur*. London: Weidenfeld and Nicolson, 1973.

"Nennius." In *History from the Sources*. Vol. 8, *British History and the Welsh Annals*, ed. and trans. John Morris. Chichester: Phillimore, 1980.

Padel, O.J. "Tintagel: An Alternative View." In *A Provisional List of Imported Pottery in Post-Roman Western Britain and Ireland*, ed. Charles Thomas. Redruth: Institute of Cornish Studies, 1981.

Phillips, Graham, and Martin Keatman. *King Arthur: The True Story*. London: Century Random House, 1992.

Rahtz, Philip. *Glastonbury*. London: Batsford/English Heritage, 1993.

Scott, John. *The Early History of Glastonbury*. Woodbridge: Boydell and Brewer, 1981.

Tatlock, J.S.P. (1) "The Dates of the Arthurian Saints' Legends." *Speculum*, 14 (1939), 345–65.

————. (2) *The Legendary History of Britain*. Berkeley: University of California Press, 1950.

Tolstoy, Nikolai. *The Quest for Merlin*. London: Hamish Hamilton, 1985.

Westwood, Jennifer. *Albion*. London: Granada, 1985.

Wood, Ian. "The Fall of the Western Empire and the End of Roman Britain." *Britannia*, 18 (1987), 251–62.

CHAPTER II: EARLY ARTHURIAN LITERATURE

A. SELECTED EDITIONS AND TRANSLATIONS

Collections

Barber, Richard, ed. *The Arthurian Legends: An Illustrated Anthology*. New York: Littlefield Adams, 1979.

Brengle, Richard L. *Arthur, King of Britain: History, Romance, Chronicle, and Criticism*. New York: Appleton-Century-Crofts, 1964. [Medieval texts and a selection of critical essays.]

Goodrich, Peter, ed. *The Romance of Merlin: An Anthology*. New York: Garland, 1990. [Merlin texts from early Welsh to the twentieth century.]

Wilhelm, James J., ed. *The Romance of Arthur: An Anthology of Medieval Texts in Translation*. New, Expanded Edition. New York: Garland, 1993. [Translations of complete texts and excerpts of others; includes works from Welsh, Latin, French, Old Norse, Italian, and Middle English.]

Celtic

Aneirin: Y Gododdin, Britain's Oldest Heroic Poem, ed. and trans. A.O.H. Jarman. Llandysul: Gomer, 1988.

Culhwch ac Olwen, ed. Rachel Bromwich and D. Simon Evans. Cardiff: Gwasg Prifysgol Cymru, 1988.

Lorgaireacht an tSoidhigh Naomhtha: An Early Modern Irish Translation of the "Quest of the Holy Grail," ed. and trans. Sheila Falconer. Dublin: Dublin Institute for Advanced Study, 1963.

The Mabinogion, trans. Jeffrey Gantz. Harmondsworth: Penguin, 1976. [Includes also *Owein*, *Peredur*, and *Gereint and Enid*.]

Nennius: British History and the Welsh Annals, ed. and trans. John Morris. Chichester: Phillimore, 1980.

French

Béroul. *Romance of Tristran*, ed. and trans. Norris J. Lacy. New York: Garland, 1989.

Chrétien de Troyes. *Arthurian Romances*, trans. William W. Kibler (*Erec* trans. Carleton W. Carroll). Harmondsworth: Penguin, 1991.

———. *Romans arthuriens*, ed. Michel Zink. Paris: Livre de Poche, 1994.

Le Haut Livre du Graal: Perlesvaus, Vol. 1, ed. William A. Nitze and T. Atkinson Jenkins; Vol. 2 (Commentary and Notes), William A. Nitze, et al. Chicago: University of Chicago Press, 1932, 1937.

Lancelot-Grail: The Old French Arthurian Vulgate and Post-Vulgate in English Translation, ed. Norris J. Lacy. 5 vols. New York: Garland, 1993–96.

Lancelot: roman en prose du XIIIe siècle, ed. Alexandre Micha. 9 vols. Geneva: Droz, 1978–83.

Marie de France. *The Lais of Marie de France*, trans. Glyn S. Burgess and Keith Busby. Harmondsworth: Penguin, 1986.

Merlin: roman du XIIIe siècle, ed. Alexandre Micha. Geneva: Droz, 1979.

La Mort le Roi Artu, ed. Jean Frappier. Geneva: Droz, 1954; 3rd ed. 1959.

La Queste del saint Graal, ed. Albert Pauphilet. Paris: Champion, 1923.

Robert de Boron. *Joseph d'Arimathie*, ed. Richard O'Gorman. Toronto: Pontifical Institute of Mediaeval Studies, 1995.

———. *Merlin*, ed. Alexandre Micha. Geneva: Droz, 1980.

Le Roman de Tristan en prose, ed. Philippe Ménard et al. Geneva: Droz, 1987–. [9 vols. to date.]

Roman du Graal, ed. Fanni Bogdanow. 3 vols. Paris: SATF, 1994.

Romance of Tristan, trans. Renée L. Curtis. Oxford: Oxford University Press, 1994. [A partial translation of the Prose *Tristan*.]

Le saint Graal, ed. Eugène Hucher. 3 vols. Le Mans: Monnoyer, 1875–78. [The Vulgate *Estoire del saint Graal*.]

Thomas of Britain. *Tristran*, ed. and trans. Stewart Gregory. New York: Garland, 1991.

The Vulgate Version of the Arthurian Romances, ed. H. Oskar Sommer. 8 vols. Washington, D.C.: Carnegie Institution, 1908–16.

Wace. *Le Roman de Brut*, ed. I. Arnold. 2 vols. Paris: Champion, 1938–40.

German

Gottfried von Strassburg. *Tristan*, ed. Reinhold Bechstein; re-ed. Peter Ganz. Wiesbaden: Brockhaus, 1978.

———. *Tristan with the Surviving Fragments of the Tristan of Thomas*, trans. A.T. Hatto. Harmondsworth: Penguin, 1960.

Hartmann von Aue. *Erec*, ed. Albert Leitzmann; 5th ed. Ludwig Wolff. Tübingen: Niemeyer, 1972.

———. *Erec*, trans. J.W. Thomas. Lincoln: University of Nebraska Press, 1982.

———. *Iwein*, ed. and trans. Patrick M. McConeghy. New York: Garland, 1984.

Heinrich von dem Türlin. *Crown: A Tale of Sir Gawein und King Arthur's Court*, trans. J.W. Thomas. Lincoln: University of Nebraska Press, 1989.

Ulrich von Zatzikhoven. *Lanzelet*, trans. Kenneth G.T. Webster. New York: Columbia University Press, 1951.

Wigamur, ed. Danielle Buschinger. Göppingen: Kümmerle, 1987.

Wolfram von Eschenbach, ed. Albert Leitzmann. Halle, 1905–06. 4 vols.; 6th ed. Wilhelm Deinert. Tübingen: Niemeyer, 1961–65. [Edition of *Parzival*.]

———. *Parzival*, trans. A.T. Hatto. Harmondsworth: Penguin, 1980.

Scandinavian

Erex Saga and Ívens Saga, trans. Foster W. Blaisdell and Marianne E. Kalinke. Lincoln: University of Nebraska Press, 1977.

Erex saga Artuskappa, ed. Foster W. Blaisdell. Copenhagen: Munksgaard, 1965.

Ívens saga, ed. Foster W. Blaisdell. Copenhagen: Reitzel, 1979.

Möttuls saga, ed. Marianne E. Kalinke, with an edition of *Le Lai du cort mantel* by Philip E. Bennett. Copenhagen: Reitzel, 1987.

Tristrams saga ok Ísöndar, ed. Eugen Kölbing. Heilbronn: Henninger; rpt. Hildesheim: Olms, 1978.

Dutch

Lanceloet: De Middelnederlandse vertaling van de Lancelot en prose overgeleverd in de Lancelotcompilatie, pars 1 (vs. 1–5530), ed. Bart Besamusca and Ada Postma. Assen: Van Gorcum, forthcoming.

Lanceloet: De Middelnederlandse vertaling van de Lancelot en prose overgeleverd in de Lancelotcompilatie, pars 2 (vs. 5531–10740), ed. Bart Besamusca. Assen: Van Gorcum, 1991.

Lanceloet: De Middelnederlandse vertaling van de Lancelot en prose overgeleverd in de Lancelotcompilatie, pars 3 (vs. 10741–16263), ed. Frank Brandsma. Assen: Van Gorcum, 1992.

Lantsloot vander Haghedochte: Fragmenten van een Middelnederlandse bewerking van de Lancelot en prose, ed. W.P. Gerritsen, with A. Berteloot, et al. Amsterdam: North-Holland, 1987.

Maerlant, Jacob van. *Historie van den Grale und Boek van Merline*, ed. Timothy Sodman. Cologne: Bhohlau, 1980.

Penninc and Pieter Vostaert. *Roman van Walewein*, ed. and trans. David F. Johnson. New York: Garland, 1992.

Hispanic

The Book of the Knight Zifar, trans. Charles L. Nelson. Lexington: University Press of Kentucky, 1983.

Cervantes, Miguel de. *Don Quijote de la Mancha*, ed. Martí de Riquer. Barcelona: Juventud, 1968.

A Demanda do Santo Graal, ed. Joseph-Maria Piel; concluded by Irene Freire Nunes. Lisbon: Imprensa Nacional-Casa da Moeda, 1988.

———. *Don Quixote*, trans. J.M. Cohen. Harmondsworth: Penguin, 1950.

Montalvo, Garci Rodríguez de. *Amadís de Gaula*, ed. E.B. Place. 4 vols. Madrid: CSIC, 1959–69.

———. *Amadís de Gaula*, trans. E.B. Place and H.C. Boehm. 2 vols. Lexington: University of Kentucky Press, 1974, 1975.

Spanish Ballads, ed. and trans. Roger Wright. Warminister: Aris and Phillips, 1987, pp. 24–25, 152–53.

Italian

Cantari di Tristano, ed. Giulio Bertoni. Modena: Società Tipografica Modenese, 1937.

Grant Queste del saint Graal. La grande ricerca del santo graal: versione inedita della fine del XIII secolo del ms. Udine, Biblioteca Arcivescovile, 177, ed. and trans. A. Rosellini. Tricesimo: Vattori, 1990.

Tavola Ritonda o l'istoria di Tristano, ed. Filippo-Luigi Polidori. Bologna: Romagnoli, 1864–65.

Tristan and the Round Table: A Translation of "La Tavola Ritonda," trans. Anne Shaver. Binghamton: State University of New York Press, 1983.

Latin

Geoffrey of Monmouth (1). *Historia Regum Britanniae*, ed. Neil Wright. Cambridge: Brewer, 1985.

———. *History of the Kings of Britain*, trans. Lewis Thorpe. London: Penguin, 1966.

———. *Vita Merlini*, ed. and trans. J.J. Parry. Urbana: University of Illinois Press, 1925.

The Rise of Gawain, Nephew of Arthur (De ortu Waluuanii nepotis Arturi), ed. and trans. Mildred Leake Day. New York: Garland, 1984.

The Story of Meriadoc, King of Cambria, ed. and trans. Mildred Leake Day. New York: Garland, 1988.

English

Avowing of King Arthur: A Modern Verse Translation, trans. Nirmal Dass. Lanham, Md.: University Press of America, 1987.

Five Middle English Arthurian Romances, trans. Valerie Krishna. New York: Garland, 1990. [The Stanzaic *Morte Arthur; The Adventures of Arthur at Tarn Wadling; The Vows of King Arthur, Sir Gawain, Sir Kay, and Baldwin of Britain; The Wedding of Sir Gawain and Dame Ragnell; Sir Gawain and the Carl of Carlisle.*]

"Lancelot of the Laik" and "Sir Tristrem," ed. Alan Lupack. Kalamazoo: Medieval Institute, 1994.

Lawman. *Lawman: Brut*, trans. Rosamund Allen. London: Dent, 1992.

Malory, Sir Thomas. *The Works*, ed. Eugene Vinaver; revised version P.J.C. Field. 3 vols. Oxford: Clarendon, 1990.

Le Morte Arthur: A Critical Edition, ed. P.F. Hissiger. The Hague: Mouton, 1975. [Stanzaic *Morte Arthur*.]

Morte Arthure, ed. Mary Hamel. New York: Garland, 1984. [Alliterative *Morte Arthure*.]

Sir Gawain and the Green Knight, ed. J.R.R. Tolkien and E.V. Gordon; 2nd ed. Norman Davis. Oxford: Clarendon, 1967.

Sir Gawain and the Green Knight, ed. and trans. William Vantuono. New York: Garland, 1991.

B. STUDIES

General

Bruce, James Douglas. *The Evolution of Arthurian Romance from the Beginnings Down to the Year 1300*. 2 vols. 2nd ed. Baltimore: Johns Hopkins Press, 1928.

Dean, Christopher. *Arthur of England: English Attitudes to King Arthur and the Knights of the Round Table in the Middle Ages and the Renaissance*. Toronto: University of Toronto Press, 1987.

Ferrante, Joan M. *The Conflict of Love and Honor: The Medieval Tristan Legend in France, Germany, and Italy*. The Hague: Mouton, 1973.

Fletcher, Robert Huntington. *The Arthurian Material in the Chronicles, Especially Those of Great Britain and France*. Boston: Ginn, 1906; 2nd ed. Roger Sherman Loomis. New York: Franklin, 1966.

Knight, Stephen. *Arthurian Literature and Society*. New York: St. Martin's, 1983.

Köhler, Erich. *Ideal und Wirklichkeit in der höfischen Epik*. Tübingen, 1956.

Korrel, Peter. *An Arthurian Triangle: A Study of the Origin, Development and Characterization of Arthur, Guinevere and Modred*. Leiden: Brill, 1984.

Krueger, Roberta L. *Women Readers and the Ideology of Gender*. Cambridge: Cambridge University Press, 1993.

Lacy, Norris J., et al., eds. *The New Arthurian Encyclopedia* (see above). Updated Paperback Edition. New York: Garland, 1996.

Lagorio, Valerie M., and Mildred Leake Day, eds. *King Arthur Through the Ages*. 2 vols. New York: Garland, 1990.

Lazar, Moshe. *Amour courtois et fin'amors dans la littérature du XIIe siècle*. Paris: Klincksieck, 1964.

Loomis, Roger Sherman. (1) *The Development of Arthurian Romance*. New York: Harper and Row, 1963.

———. (2) *Wales and the Arthurian Legend*. Cardiff: University of Wales Press, 1956.

———, ed. *Arthurian Literature in the Middle Ages: A Collaborative History*. Oxford: Clarendon, 1959; 2nd ed. 1961.

Mermier, Guy R., ed. *Courtly Romance*. Detroit, 1984.

Morris, Rosemary. *The Character of King Arthur in Medieval Literature*. Cambridge: Brewer, 1982.

Owen, D.D.R., ed. *Arthurian Romance: Seven Essays*. New York: Barnes and Noble, 1971.

Stevens, John. *Medieval Romance: Themes and Approaches*. London: Hutchinson, 1973.

Vinaver, Eugene (1). *Form and Meaning in Medieval Romance*. Leeds: Maney, 1966.

———— (2). *The Rise of Romance*. Oxford: Clarendon, 1971.

Celtic

Bromwich, Rachel, A.O.H. Jarman, and Brynley F. Roberts, eds. *The Arthur of the Welsh: The Arthurian Legend in Medieval Welsh Literature*. Cardiff: University of Wales Press, 1991.

Goetinck, Glenys Witchard. *Peredur: A Study of Welsh Tradition in the Grail Legends*. Cardiff: University of Wales Press, 1975.

Jarman, A.O.H., and Gwilym Rees Hughes, eds. *A Guide to Welsh Literature*. 2 vols. Swansea: Christopher Davies, 1976, 1979.

Lapidge, Michael, and David Dumville, eds. *Gildas: New Approaches*. Woodbridge: Boydell and Brewer, 1984.

Mac Cana, Proinsias. *The Mabinogi*. 1977; 2nd ed., Cardiff: University of Wales Press, 1992.

Murphy, Gerard. *The Ossianic Lore and Romantic Tales of Medieval Ireland*. Dublin: Three Candles, 1961.

Piriou, Jean-Pierre. "Un Texte arthurien en moyen-breton: *Le Dialogue entre Arthur, Roi des Bretons, et Guynglaff*," in *Actes du 14e Congrès International Arthurien*, ed. Charles Foulon, et al. Rennes: Presses Universitaires de Rennes 2, 1985, vol. II, pp. 473–99.

French

Baumgartner, Emmanuèle. *Le Tristan en prose: Essai d'interprétation d'un roman médiéval*. Geneva: Droz, 1975.

Blakeslee, Merritt R. *Love's Masks: Identity, Intertextuality, and Meaning in the Old French Tristan Poems*. Cambridge: Brewer, 1989.

Burns, E. Jane. *Arthurian Fictions: Rereading the Vulgate Cycle*. Columbus: Ohio State University Press, 1985.

Busby, Keith. *Gauvain in Old French Literature*. Amsterdam: Rodopi, 1980.

Frappier, Jean. (1) *Amour courtois et Table Ronde*. Geneva: Droz, 1973.

————. (2) *Chrétien de Troyes: l'homme et l'œuvre*. Paris: Hatier, 1957; trans. as *Chrétien de Troyes: The Man and His Work*, trans. Raymond J. Cormier. Athens: Ohio University Press, 1982.

———. (3) *Etude sur la Mort le roi Artu.* Paris: Droz, 1936.

———, and Reinhold R. Grimm, eds. *Le Roman jusqu'à la fin du XIIIe siècle.* Heidelberg: Winter, 1978. (Vol. IV of *Grundriss der romanischen Literaturen des Mittelalters.*)

Kelly, Douglas. *The Art of Medieval French Romance.* Madison: University of Wisconsin Press, 1992.

———. *Medieval French Romance.* New York: Twayne, 1993.

———, ed. *The Romances of Chrétien de Troyes: A Symposium.* Lexington: French Forum, 1985.

Kelly, Thomas, E. *Le Haut Livre du Graal: Perlesvaus. A Structural Study.* Geneva: Droz, 1974.

Kennedy, Elspeth. *Lancelot and the Grail: A Study of the Prose "Lancelot."* Oxford: Clarendon, 1986.

Kibler, William W., ed. *The Lancelot-Grail Cycle: Text and Transformations.* Austin, TX: University of Texas Press, 1994.

Lacy, Norris J. *The Craft of Chrétien de Troyes: An Essay on Narrative Art.* Leiden: Brill, 1980.

———, Douglas Kelly, and Keith Busby, eds. *The Legacy of Chrétien de Troyes.* 2 vols. Amsterdam: Rodopi, 1987–88.

Leupin, Alexandre. *Le Graal et la littérature.* Lausanne: L'Age d'Homme, 1982.

Lot, Ferdinand. *Etude sur le Lancelot en prose.* Paris, 1918; Paris: Champion, 1954.

MacDonald, Aileen Ann. *The Figure of Merlin in Thirteenth-Century French Romance.* Lewiston, NY: Mellen, 1990.

Maddox, Donald. *The Arthurian Romances of Chrétien de Troyes: Once and Future Fictions.* Cambridge: Cambridge University Press, 1991.

Mickel, Emanuel J., Jr. *Marie de France.* New York: Twayne, 1974.

Nykrog, Per. *Chrétien de Troyes: romancier discutable.* Geneva: Droz, 1996.

Pauphilet, Albert. *Etudes sur La Queste del saint Graal.* Paris: Champion, 1921.

Pickens, Rupert. *The Welsh Knight: Paradoxicality in Chrétien's "Conte del Graal."* Lexington: French Forum, 1977.

———, ed. *The Sower and His Seed: Essays on Chrétien de Troyes.* Lexington: French Forum, 1983.

Pickford, Cedric E. "The Maturity of the Arthurian Prose Romances," *BBSIA*, 34 (1982), 197–206.

Schmolke-Hasselmann, Beate. *Der arthurische Versroman von Chrestien bis Froissart.* Tübingen: Niemeyer, 1980.

German

Batts, Michael. *Gottfried von Strassburg.* New York: Twayne, 1971.

Bumke, Joachim. *Wolfram von Eschenbach.* Stuttgart: Metzler, 1964; 5th ed. 1981.

Clark, Susan L. *Hartmann von Aue: Landscapes of Mind*. Houston: Rice University Press, 1989.

Göller, Karl Heinz, ed. *Spätmittelalterliche Artusliteratur*. Paderborn: Schöningh, 1984.

Gürttler, Karin R. *"Künec Artûs der guote": Das Artusbild der höfischen Epik des 12. und 13. Jahrhunderts*. Bonn: Grundmann, 1976.

Jackson, W.T.H. *The Anatomy of Love: The Tristan of Gottfried von Strassburg*. New York: Columbia University Press, 1971.

Jones, Martin H., and Roy Wisbey, eds. *Chrétien de Troyes and the German Middle Ages*. Woodbridge: Brewer, 1993.

Poag, James F. *Wolfram von Eschenbach*. New York: Twayne, 1972.

Sacker, Hugh D. *An Introduction to Wolfram's "Parzival."* Cambridge: Cambridge University Press, 1963.

Schultz, James A. *The Shape of the Round Table: Structures of Middle High German Arthurian Romance*. Toronto: University of Toronto Press, 1983.

Thomas, Neil. *The Defence of Camelot: Ideology and Intertextuality in the "Post-Classical" German Romances of the Matter of Britain Cycle*. Bern: Lang, 1992.

Wapnewski, Peter. *Hartmann von Aue*. 7th ed. Stuttgart: Metzler, 1979.

Scandinavian

Barnes, Geraldine. "Arthurian Chivalry in Old Norse," *Arthurian Literature*, 7 (1987), 50–102.

Kalinke, Marianne E. *Bridal-Quest Romance in Medieval Iceland*. Ithaca: Cornell University Press, 1990.

———. *King Arthur, North-by-Northwest: The Matière de Bretagne in Old Norse-Icelandic Romances*. Copenhagen: Reitzel, 1981.

Schach, Paul. "Tristan and Isolde in Scandinavian Ballad and Folktale." *Scandinavian Studies*, 36 (1964), 281–97.

Schlauch, Margaret. *Romance in Iceland*. Princeton: Princeton University Press, 1934.

Middle Dutch

Besamusca, Bart. *Repertorium van de Middnederlandse Arturepiek: Een beknopte beschrijving van de handschriftelijlee en gedrulete overlevering*. Utrecht, 1985.

———. *"Walewein," "Moriaen" en de "Ridder metter mouwen": Intertekstualiteit in drie Middelnederlandse Arturromans*. Hilversum: Verloren, 1993.

Gerritsen, W.P., Orlanda S.H. Lie, and F.P. Van Oostrom. "Le *Lancelot en prose* et ses traductions moyen-néerlandaises." In *Langue et littérature françaises du moyen âge*, ed. R.E.V. Stuip. Assen: Van Gorcum, 1978.

Hispanic

Entwistle, W.J. *Arthurian Legend in the Literatures of the Spanish Peninsula*. London: Dent, 1925.

Lida de Malkiel, María Rosa. "Arthurian Literature in Spain and Portugal." In Roger Sherman Loomis, ed., *Arthurian Literature in the Middle Ages: A Collaborative History*. Oxford: Clarendon, 1959, pp. 406–18.

Riquer, Martí de. *Estudios sobre el "Amadís de Gaula."* Barcelona: Sirmio, 1987.

Williamson, Edwin. *The Half-way House of Fiction: Don Quixote and Arthurian Romance*. Oxford: Clarendon, 1984.

Italian

Delcorno Branca, Daniela. *Il romanzo cavalleresco medievale*. Florence: Sansoni, 1974.

———. "Sette anni de studi sulla letteratura arturiana in Italia: Rassegna (1985–1992)." *Lettere Italiane*, 44 (1992), 465–97.

Gardner, Edmund G. *Arthurian Legend in Italian Literature*. London: Dent, 1930.

Hoffman, Donald L. "The Arthurian Tradition in Italy." In Valerie M. Lagorio and Mildred Leake Day, eds., *King Arthur Through the Ages*. 2 vols. New York: Garland, 1990, I, 170–88.

Kleinhenz, Christopher. "Tristan in Italy: The Death or Rebirth of a Legend." *Studies in Medieval Culture*, 5 (1975), 145–58.

Shaver, Anne. "The Italian Round Table and the Arthurian Tradition." In *Courtly Romance*, ed. Guy R. Mermier. Detroit, Mich. 1984, pp. 203–22.

English

Aertsen, Henk, and Alasdair A. MacDonald, eds. *Companion to Middle English Romance*. Amsterdam: VU University Press, 1990.

Benson, Larry D. (1) *Art and Tradition in Sir Gawain and the Green Knight*. New Brunswick: Rutgers University Press, 1965.

———. (2) *Malory's "Morte Darthur."* Cambridge, Mass.: Harvard University Press, 1976.

Brewer, D.S., ed. *The Morte Darthur, Parts Seven and Eight*, by Sir Thomas Malory. Evanston: Northwestern University Press, 1970. [Cited here for Brewer's introduction.]

Burrow, J.A. *A Reading of Sir Gawain and the Green Knight*. London: Routledge and Kegan Paul, 1965.

Cable, Thomas. *The English Alliterative Tradition*. Philadelphia: University of Pennsylvania Press, 1991.

Clein, W. *Concepts of Chivalry in Sir Gawain and the Green Knight*. Norman, OK: Pilgrim, 1987.

Field, P.J.C. *The Life and Times of Sir Thomas Malory*. Cambridge: Brewer, 1993.

Hibbard, Laura A. *Mediaeval Romance in England*. New York: Franklin, 1963.

Howard, Donald R. "Structure and Symmetry in *Sir Gawain*," *Speculum*, 39 (1964), 425–33.

———, and C.K. Zacher, eds. *Critical Studies of Sir Gawain and the Green Knight*. Notre Dame: University of Notre Dame Press, 1968.

Ihle, Sandra Ness. *Malory's Grail Quest: Invention and Adaptation in Medieval Prose Romance*. Madison: University of Wisconsin Press, 1983.

Lumiansky, R.M., ed. *Malory's Originality*. Baltimore: Johns Hopkins Press, 1964.

McCarthy, Terence. *Reading the Morte Darthur*. Cambridge: Brewer, 1988; rpt. as *An Introduction to Malory*, 1991.

Mehl, Dieter. *The Middle English Romances of the Thirteenth and Fourteenth Centuries*. London: Routledge and Kegan Paul, 1969.

Takamiya, Toshiyuki, and Derek Brewer, eds. *Aspects of Malory*. Woodbridge: Brewer, 1981.

Whitaker, Muriel. *Arthur's Kingdom of Adventure: the World of Malory's "Morte Darthur."* Cambridge: Brewer, 1984.

CHAPTER III: MODERN ARTHURIAN LITERATURE

A. SELECTED PRIMARY TEXTS

Collections

Goodrich, Peter, ed. *The Romance of Merlin: An Anthology*. New York: Garland, 1990.

Lupack, Alan, ed. *"Arthur, the Greatest King": An Anthology of Modern Arthurian Poems*. New York: Garland, 1988.

———, ed. *Modern Arthurian Literature: An Anthology of English and American Arthuriana from the Renaissance to the Present*. New York: Garland, 1992.

French

Apollinaire, Guillaume. *L'Enchanteur pourrissant*, ed. Jean Burgos. Paris: Minard, 1972.

Barjavel, René. *L'Enchanteur*. Paris: Denoël, 1984.

Bédier, Joseph. *Le Roman de Tristan et Iseut*. Paris: Piazza, 1900.

Cocteau, Jean. *Les Chevaliers de la Table Ronde*. In *Œuvres complètes de Jean Cocteau*. Geneva: Marguerat, 1948, Vol. 6.

Gracq, Julien. *Au Château d'Argol*. Paris: Corti, 1939.

———. *Le Roi Pêcheur*. Paris: Corti, 1945.

Le Dantec, Jean-Pierre. *Graal Romance*. Paris: Albin Michel, 1985.

Pinget, Robert. *Graal Flibuste*. Paris: Minuit, 1966.

Quinet, Edgar. *Merlin l'enchanteur*. 2 vols. Paris: Michel Lévy, 1860.

Rio, Michel. *Merlin*. Paris: Seuil, 1989.

Weingarten, Romain. *Le Roman de la Table Ronde, ou le livre de Blaise*. Paris: Albin Michel, 1983.

German

Dorst, Tankred, with Ursula Ehler. *Merlin oder das Wüste Land*. Frankfurt: Suhrkamp, 1981.

Hauptmann, Gerhart. *Lohengrin*. Berlin: Ullstein, 1913.

———. *Parsival*. Berlin: Ullstein, 1914.

Immermann, Karl. *Merlin*. Leipzig: Klemm, 1932.

———. *Tristan und Isolde: Ein Gedicht in Romanzen*. Leipzig: Reclam [1841].

Muschg, Adolf. *Der rote Ritter*. 3 vols. Frankfurt am Main: Suhrkamp, 1991.

Sachs, Hans. "Meisterlieder." In Eli Sobel, *The Tristan Romance in the Meisterlieder of Hans Sachs*. Berkeley: University of California Press, 1963, pp. 256–68.

———. "Tragedia mit 23 personen, von der strengen lieb herr Tristrant mit der schönen königen Isalden, unnd hat 7 actus." In *Hans Sachs*, ed. Adelbert von Keller. Tübingen: Litterarischer Verein, 1879, Vol. 12, pp. 142–86.

Stucken, Eduard. *Der Gral, ein dramatisches Epos*. Berlin: Reiss, 1924.

English and American

Anderson, Dennis Lee. *Arthur, King*. New York: HarperPrism, 1995.

Barthelme, Donald. *The King*. New York: Harper and Row, 1990.

Berger, Thomas. *Arthur Rex: A Legendary Novel*. New York: Delacorte, 1978.

Bradley, Marion Zimmer. *The Mists of Avalon*. New York: Knopf, 1982.

Bradshaw, Gillian. *Hawk of May*. New York: Simon and Schuster, 1980.

———. *In Winter's Shadow*. New York: Simon and Schuster, 1982.

———. *Kingdom of Summer*. New York: Simon and Schuster, 1981.

Byatt, A.S. *Possession*. London: Chatto and Windus, 1990.

Cabell, James Branch. *Jurgen: A Comedy of Justice*. New York: McBride, 1919.

Canning, Victor. *The Crimson Chalice*. New York: Morrow, 1978.

Chant, Joy. *The High Kings*. New York: Bantam, 1983.

Cherryh, C.J. *Port Eternity*. New York: DAW, 1982.

Cooper, Susan. *The Dark Is Rising*. New York: Atheneum, 1973.

———. *Greenwitch*. New York: Atheneum, 1974.

———. *The Grey King*. New York: Atheneum, 1975.

———. *Over Sea, Under Stone*. London: Cape, 1965.

———. *Silver on the Tree*. New York: Atheneum, 1977.

David, Peter. *Knight Life*. New York: Ace, 1987.

Davies, Robertson. *The Lyre of Orpheus*. New York: Viking Penguin, 1988.

Deal, Babs H. *The Grail: A Novel*. New York: McKay, 1963.

Dryden, John. Libretto for *King Arthur, or the British Worthy*. In *The Dramatic Works*, ed. Montague Summers. London: Nonesuch, 1931–32, Vol. 6.

Eliot, T.S. *The Waste Land*. In *Poems, 1909–1925*. London: Faber and Gwyer, 1925, pp. 63–92.

Erskine, John. *Galahad: Enough of His Life to Explain His Reputation*. Indianapolis: Bobbs-Merrill, 1926.

Fielding, Henry. *The Tragedy of Tragedies; or The Life and Death of Tom Thumb the Great*. In *Eighteenth-Century Comedy*, ed. W.D. Taylor and Simon Trussler. London: Oxford University Press, 1969.

Gash, Jonathan. *The Grail Tree*. London: Collins, 1979.

Godwin, Parke. *Beloved Exile*. New York: Bantam, 1984.

———. *Firelord*. New York: Doubleday, 1980.

———. *The Last Rainbow*. New York: Bantam, 1985.

Griffiths, Paul. *The Lay of Sir Tristram*. London: Chatto and Windus, 1991.

Hardy, Thomas. *The Famous Tragedy of the Queen of Cornwall at Tintagel in Lyonnesse*. London: Macmillan, 1923.

Heath-Stubbs, John. *Artorius*. London: Enitharmon, 1973.

Hovey, Richard. *Launcelot and Guenevere: A Poem in Dramas*. 5 vols. Boston: Small, Maynard, 1898–1907.

Jones, David. *The Anathémata*. London: Faber and Faber, [1952].

———. *In Parenthesis*. London: Faber and Faber, [1937].

Karr, Phyllis Ann. *The Idylls of the Queen*. New York: Ace, 1982.

Laubenthal, Sanders Anne. *Excalibur*. New York: Ballantine, 1973.

Lawhead, Stephen R. *Arthur*. Westchester, Ill.: Crossway, 1989.

———. *Merlin*. Westchester, Ill.: Crossway, 1988.

———. *Pendragon*. New York: Morrow/AvoNova, 1994.

———. *Taliesin*. Westchester, Ill.: Crossway, 1987.

Lewis, C.S. *That Hideous Strength: A Modern Fairy Tale for Grown-ups*. London: Lane, 1945.

Lupack, Alan. *The Dream of Camelot*. Vista, Calif.: Green Chapel, 1990.

Masefield, John. *Badon Parchments*. London: Heinemann, 1947.

———. *Midsummer Night and Other Tales in Verse*. London: Heinemann, 1928.

Mnookin, Wendy. *Guenever Speaks*. Rochester, N.Y.: Round Table, 1991.

Monaco, Richard. *The Final Quest*. New York: Putnam, 1980.

———. *The Grail War*. New York: Pocket Books, 1979.

———. *Parsival or A Knight's Tale*. New York: Macmillan, 1977.

Morris, William. *The Defence of Guenevere, and Other Poems*. London: Bell and Daldy, 1858.

Murdoch, Iris. *The Green Knight*. New York: Viking Penguin, 1993.

Norton, Andre. *Merlin's Mirror*. New York: DAW, 1975.

Peacock, Thomas Love. *The Misfortunes of Elphin*. London: Hookham, 1829.

Percy, Walker. *Lancelot*. New York: Farrar, Straus and Giroux, 1978.

Powell, Anthony. *The Fisher King*. London: Norton, 1986.

Powys, John Cowper. *A Glastonbury Romance*. New York: Simon and Schuster, 1932.

———. *Porius: A Romance of the Dark Ages*. London: Macdonald, 1951.

Robinson, Edwin Arlington. *Lancelot: A Poem*. New York: Seltzer, 1920.

———. *Merlin*. New York: Macmillan, 1917.

———. *Tristram*. New York: Macmillan, 1927.

Saberhagen, Fred. *Dominion*. New York: Tor Books, 1982.

———. *Merlin's Bones*. New York: Tor Books, 1995.

Skinner, Martyn. *The Return of Arthur: A Poem of the Future*. London: Chapman and Hall, 1966.

Smith, Rosamond. *You Can't Catch Me*. New York: Dutton, 1995.

Spenser, Edmund. *The Faerie Queene*. In *Poetical Works*, ed. J.C. Smith and E. de Selincourt. London: Oxford University Press, 1912.

Steinbeck, John. *The Acts of King Arthur and His Noble Knights*. New York: Farrar, Straus and Giroux, 1976.

Stewart, Mary. *The Crystal Cave*. London: Hodder and Stoughton, 1970.

———. *The Hollow Hills*. London: Hodder and Stoughton, 1973.

———. *The Last Enchantment*. London: Hodder and Stoughton, 1979.

———. *The Wicked Day*. London: Hodder and Stoughton, 1984.

Sutcliff, Rosemary. *The Lantern Bearers*. London: Oxford University Press, 1959.

———. *The Light Beyond the Forest: Quest for the Holy Grail*. London: Bodley Head, 1979.

———. *The Road to Camlann*. London: Bodley Head, 1981.

———. *The Sword and the Circle: King Arthur and the Knights of the Round Table*. London: Bodley Head, 1981.

———. *Sword at Sunset*. London: Hodder and Stoughton, 1963.

———. *Tristan and Iseult*. London: Bodley Head, 1971.

Tennyson, Alfred Lord. *Idylls of the King*, ed. J.M. Gray. New Haven: Yale University Press, 1983.

Twain, Mark. *A Connecticut Yankee in King Arthur's Court*. New York: Webster, 1889.

Updike, John. *Brazil*. New York: Fawcett, 1994.

Vansittart, Peter. *Lancelot: A Novel*. London: Owen, 1978.

White, T.H. *The Once and Future King*. London: Collins, 1958.

————. *The Book of Merlyn*, ed. Sylvia Townsend Warner. Austin: University of Texas Press, 1977.

Williams, Charles. *The Region of the Summer Stars*. London: Oxford University Press, 1944.

————. *Taliessin Through Logres*. London: Oxford University Press, 1938.

————. *War in Heaven*. London: Gollancz, 1930.

Woolley, Persia. *Child of the Northern Spring*. New York: Poseidon, 1987.

————. *Guinevere: The Legend in Autumn*. New York: Poseidon, 1991.

————. *Queen of the Summer Stars*. New York: Poseidon, 1990.

Other Literatures

Kuncewiczowa, Maria. *Tristan 1946*. Warsaw: Czytelnik, 1967; 1st English-language ed., *Tristan: A Novel*. New York: Braziller, 1974.

Sōseki, Natsume. *Kairo-Kō: A Dirge*, trans. Toshiyuki Takamiya and Andrew Armour. In *Arthurian Literature* II, ed. Richard Barber. Cambridge: Brewer, 1983, pp. 92–126.

B. STUDIES

General

Baswell, Christopher, and William Sharpe, eds. *The Passing of Arthur: New Essays in Arthurian Tradition*. New York: Garland, 1988.

Brinkley, Roberta F. *Arthurian Legend in the Seventeenth Century*. Baltimore: Johns Hopkins Press, 1932. [Primarily on English literature, but includes some information on French and other texts.]

Lacy, Norris J., et al., eds. *The New Arthurian Encyclopedia* (see above). Updated Paperback Edition. New York: Garland, 1996.

Lagorio, Valerie M., and Mildred Leake Day, eds. *King Arthur Through the Ages*. 2 vols. New York: Garland, 1990, Vol. 2.

Parker, Patricia A. *Inescapable Romance: Studies in the Poetics of a Mode*. Princeton: Princeton University Press, 1979. [Studies of Ariosto, Spenser, and others.]

Reid, Margaret Jane. *The Arthurian Legend: Comparison of Treatment in Modern and Mediaeval Literature; A Study in the Literary Value of Myth and Legend*. Edinburgh: Oliver and Boyd, 1938.

French

Baudry, Robert. "Julien Gracq et la légende du Graal." In *Actes du Colloque International sur Julien Gracq*. Angers: Presses de l'Université d'Angers, 1981.

Bowden, Marjorie. *Tennyson in France*. Manchester: Manchester University Press, 1930.

Crossley, Ceri. *Edgar Quinet (1803–1875): A Study in Romantic Thought.* Lexington: French Forum, 1983.

Dakyns, Janine R. *The Middle Ages in French Literature, 1851–1900.* Oxford: Oxford University Press, 1973.

Forsyth, Louise Barton. "Apollinaire's Use of Arthurian Legend." *Esprit Créateur,* 12 (1972), 26–36.

Henkels, Robert M., Jr. *Robert Pinget: The Novel as Quest.* University, Ala.: University of Alabama Press, 1979.

German

Golther, Wolfgang. *Parzival und der Gral in der Dichtung des Mittelalters und der Neuzeit.* Stuttgart: Metzler, 1925.

Müller, Ulrich (1). "Das Nachleben der mittelalterlichen Stoffe." In *Epische Stoffe des Mittelalters,* ed. V. Mertens and Ulrich Müller. Stuttgart: Kroner, 1984, pp. 435–59.

Sobel, Eli. *The Tristan Romance in the Meisterlieder of Hans Sachs.* Berkeley: University of California Press, 1963.

Weiss, Adelaide Marie. *Merlin in German Literature.* Washington, D.C.: Catholic University of America Press, 1933.

English

Coghlan, Ronan, Toshiyuki Takamiya, and Richard Barber. "A Supplementary Bibliography of Twentieth Century Arthurian Literature." In *Arthurian Literature* III, ed. Richard Barber. Cambridge: Brewer, 1983, pp. 129–36.

Godwin, Parke. "Finding *Firelord.*" *Avalon to Camelot,* 1, 4 (1984), 24–25.

Göller, Karl Heinz. "From Logres to Carbonek: The Arthuriad of Charles Williams." *Arthurian Literature* I, ed. Richard Barber. Cambridge: Brewer, 1981, pp. 121–73.

Lewis, C.S. *English Literature in the Sixteenth Century, Excluding Drama.* New York: Oxford University Press, 1954, pp. 355–93.

Linneman, William R. *Richard Hovey.* Boston: Twayne, 1976.

Lupack, Alan C. "Modern Arthurian Novelists on the Arthurian Legend." *Studies in Medievalism,* 2 (1983), 79–88.

Merriman, James Douglas. *The Flower of Kings: A Study of the Arthurian Legend in England Between 1485 and 1835.* Lawrence: University Press of Kansas, 1973.

Müller, Ulrich (2). "Lanzelot am Broadway und in New Orleans." In *De Poeticis Medii Aevi Quaestiones,* ed. Jürgen Kühnel, Hans-Dieter Mück, and Ulrich Müller. Göppingen: Kümmerle, 1981, pp. 351–90. [On the musical *Camelot* and Walker Percy's *Lancelot.*]

Rosenberg, John D. *The Fall of Camelot: A Study of Tennyson's Idylls of the King.* Cambridge: Belknap, 1973.

Staines, David. *Tennyson's Camelot: The Idylls of the King and Its Medieval Sources.* Waterloo: Wilfrid Laurier University Press, 1983.

Starr, Nathan Comfort. *King Arthur Today: The Arthurian Legend in English and American Literature, 1901–53.* Gainesville: University of Florida Press, 1954.

Taylor, Beverly, and Elisabeth Brewer. *The Return of King Arthur: British and American Arthurian Literature Since 1900.* Cambridge: Brewer, 1983.

Thompson, Raymond H. *The Return from Avalon: A Study of the Arthurian Legend in Modern Fiction.* Westport: Greenwood, 1985.

Wildman, Mary. "Twentieth-Century Arthurian Literature: An Annotated Bibliography." In *Arthurian Literature I*, ed. Richard Barber. Cambridge: Brewer, 1983, pp. 127–62.

ChAPTER IV: ARThUR IN ThE ARTS

A. GENERAL

Lacy, Norris J., et al., eds. *The New Arthurian Encyclopedia* (see above). Updated Paperback Edition. New York: Garland, 1996.

Whitaker, Muriel. *The Legends of King Arthur in Art.* Cambridge: Brewer, 1990.

B. MEDIEVAL

Branner, Robert. *Manuscript Painting in Paris During the Reign of Saint Louis: A Study of Styles.* Berkeley: University of California Press, 1977.

Gengaro, M.L., and L. Cogliato Arano. *Miniature lombarde.* Milan, 1970.

Loomis, Roger Sherman, and Laura Hibbard Loomis. *Arthurian Legends in Medieval Art.* London: Oxford University Press, 1938.

Meiss, Millard. *French Painting in the Time of Jean de Berry.* 2 vols. London: Phaidon, 1967.

Nickel, Heinrich L. *Mittelalterliche Wandmalerei.* Leipzig: Seemann, 1979.

Scherer, Margaret R. *About the Round Table.* New York: Metropolitan Museum of Art, 1945.

Souchal, Geneviève. *Masterpieces of Tapestry,* introduction by Francis Salet. New York: Metropolitan Museum of Art, 1973.

Stokstad, Marilyn. *Medieval Art.* New York: Harper and Row, 1986.

C. MODERN

Banham, Joanna, and Jennifer Harris, eds. *William Morris and the Middle Ages.* Manchester: Manchester University Press, 1984.

Baumstark, Reinhold, and Michael Koch. *Der Gral: Artusromantik in der Kunst des 19. Jahrhunderts.* Munich: Bayerisches Nationalmuseum, 1995.

Brown University. *Ladies of Shalott: A Victorian Masterpiece and Its Contexts.* Providence: Brown University, 1985.

Casteras, Susan P., ed. *Pocket Cathedrals: Pre-Raphaelite Book Illustration.* New Haven: Yale Center for British Art, 1991.

Christian, John, ed. *The Last Romantics: The Romantic Tradition in British Art from Burne-Jones to Stanley Spencer.* London: Lund Humphries and Barbican Art Gallery, 1989.

Faxon, Alicia Craig. *Dante Gabriel Rossetti.* New York: Abbeville Press, 1989.

Fox-Friedman, Jeanne. "Messianic Visions: Modena and the Crusades," *Res,* 25 (1994), 77–95.

Gernsheim, Helmut. *Julia Margaret Cameron: Her Life and Photographic Work.* New York: Aperture, 1975.

Girouard, Mark. *The Return to Camelot: Chivalry and the English Gentleman.* New Haven: Yale University Press, 1981.

Harty, Kevin J., ed. *Cinema Arthuriana: Essays on Arthurian Film.* New York: Garland, 1991.

Lockspeiser, Edward. *Debussy: His Life and Mind.* 2 vols. New York: Macmillan, 1965.

MacCarthy, Fiona. *William Morris: A Life for Our Time.* London: Faber and Faber, 1994.

Mancoff, Debra N. *The Arthurian Revival in Victorian Art.* New York: Garland, 1990.

———. *The Return of King Arthur: The Legend Through Victorian Eyes.* New York: Abrams, 1995.

———, ed. *The Arthurian Revival: Essays in Form, Tradition, and Transformation.* New York: Garland, 1992.

———, and Bonnie Wheeler, eds. *William Morris and King Arthur.* Special issue of *Arthuriana,* vol. 6, no. 1 (1996).

Muir, Percy. *Victorian Illustrated Books.* London: Batsford, n.d.

Müller, Ulrich. (1) "Lanzelot am Broadway und in New Orleans." In *De Poeticis Medii Aevi Quaestiones,* ed. Jürgen Kühnel, Hans-Dieter Mück, and Ulrich Mück. Göppingen: Kümmerle, 1981, pp. 351–90.

———. (2) "Mittelalter-Musicals." In *Forum: Materialien und Beiträge zur Mittelalter-Rezeption,* ed. Rüdiger Krohn, Vol. 1. Göppingen: Kümmerle, 1986, pp. 319–42.

———. (3) "Das Nachleben der Mittelalterlichen Stoffe." In *Epische Stoffe des Mittelalters.* Stuttgart: Kröner, 1984, pp. 424–48.

————. (4) "Parzival und Parsifal: Vom Roman Wolframs von Eschenbach und vom Musikdrama Richard Wagners." In *Sprache-Text-Geschichte*, ed. Peter K. Stein. Göppingen: Kümmerle, 1980, pp. 479–502.

Newman, Ernest. *The Wagner Operas.* 2 vols. New York: Knopf, 1949.

Nitze, William Albert. *Arthurian Romance and Modern Poetry and Music.* Chicago: University of Chicago Press, 1940.

Pitz, Henry C. *Howard Pyle: Writer, Illustrator, and Founder of the Brandywine School.* New York: Potter, 1975.

Richards, Jeffrey. *Swordsmen of the Screen: From Douglas Fairbanks to Michael York.* London: Routledge and Kegan Paul, 1977.

Stein, Jack M. *Richard Wagner and the Synthesis of the Arts.* Westport: Greenwood, 1973.

Surtees, Virginia. *The Paintings and Drawings of Dante Gabriel Rossetti (1828 to 1882): A Catalogue Raisonné.* 2 vols. Oxford: Clarendon, 1971.

Tate Gallery. *The Pre-Raphaelites.* London: Tate Gallery and Penguin Books, 1984.

Wildman, Mary. "Twentieth-Century Arthurian Literature: An Annotated Bibliography." In *Arthurian Literature* II, ed. Richard Barber. Cambridge: Brewer, 1983, pp. 127–62. [Includes items on music and film, as well as literature.]

Wildman, Stephen, ed. *Visions of Love and Life: Pre-Raphaelite Art from the Birmingham Collection, England.* Alexandria: Art Services International, 1995.

Wood, Charles T. "*Camelot 3000* and the Future of Arthur." In *Culture and the King: The Social Implications of the Arthurian Legend*, ed. Martin B. Shichtman and James P. Carley. Albany: State University of New York Press, 1994, pp. 297–313.

INÒEX

This index includes all Arthurian authors, artists, and significant historical and legendary figures discussed in this volume. We list all Arthurian titles as well, but for works whose authors are known, we give cross-references to the author, rather than page numbers; this method permits the rapid identification of titles. We have indexed selectively; given the dozens or hundreds of allusions to common characters (e.g., Arthur, Merlin) or to major authors, themes, and places (e.g., Malory, Grail, Camelot), we index substantive discussions of items, but not passing or incidental references.

Italicized page numbers identify illustrations. An asterisk preceding an item indicates that the glossary devotes an entry to that subject.